The
Discovery of Troy
and its
Lost History

Published by
Trojan History Press,
Sami 28080,
Kefallinia, Greece

Author's website
www.trojanhistory.com

Facebook
www.facebook.com/trojanhistory

ISBN 978-1-91649-920-1

A CIP catalogue record for this
book is available from the British Library
and American Library of Congress

Pre-press production
eBook Versions
127 Old Gloucester Street
London WC1N 3AX
www.ebookversions.com

The
Discovery of Troy
and its
Lost History

BERNARD JONES

Contents

List of Maps

List of Illustrations

List of Tables

List of Plates

Acknowledgements

I started my research on Troy purely because I wanted to know about my own history. This was more than thirty five years ago. I had no computer then, and there was no internet. My notes were all handwritten as were the early chapters of my book. My research was done mostly in local libraries and my research assistants were the librarians. These are the unsung heroes of my early research and my undying thanks go to these very special people.

I pay tribute to my wife who helped with typing and manuscripts and never threw me out of the house for talking about the same subject all the time. My sincere admiration goes to my son and daughter who, despite being bombarded by my constant updates, managed to stay sane over all these years and grew up to be remarkable mature adults. Special thanks go to my dad for discussing my writings when they were in their infancy, and for accompanying me on some of my fieldwork visits. My brother too needs a special mention for reading the whole first draft of my book and for giving me my most valuable constructive feedback.

Finally, I am grateful to Childerley Estates for letting me visit on a number of occasions and wander without restriction over some of the most beautiful acreages in Britain.

Credits

MAP 7. The Sources of Homer's Metals. Ack. Wood, E.S. *Historical Britain.*; MAP 21. Geology of the Fenland. Ack. Darby, *The Changing Fenland.*; MAP 25. Rivers: Southern Fens. Ack. Astbury, *The Black Fens.*; FIG. 6. Chariots. Ack. Seyffert, O. *Classical Encyclopaedia.*; FIG. 12. Chariot Warfare. Ack. John Flaxman.; FIG. 14. The Formation of Roddons. Ack. Fowler. *Fenland Waterways Past and Present.*; FIG. 18. Danish Runic Cross. Ack. Olaf Worm 1651; FIG. 19. Tragliatella Wine Jar. Ack. Mathews, and Deeke.; PLATE 6. Greek Water Jar, British Museum (Achilles & Penthesileia). Ack. Jess Bygd.

The following images are from **Wikimedia Commons:**

MAP 19. Herodotus' World Map. This image is in the public domain. https://commons.wikimedia.org/wiki/File:Herodotus_world_map-en.svg

FIG. 1. Trojan War Scene. A public domain work of art. https://commons.wikimedia.org/wiki/File:DeathOfAchilles_Rumpf_ChalkidischeVasen.jpg

FIG. 4. Britons with coracles. A public domain image free of copyright. https://commons.wikimedia.org/wiki/File:Britons_with_coracles_-_from_Cassell's_History_of_England,_Vol._I_-anonymous_author_and_artists.jpg

FIG. 5. Druids. Engraving of a bas-relief. Public domain. https://commons.wikimedia.org/wiki/File:Two_Druids.PNG

FIG. 7. The Coming of the Milesians. Public domain. https://commons.wikimedia.org/wiki/File:Myths_and_legends;_the_Celtic_race_(1910)_(14760459036).jpg

FIG. 8. Statue of Apollo. Meyers Konversationslexikon (1885-90) 4th ed.

The Trojan War is one of the most fascinating events in human history yet no-one knows if it is really true. Was it the greatest catastrophe of the ancient world? If not, then it is certainly the greatest story ever told. My interest in the story of Troy began a long time ago after reading a little-known book on British history. This history, however, was not taught in the schools but, incredibly, it had its origins in the Trojan War!

The history of Britain most often begins with the Romans. Why is this when so many other nations have histories stretching back thousands of years? Is this just a convenient place to start or is the history of Britain prior to the Romans completely unknown? Is there a history relating to the British people prior to the Roman occupation? After all, there were people in the island when the Romans first arrived because Caesar fought with them. They were not a figment of his imagination. He tells us that the population of Britain was exceedingly large and the ground was thickly studded with homesteads.[1] The Romans spent centuries trying to subdue the island of Britain, and Caesar and other Roman writers relate how difficult a task it was. Throughout this time there was never a shortage of native Britons ready to do battle. Yet, read some of the history books and you could be forgiven for thinking that there was no one of consequence in the island, and that the people who were there were probably little more than savages anyway. Besides, how could there be a history of those early times? If anything existed at all it was probably only fairy-tales, fabrications and falsehoods. These mistaken assumptions could not be further from the truth.

A British history does actually exist and it covers the era of the Roman occupation of Britain. Furthermore, it stretches back more than a thousand years directly to the Trojan War, the cardinal point in British and European history. According to British history the ancient British kings and princes are descended from Brutus the Trojan, the great grandson of Aeneas of Troy.[2] Aeneas fought against the Greeks at Troy, and after the Greek victory he was exiled with his people to Italy. There is not much in the way of indigenous material though that can be added to the picture before the time of Brutus. On the other hand the ancient Britons, the Cymry of Wales, also derive their origin from Gomer, the son of Japhet. We are informed that they were the first to take possession of the island of Britain at the time when there were no people in it, only bears, wolves, crocodiles, and bison.[3] The Cymry came originally from Asia, from the area considered to have been Constantinople, now Istanbul.[4] The Trojan War was fought in Asia, but details of the ancient connections, if any, between the Cymry and the Trojans before the time of Aeneas are not clear and may be lost in the mists of time.

There is no scientifically proven migration of people from Asia to northwest Europe or, in other words, from the south to the north. If anything, migrations have taken place in the opposite direction. So how did the Cymry from Asia and Brutus the Trojan from Italy come to Britain? The key and starting point is Aeneas of Troy and the Trojan War.

THE LEGEND OF AENEAS OF TROY

Aeneas was a Trojan prince. During the Trojan War he behaved with valour and is mentioned a number of times in Homer's epic the *Iliad*. He is sometimes depicted in Trojan War scenes on ancient Greek vases. As an example, our first illustration (Fig. 1) shows him as a combatant in the fight over the dead body of Achilles. In the centre with his bow is Paris who, supposedly, killed Achilles with a poisoned arrow. Directly behind Paris

FIG 1. DRAWING OF TROJAN WAR SCENE ON LOST GREEK VASE from 540 BC.
A. Rumpf, ChalchidischeVasen (Berlin/Leipsig 1927), pl.12 .
Acknowledgement Wikimedia Commons. A public domain work of art.

is Aeneas. The Voyage of Aeneas of Troy is told in the *Aeneid*, a poem by Virgil. The subject matter of the poem is the settlement of Aeneas and his people in Italy, as destined by the immortal gods.

The Legend of Aeneas

In the tenth year of the Trojan War the Achaeans build a huge wooden horse that is taken inside the walls of Troy by the Trojan people. During the night Achaean warriors emerge from the belly of the horse, open the gates of the city and let the Achaean army inside. Troy is burnt to the ground. King Priam and most of the inhabitants are slaughtered, and some are taken away as slaves. Aeneas leads his son and father to safety but his wife perishes in Troy.

After building a fleet of ships Aeneas and his people set sail to the winds of destiny. They leave Troy for Thrace and then journey on to Delos, and then to Crete. They begin to make new homes but suffer plague and famine, and the Phrygian hearth-gods tell Aeneas that his true home lies in Italy. They take to the sea again, lose their way in a storm, and land eventually in the Strophades. Here they encounter the vile Celaeno and other Harpies. They flee from the Strophades over the waves past Zakynthos, Dulichium, Sami, Neritos, Ithaka and Mt. Leucata, the ships coming to rest on the Actian shore where they hold the games of Ilium.

As winter comes on the fleet departs, passing Phaeacia and the coast of Epirus to Chaonia and Buthrotum town. Here Aeneas finds Andromache, Hector's widow, and Helenus, the son of King Priam, who gives him sailing directions and advice on consulting the Sybil. During the voyage to Italy the Trojans land on Aetna's coast, encountering the terrifying Cyclopes, and afterwards narrowly escape death from the sea-monster, Scylla, and the whirlpool, Charybdis. Later, they are shipwrecked on the Libyan coast where Aeneas meets Dido, the Sidonian Queen, who as a result of her passion for Aeneas commits suicide as the fleet leaves her shores.

Aeneas' father dies in Sicily, where the Trojans return a year later from Libya, and games are held with Acestes' people. The fleet lose their helmsman overboard when approaching the Siren's reef, and Misenus is built a huge funeral mound after he drowns off the Cumae coast. Here, with the help of the Sibyl, Aeneas descends into Hades where he meets his father and is shown the souls of Trojan generations to come – Aeneas' destiny. Eventually the fleet arrives in Latium where King Latinus pledges his daughter, Lavinia, as wife to Aeneas, as the oracles have decreed. Lavinia, however, is betrothed to Turnus, a King of the Rutuli, and in his outrage he leads the whole of Latium to war against the Trojans.

VIRGIL'S *AENID* – FACT OR FICTION?

It is taken for granted that Aeneas' voyage took place in the Mediterranean and Aegean areas. It commenced at Troy, in Turkey, and ended in the river Tiber, in Italy. A number of the places may be familiar to us, such as Crete, Sicily, and so on. Even if we are not

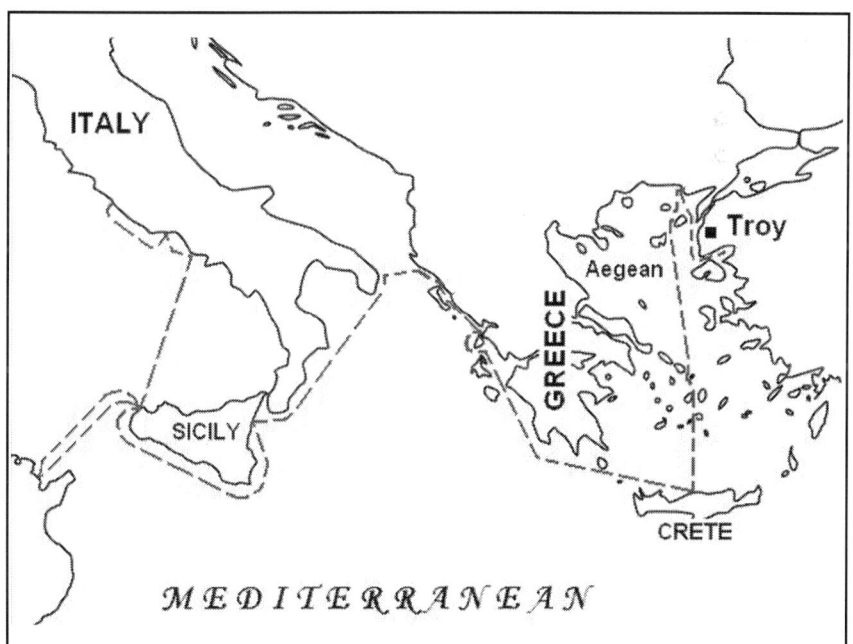

MAP 1: AENEAS' VOYAGE FROM TROY TO ITALY

too clear about the exact locations we can find them in an atlas and follow the journey ourselves. At the most basic level the names of the places visited can be listed in order and the route can be plotted quite easily. Alternatively, if the voyage is conducted in accordance with the detailed information in the text, the journey cannot be completed in its entirety. There are many occasions when such detail appears to be extraneous to the specific picture being presented to the reader at the time. In other places there is a distinct lack of information. Sometimes the detail given is irrational, leading to a ludicrous result. A great deal of information contained in the *Aeneid* does not fit into a Mediterranean/Aegean background but, here again, the minute detail is there and appears to have been most carefully inserted into the narrative. The list of anomalies and inconsistencies is quite long as the following examples will illustrate:

1. In Book 3 of the *Aeneid* when the fleet is about to leave Thrace for Delos we are told that they leave 'as soon as the ocean may be trusted, and the winds leave the seas in quiet, and the soft whispering south wind calls seaward'. Why is it that the Aegean Sea cannot be trusted? Why wait for a whispering south wind if they are going to sail south? The fleet would wish to make their journey as easy as possible and this would be achieved with a strong wind from the north so that the sails could be used. A whispering south wind would mean that they would have to use the oars.

2. During the journey from Thrace to Delos there is no mention of any other place which they passed on the way, e.g. Samothrace, Imbros, Lemnos, Lesbos, Chios, Andros, Tinos, or Mykonos, to name but a few of the many islands in the Aegean. The fleet would have travelled about 380 kilometres to Delos but there is no mention of sails being used. These omissions do not fit with the general tendency throughout the *Aeneid* of supplying minute detail to the reader. We are given further detail about the island of Delos because we are told 'the grateful Archer god chained it fast from high Mykonos and Giaros, and made it lie immovable and defy the winds'. The two islands which lie beside Delos are Mykonos on the north-east and Rinia on the west, whereas Giaros is more than 50 kilometres away to the north-west. This is completely at odds with the information given by Virgil.

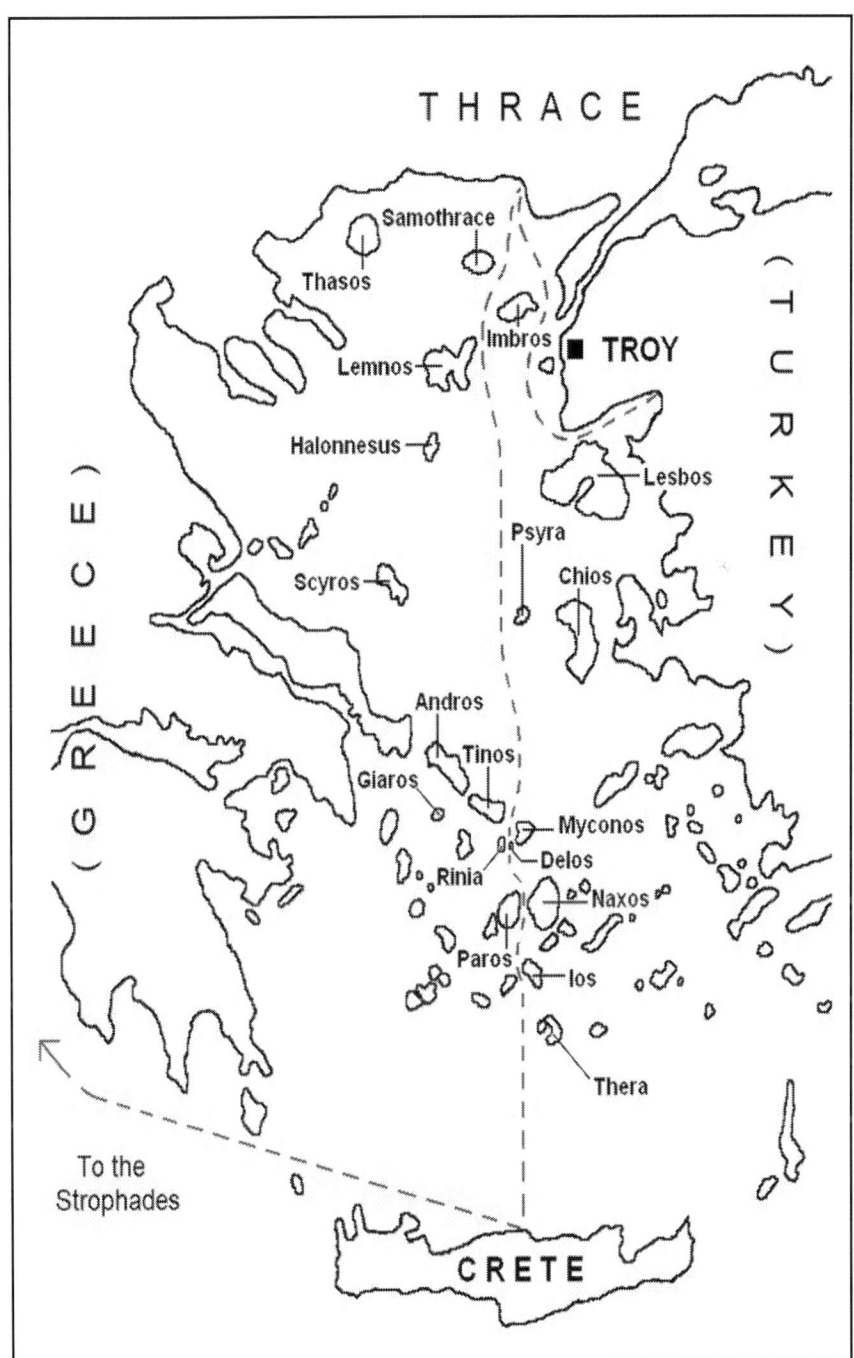

MAP 2. AENEAS' VOYAGE IN THE AEGEAN
The irrationality and inaccuracies in Virgil's account are puzzling

3. Again, before leaving Delos they made sacrifices to Neptune, Apollo the storm-god, and the favouring west winds. Why sacrifice to the west winds when the fleet is to travel south to Crete? There is a further anomaly here when Aeneas' father, Anchises, tells everyone that Crete is not far away – 'the third dawn shall bring our fleet to anchor on the Cretan coast'. Sailing time for the journey, therefore, is between 48 and 64 hours, giving an average speed of 3.5 to 4.5 kilometres per hour. This is a very slow speed indeed, particularly when we are told that they 'fly over the sea' and that 'a wind rising astern attends us as we sail'.

4. After leaving Epirus to take the shortest route to Italy we are told that Palinurus studies the heavens and marks the constellations gliding together through the sky: 'Arcturus, the rainy Hyades and the twin Oxen, and scans Orion in his armour of gold'. The directions are clearly given in the order of the constellations stated, in fact three different directions to be followed, one after the other. Why are these directions included in the text when one direction only is needed for crossing over to Italy i.e. West.

5. When the fleet passes the bay of Tarentum, Virgil describes Scylaceum as a 'wrecker of ships', yet there are no apparent dangers to navigation here. After leaving Aetna, good fortune saves them from the sea-monster, Scylla, and the whirlpool, Charybdis. No whirlpool has ever been found which corresponds to the alarming reports of the ancients.

6. In Book 8, when Aeneas goes on an embassy to Evander, he chooses two galleys and mans them with rowers. They travel up the river Tiber from its mouth to Evander's city on the Palatine Hill 'where now the might of Rome has risen high as heaven'. The water in the river is like a still pool but we are told, 'they outwear a night and a day in rowing'. This must be one of the slowest recorded journeys of all time, because it takes about 24 hours to travel an equal number of kilometres – a speed of only 1 kilometre per hour!

7. In Book 3, the fleet leaves Crete and encounters a severe storm

that lasts for three days and nights, '... a dusky shower drew up overhead carrying night and tempest, and the wave shuddered and gloomed. Straightway the winds upturn the main, and great seas rise; we are tossed asunder over the dreary gulf. Storm clouds enwrap the day, and rainy gloom blots out the sky...' Certainly, this description does not seem like the Mediterranean!

8. At the beginning of Book 1, the story opens after the fleet has left Drepanum in Sicily. Juno, in anger at the Trojans, engineers a violent tempest that she hopes will overwhelm the ships and strew the corpses over the ocean. The waves are 'raised up to heaven', the 'tide churns with sand', there are 'broken mountains of water', and the sea 'boils up from the depths'. The ships are sent spinning, the frameworks of their sides are torn, and some are hurled on the rocks. Yet again, this information is at odds with our picture of the Mediterranean. If we transferred the event to the North Sea or the Atlantic Ocean it would not be out of place. In the Bay of Biscay, for example, ships have faced waves more than 15 metres high.

9. Virgil writes of 'salt water' on a number of occasions. In Book 3, near the Fort of Minerva, 'reefs run out and foam with the salt spray'. At the start of Book 1, after leaving Sicily, 'they set their sails joyously to sea, and upturned the salt foam with brazen prow'. In Book 5, during the contest of the swift ships, we are told 'their long keels furrowing the salt water-ways'. Virgil uses the word *salsa* so there is no mistake that he is describing the briny sea, a description not normally applied to the Mediterranean.

10. Descriptions of the tides are given in various places in the *Aeneid*. In Book 3, near the Fort of Minerva, 'The harbour is scooped into a bow by the eastern flood'. Immediately before the fleet land at Aetna we are told that the wind falls with sundown, so it is surprising to find these words followed by 'In ignorance of the way, we glide on to the Cyclope's coast'. This can only be a reference to the ships being carried to the shore by the tide. In Book 10, when Aeneas returns from his meeting with Evander, he lands his allies by gangways from the high ships. Many watch 'the retreat and slack of the sea, and leap boldly into the shoal water;

others slide down the oars. Tarchon, marking the shore where he is secure of shoals and no broken surge plashes, but the sea glides up and spreads its tide unhindered…' There are other descriptions given but one is of particular interest, and it is found in Book 7 where Aeneas sends his envoys to King Latinus. Ilioneus, speaking of the shockwave of the Trojan War, says 'even he has heard who is sundered in the utmost land where the ocean surge recoils …' This is a perfect description for the Atlantic or the North Sea but not for the Mediterranean.

11. In addition to information on tides, Virgil takes great pains to give the reader details of how the ships are drawn up on a beach and from which end of the ships the anchors are cast. For example, when fleeing from the Strophades, Anchises bids them 'pluck the cable from the shore …' On their arrival on the Actian shore, 'the anchor is cast from the prow; the sterns lie aground on the beach'. When the fleet glides in to the Cumae coast we are told, 'They turn the prows seaward; the ships grounded fast on the anchor-flukes, and the curving sterns line the beach'. After leaving the Cumae coast they visit Caietas' haven where 'the anchor is cast from the prow; the sterns lie aground on the beach'. In seas that are subject to tides and currents these actions are essential to ensure the safety of the ships. Each beach, haven or harbour has its own peculiar conditions – high and low water levels, tidal force, direction of currents, sandbanks, and so on. Conditions change throughout the day, each and every day, and are further complicated by adverse weather conditions. In the Mediterranean these matters are of a relatively low significance, so why are these details provided?

All of these examples show that if we adhere to the detail of the story it is difficult to overcome many of the problems raised as a result. There are too many occasions where the information presented is illogical or, apparently, incorrect. In some circumstances the outcome is absurd. We are also given information which does not fit a Mediterranean or Aegean setting – storms and tempests, tides, grey and black seas, waves as high as mountains which hurl ships against the rocks etc.

MAP 3. AENEAS' VOYAGE IN THE MEDITERRANEAN
Yet more puzzling descriptions in Virgil's Aeneid

Caesar describes conditions such as these during his first visit to Britain in 55 BC.[5] His eighteen transport ships had been caught in a violent storm as they approached Britain, and they could not hold their course. Some were driven back to the continent and some were swept westwards down the English Channel. Caesar tells us 'It happened to be full moon that night, at which time the Atlantic tides are particularly high – a fact unknown to the Romans'. The warships that had been beached were waterlogged and the ships out at sea were being filled with water from the waves. A number of ships were shattered by the storm whilst the rest were unusable as a result of losing their cables, anchors and tackle. When Caesar came to Britain a second time, in 54 BC, he experienced similar problems.[6] When his ships were part way across the channel the wind dropped and they were driven far out of their course by the tidal current. Eventually, he managed to disembark his army and immediately marched against the Britons. We are told that he felt little anxiety about the ships because they were anchored on an open shore of soft sand. His complacency was short lived. During the night there had been a great storm and nearly all the ships had been damaged or cast ashore, requiring Caesar to return to camp with his legions and cavalry.

These are not insignificant matters and it surprises me how Virgil can describe such conditions not normally associated with the part of the world where he lived. I have my doubts, however, that they can be attributed purely to 'poetic licence'. For the majority of people who live near the coasts of the Atlantic or the North Sea these conditions are accepted as being perfectly normal. They are not seen as being in any way unusual. For someone from the Mediterranean area, however, it can be a bewildering experience encountering them for the first time. Even the most ordinary twice-daily rise and fall of the sea is a phenomenon that is truly astonishing when first experienced. The significance of such simple matters became clear to me many years ago when a Greek friend came to Britain and spent a holiday with my family.

On one particular day we visited one of our coastal areas and, arriving after the tide had gone out, all the boats in the estuary were lying motionless in the mud. After viewing the scene for a while our visitor turned to me and said, 'All these ships; what are they doing'? I knew the answer of course but nobody ever asks the question. 'They are waiting for the tide', I replied.

'The tide', exclaimed our visitor! 'Yes', I said, 'They are waiting for the water'. Looking a little perplexed by my answer our visitor enquired, 'Where does the water come from'? This was another question I had never been asked. And then, almost like a flash of lightning, I realised that our visitor from the Mediterranean had never seen anything like this before. So I explained the process of the tides. Although we couldn't see the sea at this juncture, I gave my assurances that it would come into the estuary in a few hours time. Our visitor was clearly not convinced and looked at me as if I had taken leave of my senses. Four or five days later we visited a pretty little seaside fishing village but, once again, the tide had gone out and the boats in the harbour were lying on the sand. From our vantage point we could see that the sea was about half a kilometre away. The subject matter was discussed once more but our visitor was clearly not going to believe that the sea would move from where it was. So, with my credibility hanging by a thread, we spent most of the day sightseeing. Fortunately, we returned to the harbour in the early evening, and the tide was in! Our visitor was stunned, and the whole scene was viewed with awe and wonderment. The sea level had risen by about six metres and the boats in the harbour were floating on the water in their normal fashion. Some were tying up, having just come in to the harbour, and there were some preparing to leave. The whole harbour area was a hive of activity. For a while our friend was speechless. Then, when the enormity of it could no longer be contained, came the words, 'Oh my god, oh my god, oh my god; I never would have believed it if I hadn't seen it with my own eyes'. This shows very simply how an ocean that is subject to tides is very different from an inland sea like the Mediterranean.

From these initial findings it would appear that there are defects in the text of the *Aeneid*. Would Virgil allow such flaws to exist in his work, or is there some other explanation? Before we try to answer these questions it would be helpful if we looked at the problem from a different viewpoint, namely that of Homer and of Troy.

HOMER'S *ILIAD*

As we know, Aeneas' voyage commenced at Troy. Homer's epic, the *Iliad*, covers a period of fifty days in the ten years war that was waged against the Trojans. Here we will find much useful information that will help in the investigation of Aeneas's voyage. Homer gives detailed information on an infinite number of matters relating to the natural world in which he lived. It is quite likely though that when reading the *Iliad* for the first time many people may not even notice the information because it is embodied in the text in very subtle ways and is easily missed. From the outset it is undoubtedly the battle scenes that impress themselves on the mind. The enormity of the war, the vast numbers of ships and men and chariots and horses, the violence of battle, the never-ending struggle for glory, the brutality, death, blood and gore. It is overwhelming. Under such a bombardment it is impossible to take in the many microscopic and beautiful details of the natural world that present themselves fleetingly through the carnage of the battlefield. Even after two, three, or four readings of the *Iliad* many of these details can still be missed. Unfortunately, most translations of the *Iliad* do not help us to find this important information because their indexes contain little more than a list of names and places. It has been necessary, therefore, to search and scrutinize Homer's work repeatedly and in a slow methodical manner in order to identify the myriad details that otherwise could easily escape our attention. From this mass of information a purpose-made index has been developed for use with the *Iliad*. Initial location of appropriate details and continuous referencing is now made much easier whilst the index also provides the means for appraising this information. This index can be found in Appendix 1, 'The Natural World in Homer's *Iliad*'.

Throughout the *Iliad* Homer describes the seas as being salty. He uses the terms 'grey' sea and 'wine-dark' sea, the 'sounding' sea, and the 'roaring' sea. He tells us of the black rollers which pile up seaweed all along the beach, the grey and thundering surf, and the hissing waves. He describes squalls, choppy seas, and the storm-tossed sea when billows tumble over the bulwarks of a ship. He also tells us that the much-travelled seagoing ships of the Achaeans were fast 'salt-watercraft', and when they reached land the sailors cast anchors and made the hawsers fast. The picture that emerges from the *Iliad* is unambiguous. It is a picture of a sea that is continually in tumult, and the predominant colour is grey. These are accurate descriptions for the Atlantic but not for the Mediterranean. Of course, it is not only the sea that Homer describes in the *Iliad*. He gives an account of the weather in such detail that any reader could be forgiven for thinking that the Trojan War must have taken place in the North Sea. He tells us of dark clouds, blustering winds, the thunder-laden sky, heavy rain and winter torrents. There is fog, chilling hail, and mist which is so thick that 'a man can see no further than he can heave a rock'. He also describes snow by comparing it to stones being thrown in the thick of battle:

> "Stones were falling thick as snowflakes on a winter day when Zeus the thinker has begun to snow and let men see the javelins of his armament; when he has put the winds to sleep and snows without ceasing till he has covered the high hilltops and the clover meadows and the farmers fields; till even the shores and inlets of the grey sea are under snow and only the breakers fend it off as they come rolling in – everything else is blanketed by the overwhelming fall from Zeus's hand".[7]

Such an overwhelming blanket of snow that covers the whole land excepting only the rolling waves appears to indicate some northern land. This is borne out by Homer's descriptions of Trojan and Achaean skin colouring. The Danaan Captains and Counsellors all had white flesh, as did all of the warriors involved in the war. The Trojan Lycaon had white flesh, whilst Helen and Andromache were called 'white armed'. Aias is referred to as having 'lily white skin', an epithet at odds with a Mediterranean/Aegean skin colouring. In addition, Homer always refers to the Trojan and Achaean spears as 'long shadowed', possibly indicating the fact that the sun shone at an oblique angle, hence a northern land again seems probable.

So far Homer does not tell us anything different from Virgil. At least as far as the descriptions of the seas and the climate are concerned Homer's information reinforces what Virgil has told us. Are they both wrong, or could they both be describing a place that is somewhere other than the Mediterranean? Let us see what else Homer has to tell us.

THE BOUNTIFUL EARTH

Homer gives us valuable information about the homelands of the various contingents in the Trojan and Achaean armies. Throughout the *Iliad* he uses the phrase 'bountiful earth' when referring to them, and his descriptions indicate a veritable Garden of Eden. There are rich estates in a fertile countryside, wooded peaks and forests. He tells us of the deep meadows and reedy banks of Asopus, the spreading lawns of Mycalessus, grassy Haliartus, and flowery Pyrasus. The rolling lands of Lacedaemon are deep in the hills, whilst Pteleus is deep in grass. There is Sicyon of the broad lawns, and Mount Phthires of the myriad leaves. He tells us also of the fertile lands of Tarne and Achaea, and the deep-soiled lands of Thrace, Paeonia, Larissa, Phthia, Ascania and Troy. We are told of the corn-lands of Buprasion, and Argos with its corn-lands and orchards. Phrygia is the land of vines and galloping horses, whilst Lycia is a broad and fertile realm with lovely orchards and splendid fields of wheat.

These countries are rich in grazing lands, plough lands, tilled fields, farms, farmyards, threshing floors, reaping, fishing, hunting and horse breeding. The land is so rich and fruitful that it is impossible for it to be the modern Greece of today, where thin rocky soils are typical of the whole area and less than 25% of the land could ever be cultivated. The south and west Mediterranean areas of Turkey are characterised by thick scrubby undergrowth, whereas the interior is semi-arid. There are rolling plains in European Turkey (Thrace) and dense forest along the Black Sea coast but nowhere else matches the detailed descriptions given by Homer. As far as the last 5,000 years are concerned, aromatic herbs, cork oak and bare white limestone are considered to be the embodiment of the natural Mediterranean world. The summer-dry evergreen forest, scrub and dry heath are distinctive features. Neil Roberts, in his environmental history of the Holocene,[8] states that Mediterranean-type environments are also distinguished by their stark, often memorable landscapes. He gives as an example an Aegean island – bare white limestone and blue sea. What we can say with certainty is that it is not a Mediterranean environment that Homer is describing in the *Iliad*.

The homelands of the Achaeans and of the Trojans and their allies were 'rich in flocks and cattle'. Iton was known as the 'mother of sheep', whilst Athens was known for its bulls and rams. Orchomenus was rich in sheep, Argos in horses, and Cilician Thebe in shambling cattle and white sheep. Homer refers to 'unnumbered flocks' and describes the booty when Nestor raided the herds of Itymoneus in Elis. He took away with him fifty herds of cattle, fifty flocks of sheep, as many droves of pigs, the same of herds of goats, together with one hundred and fifty mares and a large number of foals. In addition to those already mentioned, Homer describes other animals as well as many different birds, fish, insects and a wide variety of trees and plants.

These lands produced wheat, corn, barley, rye, honey, wine and bread. There were farmers, farm hands, shepherds, physicians and surgeons. Homer describes weaving, spinning, dyeing, sewing, embroidery, basketwork, wickerwork and the exquisite works of craftsmen, in wood, leather and metals. Trojan and Achaean warriors were clad in bronze; and gold, silver, tin and copper were used on their shields, helmets, greaves and swords. Iron was used for axes, and a quoit of pig iron was highly valued. These metals, however, were not available together in the Aegean world, so where did they come from? It is a mystery that continues to perplex many scholars even today. There were market places in the cities, widespread trading and the currency in use was the ox. When describing life in the Achaean camp, in Troy and other cities, Homer tells us of slaves, servants, maids, nurses, ladies-in-waiting, priests, prophets, heralds, chieftains, lords, princes and sceptered kings. There were codes of honour and respect to be observed and generally accepted rules of hospitality. Throughout the *Iliad* there is an innate love of story telling and knowledge of family history and genealogy, and this is demonstrated time after time by many of the participants in the war. Here again it is puzzling that the society that Homer describes is a warrior aristocracy more easily recognisable in that of the early Celts. This heroic age is reflected in the Irish tales commonly known as the Ulster Cycle.[9]

In due course we will have to pay attention to the problem of where Homer's metals came from. We will also need to discuss the Celts in a little more detail. So far though there is nothing in Homer's descriptions to dissuade us from thinking that Troy was not in the Mediterranean area. Wherever Troy was located, however, it was certainly not a land-locked region because Homer describes headlands, coasts and beaches, as well as the shores and inlets of the sea. The detail provided by Homer certainly indicates that it may have been elsewhere, possibly a northern country on the shores of the Ocean. These findings add considerable weight to the doubts expressed earlier in relation to the voyage of Aeneas of Troy. Both the *Iliad* and the *Aeneid* cover events supposedly in the Mediterranean area and Aeneas' voyage began at Troy, which is the setting for Homer's *Iliad*. Later, we will discover the significance of many of the pieces of information that are imparted to us by Homer, but first, let us consider what he says about the city of Troy.

HOMER'S TROY

Homer's Troy was an extensive city with mighty walls and towers. It had broad streets and there was an open square in the upper part of the citadel. The temple of Athena stood in the upper part of the city, and there was a temple of Apollo high in the citadel in the holy Pergamos. There was also a market place.

Homer tells us that King Priam's palace was a magnificent house and it was fronted with marble colonnades. Here stood the King's private apartments, complete with courtyard, stabling for horses and mules and accommodation for chariots and carts. In the main building behind, there were fifty apartments of polished stone, adjoining each other, where the King's sons slept with their wives. On the other side of the courtyard there were twelve adjoining bedrooms for his daughters and sons-in-law. Paris had a house near to Priam's palace, which had sleeping quarters, a hall and a courtyard. Nearby was the many-roomed abode of Hector, with its spacious halls. In addition, the house of Deiphobus, another of Priam's sons, is mentioned as having several rooms.

Homer also informs us that there were fifty thousand men on the Trojan side, fighting on the plain. In addition, there was a large civilian population in the city. All of these were accommodated inside the walls, so the city of Troy must have been of a vast size. It was situated on a hill, and Homer refers to it as steep and windy.

Let us now compare this with the site of the archaeological Troy in Turkey.

THE ARCHAEOLOGICAL TROY

On the evidence of inscriptions discovered in the area, a ridge known to the Turks as Hissarlik was identified nearly 200 years ago as the site of Hellenistic and Roman Ilion. Hissarlik is situated in the Bunar-Bashi valley in Turkey, about 5 kilometres from the Aegean Sea and the Hellespont, now called the Dardanelles. The mound of Hissarlik had a maximum length of 200 metres and was less than 150 metres wide. It rose just over 30 metres above the level of the plain.[10]

In 1865 Heinrich Schliemann decided to excavate the mound. Eventually, he distinguished seven and then nine main layers that corresponded to the ruins of towns. He started with the assumption, gained from Homer, that the Troy of King Priam was the original establishment on the hill. The lowest layer, however, produced only rude stone, primitive pottery and bone. Schliemann shifted his attention to a burnt third layer where he found treasures of gold, silver and copper or bronze. This treasure, which included weapons, vessels and ornaments, has since been dated to pre-2200 BC. In 1882, Schliemann shifted his identification to another layer, and yet again to another in 1890. Schliemann died that year but Professor Dorpfield continued excavating and discovered the fortification walls and houses of Troy VI and a lot of Mycenaean pottery. He pronounced this settlement as the Troy of Homer and Priam. After Dorpfield's excavations, Blegen led an Archaeological Expedition from the University of Cincinnati in an investigation of the site. This showed that there were no contemporary written records to throw light on the history, religion, social organisation, economic life or other aspects of Trojan culture. There have been Archaeological finds in Mesopotamia, Syria, Egypt, Crete and Greece but not a single document at Hissarlik. Blegen, however, found evidence that the layer of Troy VIIa was destroyed by human violence.

In his book *Troy and the Trojans*, Blegen stated that it could no longer be doubted that there was an actual historical Trojan War.[11] This drew fierce criticism from Finley who said that there was nothing in the archaeology of Troy that gave the slightest warrant for such an assertion. Blegen's team had found nothing that pointed to an Achaean coalition, an overlord king, Trojan allies or the destroyers of Troy. Mainland Greek archaeology and the Mycenaean tablets were equally devoid of information.[12] According to Caskey, the physical remains of Troy VIIa do not prove that the place was captured at all, and if the citadel was not sacked we are left without a compelling reason even to go on calling it Troy.[13] On archaeological grounds there is nothing to connect the mound at Hissarlik with the bronze-age city of King Priam. As stated by Donald Easton, it has never been proved that Hissarlik is the site of Homer's Troy.[14] Neither does the mound correspond with Homer's descriptions. How could an extensive city with broad streets, temples and palaces fit onto such a small mound? How could it contain thousands of fighting men, their horses and chariots and the whole population of Troy?

It appears that there is just no evidence capable of supporting the theory that Homer's Troy was in Turkey. There is nothing in the archaeological evidence, and nothing in Homer's descriptions to substantiate the fact that Troy was even in the Mediterranean or Aegean areas. Neither is there anything in Virgil's account to validate Aeneas's voyage in the Mediterranean, a voyage that we are told commenced at Troy. Conversely, there is evidence in Virgil and Homer in favour of Troy being elsewhere. The *Aeneid* and the *Iliad* more accurately reflect a north Atlantic, temperate, oceanic climate.

At the beginning of this chapter our intention was to investigate how the Cymry from Asia and Brutus the Trojan from Italy arrived in Britain. If Troy was not in Asia or anywhere in the Mediterranean or Aegean, and Aeneas' voyage did not take place in the Mediterranean either, then it is highly unlikely that the Cymry or Brutus the Trojan came from these areas. This presents us with a particular problem, and it is one that cannot be answered at this stage. Nevertheless, although we cannot alter our findings regarding the location of Troy or Aeneas' voyage, we will find that in due course this problem too will be resolved.

NOTES

1. Caesar, *The Conquest of Gaul*, V, 12
2. Nennius's History of the Britons, pp. 38-39
3. Probert, *The Ancient Laws of Cambria*, Triad No. 1, p373
4. See Woodward, *The History of Wales*, p33
5. Caesar, *The Conquest of Gaul*, IV, 28-29
6. Ibid. V, 8-10
7. *Iliad*, 12. 278-287
8. Roberts, *The Holocene*, pp 186, 187 and 192.
9. See Dillon and Chadwick, *The Celtic Realms*, Ch. 10, 'Irish Literature'.
10. See Easton, *The Quest for Troy*.
11. Blegen, *Troy and the Trojans*, p20.
12. Finley, 'The Trojan War', Journal of Hellenic Studies Vol. LXXXIV. 1-9.
13. See Finley, *The World of Odysseus*, p170.
14. Easton, *The Quest for Troy*.

2

THE LAND
OF
THE BEAR

CLIMATE

In Chapter 1 we found that the voyage of Aeneas of Troy could not have taken place in the Mediterranean – that the probable location was a temperate climate, in the North Atlantic or North Sea area. In order to pursue these observations we now need to examine the regions of northwest Europe that have a temperate climate. We will then be able to identify countries as possible candidates for the land of Troy. A temperate oceanic climate means moderate rainfall every month, cool summers and mild winters. The necessary information is provided in the illustrations that follow. Let us begin with the areas subject to moderate rainfall.

It can be seen from the first illustration that the countries that are subject to moderate rainfall include Iceland, Norway, Sweden, part of Finland, Denmark, Ireland, Britain, The Netherlands, Belgium, most of France, most of Germany and a part of Poland.

The areas having cool summers and mild winters, include Iceland, the south-western part of Norway, Ireland, Britain, The Netherlands, Belgium and the extreme north of France – quite a restricted geographical coverage.

As a strict test of compliance a country will not be considered as having a

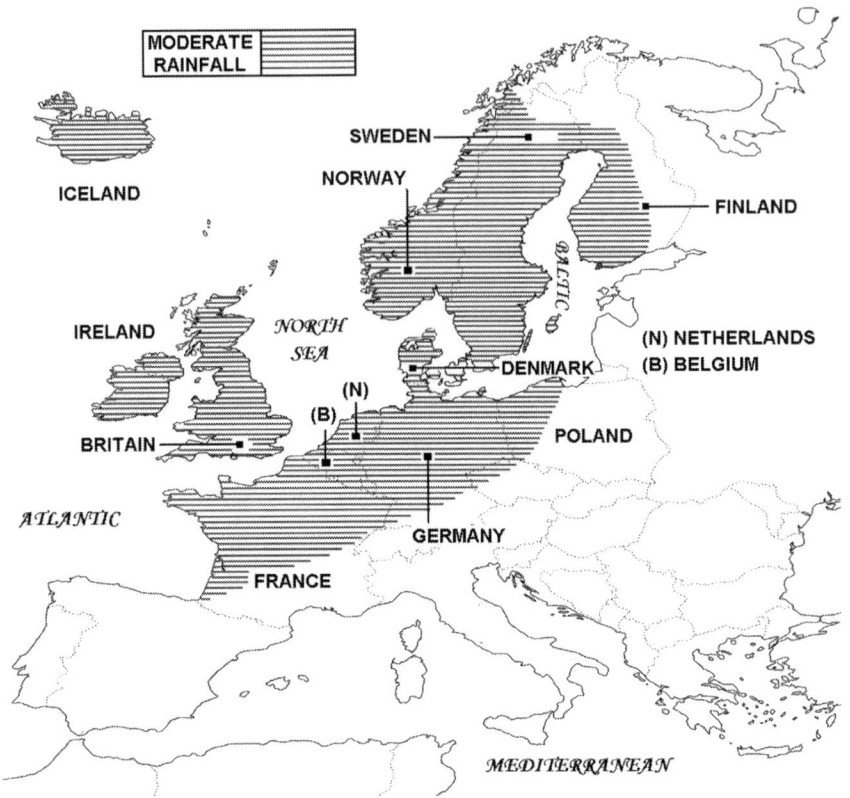

MAP 4. MODERATE RAINFALL: NORTH-WESTERN EUROPE

temperate climate unless it has cool summers and mild winters and moderate rainfall. This means that not all of the above countries satisfy the climate test. We are left with Iceland, Ireland, Britain, The Netherlands, Belgium and parts of France and Norway. But of course, it is not only climate that Homer describes in detail in the *Iliad*. As we saw in the first chapter he provides a great deal of information on the landscape too.

LANDSCAPE

Let us now consider what Homer has told us about the homelands of the participants in the war. There are a number of countries in north-western Europe close to the Atlantic Ocean or the North Sea, which could be considered as possible candidates for the land of Troy. These are Iceland, Norway, Sweden, Denmark, Ireland, Britain, The Netherlands, Belgium and France. How many of these countries though have landscapes that match Homer's descriptions?

Iceland, Denmark and The Netherlands do not meet the basic criteria because the physical features are totally different. The Netherlands is a predominantly flat landscape; Denmark averages only about thirty metres above sea level; and Iceland has glaciers, volcanic areas and hot springs, and nowhere does Homer mention the Aurora Borealis.

Norway can be excluded because the physical features do not match. It is a spectacular rugged land with high mountains, deep valleys and Fjords, more than 160,000 lakes and 50,000 islands. Northern Norway lies above the Arctic Circle and only the western part has a relatively temperate

MAP 5.
COOL SUMMERS/MILD WINTERS: NORTH-WESTERN EUROPE

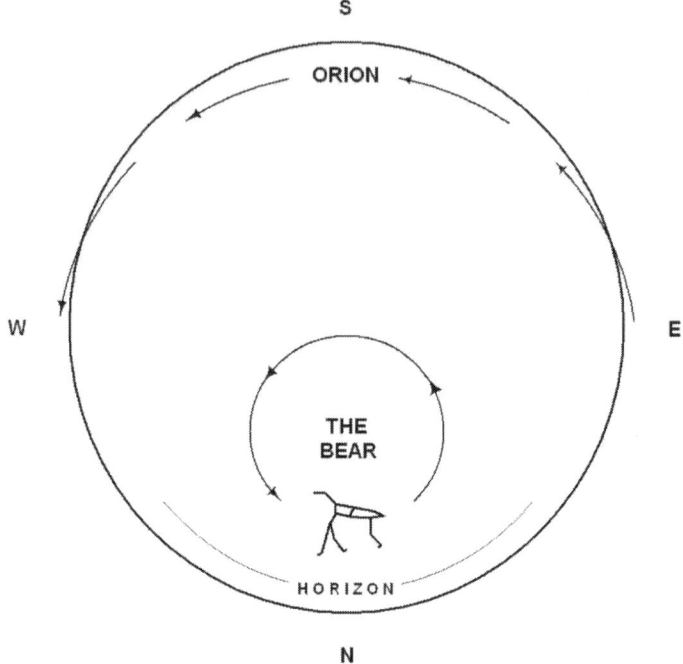

FIG. 2. THE CIRCULAR MOTION OF THE BEAR

climate. Sweden can be excluded for similar reasons. Northern and central parts are mountainous, and 15% of the land lies within the Arctic Circle. The north and east is affected by cold air from Siberia, and the northern or feature of the country, covering one twelfth of the total area.

Of the four countries that are left, Ireland, Belgium and north-western France all have landscape characteristics that match some of Homer's descriptions. Britain, however, meets these conditions to the greatest extent. Its physical features consist of a diverse landscape of highlands, lowlands, moors, rolling hills and plains. It is a country of fertile arable and pastoral lands, agriculture, livestock and fishing. It has a generally mild climate with strong regional variations in snow, wind, rain and temperature.

Using **both** climate and landscape as a test of compliance it is only the island of Britain that fully satisfies Homer's descriptions and, as such, must be considered as the prime contender in our search for Troy. Two other countries, Ireland and Belgium, partially satisfy the combined criteria. There is, however, one more piece of information that is of major significance and yet again it can be found in the *Iliad*.

THE SHIELD OF ACHILLES

Achilles had lent his armour to Patroclus who went into battle and was killed by Hector. Thetis, the mother of Achilles, then went to Hephaestus to ask him to make a new set of armour for Achilles, who was soon to die. Hephaestus began by making a large and powerful shield:

"The Shield consisted of five layers and he decorated the face with a number of designs executed with consummate skill and representing, first of all, Earth, Sky and Sea, the indefatigable Sun, the Moon at the

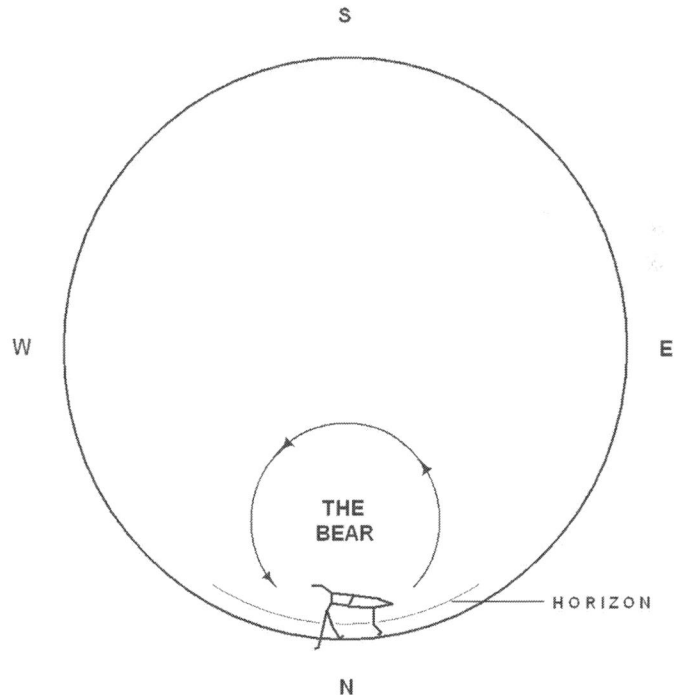

FIG. 3. THE BEAR: VIEW FROM TROY IN TURKEY

full, and all the Constellations with which the heavens are crowned, the Pleiads, the Hyads, the great Orion, and the Bear, nicknamed the Wain, the only constellation which never bathes in Ocean Stream, but always wheels round in the same place and looks across at Orion the Hunter with a wary eye.'[15]

Now, the Bear (Ursa Major) is found in the northern sky. It has a small, circular, anti-clockwise journey through the heavens. Imagine yourself facing north, looking up at the night sky. West is to your left, east to the right, and south is behind you. What you see in the night sky is shown in the illustration. It takes Orion approximately ten hours to traverse the sky and it can be seen that the Bear never crosses the horizon. As Homer tells us, the Bear always wheels around in the same place. This drawing gives a general impression only and we need to test it by looking at the movement of the Bear when viewed from Turkey.

The illustration shows that the circular motion of the Bear has moved north and it can be seen to partially cross the horizon. In other words part of the constellation will not be seen for a period of time.

If Homer depicted the constellations as they were, and there is no reason to believe that he did not, then it is impossible for Troy to have been in Turkey. For the constellation of the Bear **not** to cross the horizon it is necessary to be north of Lyon, Zagreb or Odessa; that is, north of the line of Latitude 45 degrees. As a result this excludes all of Greece and Turkey and the whole of the Mediterranean and Aegean areas.

Even if we exclude the horizon from the picture, which we cannot do in the real world, we still need to be north of Marseilles, Florence or Sofia (Latitude 43 degrees North) in order to view Ursa Major in accordance with Homer's descriptions. This means that Homer's viewing point could never have been in the Mediterranean area, or in Greece or in Turkey. It must have been much further north. In a roundabout way this is confirmed by Herodotus, who was writing in the middle of the fourth century BC. Known primarily for his history of Persia's wars with Greece his work covers many categories of knowledge, including geography, anthropology, fable and folklore. He is believed to have travelled widely throughout the Mediterranean, the Black Sea, Egypt and Africa. He tells us that of the

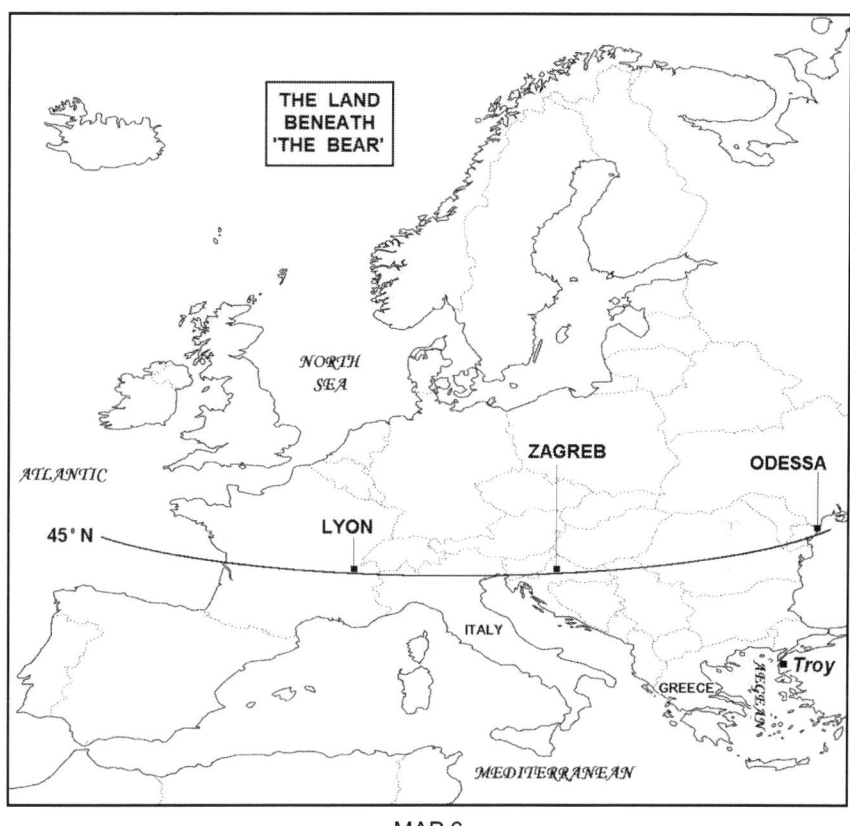

MAP 6

THE LOCATION OF TROY: NORTH OF THE LINE OF LATITUDE 45°

peoples who lived in the countries north of Thrace he had no precise information but it was his own belief that 'it is cold which prevents men from living under the Great Bear'.[16] Here, Herodotus verifies the fact that people who lived under the Great Bear were located north of Greece and Turkey.

The 45-degree latitude line is the limit at which the constellation of the Great Bear can be seen to dip below the horizon. In very basic terms, south of this line it does but north of the line it does not. I have used the word 'horizon' for the sake of simplicity, because Homer actually said that the Great Bear 'never bathes in Ocean Stream'. This indicates that Troy was located in a real ocean that was subject to tides, and not an inland sea. Also, it indicates that this land was surrounded by the ocean; otherwise Homer could not say '**never**' bathes in ocean stream. His words reflected

TABLE 1.
COMPLIANCE WITH HOMER'S DESCRIPTIONS

COUNTRIES	CLIMATE	LANDSCAPE	ASTRONOMICAL
Iceland	♦	—	♦
Norway	Only S.W.	—	—
Sweden	—	—	—
Finland	—	—	—
Denmark	—	—	—
Ireland	♦	Partial	♦
Britain	♦	♦	♦
Netherlands	♦	—	—
Belgium	♦	Partial	—
France	Only N.W.	Partial	—
Germany	—	—	—

♦ Countries in northwest Europe that satisfy Homer's
astronomical specifications and descriptions of climate and landscape.
Only the island of Britain fully satisfies all criteria.

a fact of life, which came from the study of the heavens and knowledge of the land where the Trojan War took place. In other words, from whatever shore of this land the constellation of the Great Bear was viewed it never dipped in the ocean. This tells us that **the land where Troy was situated was an island.**

Previously, we had three countries variously satisfying Homer's descriptions for climate and landscape. These were Ireland, Britain and Belgium. We can now exclude Belgium because it is not an island. This leaves Ireland and Britain for further consideration, although it is only Britain that satisfies all the criteria.

BRITAIN: THE LAND BENEATH THE BEAR

There are a number of historical references to the 'Great Bear' and the 'Little Bear' and, surprisingly most of these relate to the georgraphical location of Britain. These references indicate that the primary means of locating the island in a much larger world was astronomical. The information has been recorded by various authorities down through the ages. The underlying astronomical knowledge appears to stretch back into ancient times and was possibly indigenous to Britain. The evidence may reveal an historical convention.

BRITISH AUTHORITIES

Raphael Holinshed was an English chronicler and a translator in the printing office of Reginald Wolfe. He continued the compilation of their universal history after Wolfe's death, but it was pared down to cover only the British Isles. Holinshed's chronicle was first published in 1958. In treating of the ancient names or denominations of the island of Britain, Holinshed finds that at the first it seemed to be a parcel of the Celtic kingdom whereof Dis, otherwise called Samothes, one of the sons of Japhet, was the original beginner. Japhet the third son of Noah was the first that peopled the countries of Europe, which afterwards he divided among his sons. Tuball obtained the kingdom of Spain, Gomer had dominion over the Italians and Samothes was the founder of Celtica, which contained in it a great part of Europe but especially those countries, which now are called by the names of Gallia and Britannia. Of the offspring of Japhet, the isles of the Gentiles (whereof Britain is one) were sorted into regions in the time of Phaleg the son of Hiber, who was born at the time of the division of languages. Here, Holinshed cites the words of Theophilus (AD. 160):

> "When at the first there were not many men in Arabia and Chaldea, it came to pass, that after the division of tongues, they began somewhat better to increase and multiply, by which occasion some of them went toward the east, and some toward the parts of the great main land: divers went also northwards to seek them dwelling places, neither staid they to replenish the earth as they went till they came unto the Iles of Britaine, lying under the north pole".[17]

This refers to the pole star, or Polaris, the brightest star in the constellation Ursa Minor, known as the Little Bear. It lies one degree from the North celestial pole.

Other much earlier authorities have used similar terms to describe the geographical position of Britain. At the end of the fourteenth century Richard of Cirencester, writing on the ancient state of Britain, says that it is 'situated almost under the north pole'.[18] More than six centuries before this, however, Bede had completed his ecclesiastical history in 731, and he informs us that '…Britain lies far north toward the pole…'[19] Gildas was Britain's most ancient author and he flourished almost two centuries before the time of Bede. Gildas tells us that the island of Britain 'stretches out from the south-west towards the north pole'.[20]

Geoffrey of Monmouth translated his History of the Kings of Britain into Latin from a very ancient book written in the British language. The history relates that in the fifth century the British King, Aurelius Ambrosius, was poisoned and the continuing struggle against the Saxons was shouldered by his brother, Utherpendragon. The Saxons had begun to besiege York when Uther met them in battle. At the end of the day the Britons had been driven back and they spent the night on a mountain among the rocks and hazel-bushes. In order to receive advice on how best to attack the enemy Utherpendragon summoned his leaders and princes to him 'as the plough began to revolve its pole'.[21] Here, the reference is to the plough, another name for the Great Bear.

PYTHEAS OF MARSEILLES

Pytheas was an eminent mathematician who was famous for his measurement of the declination of the ecliptic, and for the calculation of the latitude of Marseilles. He was also known for his studies on the influence of the moon upon the tides. Pytheas was chosen as the leader of an expedition to explore the Iberian coast then to proceed north to the Celtic countries, and then as far as seemed expedient. His expedition took place about 300 BC, the course being from Cadiz round Spain to Brittany, then to Kent and other parts of Britain, around Jutland and along the Baltic, then up the Norwegian coast to the Arctic Circle. He returned via the Shetlands and the north of Scotland, then again to Brittany and so to the mouth of the Garonne, where he found a route leading to Marseilles. A good many fragments of his diary were preserved by Eratosthenes and other geographers, as well as in the criticisms of Polybius (preserved in Strabo's work).

Pytheas remained for some time in Britain and, apparently, paid more attention to it than to any other country that he visited in the course of his travels. The following description is given by Diodorus Siculus, based partly on the voyage of Pytheas:

> "As for the inhabitants, they are simple and far removed from the shrewdness and vice which characterise our day. Their way of living is modest, since they are well clear of the luxury, which is begotten of wealth. The island is also thickly populated and its climate is extremely cold, as one would expect, since it actually lies under the Great Bear".[22]

Here we have confirmation of the geographical location of the Isle of Britain via reference to the Bear, or in other words to the constellation of Ursa Major.

HIMILCO

Himilco was a Carthaginian who made a voyage round the west coast of Europe about 500 BC. Himilco and his brother Hanno were sent by the Senate to find new trading stations and to found new colonies. Each had a powerful fleet to command. Hanno was directed to go south from the Pillars of Hercules and to follow the African coast, whilst Himilco was told to keep to the coast of Spain. Himilco's own account of his expedition was translated into Greek by Eratosthenes (circa 275-195 BC) and a copy of the Greek version was translated into Latin by Rufus Festus Avienus of which some 4015 lines have come down to us.[23]

It appears that Himilco may have travelled north as far as the Scilly isles or 'Oestrymnides'. He tells us that Hibernia (Ireland) is two days sail from here and near to this again is the broad island of Albion (Britain):

> "Beneath this promontory spreads the vast Oestrymnian gulf, in which rise out of the sea the islands Oestrymnides, scattered with wide intervals,

rich in metal of tin and lead. The people are proud, clever and active, and all engaged in incessant cares of commerce. They furrow the wide rough strait and the ocean abounding in sea-monsters, with a new species of boat. For they know not how to frame keels with pine or maple, as others use, nor to construct their curved barks with fir; but, strange to tell, they always equip their vessels with skins joined together, and often traverse the salt sea in a hide of leather. It is two days sail from hence to the Sacred Island, as the ancients called it, which spreads a wide space of turf in the midst of the waters, and is inhabited by the Hibernian people. Near to this again is the broad island of Albion".[24]

It has been a common belief that the tin islands or cassiterides were the Scilly Isles, discovered in very early times by the Carthaginians. Kenrick states, 'That by the Cassiterides, or Oestrymnides, the ancients meant the Scilly Islands is highly probable, because, though they do not in all points correspond with their description, no others answer so well...'[25] The exact location of the Oestrymnides, however, does not concern us here. A general location somewhere between the Bay of Biscay and the southwest coast of Britain will suffice because we can then take advantage of the astronomical information provided later in the poem of Festus Avienus:

"...he who shall dare to urge his bark beyond the Oestrymnic isles into the wave, where 'neath the Great and Little Bear the air grows rigid, shall reach the Ligurians' land, tenantless now, and wasted long ago by bands of Celts..."[26]

Now, regardless of the exact location of the Oestrymnides, if we sail past them we will be beneath the Great and Little Bear. We can in fact sail between Ireland and Wales towards Scotland or up the English Channel to the shores of the North Sea. Either way we will be beneath the Great and Little Bear.

It is a known fact that the ancient mariners navigated by the stars. As time progressed there was a shift away from using the constellation of Ursa Major to the bright star of Polaris in Ursa Minor because it was more accurate for navigation. If Pytheas uses the term the 'Great Bear' to pinpoint the geographical location of Britain around the third century BC and Himilco gives us the 'Great and Little Bear' to indicate the whereabouts of the

FIG. 4. BRITONS WITH CORACLES[27]
British coracles were described by Himilco in 500 BC.
These traditional boats can still be seen on rivers in Wales, South West
England, Ireland and Scotland. Coracles have actually sailed
the English Channel.

of the Ligurians land about 500 BC, should we give less credit to Homer when he uses the term the 'Bear' in his epic the *Iliad*? We have seen in the previous chapter how the voyage of Aeneas could no have taken place in the Mediterranean and also that Troy could not have been in Turkey. It is my contention that both Homer and Virgil are giving us factual information but we have not been able to appreciate it because we have been looking for the clues in the wrong part of the world.

All of the above authorities refer to the same constellations, and in the vast majority of cases the astronomical references are used to identify the geographical position of Britain. As we have discovered, this is the only country that matches Homer's descriptions of climate **and** landscape **and** fully satisfies Homer's astronomical specifications. Is it possible that Homer's astronomical description actually refers to Britain? Our findings in the previous chapter indicated that the scene of Aeneas' voyage was more likely to have taken place around the shores of the Atlantic or the North Sea. Our recent attention to climate, landscape, and astronomical information places us quite firmly in North West Europe with Britain in the centre of the picture. This is the part of the world that lies 'beneath the Bear'.

ENDNOTES

[15] *Iliad* 18. 483-489

[16] Herodotus, *The Histories*, 5. 9-10

[17] Holinshed, *The First Book of the History of England*, Ch. 1. p428

[18] Richard of Cirencester, Ch. V.7, in *Six Old English Chronicles*, Ed. J.A.Giles.

[19] Bede, *A History of the English Church and People*, Bk. 1, Ch. 1

[20] The Works of Gildas, Ch. 3, in *Six Old English Chronicles*, Ed. J.A.Giles.

[21] Geoffrey of Monmouth, *The History of the Kings of Britain*, viii. 14-18

[22] Diodorus Siculus, Vol. III, pp 151-159

[23] See Dinan, *Monumenta Historica Celtica*, p10

[24] Ibid. p21. See also Elton, *Origins of English History*, p20

[25] See Elton, p20

[26] See Dinan, *Monumenta Historica Celtica*, p25

[27] Illustration from Cassell's History of England Vol.1. (Author / llustrator unknown). Acknowledgement Wikimedia Commons (Public Domain)

WHERE DID
THE GREEKS
COME FROM?

3

At the time of Herodotus the Greeks were in the Mediterranean and Aegean and their history, as we know it today, began. It began as a result of Herodotus' pioneering work in the field of historical research and method. Writing about 700 years after the Trojan War his collection of oral traditions has been a font of knowledge for anyone seeking information on the early Greeks. This accumulated tradition of centuries of myths and legends was all that there was in the way of early Greek history.[28]

Surprisingly, 'the Greeks had no legends about their entry into the land in which they lived'.[29] Prior to about 2500 BC the Greek language, and even its ancestor, had probably never been heard in the Aegean world. In fact, very few of the ancient place-names in Greece belong to the Greek language. The people who brought this language into Greece appear to have arrived as relatively primitive people.[30] But, where did they come from? Nothing is known with certainty. What is known, however, is that the Greek language belongs to the Indo-European family of languages that had its origin in the north.

A CELTIC CONNECTION

Many of the cultural themes from Homer, however, are characteristic of the Celts. In the first chapter we mentioned the heroic warrior class, distinctive laws of hospitality, codes of honour and respect, the innate love of story telling, knowledge of family history and genealogy, worship of the oak, priests and prophets.[31] The word, 'Celt', was first used by the Greeks to refer to people living to the north of the Greek colony of Marseilles in Southern France. As an ethnic attribute the meaning is unclear. The Greek literary source is embedded in a poem, *Ora Maritima*, which is a description of the shores of the known world. In this poem the Latin author, Rufus Festus Avienus, tells us that the Ligurian land is deserted because it has been emptied by the power of the Celts. It appears that the Ligurians were displaced from around Marseilles and may have moved into northern Spain and then the Mediterranean. David Rankin is of the opinion that Avienus is the carrier of some very early information about the Celts, his earliest sources representing current knowledge at the end of the sixth century BC.[32]

The original home of the Celts may have been in the areas now called Bavaria and Bohemia. A new culture appears about the fourteenth century BC which is thought by some to be the emergence of the Celts. We are told that they spread west to the Atlantic coast and into Spain, north into the British Isles, south into Italy and east along the Danube. The earliest migrations date from the Bronze Age with later separate migrations around the sixth century and the third century BC.[33]

When we speak of Celts we have to look at some late Bronze Age and Iron Age peoples of Europe who appear to have spoken dialects of Indo-European, akin to what we now call Celtic.[34] The modern Celtic languages are Irish, the Gaelic of Scotland, the Manx of the Isle of Man, Welsh, Cornish (which died out at the end of the eighteenth century) and Breton. Old Irish is known from inscriptions written in the Ogham alphabet, and in Latin characters, and from copious glosses of the eighth and ninth centuries. Ancient British is known from much briefer glosses of the same period and from proper names preserved in Christian inscriptions of Britain and in Breton tradition. Gaulish or Gallic covers the remnants of several ancient dialects which were spoken on the continent and in Britain. These remnants include inscriptions written in Etruscan, Greek, and Latin characters.[35] French is Latin pronounced by Celts. Latin comes from the Italic group and it is probable that Celtic and Italic were spoken in neighbouring regions in prehistoric times. Celtic and Italic are two languages born of a parent tongue which lies not very far behind. In its Mediterranean evolution Italic drew close to Greek, but many similarities prove that it is connected with the languages of the North.[36]

In 186-185 B.C. Gauls appeared in the army of the Lagids which besieged Abydos in Upper Egypt. They left an inscription on the walls of the temple of Seti I, in the small chapel of Horus. Although those Galatians could write, they did not think of writing in Gaulish; they wrote in Greek. Greek was the language of the Gallic troops and, likewise, the official language of the Gauls of Asia Minor.[37] Tacitus says in his Agricola that Gaulish and British are very little different. Bodinus writes that the British and Celtic language was all one. Holinshed[38] says, 'Of so much are we certain, that the speech of the ancient Britons, and of the Celts, had great affinity one with another', and, 'some are of the opinion that the Celts spoke Greek'. The Celtic Druids knew Greek writing from about 600 BC, and the Druid Abaris, mentioned by Diodorus Siculus, is recorded as speaking Greek perfectly. It is a mixture of Celtic and Greek that survives in the Black Book of Caermarthen.[39] Henry Hubert takes it as proved that the Greeks came from the north, that is, Central Europe, with the likelihood that they were once neighbours of the Italo-Celts, and even of the Celts.[40]

Poseidonius of Apamea tells us that the tribes in the north of Gaul and the Britons inhabiting Ireland were known first as Cimmerians, and afterwards under the corrupted form, Cimbri. The Pictish Kings had Welsh names, or to be more precise, they were the 'Old Cymry'. The national name of the Welsh or Britons is Cymri, and according to the Rev. R. W. Morgan[41] the Kymric language prevailed in different dialects over the whole of Europe and a large part of Asia. It is the substructure of all the Keltic tongues and the archaic element in the Greek, the Latin, the Sanscript and the hieroglyphic Egyptian. Hubert doubts that 'Cimbri' has anything to do with the Cymry but says there is no doubt at all about that of the Cimmerians – they were Thracians, or a kindred people.[42]

There is a difference between the dialects of Irish on the one hand and Welsh, or British, on the other. This is interpreted as a kind of prehistoric cleavage of the Celtic body, resulting in a separation into two groups of peoples. The one group is called the Gaelic (Goidel or Irish) branch, and the other is called the Brythonic (British) branch which includes the Gauls.

According to Hubert the dividing of the Celtic peoples into two groups is an ancient event of very great importance, connected with the great facts of European prehistory.[43] A certain theoretical assumption suggests that the two representative forms, Irish and Welsh, would originally have been the same language in the eighth century BC.[44]

So here we have Latin from the Italic group, with Italic and Celtic born of the same parent tongue, and Italic connected with the languages of the North. The Celts and Gauls wrote and spoke Greek, and Gaulish was very little different to British – a mixture of Celtic-Greek surviving in Welsh annals. The Greeks also came from the North and were probably neighbours of the Celts. As to the original homeland of the Celts, Hubert says, 'Modern theories of the origin of the Celts, whether based on the observation of archaeological facts or on the interpretation of historic-linguistic facts, are falling into line with the ancient belief – that the Celtic cradle was either in Gaul or on the very shores of the North Sea'.[45] David Rankin adopts a more cautious approach in his opinion that Celtic probably achieved its historically recognisable form in the region north of the Alps.[46]

As we can see from this short introduction, tracing the Celts is not an easy task. These people may have been the ruling power in what is called 'barbarian Europe', between the fifth and first centuries BC. Prior to this era is the Halstatt culture which, again, is commonly associated with a Celtic civilization in central Europe, between 800 and 500 BC. This period takes its name from the beautiful lakeside village of Halstatt in Austria where archaeoligists found more than 1,000 burials and many fine artefacts. Material artefacts that are considered to be Celtic have been found all over Europe. One of the most famous is the Gundestrup Cauldron, which was discovered in a peat bog in Denmark. Another is the Battersea shield, found in the River Thames at Battersea, London. A further artefact described as late La Tene Celtic design is the famous Birdlip bronze mirror from Gloucestershire in England. The Basse Yutz Flagons are a pair of Iron Age ceremonial drinking vessels. They are made of bronze and are believed to be amongst the finest examples of Celtic works of art. The Glauberg Prince is a figure of a Celtic warrior from a burial mound in Glauberg, Germany. It is a spectacular life-size sandstone statue from one of the most important early Celtic centres in Europe. The Vix Torc and Vix Crater were found in a burial mound on the site of a fortified Celtic settlement at Vix, in

Burgundy, France. They are magnificent examples of Celtic craftsmanship. It is easy to see that when it comes to the Celts we are fortunate to have an abundance of archaeological matter available to us for further study. We are not so blessed, however, when faced with questions of ethnic, cultural, or linguistic relationships because it appears that there is no settled opinion and much is disputed.

In addition to the many questions we may have it remains a fact that no one really knows what the Celts looked like. The earliest description we have is that of Diodorus Siculus in his first century history, although he may have had his information from Posidonius. Diodorus tells us that Celtica was part of Gaul and those that inhabited the inland parts beyond Marseilles and about the Alps are called Celts. He says that below Celtica the people were called Gauls. Caesar gives us a detailed account of the geography at the time of his Gallic Wars as it related both to Gaul and the Celts:

> 'Gaul comprises three areas, inhabited respectively by the Belgae, the Aquitani, and a people who call themselves Celts, though we call them Gauls. All of these have different languages, customs, and laws. The Celts are separated from the Aquitani by the river Garonne, from the Belgae by the Marne and Seine.'[47]

There is no mistaking the fact that the Celts are called Gauls by the Romans. Although he does not call the country Celtica Caesar goes on to give the boundaries of the Celts. North east of the river Seine are the Belgae, and south of the Garonne are the Aquitani. The vast majority of the country, therefore, is occupied by the Celts. It is 'Celtica', as described by Diodorus Siculus. In book 5 of his history Diodorus describes the Gauls as being tall in stature, with pale skin and blond hair. He tells us that some shave their beards whilst others let them grow a little. Persons of quality shave their chins close but let their moustaches grow. Is Diodorus really describing a Gaul or a Celt? Either way, it seems to me that the description matches that of the famous Roman marble statue 'The Dying Gaul', with flowing hair and moustache.

A CELTIC CONUNDRUM

At this stage in our investigation it is clear that no serious obstacles have been placed in our way that adversely affect our findings or the general direction of our enquiry. The fact that many of the cultural themes in Homer are Celtic leads us to pursue this Celtic connection further. At the end of Chapter 2 the British Isles took centre stage in our search for Homer's Troy. The present location of the Celtic-descended peoples is also in the British Isles so it is in this direction that we now turn our attention. Whether the Greeks came from 'the North' or from 'the shores of the North Sea' is of little consequence at this time. When dealing with the Celts and the British Isles, however, all is not what it seems.

The introduction of a 'Celtic' ancestry for the British, Scots and Irish was insidiously introduced into British literature. Waddell[48] explains that it is a striking example of the inception and growth of a false theory. The catalyst seems to have been a French book by Pezron, issued in 1703. It was called *Antiquity of the Nation and of the Language of the Celts.* An English translation was published in 1706 but now with the title *Antiquities of Nations, more particularly of the Celtae or Gauls, taken to be originally the same people as our Ancient Britons.* The seed for a 'Celtic' ancestry of the British, Scots and Irish had thus been planted. In the sixteenth century George Buchanan used the name as an embracing ethnic and cultural term. He thought that Gaelic had been introduced into Ireland by the Celts.[49] In 1757, in a translation of Rapin's *History of England,* Tindal says 'Great Britain was peopled by the Celtae or Gauls'. The theory grew over the next century until the transformation of the people of the British Isles into 'Celt' was complete. But unfounded assumptions rested on further unfounded assumptions. At the beginning of the eighteenth century the term was taken up by Edward Lhuyd who noticed similarities between the Welsh and Irish languages. By 1851 Sir Daniel Wilson the Antiquary was calling the British Isles 'the insular home of the Celtai'. Since then the term has often been used indiscriminately by commentators and this has resulted in a great deal of confusion. Waddell says that the older philologists were mainly responsible for the arbitrary extension of the name 'Celtic' in a racial sense to the earlier inhabitants of the British Isles. Whereas anthropologists eventually gave up the use of the misleading term 'Celtic', philologists still appear to cling to the title. The result is that today the British Isles is awash with the 'Celtic' theme. There are Celtic kings, Celtic churches, Celtic crosses, Celtic history and mythology, Celtic arts and crafts, and so on. No purposeful long-term marketing campaign could ever have been so successful

In reality, the term 'Celt' is entirely unknown as a designation of any race or racial element or language in the British Isles until arbitrarily introduced there. The name does not even exist in the so-called 'Celtic' languages of Gaelic, Welsh and Irish.[50] Further, the inhabitants of Britain and Ireland were never called 'Celts', whether by the classical writers or the Anglo-Normans or English.[51] The once-held belief that there was massive Celtic immigration into the British Isles is no longer tenable. No traditional or historical reference or record whatever exists of the migration of any people called 'Celts' into Early Britain.[52] The common opinion among archaeologists suggests there was no large-scale immigration into the islands between 2000 and 600 BC.[53] Francis Pryor tells us that the 'Celtic' history people had been fed is now proved to be pure myth. The oldest complete skeleton found at Cheddar Gorge in Britain is nine thousand years old but is identical to people living in the area today. DNA tests prove that the population had not been replaced.[54] It is clear that a Celtic historical background to the British Isles is erroneous.

After reviewing the above problems the question now arises, where do we go from here? Most of the avenues where we would have liked to have made some progress on this 'Celtic' question now appear to be fraught with difficulty, and it is apparent that we are not going to profit any further in trying to find Celts in the British Isles. The reason for pursuing this Celtic connection, of course, was to make some headway in tracking down the Greeks but this is not proving to be as productive as we would have wished. In his Introduction to *The Coming of the Greeks* Robert Drews says, 'One of the chief attractions of the early Indo-Europeans, including the Greeks of the Bronze Age, is their magnificent obscurity.[55] How true!

A SOURCE OF EARLY GREEK

From our brief look at the Celts, however, there is one aspect which appears particularly significant and that is the use of the Greek language. Whether we call these people Celts, Galatians, or Galli, they used Greek letters and spoke Greek. Where did the Greek language come from? Did the Celts learn the language from their Greek neighbours in Marseilles? In 53BC Caesar informs us that although the Druidic teachings were forbidden to be put in writing the Gauls used the Greek alphabet for most other purposes. The Celtic Druids in Gaul knew Greek writing but their Druidic homeland had always been in Britain. And this is where those who wanted to make a profound study of the doctrine generally went for the purpose.[56] Is it possible that Britain was also a native abode of the Greek language? If a mixture of Celtic and Greek survives in the Black Book of Caermarthen, one of the Ancient Books of Wales, it follows that the ancient Britons must have used the Greek language. Giraldus Cambrensis who wrote his *Description of Wales* in 1188 tells us that all the words in the Welsh language are cognate with either Greek or Latin.[57] The Latin language is one of the legacies of the Roman occupation of Britain. Although at first it was distasteful to the Britons it appears to have become acceptable in the days of Agricola.[58] There is no evidence, however, that the Romans brought the Greek language with them and it did not arrive in Britain in the post Roman period. The only other explanation is that it was in use in Britain prior to the first arrival of the Romans in 55BC. In referring to the Welsh people as Cymry Giraldus Cambrensis informs us that their language is 'cam Graecus' or Crooked Greek.[59] This is confirmed by Geoffrey of Monmouth[60] who tells us that Brutus, the great grandson of Aeneas of Troy, came to Britain when the island was called Albion:

> "Brutus then called the island Britain from his own name, and his companions he called Britons. His intention was that his memory should be perpetuated by the derivation of the name. A little later the language of the people, which had up to then been known as Trojan or Crooked Greek, was called British for the same reason".

This legendary account gives details of ancient connections with the Trojans but as we cannot pursue this matter here it will be necessary to return to it later. What we can say, however, is that we have indications that Greek, or some sort of Greek, was actually used by the ancient Britons.

ANCIENT ACCOUNTS OF THE BRITISH ISLES

In order to build on this evidence we need to examine the ancient accounts of the peoples of the British Isles. There is much to interest us here and many, many surprises. Most profess a history and genealogical record that stretches back thousands of years. Some assert first-hand knowledge of, and historical connections with, Old Testament figures. Others claim close associations with Greeks and Trojans.

Many commentators, however, seem to have had difficulty in coping with these accounts whilst others have refused even to acknowledge them. It appears that this may be due to the nature of the contents and the early epochs encompassed by them. Paradoxically, when dealing with the early history of the British Isles many scholars have turned to Greek and Roman authorities and have ignored the native Irish, Scottish and British records. At best this is unbelievable; at its worst it is inept, because the historical evidence is substantial and easily available. Because the Irish, Scottish and British records go back to very early times a common assertion by scholars is that they were invented or forged by the Christian monks. As a result of painstaking research by Bill Cooper into the veracity of the book of Genesis, however, these records have now been shown to be astoundingly accurate.

Bill Cooper has spent more than 25 years researching the early post-flood history of Europe and his research has revealed the tenth and eleventh chapters of Genesis (The Table of Nations) to be an astonishingly accurate record of events.[61] This exactitude is attested by the records of all the nations of Mesopotamia, Arabia, Egypt, Turkey and Greece. In a test that he describes as "unreasonably severe" he then carried the research into the records of the early peoples of Europe. A stringent pre-requisite was that the documents and records had to date from before the time that any given European nation was converted to Christianity. This was to combat the allegations that the early Christian Church and the monastic community were given to forgery and invention. He found that the same patriarchs mentioned in Genesis were evident in their most ancient genealogies and chronicles.[62] The records included those of the ancient Britons, Irish and Scots, which we will look at later. For us to be able to appreciate the degree to which these records have been vindicated and their current standing following such critical examination we need to look at some of the author's specific findings.

Bill Cooper tells us that the Britons left a clear written record of themselves dating back to the very earliest years of their existence as a nation.[63] Nennius' *Historia Brittonum* includes 'one of the most important documents of the ancient world' which 'records the descent of a considerable number of early European nations'. Nennius' source and Genesis were found to be in remarkable agreement with one another.[64] The *Tysilio Chronicle*, he says, 'contains historically verifiable accounts that overturn many modernist assumptions and teachings about our past. More importantly, the material that it contains reveal an antiquity for itself that carries contemporarily recorded history back to uncomfortably early times'.[65] We are informed that the history of the early British kings 'spans over two thousand years, and its survival to the present day, being little short of a miracle, is a tribute to those Welsh scholars of old who recognised its importance and preserved it entire for our reading'.[66] We are told also that in these pre-Christian records the Britons traced their ancestry back to patriarchs that are known to us from the Genesis record, and much of it can be historically verified.[67] As far as the Irish and Scots records are concerned the author tells us that, as with the British account, the modern 'student will be taught nothing concerning the chronicles and genealogies that have survived from the very earliest times'.[68] 'Nor is any account given of the surprisingly detailed chronology that the pagan scholars of Ireland were careful to weave into their histories'.[69] Quoting Cusack, he says:

"The Books of Genealogies and Pedigrees form a most important element in Irish pagan history. For social and political reasons, the Irish Celt preserved his genealogical tree with scrupulous precision. The rights of property and the governing power were transmitted with patriarchal exactitude on strict claims of primogeniture, which claims could only be refused under certain conditions defined by law…. and in obedience to an ancient law, **established long before the introduction of Christianity,** all the provincial records, as well as those of the various chieftains, were required to be furnished every third year to the convocation at Tara, where they were compared and corrected." [70]

In his concluding remarks on these records Bill Cooper informs us that they can be relied upon to be as accurate as any record can be. This brief insight into the ancient accounts of the peoples of the British Isles helps us understand the wealth of information available to us as well as the authenticity of the records. In later chapters we will explore for ourselves these extraordinary accounts of the early Irish, Scots and Britons, and discover that a major segment of history appears to have been lost and forgotten. And amazingly, we will find that these records will be instrumental in providing us with important clues to the original Bronze Age locations of the Greeks and Trojans.

ENDNOTES

[28] Finley, *World of Odysseus*, p24.

[29] Drews, *The Coming of the Greeks*, p9.

[30] Burn, *The Penguin History of Greece*, pp. 30-31.

[31] For Celtic Cultural Themes see Rankin, *Celts and the Classical World*, p11.

[32] Ibid., pp.2-5.

[33] *The Celtic Realms*, pp.3-4.

[34] *Celts and the Classical World*, p1.

[35] Hubert, *The History of the Celtic People*, p34.

[36] Ibid., pp. 14, 55, 58, 67 and 69.

[37] Ibid., Bk. 2. p52.

[38] *Description of Britain*, p22. (Chronicles of England, Scotland and Ireland).

[39] Nichols, *The Book of Druidry*, p42.

[40] *The History of the Celtic People*, p135.

[41] Morgan, *The British Kymry*, p23.

[42] *The History of the Celtic People*, p26.

[43] Ibid., p139.

[44] *Celts and the Classical World*, p23.

[45] *The History of the Celtic People*, p142.

[46] *Celts and the Classical World*, p21.

[47] Caesar, *The Conquest of Gaul,* i.1.

[48] Waddell, *the Phoenician Origin of Britons, Scots and Anglo-Saxons*, pp. 128-138.

[49] *Celts and the Classical World*, p2.

[50] Waddell, p128.

[51] Rankin, *Celts and the Classical World*, p2.

[52] Waddell, p138.

[53] *The Celtic Realms*, p4.

[54] British Channel 4 TV Documentary, *Britain BC*, 20TH February 2003.

[55] Drews, p xi.

[56] Caesar, *The Conquest of Gaul*, vi.14.

[57] Bk. 1.15.

[58] Tacitus, *Agricola*, 21.

[59] *Description of Wales*, Bk. 1, Ch. 7.

4

A
GREEK AND
TROJAN
THREAD

THE ANCIENT TAPESTRY OF THE BRITISH ISLES

So far we have dealt with Virgil's and Homer's descriptions of the oceans and the tides, and Homer's information on climate, landscape and environment. We have also seen how Homer identified the location of the land of Troy by astronomical means. Subjected to the above criteria it is only the isle of Britain that meets all of the conditions for consideration as the home of the Trojan War. Ireland is the only other country that has not been excluded so far, and as it meets some of the conditions we will include it with Britain for further examination. The knowledge that Homer's work incorporated Celtic Cultural Themes led us to enquire about the Celts. This, in turn, enabled us to see that the Greek language was not only used by the Celts in Gaul but the ancient Britons too.

Digging beneath the surface of the ancient and complex tapestry of the British Isles there was a thread that linked Britain and Ireland with the world of Homer, the Greeks and the Trojans. This thread is comprised of a number of remarkable and inter-related elements of historic importance. They include the worship of Apollo, the Hyperboreans, Homer's priests and prophets, a warrior aristocracy, chariot fighting, the sources of Homer's metals, a British-Trojan lineage, Irish-Greek origins, and the foundations of Britain's ancient laws. The following pages will serve as an introduction.

47

FIG. 5. DRUIDS (HOMER'S PRIESTS AND PROPHETS)
Acknowledgement: Wikimedia Commons

LINKS WITH HOMER'S GREEKS AND TROJANS

APOLLO AND THE HYPERBOREANS.

The gods and goddesses play a significant part in the *Iliad*. Homer relates how man went to war against man, and god went to war against god. Apollo took the side of the Trojans and their allies. He was the god of the Hyperboreans and Hecataeus clearly identifies him with Britain, where he had a sacred precinct and temple.[71] Apollo was the acknowledged god of music and song, playing on his seven-stringed lyre. Historically both Wales and Ireland are associated with the harp, and Wales has for a long time been known as 'the land of song'. The ancient British Kings were known to have been patrons of the Bards, and the Bard and the harp were held in high honour by both Gael and Cymri. The Hyperborean Triple-goddess Brigit became Christianised as St. Brigit, or St. Bride. She was the Irish goddess who presided over poets, smiths and physicians.

PRIESTS AND PROPHETS.

Homer tells us of priests and prophets and the worship of Zeus the Oak-god. The priests and prophets are the Bards and Druids of Britain and Ireland. The Druids worshiped the oak, and their name in the British (i.e. Welsh) language is 'Derwydd' meaning 'Oak-Wood'. In the *Iliad* there is an inbred love of story telling and knowledge of genealogy, a peculiar British and Irish trait. In former times it was a requirement that every free born person was capable of reciting their lineage to the ninth degree.[72] Genealogy was the domain of the Bards who framed historical matter into lines of poetry according to strict metre, and were capable of drawing pedigrees stretching back thousands of years. They were also trained to recite thousands of lines of poetry from memory. Such was the *Iliad* before it was written down.

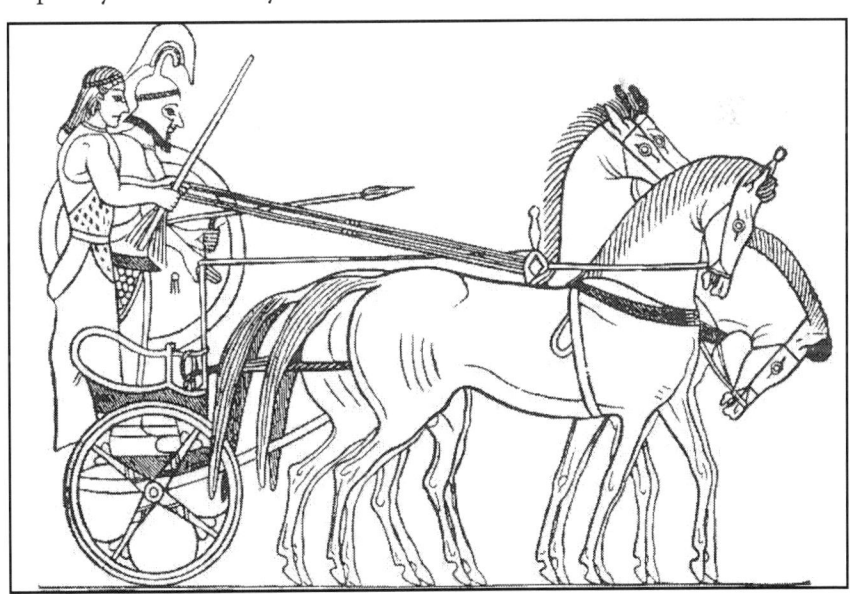

FIG. 6. CHARIOTS
Acknowledgement Seyffert

THE TRIBAL SYSTEM

Homer describes tribal chieftains, lords, princes and sceptered kings, a system which still existed in Britain at the time of the Roman occupation. Agamemnon had been made supreme commander of the Achaean expedition against Troy and this was a typical British custom. The Institutional Triads, codified 400 years before the Christian era, states that this paramount sovereign is he who is most illustrious by his bravery of the kings and princes. He had the right to assemble the country in power and his commands were binding on all others. It was in accordance with this system that Cassibellaunus and Caractacus were elected to oppose the Romans.

CHARIOT FIGHTING

Many scholars have been at a loss to explain Homer's battle scenes in the *Iliad* and, in particular, the chariot warfare. It is self-evident that in Greece the terrain is completely unsuitable for this type of warfare anyway. A. R. Burn confirms the fact that chariots were useless in the mountainous majority of the country.[74] In The World of Odysseus, Finley said the poets knew only that there was a tradition of chariots and what we read in the poems is nonsense.[75] Homer's chariot warfare was a peculiar British custom. The method of fighting is commented on by Caesar, who was clearly impressed by the skill and dexterity of the British charioteers and the javelin-throwing warriors.[76] Caesar reproduces Poseidonius' view on the British use of chariots and it accurately reflects the descriptions in the Ulster cycle of the principal heroes' mode of fighting.[77] Two-horse chariots were used carrying charioteer and chieftain. Freemen from among the poorer classes were brought into battle as attendants and used as charioteers and shield-bearers. Invariably, the chariots advanced before the battle-line and the bravest opponents were challenged to single combat. These descriptions mirror what we are told in the *Iliad*. When a challenge was accepted the opponents would loudly proclaim the valorous deeds of their ancestors and their own heroic qualities. At the same time they would verbally abuse and belittle their opponents to try and rob them of their fighting spirit.[78] As part of the challenge the warrior would recite his distinguished genealogy, authenticating his right to challenge a noble adversary. A prime example is given in the *Iliad* when Aeneas meets Achilles on the battlefield.[79]

MAP 7
THE SOURCES OF HOMER'S METALS IN BRITAIN
Acknowledgement: Wood, E.S., *Historical Britain*, pp.6-7

METALS

A number of different metals are described in the *Iliad*. These include gold, silver, iron, tin and bronze (an alloy of copper and tin). In *The Place of Troy Among Bronze Age Civilizations* Prof. James C. Wright comments on the sources of the ore used by Trojan metallurgists. Although a great deal of analytical study had been carried out to determine the major sources of copper ore the problem had not been resolved although there had been assertions in favour of tin being sourced from Afghanistan.[80] We now know, of course, that Troy could not have been in Turkey so any investigation into the sourcing of metals in this part of the world is bound to be problematical. Britain is the only country that has so far met all of the conditions for consideration as the home of the Trojan War. But what about these metals? Could they be obtained in Britain? According to Comyns Beaumont, there was nowhere else in Europe where these metals were available together.[81]

Holinshed tells us that Britain was not void of gold or silver and tin and lead were plentiful. He says that in Pliny's time there was so much lead that the Romans restricted the quantities that could be mined and transported to Rome.[82] Much of the lead, of course, contained a high proportion of silver and this was the prime reason for its extraction. Bede confirms in book 1 of his *Ecclesiastical History* that Britain was rich in copper, iron, lead, and silver.[83]

In recent years many prehistoric copper mines have been identified in the British Isles which were in use in the Bronze Age. The Great Orme Copper Mines, in Wales, date back 4000 years and may be the earliest and most extensive in the world.[84] The Cornish tin and copper mines have always been known to historians. Poseidonius of Apamea who wrote about life in Britain circa 100BC says 'the Britons of Cape Belerium prepare the tin working with skill the mine that yields it'.[85] The tin was then transported to Gaul. The Scilly Isles are mentioned by Himilco in the account of his voyage which took place about 500BC. Known also as the Cassiterrides and Oestrymnides these islands were famous. 'Scattered they lie, and rich in the metals tin and lead. A vigorous race inhabits them, noble-minded and skilful at their trades', he tells us.[86]

The Romans extracted gold from Devon, Cornwall and Wales, and at Dolaucothi in Wales, archaeologists believe that gold mining was carried out as early as the Bronze Age. We have confirmation that gold was available and in use in Britain prior to 400BC because the ancient laws prevented it from being taken to another land without permission from the lord and the country.[87] And it is an interesting fact that in Britain, gold is still sold by 'Troy' weight.

SCOTS, IRISH AND WELSH

When describing the Achaean forces, Homer tells us that Thoas, Andraemon's son, led the Aetolians from 'mountainous Calydon'.[88] This can only refer to Caledonia in Scotland. The Scottish flag is a white diagonal cross on a blue background and the Greek flag bears the same colours. St Andrew, from whom the cross takes its name, is the patron saint of Scotland as well as Greece. The Locrians of the *Iliad* are the ancient British tribe known as Lloegrians, (Lloegrwys by the Welsh), and 'Lloegria' is still the Welsh name for the portion of Britain now known as England. The Irish and Welsh connected themselves to Greeks and Trojans by lines unknown to the modern historian. Admittedly, the Irish and Welsh records are dated to uncomfortably early times and this presents its own set of problems. It is a sad fact, however, that these records are often disregarded by modern historians. It was Robert Graves' view that it was easier for historians to dismiss the records as fabrications rather than take on the study of Old Goidelic and Old Welsh.[89] Yet, unbelievably, a British-Trojan lineage and Irish-Greek origins do actually exist.

DARES PHRYGIUS

Dares Phrygius, or Dares the Phrygian, was a priest who took part in the Trojan War and wrote a history of the destruction of Troy. The Phrygii or Brygii are the same people as the Brigantes of southern Britain at the time of the Roman occupation. Although Dares' history is uncomplimentary to Aeneas of Troy it has always been regarded as a national treasure within Wales. Dares has always been regarded as British and he is credited with erecting a college at Cirencester in England.

THE TRIADS OF BRITAIN

The Triads of Britain are an ancient and authoritative source for early British history.[90] Essentially, they were a catalogue of orally preserved narrative, formed for the benefit of those whose professional duty it was to preserve and hand on the stories which embodied the oldest traditions of the Britons about themselves. Grouped in threes under distinguishing epithets, the Triads served as an index to the bards' knowledge of past history and legend. As surprising as it may seem some of the Triads commemorate royal personages of the House of Troy.

THE ENGLISH LEGAL SYSTEM

The original laws of Britain were composed of elements taken from the ancient Greek and Trojan Institutions and were a mixture of the regal and democratic. Introduced by Brutus the Trojan and codified in the 5th century BC they still form the basis of English Common or Unwritten Law.

These are some of the more important topics having particular relevance at this stage in our investigation. We will cover these and many other links in more detail later. This brief introduction, however, allows us to see the Greek and Trojan thread that exists in the ancient and complex tapestry of the British Isles. Each link is significant in itself but taken together they paint a picture that is unmistakeable, the import of which may be as momentous as it is incredible. The world of Homer, the Greeks and the Trojans may well be found in the British Isles.

ENDNOTES

[71] Diodorus Siculus, II.47.
[72] *Ancient Laws of Cambria*, p5.
[73] Triad No.68, *Ancient Laws of Cambria*, p28.
[74] *Penguin History of Greece*, p64.
[75] *The World of Odysseus*, Appendix I, p149.
[76] *The Conquest of Gaul*, iv.33.
[77] *Celts and the Classical World*, p77.
[78] Diodorus Siculus, v.29.
[79] *Iliad*, 20.156-258.
[80] See 'The World of Troy', *Homer, Schliemann, and the Treasures of Priam*.
[81] *The Riddle of Prehistoric Britain*, p189.
[82] *The Description of England*, Ch.XI., pp398-9.
[83] Bede, trans, Sherley-Price.
[84] For information see: www.data-wales.co.uk/orme
[85] See *Monumenta Historica Celtica*, p302. (Fragments of his work are found mainly in Diodorus Siculus and Strabo).

86 Ibid. p21.

87 Triad No.103, *Ancient Laws of Cambria*, p50.

88 *Iliad*, 2.638.

89 *White Goddess*, p241.

90 See *Trioedd Ynys Prydein*, (Triads of the Isle of Britain), Translated by Rachel Bromwich.

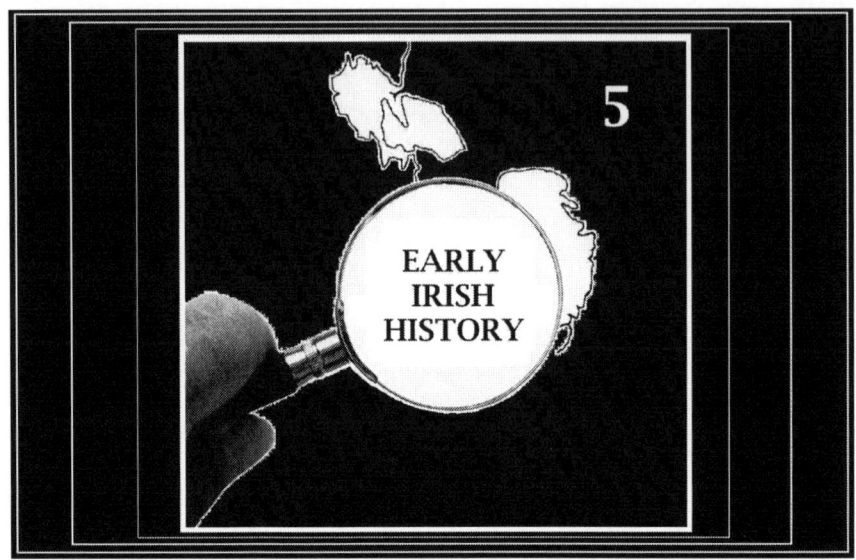

Compared to other countries in Western Europe Ireland is unusual inasmuch as it remained free from invasion or domination by foreigners until Norman times. As a result, we find that 'Ireland possessed a greater wealth of carefully preserved oral tradition from the earliest period of our era than any other people in Europe north of the Alps'.[91] The **Lebor Gabala Erenn**,[92] or *Book of Conquests*, claims to be an accurate historical account of the Irish race. It has not been free of criticism, of course. Geoffrey Keating utilised it when writing his *History of Ireland* and he referred to it as a semi-bardic and semi-historic work. He tells us that the authors of the ancient records framed their historical compilations in poems so that they were more easily committed to memory by their students, and for the purpose of ensuring accuracy.[93]

IRISH COLONIES

According to these records, Ireland was desert for three hundred years after the flood, before the arrival of Partholon. Here is what the historian Finton[94] relates:

I was then in Ireland
Pleasant was my condition
When Patholon arrived
From the Grecian country in the East

I was also in Ireland
While it was uninhabited
Until the son of Agnoman arrived
Neimead of pleasant manners

Fir Bolg and Fir Gaillian
Arrived a long period afterwards
The Fir Domman then arrived
And landed in Irrus westward.

After them the Tuatha De arrived
Concealed in their dark clouds
I ate my food with them
Though at such a remote period.

Then came the sons of Milead
From Spain southward
I lived and ate with them
Though fierce were their battles.

So Ireland was peopled by successive colonies known as Patholon; Neimead; Fire Bolg, Fir Gaillian and Fir Domnan; the Tuatha De; and the sons of Milead. At this stage we can ignore references to dates and intervals of time between the colonies because this information does not really concern us. The basic information, however, is extremely valuable and can be supplemented from other directions. We will soon see a picture begin to develop which will surprise us and challenge our accepted notions of history. Let us begin with the colony of Patholon.

PARTHOLON

Partholon and his colony came from Mygdonia in Greece. He came through the 'Muir Torrian' or Mediterranean, by Sicily, and leaving

> Spain on the right, arrived in Ireland with his three sons and a thousand
> soldiers, but after three hundred years this colony was entirely swept off
> by a plague.
> *Book of Conquests.*[95]

Nennius confirms that Partholon came with a thousand men and women and they increased to four thousand. A mortality came suddenly upon them and they all perished in one week.[96] Geoffrey of Monmouth informs us that the British king, Gurguit Barbtruc, was returning home from Denmark via the Orkney Islands when he came upon thirty ships full of men and women. Their leader was Partholon; they had been expelled from Spain and were called Basclenses. The British king granted them the island of Ireland which at that time was an uninhabited desert.[97] The information in Nennius and Geoffrey does not synchronise with the Irish records but, otherwise, there is substantial corroboration of events.

Partholon came from Mygdonia in Greece, via the 'Muir Torrian' (or Mediterranean), Sicily and Spain. Now, Mygdonia was a province near Thrace, whose inhabitants migrated into Asia and settled near Troas where the country received the name of their ancient habitation. Thrace, of course, was the first place where Aeneas disembarked after leaving Troy. There was also a Mygdonus or Mygdon who was a brother of Hecuba, King Priam's wife, and he reigned in part of Thrace. Heracles, during his ninth labour, sailed through the Hellespont, and was entertained in Mysia by King Lycus. In return, he supported Lycus in a war with the Bebrycans and killed their King Mygdon.[98] Heracles was contemporary with Laomedon, King Priam's father. If we refer back to Finton's poem we will see that he tells us that Partholon arrived from the Grecian country in the East. This does not appear to be an accurate direction for a colony that, supposedly, came from the Aegean Sea area. Keating tells us, however, that the colony of Partholon is said to be 'Greeks of Scythia', as are the other colonies.[99]

NEIMEAD

> Thirty years after, Neimead landed with a colony in Ireland. He came
> from Scythia, through the Euxine Sea, past the Rhiphean Mountains,
> to the North Sea, whence he sailed with his four sons. After Neimead's
> death, his followers were expelled by a people called Fomhoruigh, or sea

robbers, and they left Eirin in three bands. The first, under Simon Breac, went to that part of Greece called Thrace. The second, under Jobaath, went to the regions of the north of Europe. The third, under Briotan Maol, went to Dobhar and Iardobhar in the north of Alban and dwelt there.
Book of Conquests.[100]

Nennius calls the Irish Neimead, Nimech, and he says that he was the second who went to Ireland. He continued there several years but returned at length with his followers to Spain.[101]

Neimead came from Scythia, through the Euxine Sea, past the Rhiphean Mountains, to the North Sea and then to Ireland. As far as directions are concerned, this information appears ludicrous – the geographical accuracy is absurd, yet we are told that the histories were framed in poems for the very purpose of ensuring accuracy. This colony again comes from Scythia, however, and the Euxine Sea, now known as the Black Sea, was traversed by Heracles (Ninth Labour) after he killed King Mygdon. Heracles sailed to the mouth of the river Thermodon in order to obtain the golden girdle of Ares which was worn by the Amazonian queen, Hyppolyte. The Amazons were called 'oeorpata' by the Scythians, and the Amazonian queen, Myrine, was killed on the Thracian mainland fighting against King Mopsus and his ally, the Scythian Sipylus.[102]

After Neimead's death, his followers were expelled and they left in three bands. Simon Breac went to Thrace but his descendants came back as the Fir Bolg. It is difficult to believe that a colony sailed all the way from Ireland, through the Atlantic, then the Mediterranean and into the Aegean Sea, and a few generations later another colony sailed back again. Nevertheless, we have Thrace mentioned once more.

The second band, under Jobaath, went to the regions of the north of Europe. In Keating's History we are informed that some antiquaries say it is to 'Boetia' he went. Now, because of the improbability that it was Boeotia in Greece it has been suggested that some northern region is intended, possibly Bothnia.[103] On the other hand, Boeotia in Greece would maintain continuity with the general theme of the colonies being Greek. Boeotia was named after Boeotus, and his great grandsons were the leaders of the Boeotians in the expedition against Troy.

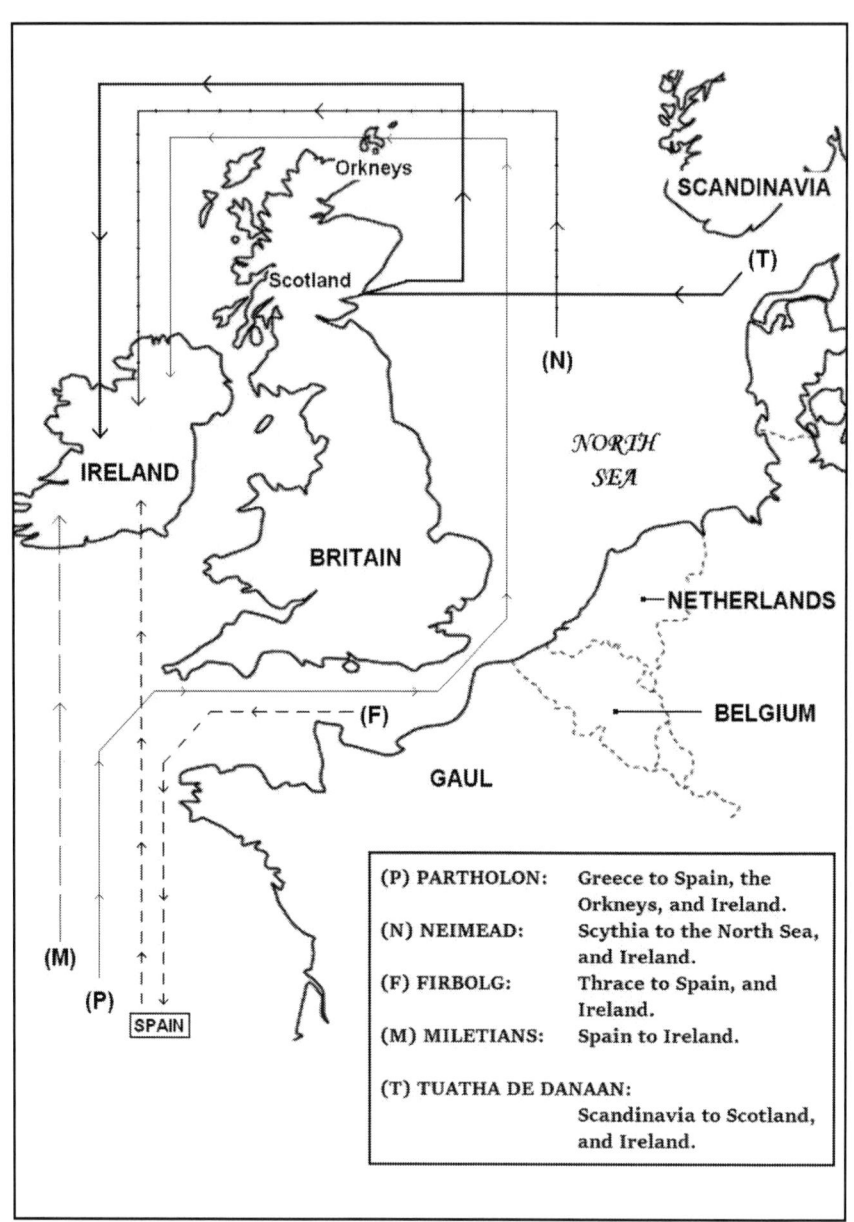

MAP 8. THE IRISH MIGRATIONS

The third band, under Briotan Maol, went to Dobhar and Iardobhar in the north of Alban and dwelt there. Alban is the ancient name of the northern part of Britain now known as Scotland. Skene identifies Dobhar and Iardobhar as the rivers Tay and Forth.

FIR BOLG, FIR GAILLIAN AND FIR DOMNAN.

The descendants of Simon Breac are supposed to have returned to Ireland from Thrace about four hundred years later, under the names of Fir Bolg, Fir Gaillian and Fir Domnan. The Greeks had subjected them to slavery, obliging them to dig the earth and raise mould and carry it in sacks or bags of leather, termed 'Bolgs' in Irish. The Fir Domnan are so called from the 'Domhin' or pits they used to dig, and the Fir Gaillian, or men of the spear, from the 'Gai' or spears they used to protect the rest at work.
Book of Conquests.[104]

Because the Greeks put bondage and great tyranny on them five thousand of them resolved to leave. They sailed over the broad Torrian Sea to Spain and then to Ireland:

> 'Thirty ships on one hundred
> And a thousand – it is not a lie
> It is the number who came from the east
> The good Slainghe with his hosts:
> Many were the Firbolg, without a lie
> At their coming out from Greece'.[105]

So these people sailed over the 'Torrian' Sea just as Partholon did. 'Torrian' has been taken to mean 'Mediterranean' but this is a mistake. The word 'Mediterranean' was not known at this time. In the classics this sea is occasionally called Internam or Nostrum, but the word 'Mediterranean' does not occur. Later, we will find that the Torrian Sea was a long way from the Mediterranean. Again, we are told that they came from the East, but this is not a good geographical indicator in relation to the Mediterranean area. Henry Hubert states that the Fir Bolg, Fir Domnan and Fir Gaillians are simply colonies of Belgae, Britons and Gauls,[106] and this would mean that, in relation to Ireland, they would indeed have come from the East. This means that these people may have come from Britain or the shores of the English Channel. If Simon Breac's descendants had returned from here then he could not have gone originally to Thrace in the Aegean area. Did he go to another Thrace, which was at that time located near Britain? If that is the case then it would equate with our findings that the voyage of Aeneas of Troy and the Homeric Troy are, most probably, to be located in these areas.

TUATHA DE DANAAN

> The Tuatha De are the Tuatha De Danaan, who arrived in Ireland about thirty-six years later. They were descended from Jobaath, who went to the north of Europe and lived in the land of Lochlin where they had four cities. After they had continued a long time in these cities they passed over to the north of Alban where they dwelt seven years in Dobhar and Iardobhar and then returned to the north of Ireland where they wrested the sovereignty from the Fir Bolg.
> *Book of Conquests.*[107]

As previously discussed, Jobaath went to Boetia, or to Boeotia. Keating informs us that it was here that the Tuatha De Danaan were located before they went to Lochlin (i.e. Scandinavia or the country of the Danes or Norsemen). He says, 'according to some antiquaries, the place which was inhabited by them was Boetia in the north of Europe. Some others say that it is in the Athenian territory they dwelt, where the city of Athens is. Understand, O reader, that Boeotia and the city of Athens, according to Pomponius Mela, are in the district of Greece which is called Achaia….'[108]

Clearly, Keating saw a problem in a reader believing that the Tuatha De Danaan were located in the Athenian country before they went to Scandinavia. This would mean that Jobaath sailed through the Atlantic and the Mediterranean to Boeotia, and his descendants sailed all the way back again to Scandinavia. On the other hand, if Jobaath actually went to the regions of the north of Europe then he would have been in the same part of the world as Briotan Maol who went to Scotland. The Tuatha de Danaan, as descendants of Jobaath, would then have a logical and completely believable voyage to Scandinavia and then back across the North Sea to Scotland.

Ross Nichols says that the Tuatha De Danaan is the Children or Tribe of the goddess Dana, and they link most plainly with Greece. The name, Dana, is one of the clearest evidences of ancient identity between the two races, the Danaans of Eire and the Danaoi of Greece, both being the sons of Dana.[109] Holinshed[110] chronicles the history of Danaus and his fifty daughters, who fled from Egypt to Greece and reigned in Argos with the assistance of the Argives. These Greeks, in remembrance of Danaus, were afterwards known as Danai. Danaus had refused the marriage of his fifty daughters to the fifty sons of his brother, Aegyptus. As a result, Aegyptus sent a great army to make war on Danaus, and his daughters were finally married to his nephews. Danaus, however, delivered a sword to each of his daughters on the first night of their marriage and each daughter, except Hypermnestra, slew her husband. Lynceus, the sole survivor, went back to Egypt and returned to Greece with men and ships to avenge the death of his brothers. All of the daughters, except Hypermnestra, were set adrift on the ocean :

> "These ladies thus embarked and left to the mercy of the seas, by hap were brought to the coasts of this Isle then called Albion (Britain)..."

Previously, we have been asked to believe that colonies, which inhabited Ireland, traversed the Atlantic Ocean and the Mediterranean and Aegean Seas as a matter of course, however improbable. Here, however, it is impossible to believe that these ladies were cast adrift in the Mediterranean and, just by chance, landed on the coasts of Britain! How is it that the Danaan myth is embedded in the chronicles of Irish and British history? Was there an ancient past which connected the Greeks, in particular, with the ancient inhabitants of the British Isles? It certainly seems that way.

SONS OF MILEAD

> The Tuatha De Danaan remained one hundred and ninety-seven years in Ireland when the sons of Milead (Miletians) arrived from Spain with the Scots and took the kingdom from them. This Milead was said to have originally born the name of Galamh, and to be the son of Bile, son of

> Breogan who took possession of Spain. He had sons by Seang, daughter
> of Refloir, King of Scythia, and also by Scota, daughter of Pharaoh, King
> of Egypt, from whom the Scots take their name.
> *Book of Conquests.*[111]

Nenius does not confirm the name of the Irish Milead, but the name means 'soldier'. He does tell us, however, that after him came three sons of a Spanish soldier with thirty ships, each of which contained thirty wives.[112]

Having remained in Ireland for a year:

> "there appeared to them, in the middle of the sea, a tower of glass, the
> summit of which seemed covered with men, to whom they often spoke,
> but received no answer. At length they determined to besiege the tower;
> and after a year's preparation advanced towards it, with the whole
> number of their ships, and all the women, one ship only excepted, which
> had been wrecked, and in which were thirty men, and as many women;
> but when all had disembarked on the shore which surrounded the tower,
> the sea opened and swallowed them up. Ireland, however, was peopled,
> to the present period, from the family remaining in the vessel which was
> wrecked".

Now, the Milesians were a Cretan colony who came to Caria and founded a city which was called Miletus, after the name of their leader. They applied themselves to navigation and planted many colonies in different parts of the world. Miletus is mentioned by Homer, in book two of the *Iliad*, when opposing armies assemble on the plains of Scamander.[113]

SCOTS

From the earliest times the Scots are inextricably linked to the Irish. The ancient language of both nations is Gaelic, which is derived from the name of Gaythelos from whom the Scots claim their origin. Whether inhabiting Ireland or Britain they were known by the name of Scoti but Scotia, the mother country of the Scots, is Ireland. The first formal history of Scotland was compiled in the fourteenth century by John of Fordun but he lived only to complete five books. William Skene,[114] however, acquaints us with the main features of early Scots History, as related by Fordun:

FIG. 7. THE COMING OF THE MILESIANS
Acknowledgement Wikimedia Commons.
Myths and Legends; the Celtic Race (1910) Rolleston.

"The Scots derived their origin from Gaythelos, the son of Neolus, King of Greece, who went to Egypt in the days of Moses, where he married Scota, daughter of Pharaoh, King of Egypt, and led the Scots from thence to Spain. From this country several colonies went to Ireland, the last under Symon Brek, son of the King of Spain, who brought the marble chair on which the Kings were crowned to Ireland, and under his great-grandson, Ethacius Rothay, the Scots passed over into Scotland, and gave the name of Scotia to that part of the island formerly called Albion. Some time after, the Picts settled in Scotland, and married wives of the Scots. In the year 330 before the Christian era, the Scots, who had come over from Ireland and settled in Scotland, elected Fergus, the son of Ferehard, their King, who brought over from Ireland the marble chair and whose kingdom extended from the sea and the Western Isles to Drumalban".

The Chronicle of the Scots gives us the name of Neolms as the father of Gaythelos, and he was King of Athens.[115] Holinshed provides us with additional information from the old Scottish historiographers that Gaythelos was either the son of Cecrops or the son of Argus Nealus, the fourth King of the Argives.[116] Argus was indeed the fourth King of Argos, and hence the Argives also. Nealus is, clearly, the same person as Neolus and Neolms, which is an epithet, probably meaning 'youthful' or 'vigorous' (Gr. Νεαλης). Argus had an incredibly long reign of seventy years so it appears that he may well have become king in his youth.

Most records appear to give the history of Gaythelos after he reaches Egypt. *The Chronicle of the Scots*, however, tells us that he arrived in Egypt with a great power of men. Finally, there is another record that informs us where the Scots came from and it appears to relate to the Scots as a national entity.[117] The Scots were Greeks from the town of Choriscon upon the river Pactolus, which separates Choria from Lydia. Having obtained ships they went by Pathmos, Abidos and the islands of the Hellespont, to Upper Thrace, and being joined by the people of Pergamus, and the Lacedaemonians, they were driven by the north wind past Ephesus, the island of Melos, and the Cyclades to Crete, and thence by the African sea they entered the Illyrian gulf. Then by the Balearic Isles they pass Spain, and through the Columns of Hercules to remote Tyle and finally land in Ireland.

Here again, we have a so-called Mediterranean origin. Aeneas of Troy sailed via the Hellespont, Thrace and the Cyclades to Crete. So if we can locate some of these places we will also be able to shed light on Aeneas' voyage.

IRISH-GREEK BEGINNINGS?

The whole of Neolithic Europe had a remarkably homogeneous system of religious ideas based on worship of the many-titled mother-goddess. Throughout successive stages the throne remained matrilineal, but the Achaean invasions of the thirteenth century B.C. seriously weakened this tradition. With the Dorian invasion of approximately 1050 B.C. patrilineal succession was established. A three-tribe system is the general rule in matriarchal society, and this phenomenon occurs throughout the Irish histories. All of the Irish colonies are said to be Greek (Grieg). According to Graves, 'Graeci' means 'worshippers of the crone' i.e. the Earth-Goddess and when the first two waves of patriarchal Hellenes invaded Greece, they were persuaded by the Hellads to change their customs and become Greeks. Later, the Achaeans and Dorians succeeded in establishing patriarchal rule. The Parian Chronicle records that this change from Greeks to Hellenes took place in 1521 B.C.[118]

The Danaus myth, which equates with the Tuatha De Danaan, records the early arrival in Greece of Helladic colonists from Palestine, and their introduction of agriculture into the Peloponnese.[119] The Tuatha De Danaan colony then was also matrilineal. Further evidence of matrilineal society is given to us in the *Chronicles of the Picts and Scots* where Gaythelos went from Greece to Egypt to marry Scota – when patriarchal rule was established, the woman went to the man. It is interesting to note that one of the titles of Aphrodite, as Goddess of Death-in-Life, was Melaenis ('black one') and Scotia ('dark one'), so it is possible that Scota, the daughter of Pharaoh, may have been a Priestess.

The main participants fighting against the Trojans in the war at Troy were the Achaeans, Danaans, and Argives. The Scots claimed Greek origin from Gaythelos, who, it seems, was the son of Argus Nealus, the fourth King of the Argives. If the Scots are descended from the Argives and the Irish Danaans are the same as the Homeric Danaans then it means that the ancestors of today's Irish and Scots were the same people who are immortalised by Homer in the *Iliad*. But what about the Achaeans who fought alongside the Danaans and Argives? There does not appear to be a record that relates anything about the Achaeans, and no genealogical tree or other description that I can find. One important piece of information, however, comes to our notice via Keating, which makes the Irish the same people. We are told that the colonies of Partholon, Neimead, the Fir Bolg and Tuatha de Danaan were called Greeks of Scythia; they all had the Scotic i.e. Gaelic language, and they obtained dominion in Gothia, Thracia and Achaia.[120] If they obtained dominion in Achaea they would be known as Achaeans. Thus we seem to have in the ancestors of the Irish and Scots the very same people who were the Bronze Age Achaeans, Danaans, and Argives. In addition, all of the Irish tribes had one language, and this is exactly what Homer tells us about the Achaeans, Danaans and Argives. This was in direct contrast to the Trojans and their allies where there were a number of different languages. At the beginning of the *Iliad* the Achaean army assembles on the plain ready to do battle. The Trojans are inside the city and Iris, having been sent by Zeus, advises Hector how to manage all of the Trojan allies:

> "In his great city, Priam has many allies. But these foreigners all talk different languages. Let their own captains in each case take charge of them, draw up their countrymen, and lead them into battle." [121]

Later the Trojan and Achaean battalions go into battle. The Achaean captains shouted their orders and their men marched silently forward like an army of the dumb. Homer relates that it was otherwise with the Trojans. They were like sheep in their thousands, bleating incessantly:

> "Such was the babble that went up from the great Trojan army, which hailed from many parts, and being without a common language used many different cries and calls." [122]

Much of the action in the Irish histories clearly takes place around the British Isles. A great deal appears to take place in the Mediterranean, the Aegean and the Black Sea (Euxine), yet there are serious anomalies – some of the voyages defy belief, others are quite impossible. Many of the locations and place-names are familiar to us in a modern Mediterranean setting and there is difficulty in believing that they were not in the same place in ancient times. There are many connections with the Greece of Homer's day but we know that Homer's Troy and Aeneas' voyage could not have taken place in the Mediterranean; that the most likely location is in the vicinity of the British Isles. Could all these familiar locations also have been in the same place at this time? Let us continue to find out more about the inhabitants of these islands. There are many more surprises in store!

ENDNOTES

[91] *The Celtic Realms*, p34.

[92] The *Lebor Gabala Erenn* (The Book of the Taking of Ireland), translated by R.A.Stewart Macalister, Irish Texts Society, Dublin, 5 Vols. (1938, 1939, 1940, 1941, 1956).

[93] Keating, *The History of Ireland*, p91.

[94] Skene, *Celtic Scotland*, Bk.3, Ch.3.

[95] *Celtic Scotland*, p172.

[96] Nennius's *History of the Britons*, III.13.

[97] *The History of the Kings of Britain*, 3.12.

[98] Graves, *The Greek Myths*, 131.

[99] *The History of Ireland*, p231.

[100] *Celtic Scotland*, p172.

[101] Nennius's *History of the Britons*, III.13.

[102] *The Greek Myths*, 131.

[103] *The History of Ireland*, p187.

[104] *Celtic Scotland*, p173.

[105] *The History of Ireland*, p193.

[106] Hubert, *The History of the Celtic People*, p223.

[107] *Celtic Scotland*, p173.

[108] *The History of Ireland*, p203.

[109] *The Book of Druidry*, p57.

[110] See The First Book of the History of England, Ch.3, pp.434-436.

[111] *Celtic Scotland*, p174.

[112] Nennius's *History of the Britons*, III.13.

[113] *Iliad*, 2.868.

[114] Skene, Preface, *Chronicles of the Picts; Chronicles of the Scots*.

[115] Ibid. p378.

[116] *Chronicles of England, Scotland and Ireland*, Vol.5, Scotland, p33.

[117] Supplied by Skene from the Acts of St. Cadroe, *Celtic Scotland*, Ch.4, p182.

[118] Graves, Introduction, *The Greek Myths*, pp.11-24.

[119] *The Greek Myths*, 60.1

[120] *The History of Ireland*, p231.

[121] *Iliad*, 2.802-806.

[122] *Iliad*, 4.433-438.

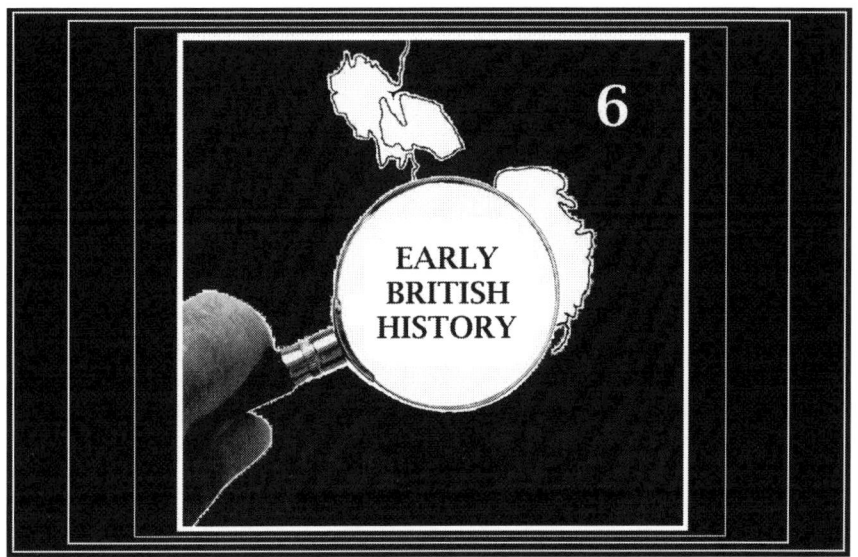

EARLY
BRITISH
HISTORY
6

The Britons, Picts, Scots and Saxons were colonies of foreign races, although those of the Britons and Picts took place at a very remote period. We dealt with the Scots under Early Irish History. The Saxons will not be considered here because of their late arrival in Britain. This leaves us with the Britons and Picts.

PICTS AND CRUITHNE

The settlement of the Picts is represented by the Welsh traditions as a people coming from Scythia, and acquiring first Orkney and afterwards Caithness and then spreading over Scotland from the north. In the 'Pictish Chronicle' the Picti and Scotti are both derived from the Albani of Albania in Asia, and are made two branches of the same people. In the additions to the Irish Nennius they appear under the name of Cruithne, and are said to have been originally Agathyrsi and to have taken possession of the islands Orkney, from whence they spread over the north of Britain.[123] In a Tract on the Picts[124] we are told that they were of the clan Geleoin, son of Ercal, and Icathirsi was their name. Cruithne was the father of the Cruithnec and he was a hundred years in the sovereignty. He had seven sons who divided Alban (Scotland) into seven portions. It appears that they spread over the north of Britain and in later years six brothers left and went eventually to Ireland. Their names were Solen, Ulfa, Nechtan, Drostan, Aengus, and

Leithenn. The story is taken up in the *Irish and Pictish Additions to the Historia Britonum*. It records the origin and deeds of the Cruithne from the time of the departure of these six brothers:

> Thrace was the name of their country
> Till they spread their sails
> After they had resolved to emigrate
> In the East of Europe.
>
> Agathyrsi was their name
> In the portion of Erchbi
> From their tattooing their fair skins
> Were they called Picti.
>
> The Picts, the tribe I speak of
> Understood travelling over the sea
> Without mean, unworthy deeds
> The seed of Geleoin, son of Ercoil.
>
> Six brothers of them
> With alacrity, unflinching
> For glory's sake set out;
> The seventh was their sister.[125]

The Cruithne had left Thrace because Policornis, King of Thrace, fell in love with the sister and he attempted to get her without a dowry. They set out for France and built the city of Pictavis, or Poitiers, and when the King of France fell in love with her, they left and went to Ireland. At the end of two tempestuous days at sea they reached Ireland and landed at Inver Slaine. Their sister, however, had died and they found themselves embroiled in bloody wars in their new country:

> They cut down the plundering host of Fea,
> Who were aided by poison,
> By their fierce deeds,
> In the battle of Ardleamnacht.

The heroes, valiant and numerous,
Cut down knotty woods,
With wonderful arts,
From the Britons their origin.

Dead was everyone they followed,
If but his blood they shed,
So that he wasted away on that account,
Whether a dog or whether a man.[126]

In another version, we are told that when the fleet of the sons of Milidh (Miletians) came to possess in Germany in the east, there came twice eighteen soldiers of the soldiers of Thrace in ships to the sons of Milidh, that is, from the fame and renown of that fleet, till they united with the sons of Milidh, who promised them that they should obtain lands with them if they should themselves acquire a country. The Gaidhil afterwards landed them by force in Ireland, in the land in which are the Cruithneachu.[127]

One common feature is that the Picts and Cruithne were a colony of soldiers who married wives of whom they had obtained from the Irish:

"And it was of the race of the sons of Mileadh they took wives afterwards. They received the daughters of chieftains from the sovereign champions of Erin, and when they had cleared their sword land yonder among the Britons, so that it is in right of mothers they succeed to sovereignty and all other successions to which they were bound by the men of Erin. They took with them from Erin (to north Britain) thrice fifty maidens to become mothers of sons..." [128]

The Greeks called Britain and Ireland the 'Pretanic' islands, and it has long been recognised that 'Pretani' is the Gallo-Brittonic equivalent of the name which in Old Irish is 'Cruithin'. The Irish equivalent enables us to identify the Pretani with the people who are now commonly called Picts.[129] So the Picts and the Cruithne are one and the same.

The Picts of northern Scotland are veiled in obscurity until St. Columba comes among them in the third quarter of the sixth century. Prior to the settlement of the Scots, Cruithne or Picts formed the sole inhabitants of Britain north of the Firths of Forth and Clyde. It seems to have been known to the Romans as early as the first century by the distinctive name of Caledonia, and it also appears to have borne from an early period the Celtic appellation 'Alban', and it's Latin form Albania. Ptolemy located the Caledonii as ranging along the entire boundary of the Highland portion of Scotland, and the Romans called them 'Caledonii Britanni' or Caledonian Britons. On the abdication of Diocletian in 305, Constantius Chlorus became Emperor of the West. In the first year of his reign he appears to have defeated the Picts, who are said by one of the panegyrists to have consisted of the Caledones and other nations. The poets clearly indicate that they considered the Picts the indigenous inhabitants of Caledonia. A twofold division of the Picts existed among them till at least the eighth century. Apparently, the southern division of the Picts bore the name of Caledonians. Bede records the fact that the northern Picts were only converted to Christianity in the year 565 whereas the southern Picts had become Christian more than a century earlier.[130]

SONS OF HERCULES

The Cruithne had descended from the seed of Geleoin, son of Ercoil, or Gelonus, son of Hercules. The ancestry of Cruithne, then, must have been from Gelonus on the male side and Agathyrsi on the female – and they were called Picti from tattooing their skins. Hercules, in his tenth labour, visited Scythia and made love to a serpent-tailed woman, and she gave birth to triplets – Agathyrsus, Gelonus and Scythes. Graves says the serpent-tailed woman was an Earth Goddess, and mother of the three principal Scythian tribes.[131]

Matrilineal succession to the throne is the condition upon which the men of Erin gave wives to the Cruithne. This may indicate that the colony of the Cruithne were of a much later date than the other colonies which had settled in Ireland and, possibly, of a patriarchal persuasion. The Cruithne came from Thrace in the east of Europe. They went direct to France and then to Ireland. The soldiers of Thrace went direct to Germany and then to Ireland. There is no mention of the Cruithne voyaging through the Aegean, the Mediterranean, or the Atlantic. This appears very suspicious in view of the fact that their original home was in close proximity to some of the Irish colonies that came from the same place! Has all reference to their voyage been deleted, or is it possible that in ancient times, Thrace was only a short voyage away from France and Germany? We know that the Picts or Cruithne were originally in the north of Britain and some time later six brothers went to France. Is there a gap in the history at this point or did they come from a Thrace that was actually in Britain at this time? If we refer back a page or two we will see that the answer is given in the words of the Cruithne themselves who, after the battles of Ardleamnacht in Ireland,

> Cut down knotty woods,
> With wonderful arts,
> *From the Britons their origin*

So, Thrace was the name of their country, and it was in Britain.

BRITONS

The Britons deduce their origin from Greeks and Trojans via Brutus the Trojan and his great grandfather, Aeneas of Troy. After the Trojan War Aeneas and his son, Ascanius, arrived in Italy and, having vanquished Turnus the king of the Rutuli, married Lavinia the daughter of king Latinus. Aeneas and Lavinia had a son, Aeneas Silvius, who afterwards ruled Italy. Ascanius married and had a son to whom, out of affection for his younger brother, he gave the same name, Silvius. This Silvius had a son by a niece of Lavinia's, and he was called Brutus. It was Brutus the Trojan who we were told had changed the name of the ancient language in Britain, previously known as Trojan or Crooked Greek, to British. To perpetuate his name he had also called the island Britain and his people Britons. The name of Brutus is found in most, if not all, of the chronicles and genealogies of the early Britons. In particular, it is attested in both Nennius' *Historia Brittonum* and the *Tysilio Chronicle*.[132] All early British history and the genealogical record is traced back from the seventh century AD to Brutus the Trojan, circa 1100BC, and thence to Aeneas of Troy, his great grandfather (See Appendix 3). It was Aeneas who, following the destruction of Troy, led his people on a seven-year voyage in quest of a new settlement. The story is told in Virgil's *Aeneid*, where his destiny is decided by the immortal gods.

During the Trojan War, whilst in the midst of battle with Achilles, the god Poseidon had removed Aeneas to a place of safety because it was fated for

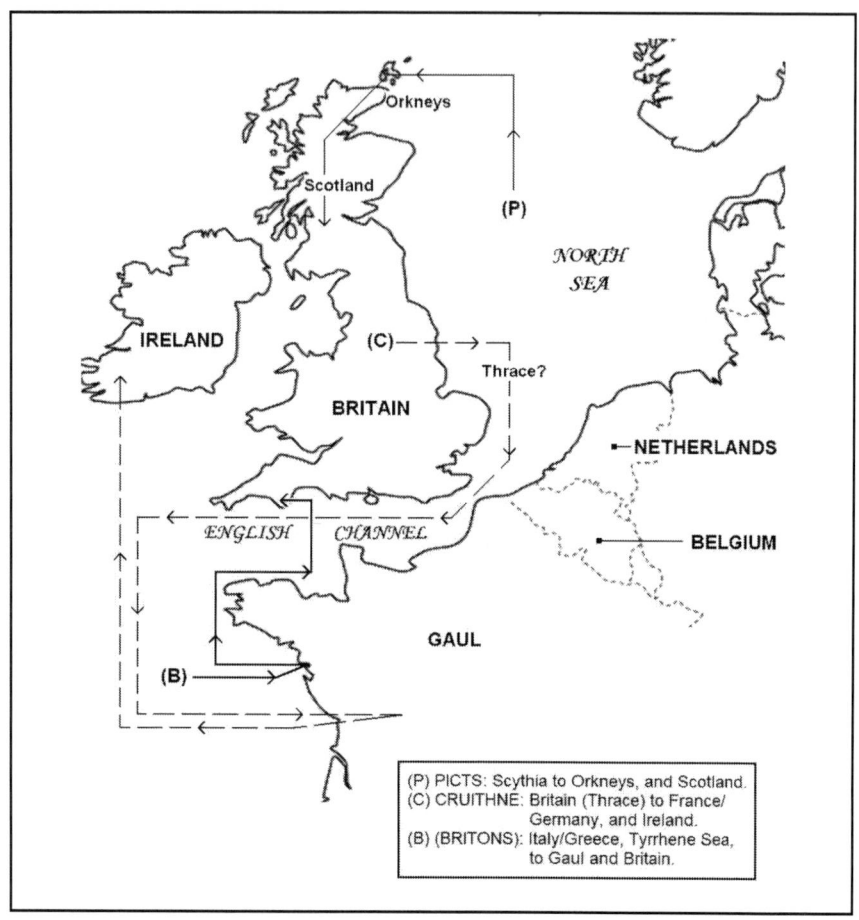

MAP 9.
MIGRATIONS OF PICTS, CRUITHNE, AND BRITONS.

him to escape so that the race of the Dardanians should not perish. 'Aeneas will be king among the Trojans and his sons' sons who will be born in days to come'.[133]

The previous age ends with Aeneas of Troy. As such, Brutus is the new dawn, the beginning of a new age. But, regardless of how he is seen in the British records, he is viewed rather differently in the *Chronicle of the Scots*.[134] Although we do not know the reasons for what is said, the name of Brutus is clearly unpalatable whilst his Trojan lineage is reviled. The Scots come from the most worshipful nation of Greeks and Egyptians, we are informed, whereas Brutus comes from the traitors of Troy......them that bear the foul surname of Anthenor and Aeneas and Helenus, which three procured the treason of Troy. Did the Scots have first-hand knowledge of the destruction of Troy and how it came about? Whether they did or not they independently corroborate the existence of Brutus. In another part of the chronicle we are told that the Scots name was founded and their land inhabited a long time before Troy was destroyed or Brutus was born, and long after that came Brutus in our isle and called it Britain.

When Brutus was in his adolescence, he accidentally killed his father with an arrow:

> "He was, for this cause, expelled from Italy, and came to the islands of the Tyrrhene Sea, when he was exiled on account of the death of Turnus, slain by Aeneas. He then went among the Gauls, and built the city of Turones, called Turnis (Tours). At length he came to this island, named from him Britannia, dwelt there, and filled it with his own descendants, and it has been inhabited from that time to the present period." [135]

THE TYRRHENE SEA

Now, Nennius tells us that Brutus came from Italy to the islands of the Tyrrhene Sea, then to Gaul, and afterwards to Britain. There is no mention of a long voyage through the Mediterranean and Atlantic, a point which we noticed before with the history of the Cruithne and Thrace. The Tyrrhene Sea is mentioned by Virgil in Book I of the *Aeneid*, where Juno in her wrath tries to exterminate the Trojans in a tempest on the waves. But, as we stated before, this tempest is typical of an Atlantic or North Sea environment and not of the Mediterranean – the sea and sky is black, the waves are high as mountains, ships are spun around and hurled on the rocks. Gaul and Britain are both in the location where we consider the voyage of Aeneas to have taken place, but what about the islands of the Tyrrhene Sea where Brutus had just come from? Well, here we have a major clue from the pages of Nennius, a contemporary account giving the British viewpoint of the first occasion when the Romans came to Britain. The Romans had sent ambassadors to the Britons to receive hostages and tribute from them, but the embassy was treated with disdain:

> "At that time Julius Caesar, inasmuch as he was the first to receive and to

hold sole rule, was highly incensed and came to Britain with sixty keels and landed at the mouth of the Thames, where his ships suffered shipwreck, while he himself was fighting with Dolobellus who was proconsul to the British King, who was called Bellinus and was the son of Minocannus, who held all the islands of the Tyrrhene Sea. And Julius returned without victory, his soldiers slain and his ships broken". [136]

So there was a Tyrrhene Sea which belonged to Britain at the time of the first Roman incursion. Of course, it would be absurd to believe that in 55 BC, when the Romans first came to Britain, King Bellinus was the British King but his father, Minocannus, ruled the islands of the Tyrrhene Sea in the Mediterranean. If Minocannus had ruled islands in the Mediterranean then he would have been in the wrong part of the world. He could not have played even the most insignificant part in the defence of the island and would not have been mentioned by Nennius. The British forces took up position along the southern shores of Britain so that they could observe the Roman galleys out in the channel and be ready to do battle wherever they came ashore. It is here, somewhere off the southern shores of the island, that we will find the Tyrrhene sea.

It appears that Nennius is correct when he tells us that Brutus went from the Tyrrhene Sea to Gaul, and then to Britain. The name of this sea goes back from the time of Caesar to Brutus the Trojan and, probably, to much earlier times. This is indicated by the suffix 'hen', which means old or ancient, so 'Tyrr-hen' would mean ancient Tyrr (or Tyrri). The sea was probably named from a person or people called Tyrr or Tyrri. Initially it would have been referred to as Tyrrian but in the course of time the descriptive ending 'hen' would have been added to show that it was then ancient. Tyrrian equates to the Irish Torrian in the same way that the British words Scyti and Lychlyn (Scandinavia) equates to the Irish Scoti and Lochlyn. The Tyrrian (Tyrrhene) Sea is therefore the Torrian Sea, traversed by Partholon on his way from Spain to the Orkneys, and by the Firbolg on their way from Thrace to Spain. So, the Irish histories are correct when they tell us that these colonies sailed over the Torrian Sea. Not only does this make perfect geographical sense, it helps put the wanderings of the Irish colonies into their true Bronze Age setting where they become completely logical and understandable. As we can see, the Torrian/Tyrrhene Sea was the English Channel, a long way from the Mediterranean and Aegean.

In the *Tysilio Chronicle*[137] Brutus is said to have come from the Tyrrhene Sea to Aquitain and/or Angyw (Anjou Province), France. From here his fleet came to the mouth of the Loire and the army of liberated Trojans spent seven days reconnoitring the country. Brutus did battle with Goffar the Pict, king of Poictou, now Poitiers, and it was whilst fighting that his nephew, Tyrri, was killed. From him the place was called Tyrrhi, now Tours. We were informed earlier that the Picts had built Pictavis (Poitiers) when they were in France so it is perfectly logical that Brutus encountered a king of the same city who was indeed a Pict. Furthermore, the Picts were still there a thousand years later when Pliny was enumerating the tribes of Gaul.[138] During his wanderings over the seas Brutus had already visited Greece where he became acquainted with descendants of Helenus, Priam's son, who were in a state of slavery under a king called Pandrasus. After a while Brutus was elected leader of this force of Trojans and Pandrasus was defeated in battle. In order to regain his life and liberty the king agreed to the ransom demands laid down by Brutus.

Pandrasus gave Brutus his daughter, Inogen, as wife in dower, and furnished the Trojans with ships, gold, silver, horses, wine, and wheat. Thus it was that Brutus and his Trojans departed Greece and arrived eventually in Gaul. From here they set sail once again and landed at Totnes in Devon in the Isle of Albion (Britain). Later, Brutus built a city on the Thames called Trinovantum, or New Troy, which is now called London. He married Inogen and had three sons, Locrinus, Kamber, and Albanactus. It is said that Loegria (the Welsh name for England), Cambria (Wales), and Alban (Scotland), received their names from his sons. These were the kingdoms they inherited after their father's death. I am more inclined to believe that Brutus purposefully took pre-existing names of historical significance in the island and endowed his sons with them. It demonstrated his statesmanship and vision in bringing the island together under one supreme sovereign. Whatever the truth of the matter Brutus, the first king of Britain, reigned over the island for twenty four years. He was buried in the city he founded.[139]

The legendary descent of the Britons from Brutus and Aeneas of Troy has always been consistently maintained by native authorities, and it is found to receive ample and unexpected confirmations from the earliest documents of Italy, Gaul, Bretagne, Spain and even Iceland.[140] The ancient Britons are the Cymry, the Welsh of today. Their language, according to an English-Welsh Dictionary by William Evans (Carmarthen 1812), 'is allowed to be one of the most ancient in this western part of the world'. The only two national names acknowledged by the ancient Britons are 'Cymry' and 'Y Lin Troia' (the race of Troy).[141] Taliesin was a 6th century Welsh poet and in his poem 'Hanes Taliesin' he had been carrying out the doctrine of the transmigration of souls. He says that he has existed many times before – he was with the Lord when Lucifer fell, he carried the banner before Alexander, he was in Canaan when Absalom was slain, he was in the Ark with Noah, and he saw the destruction of Sodom and Gomorra. In the middle of the poem, Taliesin speaks of his present incarnation:

> I was in Africa
> Before the building of Rome
> I am now come here
> To the remnants of Troia.[142]

The Romans, who also claimed Trojan descent, had left Britain a century before Taliesin wrote, so the 'remnants of Troia' can only apply to the Britons.[143]

BRITISH-GALLIC RELATIONS

It is difficult to disentangle what appears to have been an extensive and intimate historical connection between the early British and the early Gauls. As far as the language is concerned Gaulish is always considered as a part of the Brythonic branch along with the British i.e. Welsh language. We have been told that Gaulish and British were almost the same. Geography, of course, afforded a not too difficult means of communication across the English Channel and we know that from very early times trade was carried on between Britain and Gaul. In almost all of Caesar's Gallic campaigns the Gauls had received reinforcements from the Britons,[144] but it is not clear if revenge was the real reason for Caesar's invasion of Britain. A kernel of truth may perhaps be found in the *Triads of the Isle of Britain*[145] where it is recorded that Caswallawn, Son of Beli, went to Gaul to retrieve Flur, the daughter of Mygnach the Dwarf. She had been taken there clandestinely to the emperor Caesar by Mwrchan the Thief who was king of Gascony

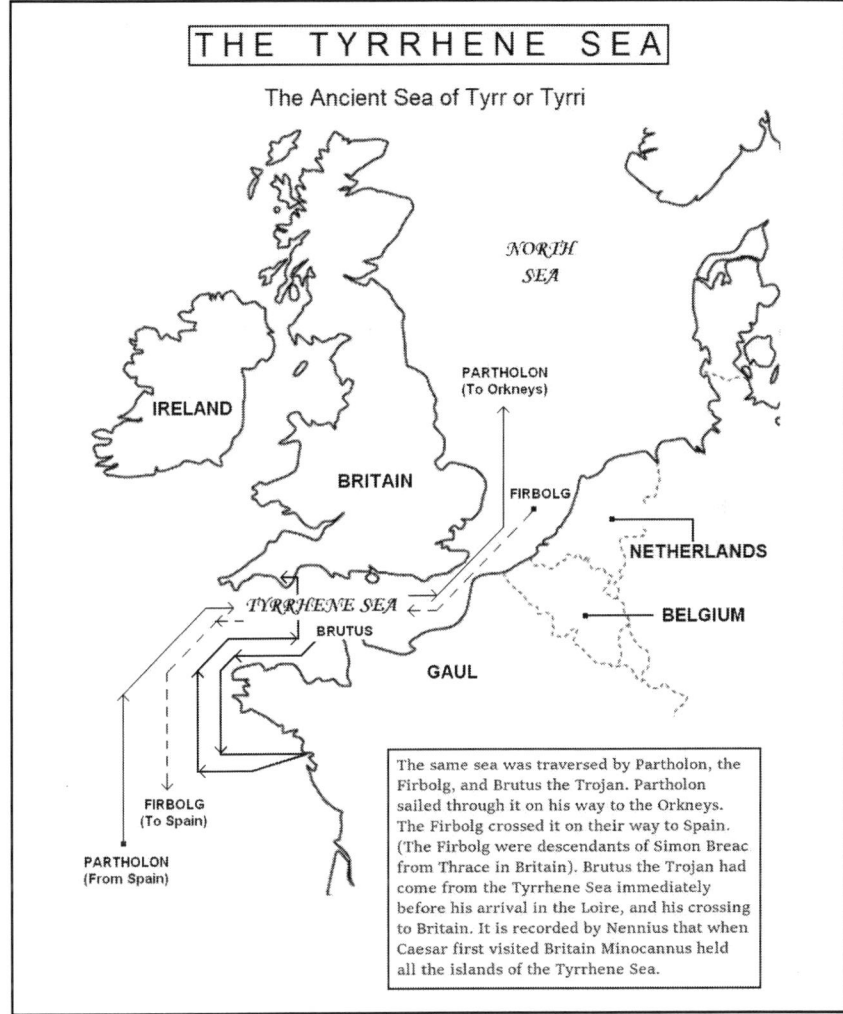

The same sea was traversed by Partholon, the Firbolg, and Brutus the Trojan. Partholon sailed through it on his way to the Orkneys. The Firbolg crossed it on their way to Spain. (The Firbolg were descendants of Simon Breac from Thrace in Britain). Brutus the Trojan had come from the Tyrrhene Sea immediately before his arrival in the Loire, and his crossing to Britain. It is recorded by Nennius that when Caesar first visited Britain Minocannus held all the islands of the Tyrrhene Sea.

MAP 10.

and Caesar's friend. Caswallawn went to Gascony against the Romans and brought her away. It is said that in revenge for Caswallawn killing six thousand Caesarians the Romans invaded Britain. Caswallawn, the Cassivellaunus of Caesar, was paramount sovereign of Britain at the time of the invasion.

The ships of the Gauls were built for sailing the oceans. Caesar describes them at length because they were very different from the ships he was accustomed to in the Mediterranean. They had exceptionally high bows and sterns, which meant that they could be used in heavy seas and violent gales. The hulls were made entirely of oak with cross-timbers a foot wide fastened with iron bolts as thick as a man's thumb. The anchors were secured with iron chains instead of ropes, and sails were of hide or thin leather. The Romans had difficulty coping with the ocean; they found sailing was hazardous at high tide, the ships ran aground at low tide and they did not weather storms easily. For much of the time the Roman ships were weather-bound.[146] At the time of Caesar's campaigns in Gaul the Veneti had the largest fleet of ships and they excelled all in knowledge and experience of navigation.[147] Britain too had its fleets and the most illustrious of these are mentioned in the Triads:

Triad No. 68

The three fleet-owners of the Isle of Britain: Gereint the son of Erbin; Gwenwynwyn the son of Nav; and March the son of Meirchion. Each of these admirals had one hundred and twenty ships, and one hundred and twenty sailors in each ship.[148]

Triad No. 86

The three roving fleets of the Isle of Britain: the fleet of Llawr son of Eidriv; the fleet of Divwg son of Alban; and the fleet of Dolor son of Mwrchath King of Manaw.[149]

It is evident from the *Tysilio Chronicle* that there was frequent intercourse across the English Channel and the North Sea from the earliest of times. Evrauc the King of Britain, around 990 BC, took a fleet and attacked Gaul. He ravaged the country with fire and sword and returned victorious and rich in booty. During his forty-year reign he had by his twenty wives, twenty sons and thirty daughters. His sons went with their fleet to Germany where they gained possession of the country and settled there.[150] In 861 BC King Lear ascended the throne. He had three daughters of whom the youngest, Cordelia, married Aganippus the King of Gaul. King Lear had divided his dominions between his two other daughters but they treated the King with contempt and he was left impoverished. Unable to bear his misfortune any longer he put to sea for Gaul and presented himself shamefully to Cordelia, because he had given her in marriage without a dowry, wealth and honour. Such was the love of Cordelia for her father, however, that Lear was treated with the greatest of respect. Aganippus levied a large force throughout Gaul, sailed to Britain and recovered King Lear's kingdom.[151] About 650 BC we see Ferrex going to Siward, King of Gaul, and having obtained forces from him returned to Britain to defeat and slay his brother in battle.[152] This was the beginning of a 200-year period of civil war in Britain.

About 420 BC the tranquillity of the realm was re-established by Dyfnwall Moelmud, one of the most celebrated Kings of Britain, but after his death his sons Beli and Bran began a violent contest for Sovereignty. Eventually the brothers agreed that Beli, as eldest son, would inherit the sovereignty but Bran would receive a portion of the kingdom. Peace ensued for five years until Bran was incited to renege on the agreement with his brother. Bran sailed for Lychlyn (Scandinavia), married the King's daughter, and was returning with a great force when he encountered the King of Denmark who had pursued him for the sake of the princess. A severe battle took place at sea but then the fleets were dispersed by a severe storm. After landing in Britain, Bran did battle with his brother but was defeated. He then sailed to Gaul and was received kindly by Seguin, the Prince of Burgundy, whose daughter he later married. When Seguin died Bran became Prince of Burgundy and he lost no time in assembling a large force and sailed to Britain to wreak vengeance on his brother. When the two armies were about to engage, Tonwen, their mother, rushed in between the lines and with wise words achieved reconciliation.[153] Later, Beli and Bran together led their armies to Gaul and subjugated the whole Kingdom. They then marched on Rome. The British version of what happened at Rome is given in the *Tysilio Chronicle*[154] and the Roman version in *The Early History of Rome*.[155]

In 374 BC Gwrgant, the son of Beli, succeeded to the sovereignty after his father's death. We are told that he took a fleet to Denmark because the King attempted to shake off the tribute that was due to Britain.[156] In 113 BC Beli Mawr (Beli the Great) succeeded to the throne. He had four sons, of whom Llefelys, because of his prudence and eloquence, Beli was more attached. When the King of Gaul died leaving only a daughter Beli requested her in marriage, of the Gallic Princes. Llefelys was furnished with ships and he sailed to Gaul where he obtained the princess in marriage and her dominions in dower.[157] Lludd was brother to Llefelys and when Beli Mawr died in 73 BC, after a reign of over forty years, Lludd became King. During Lludd's reign three calamities such as had never hitherto been known fell upon the island. Causes were sought in vain and Lludd was greatly distressed. We are told that he sailed to Gaul, consulted his brother and received the solutions to the afflictions affecting Britain.[158]

It can be seen from the above that the British-Gallic connection had a long history and, as with other nations, it included conflict and discord as well as the most glorious of periods. The English Channel and the North Sea were not such serious obstacles to communication and trade, certainly not for experienced mariners. And Britain it seems had had many fleets that were worthy of being celebrated in the historical triads. But it was not only communication and trade that went on across the channel but royal marriages too. And the enduring nature of this intimate connection is such that even today the French call Wales 'Pay de Galles', the land of the Gauls. In the next chapter we will discover that the reasons for this age-old link between the Britons and the Gauls are closely connected to the aftermath of the Trojan War.

ENDNOTES

[123] See Skene, Preface III, *Chronicles of the Picts; Chronicles of the Scots.*

[124] Ibid. pp.322-325.

[125] Ibid. pp.30-33.

[126] Ibid. pp.36-37.

[127] Ibid. Tract on the Picts, p322.

[128] Ibid. pp.319-320.

[129] See 'The Pretanic Background in Britain and Ireland', p127, in *A Celtic Reader*, Ed. John Mathews.

[130] See Skene, *Celtic Scotland*, Ch. 1-3.

[131] *The Greek Myths*, 132.6.

[132] See *The Chronicle of the Kings of Britain.* The Welsh copy, attributed to Tysilio, was translated into English in 1811 by Peter Roberts.. A facsimile reprint is available from Llanerch Publishers, Lampeter, Wales.

[133] *Iliad*, 20. 300-308.

[134] See Skene, *Chronicles of the Picts;Chronicles of the Scots*, p378.

[135] Nennius 10.

[136] Nennius 19.

[137] See Roberts, *Chron. Kings Brit.*, pp. 20-25.

[138] Pliny, *Natural History*, XIX.

[139] See Roberts, *Chron. Kings Brit.*, pp. 30-31.

[140] See Introduction, *The British Kymry*.

[141] Ibid. p22.

[142] See Nash, *Taliesin; The Bards and Druids of Britain*, p162.

[143] Beale Poste, *Britannic Researches*, p220.

[144] Caesar, *The Conquest of Gaul*, iv.20.

[145] See Triads 102 and 124, *The Ancient Laws of Cambria*, pp. 408 and 413.

[146] Caesar, *The Conquest of Gaul*, iii.12-13.

[147] Ibid. iii.8.

[148] *The Ancient Laws of Cambria*, p400.

[149] Ibid. p404.

[150] See Roberts, *Chron. Kings Brit.* pp. 36-38.

[151] Ibid. pp. 41-44.

[152] Ibid. p46.

[153] Ibid. pp. 50-56.

[154] Ibid. pp. 56-59.

[155] Livy 5. 36-55.

[156] See Roberts, *Chron. Kings Brit.* p60.

[157] Ibid. pp. 66-67.

[158] Ibid. pp. 66-71.

In the last chapter we found that the British-Gallic connection had a long history stretching back to at least 900 BC. In this chapter we will see that there is considerable verification of these events from the continent and, particularly, from Gallic sources.

In Gaul also there were elements of the Gallic population who maintained that they were connected with or descended from Trojan stock. In addition, a number of notices have come down to us respecting fugitives from Troy and the founding of new Trojan cities in Gaul. We will find that most of these stories are not myths but legitimate accounts, and they are supported by historical records. These records paint a picture that is truly astonishing. It shows that the north western part of Europe was subjected to an influx of vast numbers of immigrants in the centuries following the Trojan War. These people were fugitives from Troy and the princes and kings from these Trojan lines would go on to rule the greater part of Europe. For our purposes we shall consider Gaul in early times to have been not much different to what it was at the time of Caesar's death. The mountain ranges of the Pyrenees and the Alps were great natural boundaries, as were the Mediterranean and Atlantic. The other natural boundary was the river Rhine as its north eastern border. Gaul then comprised modern France and Belgium, together with parts of Holland, Germany and Switzerland.

THE GAULS

At the beginning of the third century B.C. the name of 'Galations' appears for the first time in the historian Hieronymos of Cardia who wrote of their invasion of Macedonia and Greece and their settlements in Asia Minor.[159] Diodorus Siculus tells us that the most savage people among the Gauls are those who dwell beneath the Bears and on the borders of Scythia:

"...some men say that it was they who in ancient times overran all Asia and were called Cimmerians, time having corrupted the word into the name of Cimbrians, as they are now called".[160]

Diodorus then continues:

"For they are the people who captured Rome, who plundered Delphi, who levied tribute upon a large part of Europe and no small part of Asia, and settled themselves upon the lands of the peoples they had subdued in war, being called in time Graeco-Gauls, because they became mixed with the Greeks, and who, as their last accomplishment, have destroyed many large Roman armies."

Diodorus clearly distinguishes between what he has heard about the Gauls in ancient times and what he knows about them in recent times. In ancient times they are said to have overrun all Asia – and it was in Asia where the Trojan War took place – so, is it possible that this is a recollection of those times? Virgil tells us of the Gauls in the eighth book of the *Aeneid*, when Venus delivers to Aeneas a suit of armour fashioned by Vulcan. On the shield were portraits of the history to follow. Rome was depicted when Porsena held the city in the grasp of a strong blockade, and a silver goose cried that the Gauls were on the threshold:

"Their clustering locks, are of gold, and of gold their attire; their striped cloaks and their milk-white necks are entwined with gold. Two alpine pikes sparkle in the hand of each, and long shields guard their bodies". [161]

The Gauls claim descent from Heracles' union with a tall princess named Galata, or Galatea, and she was the mother of the Gauls, the Celts, and the Illyrians. According to Caesar's Commentaries, the Gauls boasted that they had sprung from father Dis, and that they derived their information from the Druids. Of the two classes of persons who enjoyed honour and estimation among the Gauls, one of these was the Druids. Gaul got her classical culture from Gallic teachers trained by the Druids, and some of them were fit to teach in Rome.

TROJAN TALES

Between the fifth and seventh centuries AD the Merovingians ruled large parts of what are now France and Germany. The dynasty was mantled in an aura of magic, sorcery and the supernatural. According to tradition, Merovingian monarchs were occult adepts, initiates in arcane sciences, and practitioners of esoteric arts. They were frequently called 'the longhaired kings' and, like Samson's, their hair supposedly contained the essence and secret of their power. They were regarded as priest-kings, embodiments of the divine, similar to the ancient Egyptian pharaohs. The Merovingians claimed direct descent from ancient Troy, with a pedigree that could be traced back to the Old Testament. We are told that the ancestors of the Merovingians were connected with Arcadia's royal house in ancient Greece.[162] Later, we will see just where the Merovingians came from and the line of Troy that they claimed as their descent.

Ammianus Marcellinus, in chapter xv of his history, informs us of a tale that prevailed among the Gauls relating to their Trojan origin. 'They say that a few Trojans, fleeing from the Greeks, and dispersed, occupied these places, then uninhabited'.[163] Elton tells us in his *Origins of English History* that of the ancient tribes of Britain there were Damnonians in central Scotland as well as in Cornwall and Devon. A third Damnonia can be traced in the midland and western parts of Ireland. Another home of the race was founded in Brittany near the Forest of Broceliande. It appears that they were exiles from Britain who carried the old names and built a replica of the Trojan citadel in their new land.[164] Why would exiles from Britain build a replica of a Trojan citadel in France? The answer, perhaps, is that they were connected in some way with the original city of Troy. Is this an indication that Troy was not only near Britain but actually **in** Britain?

Hubert comments that the tribes of the Aedui and Arverni of Gaul connected themselves with Trojans by lines unknown to us.[165] The Arvernian people considered themselves brothers of the Romans because of their Trojan blood, but Sidonius Apollinaris appears to be the only writer to provide us with an insight into their ancient connection. Sidonius was a poet and diplomat who became bishop of Auvergne. He was born about 430 AD into an aristocratic Gallo-Roman family. He married the daughter of a consul, became a Prefect of Rome and a Senator. In a letter written to his friend Domitius he describes the lake on his estate and tells him 'Our fathers used to hold boat races here in imitation of the Trojan ceremonial games at Drepanum'. In another letter to the Lord Bishop Graecus he declares that the Auvergne region is in an unhappy and miserable state. Their enslavement was shameful to 'those Arvernians who by old tradition claimed brotherhood with Latium and descent from the sons of Troy'.[166]

Diodorus Siculus gives us another account:

"For a similar reason, they say, the city of Troy likewise, which even to this day exists on the bank of the Nile, received its name: for Menelaus, on his voyage from Ilium with a great number of captives, crossed over into Egypt; and the Trojans, revolting from him, seized a certain place and maintained a warfare until he granted them safety and freedom, whereupon they founded a city, to which they gave the name of their native land". [167]

Surprisingly, the Egypt of the Bronze Age has been identified as the Seine Maritime area of northern France.[168] The Land of the Pharaohs was not known as 'Egypt' until at least 700 years after the Trojan War. It was Herodotus who first called it Egypt in the fifth century BC. And it was one hundred and fifty years later that Alexander the Great made it the official name of the country. Further, the name 'Nile' was never used in the Old Testament to describe the 'River of Egypt' in the Land of the Pharaohs. Homer's descriptions do not fit the Egypt of today, whereas they do correspond to the region near Vernon, halfway between Paris and Rouen, France, where the river Epte (Egypt?) flows into the Seine. Many of the villages in the area actually retain the word 'Nile' in their names via the French equivalent of 'Nil'; these include Mesnil, Miromesnil, Mormesnil, Frichemesnil, Longmesnil, Vilmesnil, and a number of names in Paris itself. It would appear then that the information given us by Diodorus refers to the Bronze Age Egypt in northern France. For Menelaus to cross over into Egypt (Seine Maritime) from Ilium, then Ilium (Troy) must be very close to northern France.

TROJAN MIGRATIONS TO GAUL

After the devastating war at Troy it appears that the populace in the conquered regions fled from the Greeks to various parts of Europe. This was not just a small band of fugitives but migration on a massive scale. One of the groups of fugitives was led by Aeneas, the Trojan prince whose voyage we have been investigating in order to locate the Bronze Age Troy. Another group was led by Francio, the son of Hector and heir to the line of Samothes in Gaul. A third group was conducted into Western Europe by Bavo and he governed the Celts and the Belgians. A further group of fugitives came with Francus, heir to the House of Troy, and he began a line of kings that ultimately ruled in Gaul. Yet another group migrated under Marcomirus but at a much later date. In Europe they became the kings of the Sicambrians. The evidence for all of this comes from the records of the kings of Isauria, Sicambria, Pannonia, and Agrippina (Cologne); the records of the princes and dukes of Brabant, and the kings and dukes of Frisia; the records of the kings of the Belgians, the Celts, and the Franks; and the records of the Hapsburgs, East Franks, and the dukes of Gaul. These records and related histories have been brought together by Herman L. Hoeh[169] who says, 'The evidence proves that civilized people migrated to Gaul and the Low Countries centuries before the founding of Rome'. Here is a brief summary of Hoeh's information:

SURVIVAL OF THE HOUSE OF TROY

As incredible as it may seem the House of Troy survived the ten-year war and the fall of the city. Even more incredible is the fact that the full story of the royal Trojan House that returned to power in Troy has been preserved in the records of the Spanish Hapsburgs. The reason for this is that the Hapsburgs were lineal descendants of the House of Troy. We are told one of the sons of King Priam was named Helenus and after 1149 BC his descendants captured control of the city from the Greeks. The line of Dardanus was once again restored to Troy and the descendants of this Helenus governed until a third Trojan War ended the city in 677 BC. A complete list of Trojan rulers after the Trojan War of King Priam's days may be found in the original Spanish work by Bartholome Gutierrez entitled: '*Historia del estado presente y antiguo, de la mui noble y mui leal ciudad de Xerez de la Frontera*'. It was published in Xerez, Spain in 1886. After 677 BC members of the Trojan royal family and most of the population fled, apparently to the Black Sea, where they lived until 445 BC when their leader, Antenor, fell in battle against the Goths. Antenor's son, Marcomirus, later led the Trojans to the ancient territory of the Sicambri, now called West Frieseland, Gelders and Holland. Marcomirus was the first king of the Sicambri, later to be known as Franks. We are informed that they moved to the mouth of the Rhine where they built a New Troy at Xanten. The original settling of the Franks at the mouth of the Rhine is supported by Procopius who records the fact that it was where the Germans, now called Franks, lived of old. It is at this point that Hunibald, the Frankish chronicler, begins his history. (Hunibald's Chronicle is from Johannes Trittenheim, '*Chronik von der Francken Ursprung*', Frankfurt, 1605.)

SICAMBRIAN KINGS AND KINGS OF THE FRANKS

Hunibald's genealogical list of the Frankish Kings begins with Marcomirus, the first King of the Sicambri in 444 BC, and continues down to Clovis the first Christian King of the Franks in 511AD. Hunibald states that the name 'Sicambri' was derived from Cambra the wife of Antenor I, the son of Marcomirus. Other chroniclers say it came from the name of a city called Sicambria on the Black Sea. Between 444 BC and 416 BC Marcomirus crossed the Rhine and conquered part of Gaul. Gradually he completed the conquest of the whole of Gaul. The seventeenth King of the Sicambri was Antharius who commenced his reign in 76BC. He offended Caesar by refusing to deliver up to him Roman soldiers who had revolted to the Sicambri. Antharius and 2000 of his men were slain by the Gauls. His son, Francus, succeeded to the throne in 41 AD and in the fourth year of his reign the name of Sicambri was changed to Franci by an edict at the peoples request. In 322 AD Clodomirus V, the thirty-seventh king in succession from Marcomirus, sends 30,000 colonists to the river Main and establishes the Dukedom of Franconia. The Dukedom survives up to the time of Pepin the Short in 761 AD. The Franks were now permitted to resettle themselves where Holland, Utrecht, Gelders, part of Friesia, Westphalia and Brabant now lie. The Franks now split and the East Franks settle in

Germany. The forty-sixth king was Meroveus, after whom the Franks were called Merovingians.

THE HAPSBURGS

Pharamundus was the 5th Duke of Franconia (East Franks) and he became King of the West Franks in 417 AD. He is reckoned by early historians to have been the first King of France. From Pharamundus came a princely line of rulers who intermarried with Austrian royalty. The line is preserved in the *'Historia de Xerez'* by Gutierrez. The Hapsburgs (or Habsburgs) was the most prominent European royal dynasty from the 15th to the 20th century. Rudolph II became Holy Roman Emperor in 1273. In 1516 Charles V inherited the Spanish crown with its European and American possessions. The Spanish branch ruled until 1700. In the seventeenth century the Austrian Hapsburgs became emperors of Austria and Austria-Hungary.

TROJAN KINGS OF THE HOUSE OF BRABANT

Refugees led by Francio the son of Hector fled Troy and migrated eventually to France. They became ancestors of the house of the Dukes of Brabant, an old province embracing parts of modern Belgium and the Netherlands. The histories cover the Trojan Kings of Isauria, Sicambria and Pannonia, the Kings of Agrippina (Cologne) and the Princes and Dukes of Brabant. From this family came Charlemagne, the first Emperor of the Holy Roman Empire. A complete list of these Trojan rulers from Hector down to Charlemagne is found in the work by Jhr. C. A. Rethaan Macare entitled *'Oude Kronijk van Brabant'* in the *'Codex Diplomaticus Neirlandicus'* series 2, part 3, published by Het Historisch Genootschap te Utrecht, Utrecht Holland in 1855.

TROJAN KINGS OF THE BELGIANS

Bavo led another group of refugees from Troy. He was the son of a sister of Laomedon a cousin of King Priam. These refugees reached the Rhine about 1179 BC. The little known story of the royal family that governed the Celts and the Belgians has been preserved by Jacques de Guyse in his *'Histoire de Hainaut'*, a French translation of his original Latin work

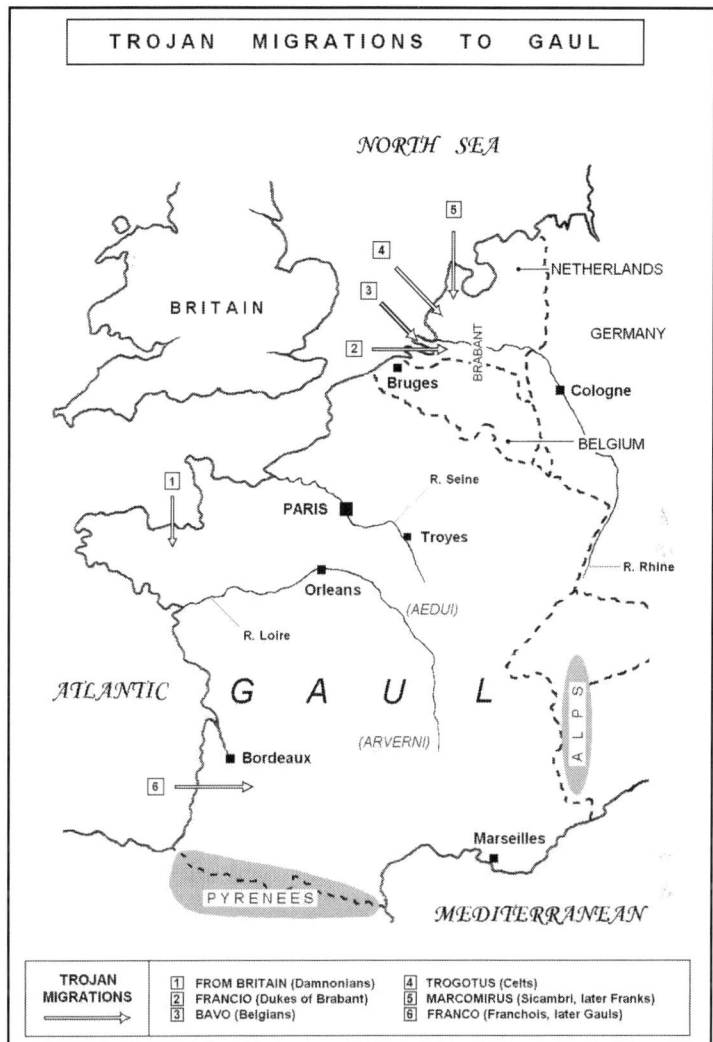

TROJAN MIGRATIONS TO GAUL

MAP 11.

of the thirteenth century. Hainaut was an ancient division of Belgium. As Herman L. Hoeh explains, archaeology may not have the answer to just who the people of Belgium, Holland, Frisia, Luxembourg and northern France are, but history certainly does. Bavo became the first priest-king of the Belgians and a line of priest-kings continued down to 776 BC when political upheaval forced a change in the form of government. A warrior king called Ursus came to the throne and he organised much of continental Western Europe under his power. This line of kings continued for another three hundred years and after a short period of annually elected dukes continued again down to 52 BC when Rome crushed Belgium and Gaul.

THE DUKES OF GAUL

At the end of the first Trojan War still another group of fugitives left Troy led by Franco the son of Hector. The story of their migration to Gaul is extant and is found in a medieval French chronicle, *'Le Myreur d'Histoir'* *(The Mirror of History)*. This line of rulers is preserved from Franco in 1181 BC down to Clovis, King of France in 511 AD. It is stated that Franco left Troy with Aeneas and Antenor but that he and 3000 of his followers settled in southern Gaul. They called the area where they settled Franche and the people were known as Franchois. After Franco's death they were known as Gauls.

TROJAN NAMES

Trojan family names are evident in nearly all of the Gallic records, the most prominent being those of Helenus, Troylus, Antenor, Hector, and Priam. These names were still being used in the genealogies in the sixth century AD. In the records of the Dukes of Gaul, in particular, it appears that the founding of cities was regarded as a significant accomplishment because there are many notices of sovereigns giving their names to cities and regions. For example, Ylion II founded Limoges c. 700 BC, Nay founded Turnay c. 670 BC, and Orlins built and gave his name to Orleans c. 550 BC. Brugen founded Bruges whilst his brother, Amyrus, founded Amiens c. 290 BC. Of names given to regions we are told that Allemania, a section of Germany, derives its name from Alemaine, the son of Bosses. The ruler Alymodes had a son called Aquitaine and he gave his name to that region of France, whilst the Auvergne derives its name from Avrengas. Frise, in Champagne, is named after Frisones, and Touraine from Turrus.

There is also an interesting entry under Ector I (1096BC – 1080BC) where it is recorded that he founded Troy in Burgogne. Troyes is situated at the edge of the modern province of Bourgogne and thus may be the Troy mentioned by Diodorus Siculus. In the lists of the Trojan kings of Sicambria and Pannonia it is recorded that in the days of Hector III (881BC – 874BC) six Sicambrian heroes or rulers migrated to France with 4,000 men. Under the leadership of Yber they built a city called Paris and called themselves Parisii.

BRITISH HISTORY VALIDATED

Not only do these records correlate to a remarkable degree, they also independently verify the authenticity of the British history. In addition, they furnish us with information about early British history hitherto unknown.

In the chronicles relating to the Dukes of Gaul we are told that Melus, a son of Franco, rebuilt Troy in 1145 BC. Knowing now that Troy was recaptured sometime after 1149 BC means that we have independent verification of important information in Britain's *Tysilio Chronicle*. Brutus the Trojan had just built his 'New Troy' on the bank of the river Thames in Britain. It is here that we are given a chronological dating statement that fixes the time within close parameters by telling us what is happening elsewhere at this time.

> "In Troy, a son of Hector's who had expelled Antenor and his family, was King; and in Italy Silvius, the son of Ascanius, and grandson of Aeneas; and the uncle of Brutus reigned the third King after Latinus".[170]

The British Chronicle gives no information about Troy being recaptured but it does confirm that there was Trojan rule in the city about 1104 BC.

In the chronicles relating to the Sicambrian Kings we are told that their original settlement on the mouth of the Rhine was where the Germans lived of old. The Trojans under Bavo had reached the Rhine about 1179 BC. They became kings of Belgium, Holland, Frisia, Luxembourg, and northern France. Alemaine (1080BC-1058BC), of the line of the dukes of Gaul, conquered all Germany and Allemania was named from him. Alemaine was the son of Bosses who had married into the Trojan-British line. Is it mere coincidence that the sons of the Trojan-British King, Efrawg, went to Germany about one hundred years later and took possession of the country?

The most natural place for them to disembark after sailing across the channel would be the mouth of the Rhine. It would make perfect sense then for the Sicambrians at a later date to settle in the same area as their compatriots.

The daughter of Melus (who rebuilt Troy in 1145 BC) was called Odela and his son was called Bosses. According to the French chronicle Odela married Silvius the King of Italy and Bosses married Grata the daughter of Ascanius. These marriages occurred during the reigns of Melus and Bosses between 1171 BC and 1096 BC. Ascanius and Silvius are part of the Trojan-British lineage. They would have reigned about 1155 BC and 1130 BC respectively. But there is no mention of Ascanius' daughter in the British Chronicles. Other marriages mentioned in the *Tysylio Chronicle*, however, are attested by chronicles from the continent. The Belgian chronicle states that Aganippus II (885 BC - 835 BC) was husband to the British Queen Cordelia. Aganippus was a priest-king of the Belgians. He died almost the same time as Cordelia's father, the British King Lear. Afterwards, Cordelia became Queen and governed Britain for five years but died in prison after an insurrection removed her from the throne.[171]

The Annals of Hainaut[172] state that Gurguncius, (the British King Gurgust) reigned over the Belgians from 741 BC to 713 BC and afterwards his son Sisillius ruled the Belgians while his father governed the Britons (713 BC – 703 BC). This is new information about these two kings from an independent source, and attests to the reigns of both kings who are only briefly mentioned in the British chronicle. Again, the Frankish chronicler, Hunibald, provides us with important information that we can use to test the veracity of the Tysilio Chronicle. Antenor I is listed as the third Sicambrian King who reigned from 416 BC to 386 BC. We are told that he married Cambra the beautiful daughter of Belinus, King of Britain. Belinus reigned in Britain from 395 BC to 374 BC and is remembered primarily for leading the Gallic armies against Rome. What is not so well known is that Belinus (Beli) was responsible for many civic works and for building Britain's first major highways of stone and mortar. There is, however, no reference to his daughter in the British history.[173]

The tenth Sicambrian King was Nicanor (234 BC–200 BC) and he married Constantina, daughter of the British King. Unfortunately we are not provided with the name of the king but Nicanor twice aided his father-in-law in a war against the Orcades (Orkneys). The twenty-seventh Sicambrian King, (now termed King of the Franks) was Marcomirus IV (125 BC – 146 BC) and he married Athilde, daughter of the King of Britain.

TROY IDENTIFIED

So, where did all the Trojan fugitives who migrated to Gaul come from? Earlier, we had narrowed down the probable location of Troy to southern Britain and the shores of the English Channel and the North Sea.[174] In our examination of the Gallic records we found a great deal of material that testified to an authentic early history of north Western Europe, including that of Britain. In this examination, however, it was not expected that any information would emerge which would finally resolve the question of where Troy was located. But this is exactly what happened. The records of the kings of the Celts had preserved an account that was electrifying. It related to Francus who began a line of kings that ultimately ruled in Gaul. When the priest-kings of the line of Bavo were ruling over the Belgians the Celts in Europe were being governed by the Trojan line of Francus. This line continued unbroken down to 776BC when Ursus the warrior-king came to power in Belgium.

It appears that the Celts lost their independence to Ursus, the Belgian king, and the two lines of kings became one. But it is the information about Francus himself that is so riveting. He was heir to the House of Troy and he supported the Trojans against the Greeks. After the Greek victory he continued to govern the Celts. But, he was more than the king of the Celts. Francus was **the last king of the Britons** until Brutus. According to the historian Freculphe, (see Vol. 19 of 'Histoire de Hainaut', sec. cclxvii.) Francus turned over the government of Britain to the Druids (until the time of Brutus). These are definitive statements. They show that Troy could only have been in Britain. Francus was **king of the Britons, in Britain,** and he was involved in the Trojan War. When all was lost he ensured that the governance of the island was in secure hands. It remained under the custodianship of the druids until a future king by the name of Brutus once again became the supreme sovereign.

This time the name of Francus is attested in British records, in a Catalogue of Kings and Princes of Britain from Samothes down to the coming of the

Romans.[175] Brutus the Trojan is listed as the twenty-sixth king of the Britons after Samothes. Brutus became king of Britain in 1104 BC, which means that Samothes must have reigned around 1800-2000 BC. The twenty-fourth king of the Britons is Francus, which corroborates the information in the Gallic records. After Francus comes Pictus, and after Pictus is appended a note, possibly indicating a gap or interregnum:

> "After whom Brute entreth into the Iland, either neglected by the Celts, or otherwise by conquest, and reigned therein with his posteritie by the space of 636 years …"

Clearly, the compilers of this information knew only that there was a gap in the continuous line of kings but they did not know why. It appears that this was the reason for appending such a note. The actual events had been lost to British history, although not to the history of Gaul.

The Gallic records also tell us that a number of Trojan colonies migrated indirectly to Gaul via certain areas of the Black Sea. We are told that 12,000 Trojan Phrygians moved to the Black Sea under a leader Friga immediately after the fall of Troy. These were joined by the descendants of Helenus in 677 BC and migrated as one colony to the Rhine in 439 BC. Exiles under Francus (the last king of the Britons) went first to the Black Sea and migrated to the Rhine in 1040 BC under their leader Trogotus. Exiles under Franco (or Francio) also went to the Black Sea area and migrated afterwards to the Rhine, but there is some confusion as to the actual date of their arrival there. This is the same Black Sea that is so closely associated with the migrations of the Irish tribes and which the evidence so far indicates was in or near Britain in the Bronze Age. We shall soon discover for ourselves the exact Bronze Age location of the Black Sea and it will become apparent just how logical and straightforward were these Trojan migrations.

ENDNOTES

[159] See Hubert, *The History of the Celtic People*, p21.

[160] Diodorus Siculus, Bk.5.32.

[161] *Aeneid*, 8. 659-662.

[162] See *The Holy Blood and the Holy Grail*, pp. 245-250 and 282-288.

[163] See Beale Poste, *Britannic Researches*, p220.

[164] Elton, *Origins of English History*, p234.

[165] *The History of the Celtic People*, p26.

[166] *Sidonius Apollinaris Letters*, pp. 34-62, Book II; and Vol. 2, pp. 95-137, Book VII.

[167] Diodorus Siculus, Bk.1.56.

[168] See Wilkens, pp. 101-103.

[169] *Compendium of World History*, Vol.2, Ch. 12 and 12A. See www.earth-history.com

[170] See Roberts, *The Chronicle of the Kings of Britain*, p31.

[171] Ibid. pp. 42-45.

[172] See note 11.

[173] Ibid. pp. 49-59.

[174] See results of Chapters 5 and 6.

[175] See *Holinshed's Chronicles of England, Scotland and Ireland*, Vol.1, 'The Description of Britaine', Ch.6, p31.

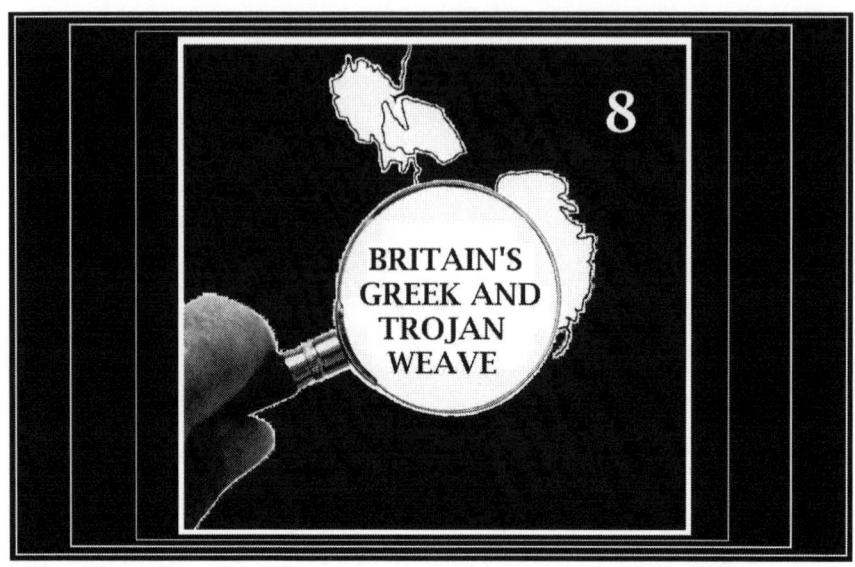

BRITAIN'S
GREEK AND
TROJAN
WEAVE

8

In Chapter 4 we began to see that there was a Greek and Trojan thread running through what we termed the ancient tapestry of the British Isles. In the last few chapters we have found that all of the Irish colonies were Greek and from the same general area of the Black Sea and Thrace. In themselves the Danaan and Milesian episodes point to a common identity for the Greeks and the Irish. The Picts and Cruithne came from Thrace and married wives obtained from the Irish. The Scots came from the Hellespontine area but they too claim descent from the son of a Greek king. The Britons and Gauls, however, claim Trojan origins. Brutus, the Grandson of Aeneas of Troy, came from Italy with a colony of Trojans to the Tyrrhene Sea and then to Britain.

Throughout these accounts references are made to place names that are familiar in a modern Mediterranean setting. Surprisingly, we will discover that in Homer's day they were to be found in a different part of the world. In due course we will locate Thrace, the Black Sea and the Hellespont in their Bronze Age setting and the various journeys of the Irish and British tribes will then no longer be unintelligible but will be found to be realistic and straightforward. In addition, the geography in these accounts will turn out to be amazingly accurate.

Our perspective has changed dramatically since we first observed a Greek and Trojan thread in the British Isles' dim and distant past. The threads have increased greatly and have woven together into a more coherent and discernible interpretation of the past. In the pages that follow we will develop our latest findings and make new discoveries whilst also covering in detail many of the topics dealt with only briefly in chapter four. Some of these fall naturally into the subject matter of their respective chapters whereas others will be discussed here. They are all part of Britain's Greek and Trojan weave.

APOLLO AND THE HYPERBOREANS

Apollo, the god of the Hyperboreans, is clearly identified with Britain. This is Diodorus' famous quotation from the historian Hecateus[176] (sixth century BC.):

"Of those who have written about the ancient myths, Hecataeus and certain others say that in the regions beyond the land of the Celts (Gaul) there lies in the ocean an island no smaller than Sicily. This island, the account continues, is situated in the north and is inhabited by the Hyperboreans, who are called by that name because their home is beyond the point whence the north wind blows: and the island is both fertile and productive of every crop, and since it has an unusually temperate climate it produces two harvests each year. Moreover, the following legend is told concerning it: Leto was born on this island, and for that reason Apollo is honoured among them above all other gods; and the inhabitants are looked upon as priests of Apollo, after a manner, since daily they praise this god continuously in song and honour him exceedingly. And there is also on the island both a magnificent sacred precinct of Apollo and a notable temple which is adorned with many votive offerings and is spherical in shape. Furthermore, a city is there which is sacred to this god, and the majority of its inhabitants are players on the Cithara; and these continually play on this instrument in the temple and sing hymns of praise to the god, glorifying his deeds. The Hyperboreans also have a language, we are informed, which is peculiar to them, and are most friendly disposed towards the Greeks and especially towards the Athenians and Delians, who have inherited this goodwill from most ancient times. The myth also relates that certain Greeks visited the Hyperboreans and left behind them there, costly votive offerings bearing inscriptions in Greek letters. And in the same way Abaris, a Hyperborean, came to Greece in ancient times and renewed the goodwill and kinship of his people to the Delians. They say also that the moon, as viewed from this island, appears to be but a little distance from the earth and to have upon it prominences, like those of the earth, which are visible to the eye. The account is also given that the god visits the island every nineteen years, the period in which the return of the stars to the same place in the heavens is accomplished; and for this reason the nineteen-year period is called by the Greeks the "year of Meton". At the time of this appearance of the god he both plays on the cithara and dances continuously the night through from the vernal equinox until the rising of the Pleiades expressing in this manner his delight in his successes. And the kings of this city and the supervisors of the sacred precinct are called Boreadae, since they are descendants of Boreas and the succession to these positions is always kept in the family."

There is no mistaking the fact that the island beyond Gaul is Britain. Apollo's mother, Leto, was born on the island, which explains the veneration for this god. He was essentially a northern deity. Despite being mentioned by Caesar the figure of Apollo doesn't belong to Roman mythology. He was introduced by the Etruscans as a deity linked to plague and epidemics, and then by the Greeks as a solar character.[177] The swan, a solar symbol linked to Apollo, is a Nordic hyperborean beast. Countless examples exist in Celtic tradition, notably the goddesses of the Tuatha de Danaan, the Irish people whom earlier we traced to Britain. Comyns Beaumont provisionally recognised the Hyperboreans as the Kimmerians.[178] In this respect it is interesting to note Plutarchs quotation from Heracleides Ponticos, which refers to the fall of Rome. Heracleides 'relates in his *Treatise on the Soul* that news came to Pontus, simultaneously with the event, that an army from the land of the Hyperboreians had taken a Greek city named Rome, situated near the Great Sea'.[179] It was the Gauls who sacked Rome, or to be technically correct, the nation of the Cymry or Cimmerians. The Hyperboreans of Britain are thus equated with the Cimmerians of Britain.

The Greek traditions concerning the founding of the Delphic cult say that prophets came from the Hyperboreans and they founded the oracle. Their names were Pagasis, Agyeus, and Olen, and Olen was the first who returned answers in heroic verse. In the old Irish books these are the names given to three ranks of Irish Druids, Bag-ois, Agh-ios, and Ollam, and Ollam is said

FIG. 8. APOLLO.
(Rome, Capitoline Museum)
Acknowledgement Wikimedia Commons.
Apollo was a purely British God.

to have been an expounder of the law of nature.[180] When Caesar speaks of the druids of Gaul he states that their doctrine was established in Britain and this is corroborated by numerous Irish sources. Irish druidism has never been claimed as being indigenous to Ireland. Indeed, it has always been stated that to complete their studies they also went to Britain.[181] Abaris was a celebrated philosopher of the Hyperboreans whom Godfrey Higgins identifies as a priest of Apollo and an Irish or British Druid.

An account in Ireland of a person called Abhras perfectly agrees with the description of the Hyperborean Abaris of Diodorus and Himerius. The Irish Abhras is said to have gone to distant parts in quest of knowledge, and after a long time to have returned by way of Scotland, where he remained seven years, bringing a new system of religion. According to Suidas he is said to have come from the Hyperborean island to the north of Gaul.[182]

The Hyperborean Apollo's arrival in Delphi represents the introduction of a new solar cult. Here, the sun played a primordial role that was regarded as essential for human survival. For the Greeks the solar character of Apollo was most important.[183] It has often been remarked that the Hyperborean island was Britain and that the Hyperboreans were British, but it never seemed to occur to anyone that the words Boreas, Boreads, and Hyperborean, were British words. *Bore* means 'the dawn', or 'the morning'. In modern Welsh 'Bore dda' is a greeting meaning, 'Good Morning'.

The *Bore*-ads were the priests of Apollo who were kings of the city and supervisors of the sacred precinct. We are told that they were descendants of *Bore*-as. The word *Hyperborean* is best understood by recalling the actions of the *Bore*-ads. They played upon the Cithara and praised Apollo in song:

(H)**y-per-bore**-an =	**Y**	=	The
	Per (Peror) =		Melodist/musician
	Bore	=	The dawn

The British Yperboreans then were musicians who praised the dawn.

DARES PHRYGIUS

Dares Phrygius was a priest who took part in the Trojan War and wrote a history of the destruction of Troy.[184] Cornelius Nepos, a celebrated historian in the reign of Augustus, says that he came upon this history at the time when he was pursuing his studies at Athens. It was 'by Dares, a Greek, in his own handwriting' and he 'translated it into Latin, word for word'. 'Dares himself lived at the time, was a person of rank, and concerned in the engagements from the first battle, until the Greeks subdued the Trojans and took Troy'.[185] This is confirmed by Homer who tells us that Dares was a wealthy citizen of high repute, and a priest of Hephaestus. He had two sons, Phegeus and Idaeus, and they were both skilled in all manner of fighting. Unfortunately, they met with Diomedes in the thick of battle and Phegeus was killed.[186]

Dares' history commences with Jason being sent to find the Golden Fleece and being treated inhospitably by Laomedon, the King of Troy. It ends with the fall of the city and the departure of the Greek forces. During the ten years of the war there were many truces called for the purpose of burying the dead, and it was not unusual for a truce to last 3 to 6 months. On these occasions intercourse was free to both sides and it appears that senior Trojans visited the Greek camp and vice versa. There is no wooden horse, however, in Dares' history. Rather we are told that in discussion in the Trojan Council Antenor, Polydamas and Aeneas besought King Priam to seek peace. They were upbraided by Priam who, being of the opinion that they would betray the city, made arrangements to have them killed. Realising now that their lives were in immediate danger Antenor orchestrated a plan and sent a messenger to Agamemnon for the agreement of the Greeks. We are told that Antenor and Aeneas opened the gate and allowed the Greeks into the city.

Ystoria Dared, the Welsh version of the history, is one of the three great historical texts of medieval Wales. It is considered to be a translation of a sixth-century Latin text entitled *Historia Daretis Phrygii De Excidio Troiae*. Despite the fact that it casts an unfavourable light on the character of Aeneas it has always been regarded as a national treasure within Wales. Dares was a Phrygian, which means he was of the same race as the Briges, Bruges, or Friges, traceable to the Brigantes of Britain.[187] If the Trojan War took place in Britain, then Dares must have been there too. It is recorded that he erected a college at Cirencester and during the reign of Membricius it was transferred to Oxford.[188] We know that he was a priest and he recorded history, which makes him one of the ancient British Bards or Druids. His name is Dar-es, *Dar* meaning Oak, the tree associated with Druids and knowledge.

THE TRIADS OF BRITAIN

The Triads of Britain are an ancient and authoritative source for early British history. The Institutional Triads were codified by the British Sovereign, Dyfnwal Moelmud, who reigned about 450 years before Christ. Dyfnwal Moelmud was a direct descendant of Brutus, the great-grandson of Aeneas of Troy. It was Brutus who introduced the constitution and laws of Troy and incorporated them with the patriarchal usages of Britain. The usages of Britain could not be altered by any act or edict of the crown or national convention. They were considered the inalienable rights to which every Briton was born and of which no human legislation could deprive him. It is to these native laws that Britons have in all ages been indebted for the superior liberties they have enjoyed as contrasted with other nations. The laws, as codified by Dyfnwal Moelmud, are eminently distinguished for their clearness, brevity, justice, and humanity. A nation ruling itself by their spirit could not be otherwise than great, civilized and free.[189]

The Triads take their name directly from the form in which the laws and historic facts were preserved by the ancient bards. They taught in verse and preserved the records of transaction through the medium of rhyme and measure. This aided the memory in recitation. As oral instruction was the chief means of conserving and transmitting the learned tradition Triads served as a mnemonic device for cataloguing a variety of information. The common feature is the arrangement in groups of three. In the Triads Dyfnwal Moelmud is referred to as one of the three 'pillars of the nation of the Isle of Britain', because he first made arrangements respecting the laws, maxims, customs and privileges of the country and tribe. He is so highly thought of that he is also called one of the three 'system formers of royalty of the Isle of Britain'.[190]

In the Preface to Dyfnwal Moelmuds Triads, William Probert comments on the frequent allusions to pedigrees and to the various relations of consanguinity. He explains that pedigrees were necessary under the conventional system because a man could neither be free nor enjoy his patrimony unless he could trace his pedigree to the ninth of his ancestors. It was, therefore, his title deed and the bulwark of his liberty and privileges. Proof of collateral relationship was also required to determine the family of a person because the whole family could be fined for the crimes of its members. Hence, he says, the Welsh still repeat their pedigrees with enthusiasm, though the cause has long since died away.[191]

It was, undoubtedly, the existence of such pedigrees which enabled Giraldus Cambrensis to give us the genealogy of the Welsh Princes. In his 12th-century *Description of Wales* he confirms the Welsh nations esteem for the genealogical record through their use of manuscript and memory.[192] The bards kept accurate copies of the genealogies in their old manuscripts. Indeed, this was such an ancient requirement that we find it written into the Institutional Triads. Of the three conventions of the country the first was the convention of the bards of the Isle of Britain:

"The privilege and office of the protégées of the convention of the bards, is to maintain, preserve and diffuse sound instruction upon the sciences of virtue, wisdom and hospitality. They are further to preserve a record of every heroic action whether of individuals or of the tribe; every event of the times; every natural phenomenon; wars; the regulations of the country and the tribe; retaliations; glorious victories. They must also preserve an authentic record of the pedigrees, marriages, nobility, privileges and institutes of the tribe of the Cambrians; ..." [193]

Of the three distinguished characters of the art of bardism the first was the chief-bard, the second was the Ovate, and the third was the Druid-Bard. Of the Chief-Bard it is written:

"He must preserve every record of the arts and sciences whilst he shall continue in his office of bard regularly inducted in dignity and privilege. He must also keep every record and memorial of the country and tribe respecting marriages, pedigrees, arms, inheritances, and the privileges of the country and tribe of the Cambrians."[194]

Giraldus Cambrensis tells us that, in addition to keeping the genealogies in manuscript form, the bards would 'recite them from memory, going back from Rhodri Mawr to the time of the blessed Virgin Mary, and then farther still to Silvius, Ascanius and Aeneas.'[195] It is Aeneas who recites his ancestry in the *Iliad*, when he encounters Achilles on the battlefield. 'You and I know each other's pedigree', he says, and relates the whole story of his bloodline from Zeus to Dardanus, Ericthonius, Tros, Assaracus, Capys, and Anchises to himself.[196] To demonstrate what was necessary in tracing one's pedigree under the ancient British system Probert shows the four different 'Scales of Lineal and Collateral Kindred'. In the 'Ascending Lineal Kindred' ancient Britons had to recite their pedigree up to their great-great-great-great-great-grandparent.[197] Is it merely coincidence that this is exactly what Aeneas does in the *Iliad*?

There are at least three Triads that commemorate royal personages of the House of Troy at the time of the Trojan War. These names will be familiar to us mainly because they are mentioned by Homer in the Iliad. They are Hector, Paris, Aeneas and King Priam. Helen herself is mentioned as well as Polixena the daughter of King Priam, and there are references to Hercules and Jason. As is the case with all the Triads they are grouped in threes under distinguishing epithets:

Triad 47. Trioedd Ynys Prydein [198]

Tri Dyn a gauas Kedernit Adaf:
Ercwlf Gadarn,
Ac Ector Gadarn,
A Sompson Gadarn.
Kyn gadarnet oedynt yll tri. Ac Adaf e hun

Three men who received the Might of Adam:
Hercules the Strong,
And Hector the Strong,
And Samson the Strong.
They were, all three, as strong as Adam himself.

In some of the manuscripts Hector is called *Ector o Droid*, so there is no mistaking the fact that the Triad refers to Hector Prince of Troy.

Additionally, Triad 47b records the names of the nine bravest and most noble warriors of the world. Egtor o Drioa is listed as one of the three Pagan warriors.

Triad 48. Trioedd Ynys Prydein [199]

Tri dyn a gauas pryt Adaf:
Absolon ab Dauyd,
A Iason vab Eson,
A Pharis vab Priaf
Kyn decket oedynt yll tri ac Adaf e hun.

Three Men who received the Beauty of Adam:
Absalom son of David
And Jason son of Aeson,
And Paris son of Priam
They were, all three, as comely as Adam himself.

Triad 50. Trioedd Ynys Prydein [200]

Teir Gvraged a gauas pryt Eva yn tri thraean:
Diadema, gordereh Eneas Yscvydwyn,
Ac Elen Uannave, y wreic y bu distriwedigaeth Tro
 Drvy y phenn
A Pholixena verch Priaf hen vrenhin Tro.

Three Women who received the Beauty of Eve in three third-shares:
Diadema, mistress of Aeneas White-Shield,
And Elen the Magnificent, the woman on whose account was the destruction of Troy,
And Polixena, daughter of Priam the Old, King of Troy.

Rachel Bromwich who carried out extensive research into the Triads of Britain shows that the original nucleus of the Triads '... consisted in an index to this Body of orally preserved narrative, formed for the benefit of those whose professional duty it was to preserve and hand on the stories which embodied the oldest traditions of the Britons about themselves ...'
[201]

ENGLISH LAW

Many centuries before the Romans set foot in Britain its inhabitants were a polished and intellectual people. They had a system of jurisprudence of their own which was superior to that of Rome. The Romans even acknowledged this. The great law authorities and the legal writers, Fortescue and Coke, affirm that the Brutus and Molmutine laws have always been regarded as the foundation and bulwark of British liberties.[202] Lord Chief Justice Coke states that 'the Original Laws of this land were composed of such elements as Brutus first selected from the Ancient Greek and Trojan Institutions'.[203] Lord Chancellor Fortescue in his British Laws declares that, 'concerning the different powers which Kings claim over their subjects, I am firmly of opinion that it arises solely from the different nature of the original institutions. So the Kingdom of Britain had its original from Brutus and the Trojans who attended him from Italy and Greece, and were a mixed Government compounded of the regal and democratic'.[204]

The royal primogeniture is known as pre-eminently 'the Trojan Law'. This meant that succession to the throne of Britain was always vested in the eldest son of the King. In all ages this remarkable law regulated the succession to the British Crown. It was adopted by the Normans and became the Law of England.[205] Another Trojan law declared that the sceptre of Britain might be held by a queen as well as a king. This is an exceptional feature of sovereignty that remains in full force today. With other nations, however, it was very different. In the Pict Kingdom succession went entirely by the female side, whereas the continental nations did not permit a woman to reign. When Ethelwulf's rebellious son, Ethelbald, placed Judith the daughter of King Charles by his own side on the throne it was contrary to the custom of the Saxon Nation. They did not allow a queen to sit beside the king or even to be called a queen.[206]

King Alfred's great friend and counsellor was Asser Menevensis, a Welsh bishop. He wrote a *Life of Alfred* and was made Abbot of Amesbury and Bishop of Sherborne. King Alfred employed Asser to translate the Molmutine Laws from the British language into Latin so that they could be incorporated into his own Anglo-Saxon code. Regarding the origin of trial by jury Probert is firmly of the opinion that it came to King Alfred from the Welsh via Asser the Welsh bishop. There is no proof, he says, of the existence of a jury amongst the Saxons before the time of Alfred the Great. The Welsh already had at that time a code of laws which distinctly specified a jury, mentioned their number and stated their qualifications.[207] From ancient times British laws and customs were different from other nations, and Henry de Bracton makes it clear that the Romans effected no change. This thirteenth-century English Judge stated that in almost all countries they use laws and written right but England alone uses unwritten right and custom. In England right is derived from what is unwritten which usage has approved, and the English have many things by custom which they have not by written law.[208] In this respect it is interesting to see how superior and enlightened were the Molmutine Laws which were set down sixteen centuries earlier:

> There are three pillars of the law:
> Custom before record and tradition;
> The King through legal authority;
> And the decision of the country by vote
> Where there has been neither custom or law. [209]

Further, it can be seen from the following that there was formal recognition of the fact that the law could be set aside or even excelled by custom:

> There are three kinds of customs which are to be maintained. First, a custom that sets the law aside. Second, a custom that excels the law by its justice whence it has authority by the decision of the King's Court and by use and obligation before memory: but its authority is limited to the place where it obtained confirmation by usage. And third, a custom which excels the law by natural event; but this kind of custom is not binding either upon the plaintiff nor defendant. It merely stops a complaint and prosecution, and transfers it to the verdict of the country, which denotes the oath of fifty men, who are elders of the tribe. If it be established by these, it cannot be subsequently opposed: and, therefore, it is called law, and is recorded and observed by the court. [210]

In his Introduction to *The British Kymry* the Rev. R. W. Morgan declares, 'Had no other monument of Kymric antiquity but the Code of British Laws of Molmutius, which still forms the basis of our common or unwritten law, descended to us, we could not doubt that we were handling the index of civilisation of a very high order'.

ENDNOTES

[176] See Diodorus Siculus, 2.47.

[177] Markale, *The Druids*, p69.

[178] See *The Riddle of Prehistoric Britain*, p70.

[179] See Hubert, *The History of the Celtic People*, Intro. P5.

[180] Higgins, *The Celtic Druids*, p121.

[181] Markale, p50.

[182] *The Celtic Druids*, p124.

[183] Markale, pp. 49 and 67.

[184] Dares Phrygius, Translated from the Welsh copy in The Book of Basingwerke. Dares Phrygius may be found as part of *The Chronicle of the Kings of Britain*. These were translated into English by Peter Roberts in 1811.

[185] 'Letter to Sallust', Introduction to the History of Dares.

[186] *Iliad*, 5. 9-29.

[187] See Comyns Beaumont, *Britain; The Key to World History*, p242.

[188] See Morgan, *The British Kymry*, p39.

[189] Ibid. pp. 33-45.

[190] See Probert, *The Ancient Laws of Cambria*, pp. 374-389.

[191] Ibid. p4

[192] Gerald of Wales, Bk.1, Ch.4.

[193] Triad 61, *The Ancient Laws of Cambria*, pp. 26-27.

[194] Triad 71, *The Ancient Laws of Cambria*, pp. 39-40.

[195] *Description of Wales*, Bk.1, Ch.4.

[196] *Iliad*, 20. 199-241.

[197] See Probert, *The Ancient Laws of Cambria*, pp. 5-6

[198] See Bromwich, *Trioedd Ynys Prydein*, p122

[199] Ibid. p127

[200] Ibid. p129

[201] See Bromwich, *Trioedd Ynys Prydein*, pIXV.

[202] See Isabel Hill Elder, *Celt, Druid and Culdee*, p22.

[203] De Laudibus Legum Angliae. Coke Preface, Third Volume of Pleadings. Fortescue *Brit. Laws*, pub. Selden, Ch. 17, pp. 38-39.

[204] Fortescue, *Brit. Laws.*

[205] Morgan, *The British Kymry*, p32.

[206] Asser's Life of Alfred, p47, in *Six Old English Chronicles*, Ed. Giles.

[207] *The Ancient Laws of Cambria*, p4.

[208] *Celt, Druid and Culdee*, p24.

[209] Triad 155, *The Ancient Laws of Cambria*, p60.

[210] Triad 228, *The Ancient Laws of Cambria*, p81.

BRONZE
AGE
THRACE

9

So much has happened since we started our investigation that we should take a little time to reflect on the great distance travelled and the amount of space and knowledge that now separates us from our starting point. From here we begin the process of locating the most important regions applicable to our search for Troy. These are Thrace, the Black Sea and the Hellespont. From here we begin to reap the benefits of our work and our patience. From here the pace may seem quicker and more rewarding. First, though, a summary of our findings so far:

1. The voyage of Aeneas of Troy could not have taken place in the Mediterranean area. The *Aeneid* and the *Iliad* more accurately reflect a north Atlantic, temperate, oceanic climate.

2. There is no evidence that Homer's Troy was in Turkey but there is evidence in favour of it being elsewhere.

3. Using astronomical means Homer identifies the location of Troy as an island lying to the north of the line of Latitude 45 degrees. This excludes the whole of the Mediterranean and Aegean areas. Historically, the same astronomical references were used to locate the geographical position of the British Isles, and Britain in particular.

4. It is only the island of Britain that fully satisfies Homer's astronomical specifications and descriptions of climate and topography.

5. Many of Homer's cultural themes are characteristic of the Celts. The Celtic-descended people are found in the British Isles. The Celts spoke Greek, and so too did the ancient Britons. It is known that the Greeks came originally from the north.

6. A Greek and Trojan weave exists beneath the ancient tapestry of Britain. This includes Irish-Greek origins and a British-Trojan lineage. Britain's ancient laws came from Greek and Trojan Institutions. Britain, too, was the home of chariot fighting, as well as the worship of Zeus and Apollo.

7. Many place names in the British and Irish histories are now familiar in a modern Mediterranean/Aegean setting. In the Bronze Age, however, these were located in the vicinity of the British Isles. Thrace was in Britain, and the Tyrrhene Sea was in the English Channel.

8. Homer's Achaeans, Danaans and Argives, were the ancestors of today's Irish and Scots.

9. Continental records document the Trojan migrations to Gaul after the fall of Troy and confirm that the Trojan War took place in Britain. The government of Britain was held by the Druids until the time of Brutus.

THE SEARCH FOR TROY: SOUTHERN BRITAIN

The summary of our findings lead us to the following conclusion – that we can now reduce the geographical area that we need to concentrate on in order to find Troy, the start of Aeneas' voyage. Previously, Britain was the centre of our attention but all of the evidence indicates that we are now dealing with the southern part of the island, and possibly the shores of the English Channel and the North Sea.[211] It is here we shall continue our search.

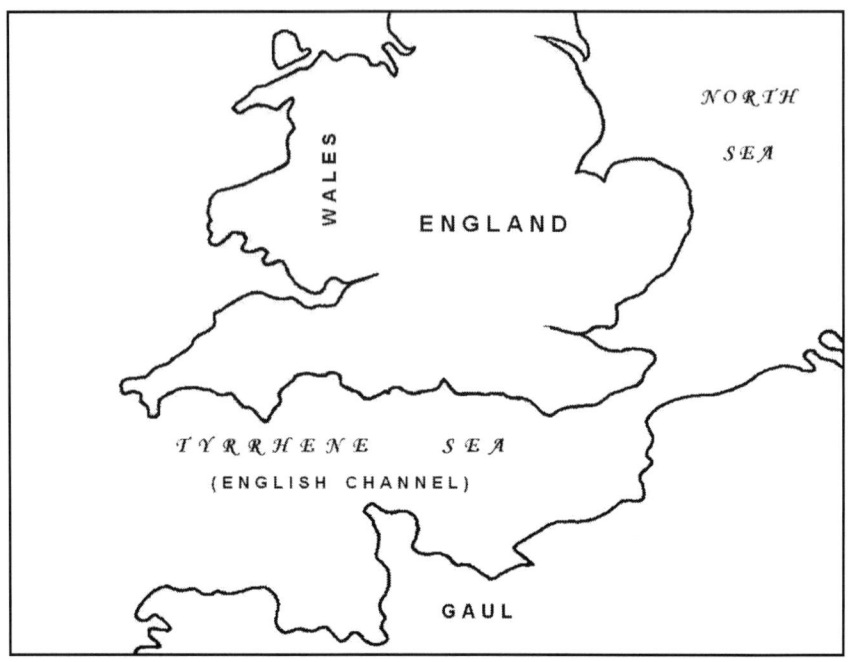

MAP 12.
THE SEARCH FOR TROY: SOUTHERN BRITAIN

LOCATING THRACE

Early on in this part of the investigation a part of southern Britain was identified as being the probable location of the Thrace of the Bronze Age. This came about mainly as a result of information provided by Homer in the *Iliad*, which helped to reduce the geographical location to only three counties in eastern England. This information covers Achilles' hut on the Trojan Plain, a town near the theatre of war that still retains its bronze-age name, eels that were present in the river Scamander, the woad that was used by the British Cruithne who actually came from Thrace, and the dykes and embankments that were present in the area where the Trojan War took place.

THE HUT OF ACHILLES

After Hector is killed king Priam decides to go to see Achilles to beg him to return his son to him for a proper funeral. Priam arrives at the Achaean encampment at night and he is taken inside Achilles' dwelling. The hut of Achilles had been built by the Myrmidons for their king. It was a towering shelter built from hewn timbers of pine with a roof of thatch shaggy with grass that had been gathered from the meadows.[212]

Of immediate significance is the description of the roof covering. In the County of Norfolk you can expect to see thatching at its best, carried out using Norfolk reed, which can last a lifetime. Remember, the Achaean army had been encamped beside their ships for ten years. The warriors and their chieftains would want good protection from the elements and there is no finer roof to live under than one made of thatch. It has excellent insulating properties that keep a dwelling warm in winter and cool in summer. Thatch also provides a good soundproofing barrier. When kept in a good state of repair thatch never gets wet beyond three to four centimetres of its thickness. Before the seventeenth century thatch was the most widespread roofing in Britain but mechanisation and the introduction of new processes and materials has now resulted in greatly reduced numbers of full-time thatchers at work.

FIG. 9. Achilles' hut may have been similar to this dwelling.
Acknowledgement: Wikipedia.com. St. Fagans Celtic Village.

Traditionally, materials for thatching were those that were most easily available such as straw, reed, heather, and turf. For a long time though the most common material was the straw left after harvesting wheat, oats, barley, and rye. Naturally, material for thatching was available in other parts of the country, but the finest material has always been Norfolk reed. It grows in water, in marshy estuaries, principally in Norfolk where the reed beds are an integral part of the landscape. Sedge is always used to ridge Norfolk-reed roofs but whole roofs of sedge can be seen in the Fen country. It is a marsh plant with a rush-like leaf.[213]

It is highly probable that Homer is describing these thatched roofs of sedge, and although we cannot pinpoint the exact location yet it does appear that he is telling us about the Fen country, the modern counties of Lincolnshire, Norfolk and Cambridgeshire.

CAISTER-ON-SEA

When the Achaeans, Danaans and Argives came out onto the plain to fight the Trojans there are so many of them that Homer likens them to the countless birds, geese, cranes, and swans on the meadow by the Kaystrian waters.[214] The streams or waters of Kaystrius (Cayster) can only be the resort of Caister on the east coast of Norfolk. This Bronze-Age name has clearly survived the ravages of time down to the modern day.

EELS

The death of Patroclus in the *Iliad* brings Achilles back into the fighting and in his rage he kills many of his opponents in the river Scamander. The dead and the dying are busily attended by eels.[215] Eels were a particular feature of Cambridgeshire and the Isle of Ely where they played a major part in the economy of the area. They were also used as currency. Later, we will find out a lot more about these eels and where exactly they were found.

WOAD

We noted in the British histories that the Cruithne came originally from Thrace and because they tattooed their skin they were called Picti. The paint they used for tattooing was made from woad, and the extraction of

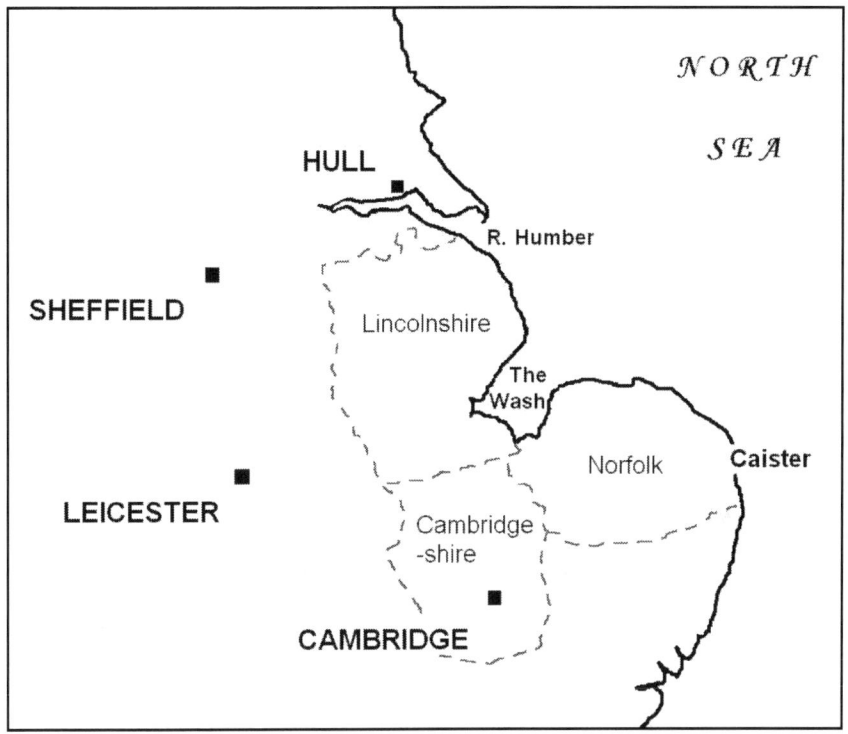

MAP 13.
LOCATING BRONZE AGE THRACE

the blue dye from the woad-plant was an extremely complicated process.

According to Robert Graves the extraction and use of the dye is such a smelly business that the woad-making and woad-dying families of Norfolk/ Lincolnshire have always been obliged to inter-marry.[216] Yet again we have Norfolk and Lincolnshire mentioned. We have reduced the probable location of Thrace to three counties in eastern England and expect to find Troy in the immediate vicinity. It will not be such a coincidence if we find that Thrace, the original home of the tattooed Picti, was in the same area where, traditionally, the woad had always been produced.

DYKES AND EMBANKMENTS

We should no longer be surprised at the incredible detail contained within the *Iliad*, yet when Homer provides us with information about dykes and embankments there is little doubt that he is illustrating life in the Bronze Age in this particular part of Britain. Historically, the low-lying land of the Fen Country has been continually at risk of inundation from the sea and freshwater flooding from the rivers. Man's answer has been to build physical defences in order to protect the land, the livestock, and himself. As a result, dykes and embankments have been perpetually constructed along rivers and in various places along the shoreline. Of all the places in southern Britain this particular area is renowned for its dykes and embankments, and Homer describes them when he tells us about one of the Danaan assaults against the Trojans. The Danaans had thrust back the Trojan line and many Trojan warriors had been slaughtered in the offensive:

"As for Diomedes himself, you could not have told to which army, Trojan or Achaean, he belonged. He stormed across the plain like a winter torrent that comes tearing down and flattens out the dykes. Against its sudden onslaught, backed by the heavy rains, nothing can stand, neither the dykes that were meant to hem it in, nor the stone walls round the vineyards and their sturdy trees. It has its way, and far and wide the farmers see the wreckage of their splendid work. Thus the Trojans in their serried lines collapsed before the son of Tydeus, unable for all their numbers to withstand him."[217]

THRACE: THE LINCOLN WOLDS

In our investigation into the true location of Homer's Troy we have relied heavily on the information provided in the *Iliad*. Aeneas' voyage from Troy, however, is described in Virgil's *Aeneid* but until now it has only been possible to apply Virgil's work in a limited way. At the beginning of this book the *Iliad* and the *Aeneid* stood in the same relationship to each other as regards the location of Troy; everything appeared wrong in a Mediterranean/Aegean setting whereas it appeared more logical in a north Atlantic or North Sea environment. Since then we have learned to respect the accuracy of Homer's information, and it is not beyond the bounds of possibility that it really is a factual account.

Can we say the same about Virgil's *Aeneid*? Certainly not at this point in time. Most commentators would insist that this magnificent work from a poet of supreme genius is, nevertheless, a work of fiction and nothing else.

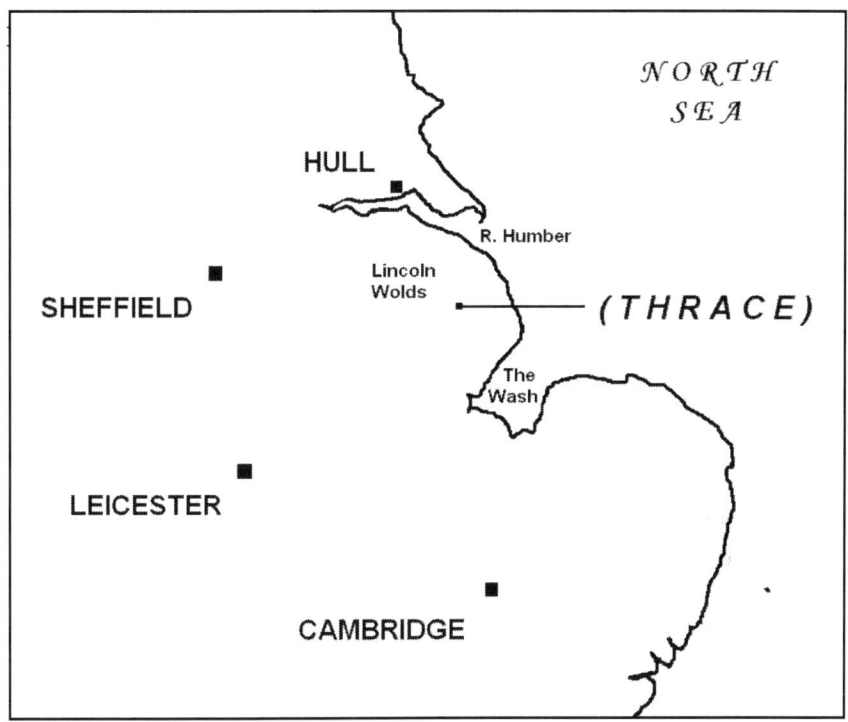

MAP 14.

THRACE IDENTIFIED AS THE LINCOLN WOLDS

When Aeneas sailed from Troy he stopped first at Thrace and then sailed on to an island normally considered as being Delos.[218] We know that Troy is near to Thrace, which itself is in the vicinity of the counties of Cambridgeshire, Lincolnshire, and Norfolk. Any voyage from this area would have to be undertaken in the North Sea and/or the English Channel. Using the information in the *Aeneid* it soon becomes apparent that there is only one place on the eastern shore that corresponds with an embarkation point that would have been Thrace.

It is only from this particular point that a sailor can comply with the directions given. This is because Aeneas would have to leave this shore at a time dictated by the tides and when the wind strength and direction were within tightly controlled parameters. Failure to do this would result in the ships being driven back to shore, dragged in the wrong direction, or becoming lost in the North Sea. Aeneas' embarkation point from this eastern shore was the Lincoln Wolds, situated between the river Humber and The Wash. Thrace, therefore, was the Lincoln Wolds.

A PERSONAL PREDICAMENT

Identifying Thrace was indeed an achievement. Furthermore, it should have been relatively straightforward after this to locate Troy itself. How wrong was this mistaken assumption? Identifying Thrace led nowhere. I retraced my steps several times and reviewed the work I had done, but still I could not move forward from this point. For some reason I was bogged down and I did not know why. I had already come so far, but now I began to question my ability. Had I made a major blunder? Was my knowledge deficient? Perhaps I was not equal to the task which I had taken upon myself? Eventually, I gave up on what appeared to be a pointless exercise. This was not so much defeat as it was pure frustration – the result of making no progress.

Then, a thought occurred to me. Did I really need to locate Troy, the starting point for Aeneas' voyage, at this precise time? No, I didn't. It would be wonderful to be able to do it immediately because I was now so close but it really was not a necessity. I could start the voyage from Thrace and, hopefully, fill in the missing information later. After all, by locating Thrace we had already tested Virgil's *Aeneid* for the first time and the information had proved to be accurate. Trying to complete the whole voyage though would not be an easy task. And what would the *Aeneid* reveal about itself? Would it stand the test we would now subject it to?

I gathered together all the information I could find in the *Aeneid* relating to geographical directions; tides; currents; speed of the ships; winds; astronomical information; descriptions of the land, waterways, bays, islands and so on. Armed with all this information I set out from Thrace, that is the Lincoln Wolds, as this was the first stop which Aeneas had made on his journey from Troy. This was the second test that Virgil's *Aeneid* had been subjected to, but this time it was a serious applied test to ascertain the true nature of Virgil's information. It was not long before I started making headway and, amazingly, in accordance with the detail given in the *Aeneid*. Eighteen months later I had completed the voyage in outline and I knew that the journey could be done in reality, in the vicinity of the British Isles, and that the information contained in Virgil's *Aeneid* was accurate. Only

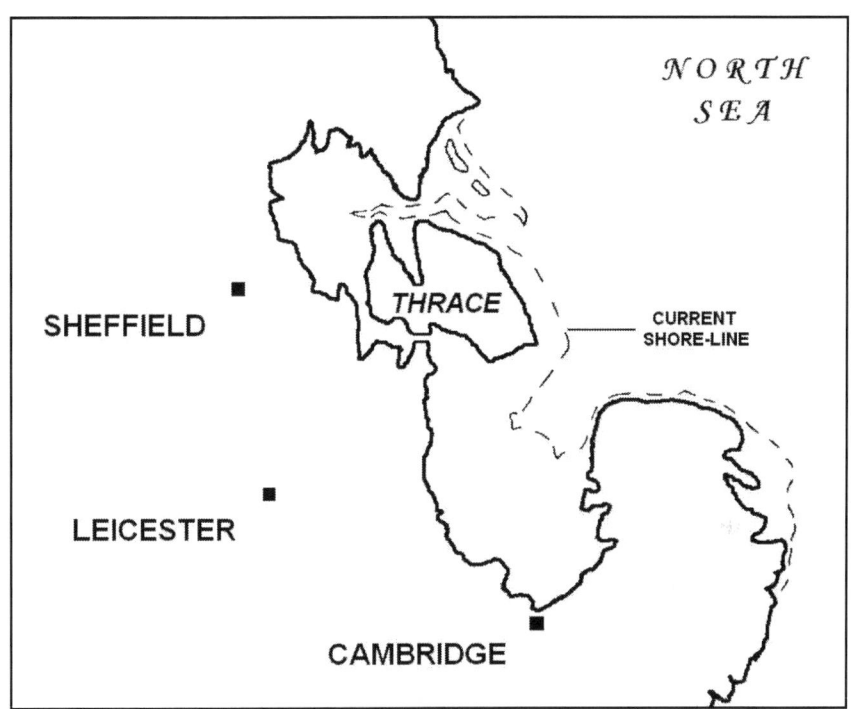

NORTH SEA

SHEFFIELD ■

THRACE

CURRENT SHORE-LINE

LEICESTER ■

CAMBRIDGE ■

MAP 15.
BRONZE AGE SEA LEVELS: EASTERN ENGLAND

in this Bronze Age geographical setting does the Voyage of Aeneas of Troy become practicable. The result of this second test was not only completely unexpected, it was a revelation. It was the strongest corroborative evidence that Homer's Troy was located in Britain and not in the Aegean. This was so unbelievable that it necessitated a further test which would be even more demanding. Could Aeneas' voyage be conducted in its entirety and in detail using Virgil's text? I was not to know at this stage though that carrying out this third test would take such a long time! Many years later, after completing all the detailed work, I was able to confirm that Virgil's work had been discovered to be a detailed historical record. This was truly astonishing. The results of all this work, however, were too great to be included here and they would have to wait until some future time.[219]

One important reason for this was that I had discovered another fact that was of crucial importance in being able to locate Troy and identify the Pontus (Euxine Sea), the Hellespont and Samothrace. It also confirmed my identification of Thrace as being correct.

Having completed Aeneas' voyage I had, naturally, identified every place where the fleet came to shore. In doing so it became apparent that in the vast majority of cases this was slightly inland from the present shoreline. This differential equates to about 5 to 7 metres in the height of the sea level. In other words, at the time of the Trojan War the sea level was 5 to 7 metres higher in relation to the land, compared to what it is now. For the majority of locations in Britain this difference in sea level is minor so far as it relates to recognising the shoreline. In the part of the country where we have identified Thrace, however, the difference is vast. Large portions of eastern England are turned into inland seas, and the shoreline becomes unrecognisable. If we look again at the maps it can be seen that the whole topography has been transformed. No wonder I had such difficulty making progress here.

BRONZE AGE SEA LEVELS: EASTERN ENGLAND

Land and sea levels are continually changing and although it appears that the sea level was 5 to 7 metres higher than at present, it may be as a result of the land falling by this amount. Britain's coastline was created more than 100,000 years before the last ice age and what we see today is the result of all the changes that have taken place since then. About 50,000 years ago glaciers several kilometres thick covered the north of Britain. Advancing glaciers moved southwards down the east coast as far as The Wash and valley ice flowed down the Vale of York, possibly as far as Doncaster. The glaciers advanced and retreated with the changing climate and deposited eroding material as they went. The mass of ice in the north of Britain pushed the landmasses downwards causing the land in the south to rise. Following the retreat of the ice, land levels in the north have been slowly rising again whereas the land in the south has been sinking. These glaciers locked up a large proportion of the world's oceans and reduced global sea level by more than 100 metres. After 18,000 years ago the major ice sheets retreated. This took about 9,000 years. Global sea levels began to rise again until, about 10,000 years ago, it was 40 metres below the current level. From about 7,000 years ago coastlines began to take on their now familiar form, and over the last 6,000 years different parts of the world have had their own local sea level histories. It is generally believed that global sea level was

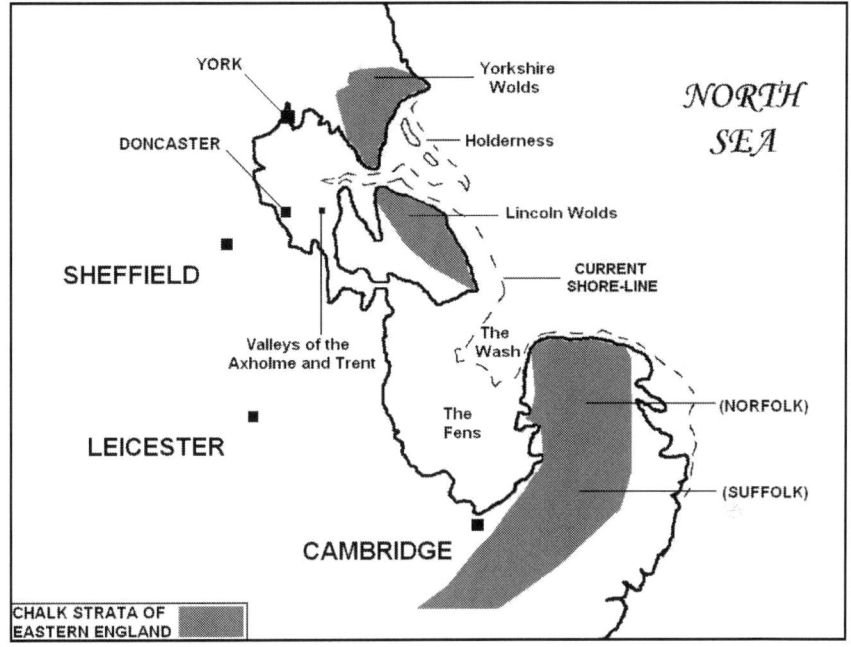

MAP 16. THE HIGHLAND AREAS OF EASTERN
ENGLAND AND THE TWO DEPRESSIONS THAT WERE
INLAND SEAS IN THE BRONZE AGE.

close to the present level by about 2,000 BC.[220]

In the part of Britain where we have identified Thrace we are dealing with
one of the most interesting yet complicated areas in the island, stretching
from the Yorkshire Wolds southwards through Lincolnshire to Norfolk
and Suffolk. The Yorkshire and Lincolnshire Wolds and the plateau of East
Anglia (Norfolk and Suffolk) are the upland areas of chalk (see map 16).
This stratum was once continuous. There are two major areas of Lowland,
one to the northwest of the Lincolnshire Wolds and one to the south. These
are referred to as 'depressions'. To the northwest of the Lincolnshire Wolds
we have the valleys of the Axholme and Trent, the greatest proportion of
which is less than 5 metres above the current sea level. The depression to
the south is known as the Fenland. This is a flat plain and most of it is less
than 3 metres above current sea level. Spring tides along this coastline are
of the order of 5.7 metres and surges of one to two metres at times of bad
weather are not unusual. Both of these depressions have clay beds.

More than 100 years ago, whilst orthodox geologists attributed the denudation of the chalk strata to marine or fluvial effects, or the action of ice, Sir Henry Howorth was arguing against it. His opinion was that the once continuous chalk was dislocated by a subterranean force. Its effect was to fold the chalk into a series of anticlinal and synclinal curves, running more or less north and south. It resulted in the raised levels of the Wolds of Yorkshire and Lincolnshire and the plateau of East Anglia. The same event produced the depressions in the areas occupied by the Fens and the valleys of the Axholme and Trent.[221] From our findings it is clearly these depressions that were inland seas at the time of the Trojan War.

Over thousands of years this coastline has been subjected to vast changes wrought by the sea. It includes Yorkshire's East Riding region and the Holderness seaboard, the Lincolnshire coast, and The Wash. Until about 6000 years ago a large part of the North Sea was a swampy area but, as sea levels rose, the deepening waters gradually eroded the shores. Ten thousand years ago the Holderness coastline was 15 to 20 kilometres east of its current position. Recent historical records suggest that the cliffs are eroding at a rate of between 1.5 to 2.0 metres per year. At least 30 villages have been lost to the sea along this coastline since Roman times. Also, the cliff line is continually being reshaped by wave and tidal forces. The whole coast is gradually developing a shape that lies at right angles to the predominant north-easterly wave direction.[222] Further south, in The Wash, it appears that the sea made its first transgression into The Fens about 8000 years ago. Four thousand years later another transgression brought an influx of sediments into the Fenland. At the beginning of the Bronze Age there was subsidence of the Fen Basin and this created shallow meres intermixed with marshland. Tidal waters reached as far south as Horningsea,[223] only 3 kilometres north of Cambridge. Further transgressions have occurred throughout history. Local sea-level history for The Wash shows a general rise in sea level over the last 7,000 years. The records, however, also show that the general rise has not been smooth and continuous. There has been a sequence of relative transgression succeeded by relative regression, and this has been repeated several times.[224]

At this stage there appears to be little doubt that Troy really was located in Britain. The participants in the war came from Britain, and large numbers of fugitives from Troy migrated afterwards to Gaul. The voyage of Aeneas of Troy can only be conducted successfully in this corrected Bronze Age environment. It follows that Aeneas of Troy was from Britain and, therefore, his great grandson, Brutus, was of British descent too. We have located the Tyrrhene Sea in the English Channel and now Thrace in eastern England. We know also that Thrace must be very close to Troy itself. Troy was located on the Hellespont (the Helle Sea) and the Euxine Sea (now called the Black Sea) was close by. The higher sea levels around Britain in the Bronze Age meant that there were inland seas in eastern England - in fact two inland seas; one to the north west of Thrace, the other to the south. Are these seas the Bronze Age Hellespont and Euxine?

Dares Phrygius, who we have identified as British, commences his history with Jason's voyage and the arrival of the Argo at Troy. Laomedon, the Trojan king, treated Jason and his friends inhospitably and they were ordered to leave his territory. To avenge this insult Hercules later led an expedition to Phrygia where he attacked Troy and killed Laomedon and his sons who were with him. Priam, the only son to survive, was away from Troy at the time but his sister, Hesione, was taken away as a captive along with the plundered riches from the city. Dares includes the story of Jason's arrival at Troy as the background and cause of conflict which would eventually result in the Trojan War. Although he mentions Jason's quest Dares does not provide any further information about the actual voyage other than to tell us that after departing they arrived at Colchis and brought home the Golden Fleece.[225]

It is known that the Voyage of the Argo took place in the Bronze Age about one or two generations before the Trojan War. This voyage too must have taken place around Britain. The Argonauts traversed the Hellespont and the Euxene so there is a possibility that we can glean some information about these two seas from the story of Jason's voyage. We will cover these events in the next chapter.

ENDNOTES

[211] See, in particular, ch. 5, p4 and ch. 6, pp 4 and 6.

[212] *Iliad*, 24. 448

[213] See Jacqueline Fearn, *Thatch and Thatching*.

[214] *Iliad*, 2. 459

[215] *Iliad*, 21. 203

[216] Graves, *Greek Myths*, 149.1, and *White Goddess*, p241.

[217] *Iliad*, 5. 84-94

[218] *Aeneid*, 3. 1-83

[219] The results of this research are included in *The Voyage of Aeneas of Troy*. At this time the book is being completed with a view to publication.

[220] See Roberts, *The Holocene*, Ch. 3, 4, and 6.

[221] Howorth, 'The Destruction and Shattering of the Chalk of Eastern England', Geological Magazine 1896, 58-66. See also www.sentex.net

[222] See 'Development of the East Riding Coastline', www.eastriding.gov.uk/aspirelinks/coastal/1development

[223] Wareham and Wright, *A History of the County of Cambridge and the Isle of Ely*, Vol. 10, pp 1-27. See www.british-history.ac.uk

[224] *An Introduction to the Coastal Geomorphology of Great Britain*, p15. See www.fettes.com/shetland/coastal_geomorphology_uk_snh.pdf

[225] Dares Phrygius, pp. xxiv-xxvi, Tr. Peter Roberts, London, 1811.

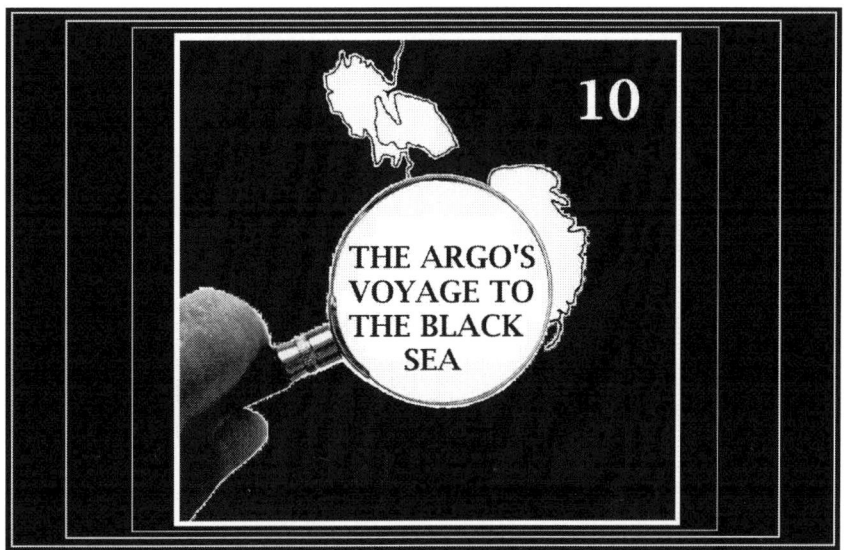

THE ARGO'S
VOYAGE TO
THE BLACK
SEA

10

The story of the Argo and Jason's quest for the Golden Fleece belongs to the very early strata of Greek myth. Homer briefly mentions the Argo as being remembered 'in mens' minds at the time of Odysseus' wanderings.[226] Essentially, the story was located in the eastern part of the Greek world but legends about the Argo existed throughout the Mediterranean. The tale was never standardised and there were many versions of the route taken. The only full account is that of Apollonius of Rhodes, and it is his only surviving work. His version encompasses as much of the known world as was possible at the time but it is a mixture of real and fabulous geography.[227] Little is known about Apollonius' sources but as Royal Librarian at the Alexandrian Library about 275-245 BC he would have had access to material which now will never be identified.

The Argonauts voyage to the Black Sea took place about eighty years before the fall of Troy. Robert Graves says that both Heracles' expedition in this area and the voyage of the Argo must not be dismissed as wholly unhistorical. Both record Greek trading ventures in the Black Sea perhaps as far back as the middle of the second millennium BC. Dubious claims were employed to justify their control of the Black Sea trade, resulting finally, in the Trojan War.[228] The Argonauts, under Jason's command, had set out to fetch the golden ram's fleece from Colchis. The fleece was hung on a tree in the grove of Colchian Ares, where it was guarded night and day by an unsleeping dragon. A few days after setting out the Argonauts found themselves near Thrace. First, they landed on the isle of Lemnos and, later, beached the ship at Samothrace where the Argonauts were initiated into the mysteries. We shall discuss Samothrace in due course but for the moment we will concentrate on the part of the voyage around Thrace and the Black Sea.

IN SIGHT OF THE BOSPORUS

Leaving Samothrace, the Argonauts approached Thrace and landed in Dolionian territory where they were received hospitably and entertained by king Cyzikus. The following morning some of the Argonauts set out to climb mount Dindymum so that they could view the sea-routes for themselves:

> "From the summit they could see the Macrian heights and the whole length of the opposite Thracian coast – it almost seemed that they could touch it. And far away on the one side they saw the misty entrance to the Bosporus and the Mysian hills, and on the other the flowing waters of Aesepus and the city and Nepeian plain of Adresteia." [229]

Now, there is only one place that is so close to Thrace that it would seem as if you could touch it; that is the peninsular immediately south of Lincoln, the southern part of Lincoln Heath. About 5km south of Lincoln the land rises to 77 metres, and there are particularly good viewing points looking west near the villages of Bracebridge Heath and Waddington. From here, the entrance to the Bosporus lies about 17 kilometres away, its northern extremity close to the town of Gainsborough. The Mysian Hills lie immediately to the west of the Bosporus.

The river Aesepus is the river Ashop which rises in the Peak District west of Sheffield, but it no longer carries the same name for the duration of its course. The Ashop becomes the Derwent before leaving the Peak District, and then, after flowing through Derby, becomes the Trent for its north-easterly route through Nottingham to Newark-on-Trent. It is thus the river Ashop, now the Trent, which could be seen by the Argonauts. The Nepeian plain can only be the current Vale of Belvoir.

After leaving the Dolionians, the Argonauts continued their voyage. Heracles was left behind in Mysia looking for his squire, and the Argo visited the island of Bebrycos and, afterwards, came to Salmydessus in Thrace where Phineus reigned. Phineus had been blinded by the gods for prophesying the future, and he was plagued by a pair of Harpies. After the Argonauts had delivered Phineus from the Harpies, Phineus instructed Jason how to navigate the Bosporus and what fortune to expect on his way to Colchis.[230]

ONWARD TO COLCHIS

After passing through the Bosporus into the Black Sea the Argonauts touched at the islet of Thynias, then sailed to the city of Mariandyne where they were welcomed by King Lycus, and then on to Sinope in Paphlagonia. They then sailed past the country of the Amazons; and that of the iron-working Chalybians who lived only on the gains of their forges; and the country of the Tibarenians, where it is the custom for husbands to groan, as if in child-bed, while their wives are in labour; and the country of the Moesynoechians, who live in wooden castles, couple promiscuously, and carry immensely long spears and white shields in the shape of ivy-leaves.[231]

Robert Graves says that 'Chalybs' was the Greek for 'iron', and 'Chalybians' seems to have been another name for the Tibarenians, the first ironworkers of antiquity. In Genesis x.2, their land is called Tubal (Tubal=Tibar), and Tubal Cain stands for the Tibarenians who had come down from Armenia into Canaan with the Hyksos hordes.[232] In this area of Britain we are in the middle of iron-working country. Iron ore deposits are found in north and south Lincolnshire, Leicestershire and Nottinghamshire, with Pig Iron production around Scunthorpe, Rotherham and Sheffield. Rotherham lies within 11 kilometres of the shores of the Black Sea.

The customs of the Moesynoechians, described by Xenophon – whose *Anabasis* Apollonius Rhodius had studied – are remarkably similar to those of the Scottish Picts and the Irish Sidhe tribes.[233] If we recall the information presented earlier on Early Irish History, the Irish Neimead came from Scythia through the Euxine Sea to the North Sea. This is not possible in the Mediterranean area but is self-explanatory when the Euxine Sea is correctly located in its Bronze Age context in Britain. Simon Breac,

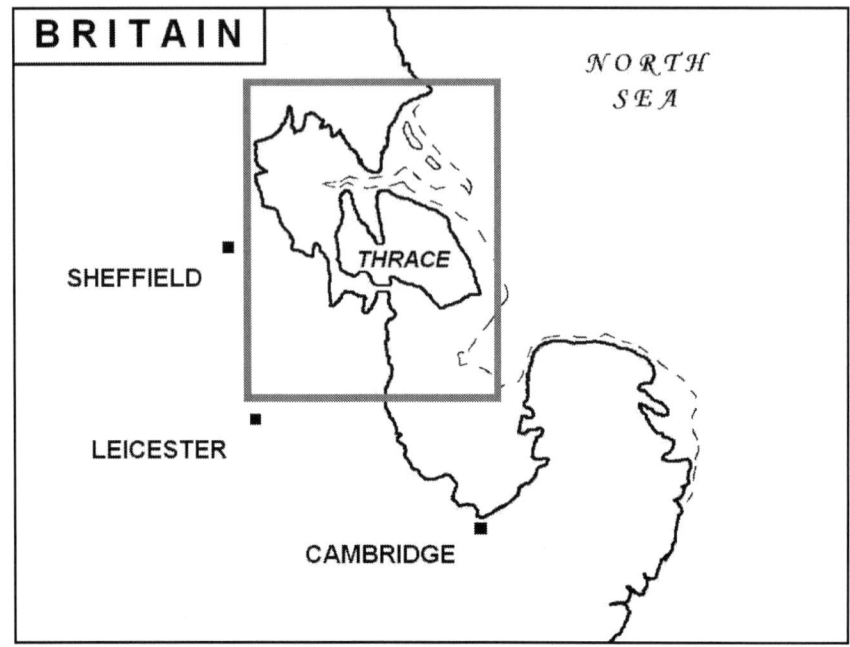

MAP 17. LOCATION MAP

one of Neimead's followers, left Ireland and went to Thrace and his descendants went back to Ireland as the Fir Bolg. This is an almost impossible journey through the Atlantic and Mediterranean but perfectly logical with Thrace situated on the east coast of England. The Fir Bolg, Fir Gaillian and Fir Domnan came to Ireland 'from the East' and this is now shown to be perfectly accurate. Now, with the Lincoln Wolds identified as the Bronze Age Thrace it should not be too surprising to find evidence of Scots habitation in the village place-names of Scotton, Scotton Common, and Scotter, on the shores of the Black Sea, about 11 kilometres north of the town of Gainsborough.

According to the '*Irish and Pictish Additions to the Historia Britonum*' the Cruithne came from Thrace in the east of Europe. Agathyrsi was their name, and from tattooing their fair skins they were called Picti. They were children of Gelonus, son of Hercules, who went to France and built Pictavis (Poitiers). Afterwards, they left France for Ireland. There is no mention of the Cruithne voyaging through the Atlantic or the Mediterranean or Aegean Seas – as we can see now, there was no necessity. The chronicles state that the Cruithne came from Thrace in the east of Europe and this fits perfectly with the Lincoln Wolds being identified as the Bronze Age Thrace. Later, we shall find exactly where the ancient divisions between Europe and Asia lay, and that Thrace really was in the East of Europe.

When the Argonauts were near the isle of Ares great flocks of birds flew over the ship, dropping brazen plumes. Phineus had advised them to put on their helmets and shout at the top of their voices, and while half of them rowed, the others protected them with their shields. The Argonauts landed on the island driving away myriads of birds until not one was left.[234] The isle of Ares is the Isle of Axholme, where the village name of Belton provides the appropriate clue – *Bel* was the British God of War, whereas *Ton* means land; Ares was the Greek God of War. The Argo then passed the island of Philyra and entered the mouth of the Phasis River, which watered Colchis. Jason told his men to row into the reedy marshes and moor the ship with anchor-stones in a spot where she could ride.[235] Colchis and its capital, Aea, were situated at the farthest end of the Black Sea, and there is only one place that answers the description. The ancient city of Aea is now the City of York (Roman Eboracum) and the river Foss, is the Phasis. To be precise, Phas = *Foss* and the ending *-is* means 'under or below'. The City of York lies 'below' the river Foss.

The voyage of the Argo passed muster until Greek geographical knowledge increased and it became impossible to reconcile the principal elements in the story. Yet, since no historian could afford to offend his public by rejecting the voyage as fabulous, the Argonauts were supposed, at first, to have returned from the Black Sea by way of the Danube, the Save, and the Adriatic; then, when explorers found that the Save does not enter the Adriatic, a junction was presumed between the Danube and the Po, down which the Argo could have sailed; and when, later, the Danube proved to be navigable only part of the way, and not to join the Po, it was held that she passed up the Phasis into the Caspian Sea, and thus into the Indian Ocean, 'Ocean Stream' and Lake Tritonis.

When the feasibility of this third route was eventually denied, mythographers suggested that the Argo had sailed up the Don, presumed to have its source in the Gulf of Finland, from which she could have circumnavigated Europe.[236] Many other suggestions followed, but none of them were realistic.

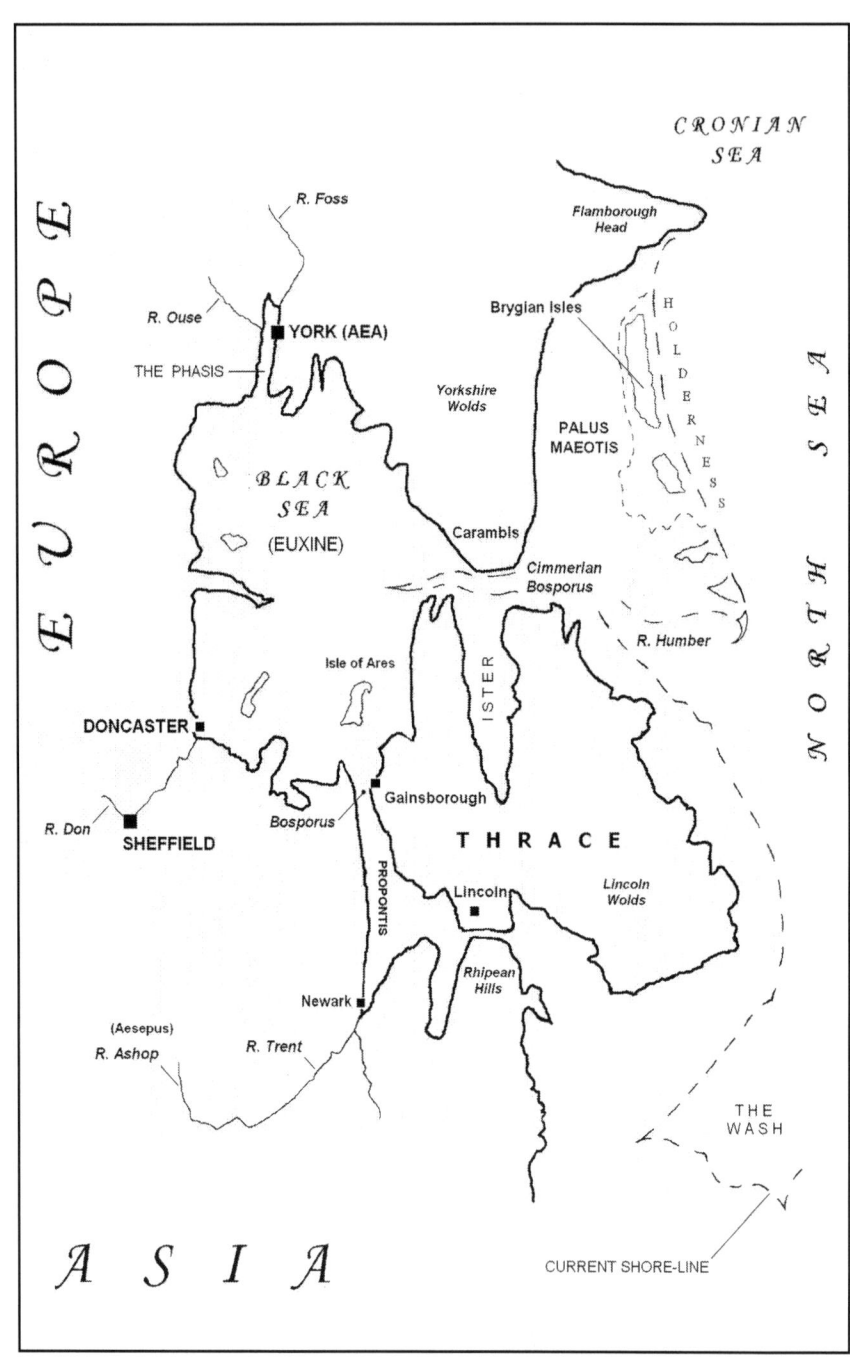

MAP 18. THE ARGO'S VOYAGE TO THE BLACK SEA

It is clear to see why these important elements have remained such a mystery. The voyage of the Argo did not take place in the Mediterranean and Aegean areas because, in the Bronze Age, these places were located around the shores of Britain.

TWO ROUTES FROM THE BLACK SEA

As can be seen, there were two routes available out of the Black Sea, the one to the south of Thrace and the other to the north. Both of these routes allowed direct access to the North Sea, the Cymric name of which was Morimarusa, whereas in the voyage of the Argo it is referred to as the Sea of Marmara. It is generally considered that these two straits were situated at the confines of Europe and Asia, and in this respect it is interesting to note the following extract from Keating's History of Ireland:

> "Neimead came from Scythia on the narrow sea which reaches from the ocean called Mare Euxinum. It is it which is the boundary between the northwest side of Asia and the northeast side of Europe. At the northwest part of Asia are the mountains of Riffe on the boundary line of the narrow sea and the northern ocean. He gave his right hand to the mountains of Riffe, till he came into the ocean to the north, and his left hand towards Europe till he came to Ireland" [237]

It is clear from this history that Neimead sailed through the narrow sea, south of Lincoln, into the North Sea and journeyed around Scotland to Ireland. The mountains of Riffe or Rhiphaean Mountains must be the southern portion of Lincoln Heath. When the Argonauts returned from Colchis and the city of Aea with the Golden Fleece they did not leave the Black Sea by the same route they had entered it. After landing first on the Paphlagonian coast, we are told:

> "At this point it was natural for Jason and all his friends to think of Phineus and how he had told them they would return from Aea by a different route." [238]

The Argonauts were being pursued by the Colchians in a fleet of ships but some of them, on a false trail had passed out of the Black Sea between the Cyanean Rocks. Sometimes called Symplegades or Planctae, the Cyanean

Rocks were perpetually shrouded in mist, and guarded the entrance to the Bosporus.[239] The Bosporus, as we now know, extended from Newark-on-Trent in the south to Gainsborough in the north. Therefore, if these Colchians were on a false trail and the Argonauts returned by a different route, then the Argo must have sailed around the north of Thrace – the current route taken by the River Humber to the Sea.

Dawn was breaking when the Argonauts left Colchis. With a fresh breeze behind them they landed on the Paphlagonian coast only long enough to sacrifice to Hecate. When they took to sea again a trail of heavenly light showed them the way to go. They did not round Carambis for the wind held and the celestial fire glowed in their van till they reached the mighty River Ister. To return from the Black Sea the Argo would have to sail from Colchis in a south-easterly direction. Shortly after dawn the trail of heavenly light would have been the reflection of the rising sun on the sea. The Argo, however, did not alter course around the headland to the ocean but took advantage of the wind all the way into the river Ister, with the sun shining in front of them all the way. It is highly probable that they took advantage of the shelter of the river Ister because the tides in the North Sea were not favourable at the time. As can be seen from the map, the river Ister was part of Thrace and a 'mighty' river it was.

When the Argonauts left the Ister, some of the Colchians had already blocked every other exit into the Cronian Sea. The Argonauts took refuge on one of the two Brygean Islands near the coast. They were sacred to Artemis. On the other island was a temple of Artemis that Brygi from the mainland coast had built. It was here that Medea and Jason committed treachery by slaughtering Apsyrtus and his Colchian crew in order to escape.[240]

EUROPE AND ASIA

The Tanais River was regarded by the ancients as the division between Europe and Asia. The Amazons lived beside this river originally when it was called the Amazon although, afterwards, it was named the Tanais after a son of the Amazon Lysippe. The Tanais is also called the Don[241] and it appears that this name may be a reference to the god of the sea. Poseidon (sometimes Poteidan) was the supreme deity of all the famous early maritime peoples of antiquity. According to Comyns Beaumont the last syllable of the name i.e. *Don* or *Dan* corresponds with Adon or Adonis, Lord, and *Don* still signifies Lord in the Spanish and Italian.[242] Sometimes it was varied to *Dan* or *Tan*, and hence Jacob's allusion to the maritime tribe of Dan, 'And, Dan shall judge his people', meaning Poseidon. On the south west shore of the Black Sea is the town of Doncaster, named after the River Don, which flows down from the Peak District, through Sheffield. The Roman name for Doncaster is Danum – hence the home of the maritime tribe of Dan. It appears then that this is the River Don which was the ancient division between Europe and Asia. Further light is shed on the ancient boundaries by the Irish histories where we are told that the narrow sea (south of Lincoln) separated the northwest of Asia from the northeast of Europe. Also the Cruithne came from Thrace which was 'in the east of Europe'.

The Trojan War was considered to be a war between Europe and Asia. It appears though that it was not the only war in which Europe and Asia were involved in ancient times.

Sesostris was the last great ruler or god-king of the nineteenth Ramses Dynasty and was famous for the conquests he carried out by land and sea. He raised a powerful army and subjugated every nation in his path. 'Thus his victorious progress through Asia continued, until he entered Europe and defeated the Scythians and Thracians ...'[243] On his return Sesostris came to the river Phasis and a body of troops from his army formed a colony at Colchis. Comyns Beaumont says that additional light seems to be thrown on the personality of Sesostris by the ecclesiastical historian Orosius, whose work Alfred the Great translated from Latin into the Saxon tongue. Calling him Vesoges, King of Egypt, he states that he conquered Asia, marched his army into the northern parts of Scythia, and was pursued in turn by the Scythians who laid Egypt waste. The Scythians were the Skutai, Scotti, or Scots and in these same Scythian lands dwelt the Parthians (exiles) who were the original Goths.

Jordanis, in his work *De Rebus Geticus*, says that Zalmoxis ruled over the Goths in Scythia, near the river Tanais. The Goths waged war with the husbands of the Amazons and met the Egyptians in battle whom they pursued to the bounds of Egypt.[244] Apollonius tells us a similar tale about an Egyptian colony being founded at Colchis in the days before the noble scions of Deucalion ruled the Pelasgian land. A certain king set out from Egypt supported by a strong and loyal force. He made his way through the whole of Europe and Asia, founding many cities as he went. To this day Aea stands, with people in it descended from the very men whom that king settled there.[245]

The Irish histories tell us that the Irish tribes were all 'Greeks of Scythia' and they obtained dominion in Gothia, Thracia, and Achaia. The Goths are descendants of the Scythians, and Jordanes informs us that their origin was in the arctic region.[246] From an island called Scandza, in the surge of the northern Ocean, the Gothic race burst forth like a swarm of bees. When the number of people had increased greatly they moved to the land of Scythia near the Sea of Pontus. There is no doubt that the island of Scandza in the northern Ocean is a part of Scandinavia, located on the other side of the North Sea from the Bronze Age Black Sea in Britain. On their first migration the Goths dwelt near Lake Maeotis; on their second they went to Moesia, Thrace and Dacia; and after the third migration they dwelt above the Sea of Pontus.[247] This is additional confirmation that the Irish histories are essentially correct. Jordanes, in referring to Josephus as a reliable relator of annals, cannot understand why Josephus has omitted the beginnings of the race of the Goths. 'He barely mentions Magog of that stock, and says they were Scythians by race and were called so by name'.[248] In an otherwise curious statement Jordanes substantiates the fact that the original home of the Goths was not the Black Sea of modern times but the very place where we have located it. 'Nor do we find anywhere in their written records legends which tell of their subjection to slavery in Britain or in some other island', he says.[249] Why single out Britain in this statement if he is talking about the Black Sea region in Asia?

The Doliones were located south of Lincoln at the time of the Argonauts' voyage and their king, Cyzicus, had recently married a woman from nearby Phrygia. Later, when the Argo arrived at Colchis, King Aeetes was told that Jason had come to take away the Golden Fleece and, in return, the Argonauts would subject the Sauromatians to Aeetes' rule. The Sauromatians were descendants of three shiploads of Amazons captured by Heracles during his Ninth Labour. They killed their guards, but knowing nothing of seamanship, drifted across to the Cimmerian Bosporus where they landed at Cremni in the country of the free Scythians.[250] Now, the straits to the southwest of Thrace can only be the Thracian Bosporus as this is connected to the Propontis where the Doliones were situated. The straits to the north of Thrace, therefore, must be the Cimmerian Bosporus which joined the Palus Maeotis to the Euxine or Black Sea. It was at Cremni on the Palus Maeotis that the Amazons landed. They drifted along the route taken by the river Ouse from York to the sea. When the Argonauts sailed up the River Ister, the various tribes in the vicinity were either Thracian or Scythian.[251] The Amazons were reputed to speak the Thracian tongue, otherwise that of the Getae or ancient Gothic.[252]

Interestingly, the Amazons were of the posterity of Magog, as were the tribes of Partholon, Neimead, The Fir Bolg, and the Tuatha de Danaan.[253] They were famous warriors and the first to employ cavalry. They carried brazen bows and short shields shaped like a half moon. Three Amazonian queens, Marpesia, Lampado, and Hippo, seized a great part of Asia and, apparently, captured Troy when king Priam was a child. Jordanes tells us that they were women of the Goths who took up arms for the defence of their own country and the devastation of other lands. Lampeto and Marpesia became their leaders and whilst Lampeto remained to guard their native land Marpesia led the novel Amazonian army into Asia and conquered various tribes in war. He also mentions the Amazons Melanippe, Hippolyte, and the Amazonian queen, Penthesilea, famed in the tales of the Trojan War.[254]

We will probably never know the original reason why the river Don was chosen as the boundary between ancient Europe and Asia. The geography of the Lincoln Wolds, however, was such that when the low-lying land in the area was flooded it became an island completely surrounded by water. Two channels were thus formed, one to the north and one to the south, both allowing direct access to the inland sea from the North Sea. These channels and the geographical features of the adjoining coastlines became easily identifiable physical boundaries. The Cimmerian Strait was about 3 kilometres across with mountains immediately inland to the north, rising rapidly to more than 160 metres. This headland was known as Carambis. To the south of Thrace the countryside was lower-lying on both sides of the sea, rising only to about 60 metres a few kilometres inland from the coast. This sea, however, was different. It was at least 7 kilometres in length and tapered gradually inwards to less than 1 kilometre wide. It was referred to

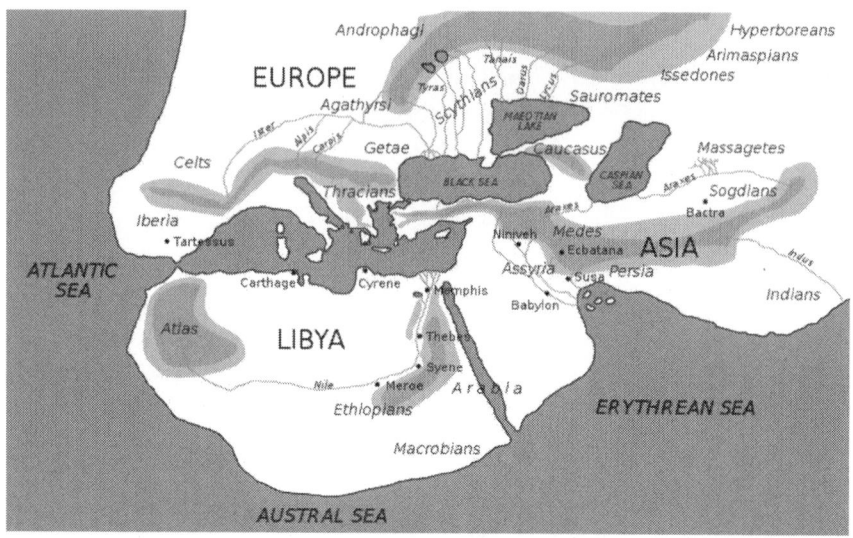

MAP 19. HERODOTUS' WORLD MAP
Acknowledgement: Wikimedia Commons, public domain.

quite naturally as the Narrow Sea. These ancient names had later been transplanted into the Aegean area because Herodotus draws our attention to them in the 5th century BC. It must be understood that the state of geographical knowledge at this time was still deficient but Herodotus takes the first steps forward in methodological enquiry. He laughed at the absurdity of mapmakers who showed ocean running round a circular earth and with Europe and Asia of the same size. He goes on to say that no one knows if there are seas around Europe or where it got its name. Furthermore, he is at a loss as to why the Maeotic Tanais and the Cimmerian Strait have been fixed upon for boundaries, and asks who marked them and from where did they get their names? [255]

BRYGES AND PHRYGES

According to Henry Hubert Phrygian is a form of Thracian.[256] Phrygia was located on the mainland north of Thrace so these people were very close neighbours. Herodotus says that, according to the Macedonian account, the Phrygians were known as Briges during the period when they were Europeans and lived in Macedonia, and changed their name at the same time as, by migrating to Asia, they changed their country.[257] These events are similar to the account given of Midas the King of Macedonian Bromium who ruled over the Brigians, and who Robert Graves equates with Mita, King of the Moschians. These people occupied the western part of Thrace, afterwards known as Macedonia. Midas entered Asia with a train of Brigians and was adopted by the childless Phrygian King Gordius. When the King of Phrygia died, Midas succeeded to the throne and his Brigians became known as Phrygians.[258]

The learned eighteenth century antiquarian writer, Thomas Baxter, describes the Phrygians as those who early became masters of almost all of Western Europe. Stating that they used the names of Briges, Bruges or Phriges, he claimed that the Brigantes of Britain, the most numerous and powerful people in England at the time of the Roman Conquest, were of that race. He related them to the Phoenicians and said they called themselves 'Bryttas' later 'Britones' or 'Britanni'.[259]

As we have seen from the foregoing, the Brygean Islands, Thrace and Phrygia have been located in close proximity to each other in Bronze Age Britain. Appollonius Rhodius tells us that the temple to Artemis on one of the Brygean islands was built by Brygi from the mainland, i.e. Yorkshire. Brygi refers to the Brigantes, and the Brigantes had their capital at York. The Phrygians or Brigians then are the same as the Brigantes who, in their own annals, claimed descent from Gad. This claim is commemorated in a bardic poem of Caedmon, the Brigantine poet, entitled, 'I sing of the origin of the Gadalians', in which he claimed that Breoganus, descended from Gad, founded Brigantia in Spain and that his posterity sailed for Ireland.[260] Skene tells us that the Tuatha de Danaan were in Ireland when the sons of Milead (Milesans) arrived from Spain with the Scots and took the kingdom from them. Milead was the grandson of Breogan (Breoganus) who took possession of Spain.[261]

CIMMERII AND CIMBRI.

We have seen that the northern route out of the Black Sea was via the Cimmerian Bosporus, which took its name from the people who were known as Cimmerians or Cimmerii. The Cimmerii are the same people as the Cymry of today. In the English language their country is called Wales. According to Josephus Gomer, the eldest son of Japeth, was the founder of the Galatai or Cimmerians.[262] At the time of the voyage of the Argo it appears that Cimmerians were located in the area which later became the East Riding of Yorkshire. This area of Britain was part of the domain of the Brigantes, which at the time of the Roman occupation covered the whole of the north of England from the line of the rivers Humber and Mersey. The Brigantes claimed descent from Gad, and the Cymry of Wales, according to the Welsh Triads,[263] have a similarly named benefactor called Hu Gadarn:

> "Before the Kymry settled in Britain, they dwelt in the Summer Country which is called Deffrobani....". "Now at this time had Britain in it no dwellers, save bears and wolves, bison and water-beasts; and it was named Clas Merddin. And Hu Gadarn led hither the nation of the Kymry from the Summer Country, Deffrobani; and it was over the Hazy Sea that they came to this island, and to Llydaw (Bretagne), and there dwelt; and none have any title therein but the nation of the Kymry, for they first settled upon it. So Hu Gadarn became 'a Pillar of the Nation'. And 'a Benefactor of the Kymry'...." [264]

Furthermore, according to Taliesin:

> "A numerous race, and fierce esteemed,
> First colonized thee, Britain, chief of Isles,
> Men of Asia, from the land of Gafis." [265]

So the Kymry (Cymri) were men of Asia, which means that they must have left their homeland north of Thrace and moved south. But, they had come from the land of 'Gafis'. Now, Cymric or Welsh names are descriptive, and Gafis (Gaf-is) can be taken to mean 'below the bent hold or hook', which is a good description for the land north of Thrace, to the east of the Palus Maeotis, now known as Holderness. The 'hook' could refer to the distinctive shape of the promontory that terminates in Flamborough Head, 54 metres above sea level. The Welsh Triads say that the Summer Country was called Deffrobani, which is best explained as follows:

De = The right side, the south
Fro = Cultivated region, lowland
Ban (*Banu*) = High, lofty (to render prominent)

In other words, 'the region/lowland to the right or the south of the promontory or high lands', possibly Flamborough Head and the Yorkshire Wolds which rise to about 240 metres above sea level. This is a good description for Holderness because it hardly rises to over 24 metres. Now, according to the Rev. R. W. Morgan the Kymry resolved to leave Deffrobani under the guidance of Hu Gadarn because the land was exposed to sea floods.[266] It is worth noting that Holderness continually loses land to the sea at an alarming rate. 10,000 years ago the coastline was 15 to 20 kilometres to the east. 30 villages have been lost since Roman times, and even now properties are being demolished because the sea cliffs have encroached to within a few feet.

It appears then that certain of the Kymry came from the Palus Maeotis area and migrated to the mainland, south of Thrace, where they became 'Men of Asia'. Part of the Kymry went to Llydaw, which is Brittany. Poseidonius of Apamea tells us that the tribes in the north of Gaul and the Britons inhabiting Ireland were known first as Cimmerians, and afterwards under the corrupted form Cimbri. According to Festus (Epitome 43) the Cimbri were called 'Brigands' in the Gallic language. Henry Hubert gives 'Kimber' as meaning Brigand.[267] I would suggest that the Brigands are the same as the Brigantes of northern England and, in this respect it is necessary to say a few words about Britain in the sixth and seventh centuries, following the Saxon invasions.

In 577 the Saxons cut off Wales from Cornwall. Later, after 613, the only other British kingdom left was that of Strathclyde or Cumbria. Cumberland was part of Cumbria, the names being pronounced Cimber-land and Cimbri-a. These were British or Cymric lands, and part of the territories of the Brigantes; Kimber and Cimbri meaning Brigand. Furthermore, one of the chief tribes of the Brigantes appears to have been the 'Gadeni' of Cumberland.[268] The Brigantes claimed descent from Gad, and Hu Gadarn (the High Gad), was a Pillar of the Cymric nation. Were the Gadeni the tribe of Gad?

VIRILE RACES DO NOT DIE

The knowledge that the sea level was 5-7 metres higher in the Bronze Age has resulted in a major breakthrough in our search for Thrace and the Black

Sea. Our findings have gone a long way to answering some of the questions that would, otherwise, remain wholly inexplicable in a Mediterranean setting. Furthermore, we have been able to substantiate many facets of history relating to the early inhabitants of the British Isles. The references in the Irish, Scottish, and British Chronicles to places such as Troy, the Hellespont, Thrace and the Black Sea, for example, have often been treated with disbelief and derision. As a result these histories have been regarded by some scholars as works of pure fantasy. We have found, however, that these chronicles deserve much credit for their historical and geographical accuracy. Taken as a whole, they provide ample confirmation that the places we have been dealing with were not located in the Mediterranean or Aegean areas. These places, and the associated events described in these chronicles all belong to the same historical period and the same geographical region – and that region is the British Isles. Comyns Beaumont, in his Foreword to *Britain – The Key to World History* says:

> "Virile races do not die without a trace. We are told by historians that the Thracians disappeared from their lands by the Hellespont and yet Herodotus says that they were the most powerful people in Europe who dissipated their strength by tribal quarrels. They did not disappear from Balkan lands for they were never there".[269]

Comyns also states, 'one cannot correctly report history unless the geography is also accurate'. This is a fact which we have also discovered for ourselves, and it will enable us to locate the Hellespont, Samothrace, the Trojan Battleground, and eventually Troy itself.

ENDNOTES

226 *Odyssey*, 12. 69-72.

227 See Hunter, Apollonius of Rhodes, *Jason and the Golden Fleece*, Introduction.

228 *Greek Myths*, 131.11.

229 Apollonius of Rhodes, *The Voyage of Argo*, p66. Tr. Rieu.

230 Ibid. pp. 70-88.

231 Graves, *Greek Myths*, 151.e.

232 Ibid. 151.3.

233 Ibid.

234 Apollonius of Rhodes, *The Voyage of Argo*, pp. 101-103, Tr. Rieu.

235 Ibid. pp. 107-108.

236 Graves, *Greek Myths*, 153.1-2.

237 Keating, *The History of Ireland*, p175.

238 Apollonius of Rhodes, *The Voyage of Argo*, p153.

239 Ibid. p155.

240 Ibid. pp. 156-160.

241 Graves, *Greek Myths*, 131.4.

242 *The Riddle of Prehistoric Britain*, p122.

243 Herodotus, 2. 102.

244 Beaumont, *The Key to World History*, pp. 148-180.

245 *Voyage of the Argo*, p154.

246 Jordanes, *The Origin and Deeds of the Goths*, III. (16), IV. (25), Tr. Mierow.

247 Ibid. V. (38).

248 Ibid. IV. (29).

249 Ibid. V. (38).

250 Herodotus, 4. 110.

251 Apollonius of Rhodes, *The Voyage of Argo*, p155.

252 Comyns Beaumont, *The Riddle of Prehistoric Britain*, p129.

253 Keating, *The History of Ireland*, p227.

254 Jordanes, *The Origin and Deeds of the Goths*, VII. (49-50), VIII. (57), Tr. Mierow.

255 Herodotus, 4.36 and 4.45.

256 *The History of the Celtic People*, p73.

257 Herodotus, 7.73.

258 *Greek Myths*, 83.

259 See Comyns Beaumont, *Britain:The Key to World History*, p242.

260 Ibid. p111.

261 *Celtic Scotland*, p174.

262 *Jewish Antiquities*, I.vi.i

263 Probert, *The Ancient Laws of Cambria*, p373.

264 Woodward, *The History of Wales*, pp.33-34.

265 Ibid.

266 *The British Kymry*, p15.

267 *The History of the Celtic People*, p104.

268 Elton, *Origins of English History*, p242.

269 Beaumont, *The Key to World History*, Foreword.

THE SEAS OF THE DEAD

The Black Sea and the Hellespont are described as 'salt seas' by Apollonius of Rhodes and Homer respectively. It was an accurate description for the Black Sea because it connected directly with the North Sea. Apollonius mentions the Cronian Sea as being the other side of the Brygean Islands from the Black Sea. We are also told that the Argonauts had sailed into the Sea of Marmara on their way from Samothrace to the Propontis. This means that the Sea of Marmara lay immediately to the north of Norfolk and The Wash. As we have already identified the Black Sea (Euxine) as the inland sea to the north west of Thrace then the one to the south of Thrace must be the Hellespont.

THE CRONIAN SEA

When Jason and the Argonauts left the Black Sea they were pursued by the Colchians in a fleet of ships. Some of these, on a false trail, had travelled through the Bosporus, south of Thrace. The others, under the command of Apsyrtus, eventually blocked every exit from the Black Sea into the Cronian Sea to prevent the Argonauts escaping. The Cronian Sea could only have been reached, therefore, by sailing through the Palus Maeotis.

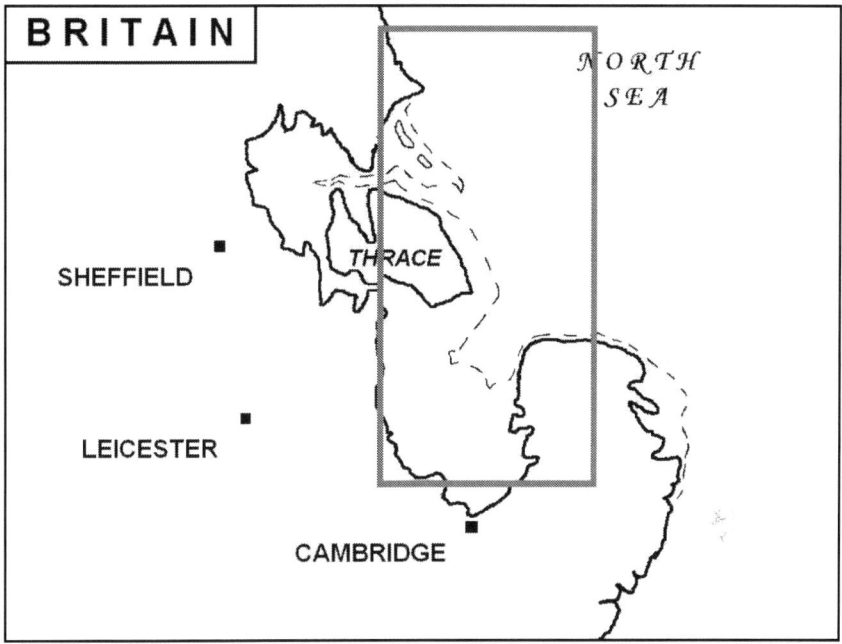

The Cronian Sea was a part of the North Sea. For it to be identified as a separate sea, as Apollonius does, it must have been the portion of the North Sea immediately to the north of Flamborough Head. This headland would have been a distinctive physical boundary marker, and it is quite possible that in the Bronze Age the sea immediately to the north of it was known as a different sea. Blocking all the exits around the Palus Maeotis would equally have prevented access beyond this headland. Pytheas sailed with Cimbric guides to the furthest of the Britannic Isles, and also made a voyage to the peninsula inhabited by the Cimbri. Shortly after, Philemon the poet recorded the fact 'that the northern ocean was called *Morimarusa*, or the Dead Sea, by the Cimbri, from their own country as far as Cape Rubeas: beyond that cape they called the ocean *Chronium*'.[270]

Chronium is the Cronian Sea, named after Cronus, who belongs to the pre-Olympean age. Cronus or 'Father Time' is always shown with a sickle, and in the company of a crow, like Apollo, Asclepias, Saturn and the early British god Bran. Cronus was the god of Death, the same as Bran. *Rubeas* means 'red' so the Cape Rubeas of Pytheas simply means the 'Red Cape'. Flamborough Head is the peninsular that separates the two seas. It appears that even in modern times the reference to the colour red has been retained in the English name, *'Flam'*-borough.

THE SEA OF MARMARA

We are told that the Argonauts had sailed into the Sea of Marmara on their way from Samothrace to the Propontis. It is clear to see that crossing over to the Thracian shore could genuinely be considered as entering the Sea of Marmara. In reality, if the tidal currents were from the north at the time of their crossing they would genuinely have had to sail northwards from Samothrace to counteract the currents and then westwards across to Thrace. Alternatively, the currents at the mouth of the Hellespont may have carried them north, immediately before the change of tides. Under such circumstances they really would have entered the Sea of Marmara. 'Marmara' is the equivalent of the Cymric name for the North Sea, which is 'Morimarusa'. It does not mean the Dead Sea but the 'Sea of the Dead'.

MAP 20. THE SEAS OF THE DEAD

This name corresponds perfectly with the Sea of Cronus – the sea of the god of death. Furthermore, Bran was the early British god of Death and his town is situated in the north western extremity of Norfolk. Known now as Brancaster, the Roman name was Branodunum, or the 'City of Bran'. It is significant that the city of Bran is located right on the Bronze Age shoreline, facing the North Sea, or the Sea of Marmara.

THE HELLESPONT

The Trojan War took place on the shores of the Hellespont, which also had direct access to the North Sea. It too was a salt sea. Homer informs us of this in various places in the *Iliad*. In book 4 he likens the steady beat of the Danaans' battalions to the beat upon beat of the thundering surf crashing against the dry land and 'spewing back the salt wash'.[271] In book 17, when the Trojans meet the Achaeans in battle the shock is compared to the outpouring of a rain-glutted river. The huge surf of the sea roars against the current and the beaches 'thunder aloud to the backwash of the salt water...'.[272] There are many other references in the *Iliad*.[273] The location of Thrace was not far away from the Achaean camp because Homer tells us that day by day Achaean ships brought wine from there in order to fill the huts belonging to Agamemnon. In addition, we are told that Thrace was 'bounded by the swift flowing Hellespont'. Samothrace was also situated near the Achaean camp and the Hellespont because Homer tells us in Book 13 that Poseidon watched the battle, spellbound, from the 'topmost peak of wooded Samothrace'.

Diodorus Siculus says that the ancient Samos came to be called Samothrace from the land of Thrace that lies opposite it.[274] The Hymn to Delian Apollo describes how Leto sought out a place to bear her son, and how Apollo, born in Delos, immediately claimed for himself the lyre, the bow, and prophecy. The hymn, which may be as old as the eighth century BC, refers to Samothrace as 'Thracian Samos'.[275] Taken together these references appear to indicate some ancient connection between Thrace and Samos that is now lost to us. Did the Thracians own Samos? Was Samos settled in ancient times by Thracians and afterwards always referred to as being 'of Thrace'?

The answer to the question lies in the geology of this area. Before the Ice

Age the chalk upland of Lincolnshire (Thrace) was continuous with that of Norfolk (Samos). It stretched right across what is now known as the Wash. Later, this barrier disappeared, either as a result of erosion or through dislocation by a subterranean force. There was subsidence of the Fen basin and, eventually, the sea broke through. But Thrace and Samos were always remembered as being one. The names 'Thracian Samos' and 'Samothrace' preserve their ancient unity.

It is clear from the above information that the Hellespont was situated south of Thrace. Samothrace lay on the east of the Hellespont – now the county of Norfolk. In ancient times Samothrace was partly devastated by a great flood when the outlet at the Cyanean Rocks was rent asunder by the force of water in the Pontus, or Black Sea. The waters burst forth violently into the Hellespont and flooded a large part of the coast of Asia and made no small amount of the level part of the land of Samothrace into a sea.[276]

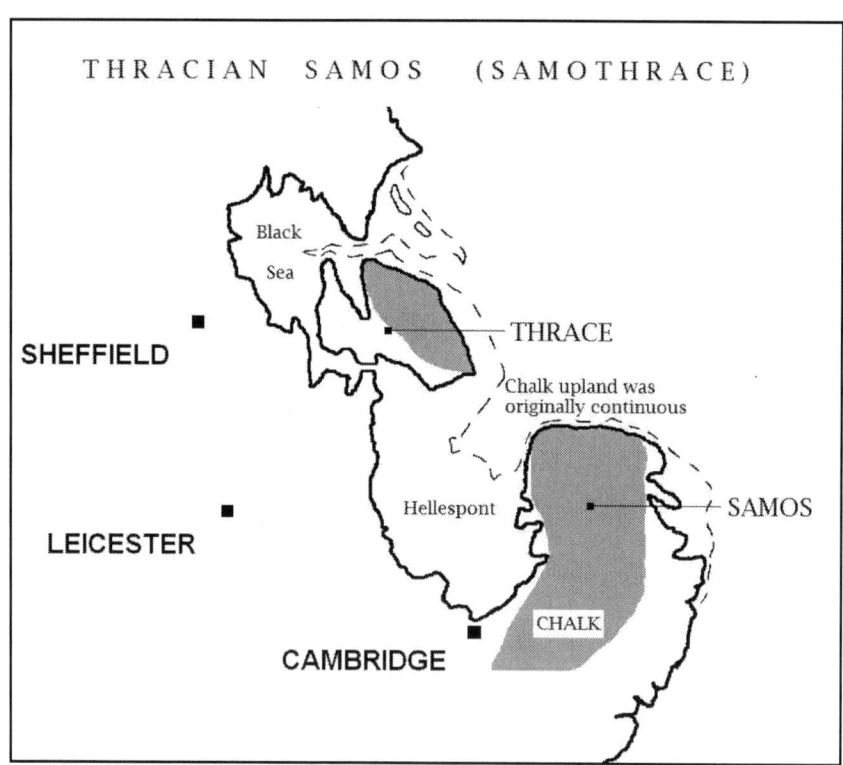

MAP 21. THE GEOLOGY OF THE FENLANDS.
Acknowledgement: Darby, *The Changing Fenland*, p2.

We have previously identified the location of the Cyanean Rocks at the entrance to the Bosporus at the south of Thrace. It is easy to see, therefore, that the opposite coast of the Hellespont, i.e. Norfolk and Suffolk, would be severely affected by such an event.

THE REALM OF HELLE

'Phrixus, the son of Athamus, the myths relate, because of his stepmother's plots against him, took his sister Helle and fled with her from Greece. And while they were making the passage from Europe to Asia, as a kind of Providence of the gods directed, on the back of a ram, whose fleece was of gold, the maiden fell into the sea, which was named after her Hellespont ...'[277]

Here again, we find that Helle and the golden ram are connected with the voyage of the Argo. Phrixus carried on to Colchis and hung up the rams fleece in the grove of Ares. It was the golden ram's fleece that the Argonauts set out to retrieve. Helle was the moon and the Helle myth represents the nightly setting of the moon and the abandonment of Helle's lunar cult in favour of Zeus' solar one.[278] Helle was a Sea goddess and this is partly confirmed by the Greek name for the sea, which is Elisponton. *El* means 'an angel or spiritual being' and *is* means 'under', so we have 'an angel or spiritual being under the sea'. We have previously identified the ancient boundaries between Europe and Asia as well as the seas around Thrace. The only portion of sea left which lies between Europe and Asia is the sea between Thrace (The Lincoln Wolds) and Samothrace (Norfolk), known today as the Wash. This then was the ancient Straits that took its name from Helle when she fell into the sea, as the place-name of Helsey, near Skegness, bears witness. Further confirmation comes from Helle as both sea goddess and moon, and the Latin name for the Wash. According to Graves[279] the Harvest Moon is the 'Reaper on High'. Ptolemy gives the Latin name for the Wash as 'Metaris', which we can transliterate via Welsh as follows:

Med(t) – Reaper
Ar – Surface
Is – Under

The name *Metaris* means nothing in Latin but when transliterated back to the original British (Welsh) language it is wholly significant. It validates the

Wash as the straits of Helle, the sea goddess and harvest moon. The 'Reaper on High' is the ancient Corn-Goddess, commemorated in the Welsh name for September – 'Mis-Medi', the month of the Reaper.

Helle, English *Hell*, is the same as the Teutonic *Hel*. The Teutonic peoples believed that the dead passed to the realm of Hel. The word *Hel* signified both the realm of the dead and the goddess who presided over it. In Greek, Roman, Scandinavian and Celtic myth we have a place of the dead, or a Hades. In Greek myth Cronus, the god of Death, was deposed by his three sons, Zeus, Poseidon and Hades. Zeus became the sky-god, Poseidon the god of the sea, and Hades the god of the underworld. Hades thus became Lord of Hell and ruled over the dead. In Homer's *Iliad* it is always to the realm of Hades that Trojan and Achaean warriors went when they were killed in battle. The Celts believed in a land of the dead, and Druidism was practised officially by a people of Celtic race. Druidism was an ancient and conservative form of the Cult of the Dead. The practice of holding funeral games was also a Celtic rite associated with the Cult of the Dead, and recalls the Trojan funeral ceremonies.[280]

Lewis Spence says that Druidism was essentially a mystery associated with the Otherworld and a belief in a process of re-incarnation.[281] The Druidic bards who lived and sang under the Welsh princes unanimously represent Ceridwen as presiding over the hidden mysteries of their ancient cult. It was essential for those bards who aspired to the Chair of Song to have tasted the waters of inspiration from her cauldron in order to have been initiated into her mysteries. Ceridwen's initiatory rites were not dissimilar to those of Greece and Rome, hence Ceridwen is of the same nature as Ceres, the Corn-Goddess, or 'Reaper on High', whom we have identified as Helle. Now, Helle was the moon, known also as Hellen or Selene, and the first tribe to be called Hellenes came from Thessaly where Helle was worshipped. Thessaly was Jason's homeland and the place of departure of the Argonauts when they set out to retrieve the golden ram's fleece. Before leaving the Hellespont on their voyage to the Black Sea the Argonauts visited Samothrace and were initiated into the mysteries. Samothrace was a centre of the Helladic religion, and hence it's moon-goddess mysteries.[282] So the realm of Helle covered Samothrace as well as the sea that was named after her.

We have identified Norfolk as the ancient Samothrace, the centre of the Helladic religion and moon-goddess mysteries, into which the Argonauts were initiated. Norfolk is the realm of Helle, or the Land of the Dead.

Helle's name is commemorated in the County in the place-names of Helhoughton near Fakenham; Hellington, south-east of Norwich; Hellesdon, north-west of Norwich; Elsden and Hell Pit. The low lying land in the north-east of the County is known as the Norfolk Broads, and is noted for its interlinked freshwater lakes, boating facilities and wildlife. At the time of the Trojan War, however, this land lay under the sea, which extended all the way up the River Yare to Norwich. Homer, in Book 2 of the *Iliad*, pictures the scene in the Asian meadow by the streams of Cayster, where there were countless flocks of geese, cranes, and long-necked swans. The seaside resort of Caister-on-Sea still retains this Bronze Age name.

On the border of Norfolk and Suffolk, at the very edge of the Hellespont, is another 'Hellesdon' in the town of Brandon, near Thetford. In Welsh *Don* means 'the wave' so we have confirmation of Helle and the height of the Hellespont. It is interesting to note that here again we have the name of Bran, the god of Death. Other place-names in Norfolk include Brancaster, Brancaster Staith, Brandon Bank, Brandon Creek, and Brandon Parva. According to the *Romance of Branwen*, Bran's head was, after his death, buried on the White Hill (Tower Hill) at London as a protection against invasion. Bran's connection with the White Hill may account for the curious persistence at the Tower of London of tame ravens, which are regarded with superstitious reverence. There is even a legend that the security of the Crown depends on their continuance there. The raven, or crow was Bran's oracular bird and denotes death and prophecy.[283]

CABIRI, CORYBANTES AND DRUIDS

The Argonauts were initiated into the mysteries of Persephone and her servants, the Cabiri. These festivals or mysteries were celebrated with the greatest solemnity and all the ancient heroes and princes were generally initiated. The Eleusinian mysteries were something similar, instituted at Eleusis in Attica. These mysteries centred on the figures Ceres, Pluto Proserpina and Bacchus. Pluto was the god of the dead and he carried off Proserpina to the nether regions whereupon she was sought for by her

MAP 22.   THE REALM OF HELLE

mother Ceres. It was ultimately agreed that she should spend half of each year below and half above ground. Proserpina is the same as Persephone. Ceres is the goddess of agriculture and the myth refers to the seasons. Bacchus was the wine god, Ceres the wheat goddess. They are the wine and bread of the Christian religion, but in a crude and natural form. The fertility cult is connected with death and resurrection, as in other religions.[284] Proserpina, or Persephone, was a Goddess of Death and Resurrection, the same as Helle. 'Cabiria' was the name given to the festivals of the Cabiri and also a surname of Ceres. The Cabiri are often confounded with the Corybantes, who were the priests of Cybele. The worship of Cybele was introduced into Phrygia by Corybas, the nephew of Dardanus who was the founder of the kingdom of Troy. Dardanus had lived in Samothrace where the initiatory rites of the mysteries had existed since ancient times. Later,

'Dardanus, Cybele and Corybas conveyed to Asia the sacred rites of the Mother of the Gods and removed with them to Phrygia'.[285]

According to W. B. Crow, Druidic mythology and culture consisted mainly of Greek traditions.[286] Druidism was primarily the worship of the mysterious Cabiri. In this was retained an ancient sacramental and initiatory system which had been inherited from the Pelasgi. The Corybantes, with whom the Cabiri were sometimes confused, were priests of Rhea Cybele or 'the Great Mother'. She was the goddess of the powers of nature and the arts of cultivation and she was worshipped upon mountains in Mysia, Lydia and Phrygia. The Corybantes were said to accompany her over the wooded hills, with lighted torches and with wild dances, amid the sound of flutes and horns, drums and cymbals.

The term *Cor-y-bantes* is pure Welsh and means 'Choir of the Heights'. On the Hellespont and on the Propontis, Rhea Cybele was the chief goddess. She was also worshipped in the Troad upon Mount Ida. Her true home, however, appears to have been Phrygian Pessinus in the district afterwards known as Galatia. The Corybantes were also called *Galli*, which is the same as Gauls. We shall see later that the priestesses of the Island of Sena were called *Gallicenae*, identified by Spence as Druidesses. The *Galli*, therefore, were Druids. Now, Caesar says that the Gauls claimed descent from Father Dis so who exactly was Dis? The answer to this question is provided by Cicero in his *Nature of the Gods*:

> 'The entire bulk and substance of the earth was dedicated to father Dis (that is, Dives, 'the rich', and so in Greek Plouton), because all things fall back into the earth and also arise from the earth. He is said to have married Proserpina (really a Greek name, for she is the same as the goddess called Persephone in Greek) – they think that she represents the seed of corn, and fable that she was hidden away, and sought for by her mother. The mother is Ceres .. Because she bears the crops; ...'[287]

So Dis is the same as Pluto, or Hades, the God of the infernal regions or of the dead. The Gallic Druids came to Britain for instruction in religion, hence the principal seat of the Dis cult could only have been in Britain. Logically, therefore, we should not be surprised to find that the seat of the Dis cult, or the Cult of the Dead, may well have been in the Land of the

Dead, at Diss, in Norfolk.

MYSTERIES OF THE WHITE GODDESS

The Mother Goddess or Great Goddess was worshipped throughout Neolithic Europe, and the moon was her celestial symbol. Graves tells us 'The priestesses of the White Goddess in ancient times are likely to have chalked their faces in imitation of the moon's white disc. It is possible that the island of Samothrace, famous for its Mysteries of the White Goddess, takes its name from scaly leprosy; for it is known that Samo means white and that the old Goidelic word for this sort of leprosy was Samothrusc'.[288] Graves writes of her as the White Goddess because white is her principal colour, and the colour of the first member of her moon-trinity. The New Moon is the white goddess of birth and growth; the Full Moon, the red goddess of love and battle; the Old Moon, the black goddess of death and divination. In Apuleius' *Golden Ass*, Lucius invokes her from the depth of misery and spiritual degradation and she appears in answer to his plea:

'Behold, Lucius, I am come; thy weeping and prayer hath moved me to succour thee. I am she that is the natural mother of all things, mistress and governess of all the elements, the initial progeny of worlds, chief of the powers divine, queen of all that are in Hell, the principal of them that dwell in Heaven, manifested alone and under one form of all the gods and goddesses. At my will the planets of the sky, the wholesome winds of the seas, and the lamentable silences of hell be disposed; my name, my divinity is adored throughout the world, in divers manners, in variable customs, and by many names. For the Phrygians that are the first of all men call me The Mother of the Gods at Pessinus; the Athenians which are sprung from their own soil, Cecropian Minerva; the Cyprians, which arte girt about by the sea, Phaphian Venus; the Cretans which bear arrows, dictynnian Diana; the Sicilians, which speak three tongues, Infernal Proserpine; the Eleusinians, their ancient goddess Ceres; some Juno, other Bellona, other Hecate, other Rhamnusia, and principally both sort of the Ethiopians which dwell in the Orient and are enlightened by the morning rays of the sun, and the Egyptians, which are excellent in all kind of ancient doctrine and by their proper ceremonies accustom to worship me, do call me by my true name, Queen Isis'.[289]

So, Persephone, Cybele, Ceres, Helle, the 'Reaper on High' and Ceridwen were the same goddess, or the moon, which was the celestial symbol of the Great Goddess, the mother of all things.

THE MYSTERIES

The mysteries were secret ceremonies and they were revealed only to the select few. Some of them were managed by special priests and assistants and ordinary people were excluded. They often included the use of holy symbols and relics, the meaning of which was revealed only to the initiated. The mysteries of the Cabiri of Samothrace were most secret and were regarded as inferior only to the Eleusinian mysteries in sanctity. The Eleusinian mysteries celebrated the descent of Persephone into the world below and her return to her mother, Demeter. These religious services were called mysteries because the initiated alone took part in them, and because the representations and usages connected with them had a hidden mystic meaning. These mysterious rites were meant to lead the novice to a rebirth of his personality through contact with his subconscious. Some mysteries had various levels of initiation through which a candidate had to progress. At the highest level the initiate had to pass through a state that resembled death in order that his subconscious being could transcend the material universe. This was a dangerous ritual, and many failed. Revelation of the mysteries to the uninitiated, or sacrilegious, was punishable by death, hence they were always shrouded in great secrecy.

Mystery schools are known to have existed in Europe and the Near East as late as the fifth century AD. The ancient language of the Mystery cults was still taught in the poetic colleges of Ireland and Wales long after its suppression by the early Christian Emperors.[290] These mystic rites were actually employed as late as the twelfth century, when Hywel, Prince of North Wales, was initiated into the lesser mysteries of Ceridwen in 1171. In a song supposed to be sung by Hywel he addresses Ceridwen as the moon, lofty and fair, slow and delicate in her descending course, and requests her to attend his worship in the mystical grove.[291] We have already identified Ceridwen as the moon-goddess, the same as Helle. She presided over the hidden mysteries of the ancient Druidic Cult of the Dead, the home of which may have been at Diss, in Norfolk. Samothrace (Norfolk) was where the Argonauts were initiated into the mysteries of the Cabiri, which, according to W. B. Crow, was Druidism. We shall now explore the ancient rites of the Cabiri through the mysteries of Ceridwen.

THE MYTH OF CERIDWEN

Ceridwen was a goddess of the underworld, also styled 'the goddess of various seeds' which equates her with Ceres.[292] She was the Barley-goddess, the White Lady of Death and Inspiration.[293] In the *Romance of Taliesin* we are told that Ceridwen had two children. Creirwy was the most beautiful girl in the world, and Afagddu was the ugliest boy. To compensate for her son's ugliness Ceridwen decided to make him highly intelligent. So she boiled up a cauldron of inspiration and knowledge, which had to be kept on the simmer for a year and a day. Season by season, she added to the brew magical herbs gathered in their correct planetary hours. While she gathered the herbs she put little Gwion to stir the cauldron. Towards the end of the year three burning drops flew out and fell on little Gwion's finger. He thrust it into his mouth and at once understood the nature and meaning of all things past, present and future. He also saw the need to guard himself against the wiles of Ceridwen who was determined to kill him as soon as he had completed his work. He fled away, and she pursued him like a black screaming hag. By using the powers that he had drawn from the cauldron he changed himself into a hare, but she changed herself into a greyhound. He plunged into a river and became a fish, but she changed herself into an otter. Gwion then flew up into the air like a bird, but Ceridwen pursued him in the shape of a hawk. He became a grain of winnowed wheat on the floor of a barn, but she changed herself into a black hen, scratched the wheat over with her feet, found him and swallowed him. When she returned to her own shape she found herself pregnant and nine months later bore little Gwion as a child. She could not find it in her heart to kill him because he was very beautiful, so she tied him in a leather bag and threw him into the sea.[294] Little Gwion was carried to a weir and rescued by Prince Elphin who renamed him 'Taliesin', the future magical bard.

THE CAULDRON OF CERIDWEN

Mythically speaking, the cauldron was designed for the preparation of a brew that induced inspiration and awoke the prophetic and bardic faculties. The myth is obviously an allegory of initiation, of which the tasting of the water was an essential rite. In the poem known as *The Chair of Taliesin* in *The Book of Taliesin*[295] a number of ingredients are enumerated, which went to compose the mystical elixir brewed in the Cauldron of Ceridwen. The water of the cauldron conferred immortality but deprived the initiate of utterance – an allusion, perhaps, to the oath of secrecy administered prior to initiation.

The use of purificatory or lustrational water was not unknown in the mysteries of Greece and Rome. In connection with the Mysteries of Ceres a decoction of laurel, salt, barley, seawater and crowns of flowers was employed. This is similar to the ingredients of Ceridwen's cauldron which according to Taliesin, contained berries, the foam of the ocean, cresses, wort and vervain which had been born aloft and kept apart from the influence of the moon. A part of this potion was also added to the sacred drink. For the British initiates this was made from wine, honey, water and malt, whereas the devotees of Ceres drank a concoction of wine, barley, water and meal. The residue of the water in the Cauldron of Ceridwen was regarded as being poisonous and accursed. It was symbolically supposed to contain the sins and pollutions of the novitiates, and was cast out, precisely as was the residue of the water employed in the mysteries of Ceres.

The mysterious cauldron is alluded to by Taliesin as having been instituted by nine maidens who 'warmed it with their breath'. These maidens were guardians of the Cauldron of Ceridwen, hereditary priestesses of her cult. They are mentioned by Taliesin as preparing their cauldron in 'the island of the strong door', which is possibly the island of Seon in the same poem. Lewis Spence equates Seon with Sena, or Ile De Sein, which is mentioned by Pomponius Mela as the abode of priestesses holy in perpetual virginity, and nine in number.

> 'They are called Gallicenae, and are thought to be endowed with singular powers. By their charms they are able to raise the winds and seas, to turn themselves into what animals they will, to cure wounds and diseases incurable by others, to know and predict the future'.

In a word, says Spence, they were Druidesses, as modern authorities have admitted.[296]

INITIATION

Baptism is a ceremony of initiation into the Christian mystery and was likewise a preliminary to participation in the Greek mysteries, on which the Christian was modelled. The same applies to the Druidic mysteries.[297] According to Lewis Spence, an ancient poem in the Welsh Archaiology supplies an old formula in obscure language, which appears to have been employed on occasions of initiation. Arthur and Kai are represented as coming to the portal, guarded by a hierophant, or priest. The poem includes an introductory dialogue for approaching the gate of the sanctuary and tells of the adventures of Arthur and Kai after their initiation. The hierophant was attended by three assistant ministers, each of whom seems to have impersonated a god. This is similar to the Eleusinian mysteries where four priests officiated – the hierophant who represented the Creator, the torch-bearer who personated the sun, the herald who took the part of Mercury, and the minister of the altar who represented the moon. In the Eleusinian Mysteries the initiate took an oath of secrecy, administered by the mystagogue. Heracles was initiated into the Eleusinian mysteries and after being cleansed and prepared he descended to Tartarus. The myth of Heracles and his twelve labours is the archetypal example of an initiation. Heracles had a ritual contact with death and was symbolically reborn. Taliesin in a poem recited immediately after he had gone through the concluding ceremony of initiation describes himself as 'thrice-born', that is, one of his natural mother, once of Ceridwen, and lastly of the mystic coracle. The rites of Ceridwen were those of initiation, and her myth is an allegory of the initiatory ceremony.[298]

ENDNOTES

[270] See Dinan, *Monumenta Historica Celtica*, p79; and Elton, *Origins of English History*, pp. 61 and 67.

[271] *Iliad*, 4.426

[272] *Iliad*, 17.265

[273] See for example, *Iliad*, 13.351, 15.619, 24.752.

[274] Diodorus Siculus, 5.47

[275] Hesiod, *The Homeric Hymns and Homerica*, 'To Delian Apollo', III.34.

[276] Ibid.

[277] Ibid. 4.47

[278] Graves, *Greek Myths*, 70.8

[279] Ibid. 70.1

[280] Lewis Spence, *The Mysteries of Britain*, p51.

[281] Ibid. p52.

[282] Graves, *Greek Myths*, 149.2

[283] Graves, *White Goddess*, p87.

[284] See W.B.Crow, 'The Mistletoe Sacrament', pp.51-56, in *A Celtic Reader*, Ed. John Mathews.

[285] Diodorus Siculus, 5.49

[286] See note 15.

[287] Cicero, *De Natura Deorum*, 2.66

[288] Graves, *White Goddess*, p435.

[289] Ibid. p72.

[290] Ibid. p12.

[291] *The Mysteries of Britain*, p196.

[292] Ibid. p200.

[293] Graves, *White Goddess*, p68.

[294] Ibid. p27.

[295] J.Gwenogvryn Evans has edited *The Book of Taliesin* and also translated poems from the book.

[296] *The Mysteries of Britain*, pp.81-85.

[297] Graves, *White Goddess*, p157.

[298] *The Mysteries of Britain*, pp.199, 205, and 237.

DRUIDISM

The mysteries of the Mother-Goddess had existed in Samothrace since ancient times, and prior to its removal to Phrygia as the worship of Rhea Cybele. The true home of Cybele in Phrygia became known as Galatia, and her priests, the Corybantes, were called Galli. The 'Galli' and 'Gallicenae' were Druids and Druidesses. The mysteries of the Cabiri are identified with Druidism, and those of the Cabiri and Corybantes with the mysteries of Ceridwen, the moon-goddess of the Druids. The Gallic Druids came to Britain for instruction in religion, and the Gauls claimed descent from Dis, the God of the infernal regions or of the dead. It was Dis who married Persephone and his name survives to this day in the place-name of Diss, in Norfolk, which we have identified as Samothrace or the Land of the Dead. Samothrace was the ancient home of the Cult of the Dead, or Druidism. Although we will be concentrating our attention on Druidism in this chapter it will be seen that there is also more to learn about ancient Samothrace.

DRUID, OAK AND MISTLETOE

Caesar is still considered the best authority respecting the ancient druids.[299] He says that the Druids act in all sacred matters, conduct public and private sacrifices, and answer all questions concerning their religion. They decide in all controversies, judge all causes, and decree rewards and punishments. Over all the Druids one presides with supreme authority and, upon his death, the next in dignity succeeds. At a certain time of the year the Druids assemble in the centre of Gaul, in a consecrated place, in order to determine the disputes of all who are at variance with one another.

The Druids are exempt from military service and from paying taxes, and are in every respect privileged. Their pupils are said to learn by heart a large number of verses, some of them taking twenty years to complete their education. The Druids considered it unlawful to commit their doctrines to writing, although they used the Greek characters for all other matters. One of their most important tenets is the Immortality of the Soul. Their other doctrines concern the motions of the heavenly bodies, the size of the earth and the universe, the nature of things, and the power and majesty of the Immortal Gods.

The Druidical system is thought to have had its origin in Britain, from where it was introduced into Gaul, and it is still customary for those who wish to study it more thoroughly to pass over into Britain for that purpose. Caesar also tells us that the Gauls boast of their descent from father Dis,

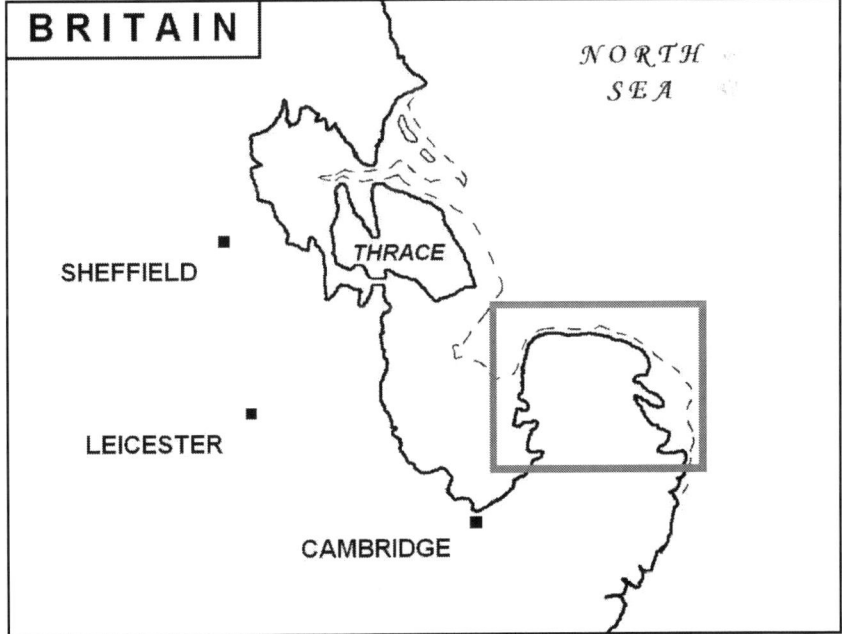

and they derive this information from the Druids. This is the reason why they measure time by nights instead of days, including birthdays and the commencement of their months and years. This measurement of time by nights persists to the present day in the Welsh language – for example one week is *Wythnos*, eight nights.

THE OAK

We are told that Druidism was practised by a people of Celtic race who worshipped Zeus, and whose image was a tall oak. The Druidical groves were composed of oak trees, and the sacred ceremonies of the Druids were invariably graced by the presence of oak branches.[300] The worship of the oak tree or of the oak god appears to have been shared by all the branches of the Aryan stock in Europe. Both Greeks and Italians associated the tree with their highest god, Zeus or Jupiter, the divinity of the sky, the rain and the thunder. The sacred marriage between Zeus and Hera was a marriage between the oak god and the oak goddess.[301]

The beginnings of Druidism, however, appear to be much earlier even than the worship of Zeus. Lewis Spence says that there is every reason to believe that it was not of Celtic origin, but a preceding population.[302] We have seen that Druidism retained an ancient sacramental and initiatory system inherited from the Pelasgians. Now, the Pelasgians took their name from Pelasgus who, supposedly, sprang from the soil of Arcadia. The name 'Pelasgians' became loosely applied to all pre-Hellenic inhabitants of Greece. Euripides, quoted by Strabo, records that the Pelasgians adopted the name 'Danaans' on the coming to Argos of Danaus and his fifty daughters.[303] It was Danaus' daughters who landed on the shores of Britain and the Danaans who took part in the siege of Troy.

We have in Apollonius of Rhodes probably one of the earliest references to the worship of the Oak. By this I mean a reference that takes us back to a generation before the Trojan War. We have seen how the Voyage of the Argo took place in Bronze Age Britain and also that Jason, and others presumably, were initiated into the Druidic mysteries at Samothrace. Later, in the country of the Doliones, strong winds blew continually for twelve days and prevented the Argonauts from sailing. In the early hours of the following morning a halcyon flew over Jason's head whilst he was sleeping.

The event was witnessed by Mopsus who understood the omen and awoke Jason:

> 'My lord, you must climb this holy peak to propitiate Rhea, Mother of all the happy gods, whose lovely throne is Dindymum itself – and then the gales will cease. I learnt this from a halcyon just now; the sea-bird flew above you as you slept and told me all. Rhea's dominion covers the winds, the sea, the whole earth, and the gods' home on snow-capped Olympus. Zeus himself, the Son of Cronos, gives place to her when she leaves her mountain haunts and rises into the broad sky. So too do the other blessed ones; all pay the same deference to that dread goddess'.[304]

Leaving a few of their comrades in the ship, they made preparations for the sacrifices and climbed the mountain:

> 'Standing in the woods, there was an ancient vine with a massive trunk withered to the roots. They cut this down to make a sacred image of the mountain goddess; and when Argus had skilfully shaped it, they set it up on a rocky eminence under the shelter of some tall oaks, the highest trees that grow, and made an altar of small stones nearby. Then crowned with oak-leaves, they began the sacrificial rites, invoking the Dindymian Mother, most worshipful, who dwells in Phrygia'.[305]

These Druidic Mysteries were those of the Mother Goddess. This (pre-Hellenic) religion was matrilineal as was succession to the throne. When the familiar Olympian system was agreed upon, it was a compromise between Hellenic (patrilineal) and pre-Hellenic views. A divine family of six gods and six goddesses was created headed by co-sovereigns Zeus and Hera.

After a rebellion of the pre-Hellenic population Hera became subservient to Zeus and the goddesses were left in a minority in the Council of the Gods.[306] It is this state of affairs which meets us in the *Iliad*. Zeus, the oak god, reigns supreme. The pre-Hellenic mistletoe and oak cult in northern Greece, Attica, and the Peloponnese, had been suppressed in Apollo's name. The goddess Athene was patroness of the cult, and her 'all-heal' was the mistletoe.

FIG. 10. MISTLETOE (VISCUS ALBUM)
Acknowledgement: Wickimedia Commons, Public Domain.

THE MISTLETOE

The Druids esteemed nothing more sacred than the mistletoe and the oak tree upon which it grew. Pliny tells us that everything which grows upon the oak is considered by the Druids as sent from heaven, and a sign that the tree is chosen by the Deity himself. The mistletoe, although very rare to find, was sought for particularly on the sixth moon because it then had abundance of strength though not yet half of its full size. When the mistletoe was found banquets were prepared under the tree and two white bulls were made ready for sacrifice. A priest clothed in a white robe ascended the tree and lopped off the bough with a golden sickle. The mistletoe, which was also termed 'All-heal', was caught in a white cloth and the bulls were sacrificed. Prayers were offered to God to prosper the gift to all who partook of it. It was believed that when taken as a drink, barren animals were made fertile and all poisons were rendered harmless.[307] The mistletoe was generally thought of as being similar to sperm. It was a fertility plant and somewhat magical inasmuch as it came from the air. The sickle shape is a symbol of the moon, and gold is that of the sun. The white bulls are sacred to the moon. Symbolically, only the symbol of sun and moon could be used in such a holy ritual.

Mistletoe can be used as a nervine, narcotic, antispasmodic and tonic, in common with a number of other plants. But what of the Druid tradition that it is the 'All-heal'? According to Ross Nichols,[308] the Steiner followers at a Swiss centre observed and experimented on mistletoe for 14 years with remarkable results, published in the British Homoeopathic Journal in 1969. Viscus Album (mistletoe) is one of the strangest of plants. It forms its flowers in winter.

The flowers appear not only at the tip of the year's growth but also at the joints with that of the previous year. As soon as the flowering of one year is over, buds form for the next. Berries with the seed kernels are not fully ripe before December. Thus, flowers and ripe berries, as well as new unripe ones, are all together on the plant in winter. In contrast, its leaves follow the usual evergreen cycle, although they are hardly normal leaves; they drop off after about four years. It is the birds, chiefly the thrush which, by eating the ripe berries in the hungry season, plant the seeds in the first three months of the year.

Steiner had indicated that the two Solstices were the times of maximum efficacy and the research confirmed this. In December the stems carry flower buds on many nodes. Berries take on a golden tint and moon forces are strong in the closed flowers. At the Summer Solstice period the power of the sap is at maximum, showing in test pictures as rose pink, a sun-filled quality. Manufacturing preparations from mistletoe garnered at these two seasons and following Steiner's advice, remedies have been found for many forms of rheumatic troubles and for cancer. All four parts of the plant are used; roots, stems, flowers and berry. But further, it has been found that the plant, after being rotated in a particular way, acts upon imbalances of all kinds in the body. It needs, however, very great care in administration, this being a highly individual matter. If this quality of healing all imbalances were known to the ancients, then the name 'All-heal' would be an exact description, not hyperbole.

DRUIDISM: ORIGIN AND FOUNDATIONS

The Druids are said by some to have been a tribe of the ancient Celts or Celtae, who emigrated, as Herodotus assures us, from the Danube towards the more westerly parts of Europe, and to have settled in Gaul and in Britain at a very early period. Accordingly, they have traced their origin, as well as that of the Celts, to the Gomerians or the descendants of Gomer, the eldest son of Japeth. But little certain is known concerning them before the time of Caesar, who says that they were one of the two orders of persons that subsisted in Gaul, the other being the Nobles. The case was the same in Britain, where it was supposed the principles and rites of Druidism originated.[309]

The Danube was considered the greatest river in Europe. It flowed into the Euxine Sea. The Greeks called it Ister. This was the river that we identified as flowing through Thrace i.e. the Lincoln Wolds, in the east of Europe in Bronze Age Britain. If the Druids emigrated to the more westerly parts of Europe it is quite clear that they moved to the western side of Britain. The Isle of Anglesey in North Wales is in the extreme west of Britain and, historically, this was always regarded as the ancient seat of the British Druids. Furthermore, Wales is the home of the Cymry, or ancient Cimmerians, who we previously located in the immediate vicinity of Thrace. The Cymry always claimed descent from Gomer, the eldest son of Japeth. Although it appears initially that there is only a tenuous connection between the Druids who emigrated from the Danube and those of Britain, we can now see quite clearly that these early references are one and the same in their origin. They refer to the Druids of ancient Britain.

PRIESTLY CLASSES

The Romans, on discovering Gaul and Britain, found an order of priests with forms and ceremonies almost new to them whose name, in the language of the country, was Druids. This name they adopted into their language as they did the word Magus from the Persians. The Druid of the

Celtae answered in every respect to the Magus of the Persians. Indeed, Pliny tells us that 'the Gauls called their Magi, Druids'.[310] All the evidence, classical and otherwise, goes to show that the Druids were a well-defined, priestly class with sub-divisions having different functions; religious, oracular, magical, administrative and bardic. Diodorus, Strabo, Timagenes, Cicero and Tacitus, allude to these classes separately or generally. The Irish evidence substantiates their existence. The Gaulish Druids, prophets and bards are reflected in the Irish Druids, Fathi or Vates, and filid or Poets. In Wales both Druids and bards are found, and long after Druidism had outwardly vanished in the Principality the Derwydd-vard, or Druid-bard, survived as a repository of Druid philosophy and belief.[311]

Both Diodorus Siculus and Cicero have named another order of men called Saronides, who were the Gaulish philosophers and divines. According to Bochart, Saron or Saronis, amongst the Greeks, was an oak, and equivalent in meaning to our Druid.[312] However, the British, i.e. Welsh, word for Druid has a much wider esoteric significance. The word Derwydd comes from *Dar-Gwydd*, where *Dar* is 'Oak' and *Gwydd* is 'wood'. The word *Gwydd* also means 'knowledge', hence *Gwyddoniad* – 'a man of science or learning'. There is no single equivalent English word for Derwydd because not only does it signify druid, but also magician, wise man, diviner, enchanter, philosopher, theologian, priest, teacher, and preacher. In fact, Druids were the font of all knowledge because it was unlawful to commit their doctrines to writing. If we remember that they worshipped Zeus, whose image was an oak tree, then it is quite logical to find these two elements combined in their name.

The word *Gwydd* also means trees, and the Druids had knowledge of all trees. In the Celtic languages all letters of the alphabet are names of trees. So the Druids who considered it unlawful to commit their doctrines to writing could employ leaves or twigs of the appropriate trees as letters. This system was kept as a profound secret and guarded from the knowledge of the vulgar. It is this system that is imparted to us by Virgil when Aeneas visits the Sybil in her Cumaean cave.[313] Aeneas had been forewarned by Helenus that the prophetess sings the fates and entrusts to leaves signs and symbols. He is told that if the breezes scatter the leaves never will she unite the verses, so Aeneas must beg the Sybil to chant the oracles and open her lips in speech.[314] The descent of Aeneas into the regions of Dis and the mysteries of metempsychosis were doctrines of pure Druidism. We know now that Aeneas' voyage took place around the British Isles so it is clear that these leaves could only be those of Irish or British Druidism. The Sybil's cave at Cumae was Cimmerian, and the Cimmerians are British. Furthermore, Virgil alludes to the mistletoe as Aeneas' passport to the Realms of Hell. The Sybil tells Aeneas that hidden in a shady tree is a bough, golden in leaf and pliant stem that is consecrate to nether Juno. To him only who first has plucked the golden-tressed fruitage from the tree is it given to enter the hidden places of the earth. This hath beautiful Proserpine ordained to be borne to her for her proper gift.[315] When Aeneas found the tree the gleam of gold shone out through its branches. Virgil tells us, 'As in winter's cold, amid the woods, the mistletoe, sown of an alien tree, is wont to bloom with strange leafage, and with yellow fruit embrace the shapely stems: such was the vision of the leafy gold on the shadowy ilex, …'[316] Virgil alludes to the mistletoe but he does not tell us openly. Is this plant really the mistletoe? And why does Virgil refer to it as being gold? The reason why Virgil does not openly tell us that it was mistletoe is because it was part of the Cimmerian druidic doctrine, which was sacred. The reason why it is referred to as being gold is that this was the meaning of the Cimmerian name. In the Cymric (Welsh) language Mistletoe is called *Pren Puraur*, the 'Branch of Pure Gold'.

Two very old alphabets are known among the ancient Greeks. These were the Pelasgic (Attic, Argive, or Arcadian), and the Ionian (Phoenician, Cadmean, or Aeolian). We are told that they were almost the same, with only 16 letters. The same number of letters is claimed by the old Latins, the old Germans, the Irish, and the British bards. It appears that there was one common origin. Surprisingly, the Hebrew, Samaritan, Irish, and Greek alphabets (as well as the old British) have all been called after British Trees.[317] Does this mean that the origin of these alphabets was Druidic, and hence Irish-British? Traditionally, we call the pages of our books 'leaves', but there are no leaves associated with ancient bark or papyrus, rolls of vellum or parchment, and writing tablets had no leaves. The Irish Beth-Luis-Nion tree alphabet, shown below, is described in Robert Graves' book, *The White Goddess*.[318] For the interested reader, Graves provides notes on each tree, explaining its significance, history and symbolism. This alphabet consists of five vowels and thirteen consonants. Each letter is named after the tree or shrub of which it is the initial.

THE BETH-LUIS-NION TREE ALPHABET

Beth	**B**	Birch
Luis	**L**	Rowan
Nion	**N**	Ash
Fearn	**F**	Alder
Saille	**S**	Willow
Uath	**H**	Hawthorn
Duir	**D**	Oak
Tinne	**T**	Holly
Coll	**C**	Hazel
Muin	**M**	Vine
Gort	**G**	Ivy
Pethboc	**P**	Dwarf Elder
Ruis	**R**	Elder
Ailm	**A**	Silver Fir
Onn	**O**	Furze
Ur	**U**	Heather
Eadha	**E**	White Popular
IdhoI	**Y**	Yew

FOUNDATIONS

Many classic writers and historians have provided us with information regarding the priestly class of men known as Druids. Simply speaking, the Druidic Order was made up of Druids, Prophets and Bards, but we are also told about Magi and Saronides. From where did these names come, and how did they have their beginnings? According to Holinshed's *Chronicles of England, Scotland and Ireland*, the first foundations of Druidism were laid down by Samothes, one of the sons of Japheth:

'In the diligent perusal of their treatises, who have written of the state of this our Island, I find that at the first it seemed to be a parcel of the Celtic Kingdom, whereof Diss, otherwise called Samothes, one of the sons of Japheth was the Saturn or original beginner, and of him thenceforth for a long while called Samothea'. [319]

Samothes is said to be the sixth son of Japheth, called by Moses, Mesech, and by others, Dis. He planted colonies of men in the country of Gallia and in the Isle of Britain. Samothes was the first King of Celtica, and the four kings who succeeded him in regiment over the Celts and Samotheans were Magus, Sarron, Druis, and Bardus. In his *Description of Britain* he mentions Magus, Sarron and Druis as being involved in philosophy, astrology, theology, religious doctrine, and teaching.

Further on in his Chronicles, in the *History of England*, Holinshed provides short treatises on each of these kings of Celtica and their respective areas of learning and knowledge. It could easily be assumed from this information that each class of men in the Druidic Order had adopted the name of its founder. Holinshed cites Berossus and Annius as sources, but he does not believe the information. He tells us that 'these stories rely only on the authority of Berossus whom diligent antiquaries reject as a fabulous and counterfeit author'. But it appears that Berossus may not have been at fault. Many books on the ancient Gauls and Druids had as their source a text attributed to Berossus but printed by Annius of Vitrebo in 1498. We are told that Annius' text is now seen as spurious. Peter Berresford Ellis says that Annius took names from Greek and Latin texts and changed them into real people, such as Druis, Bardus, Celtae and Samothes. [320] On the other hand Herman L. Hoeh, in his history of early Britain and Western

Europe, clearly regards these names as authentic and lists Samothes, Magus, Sarron, Druis and Bardus as the first five kings who ruled from 2094 BC to 1847 BC. But, this history of early Western Europe is almost wholly unknown, he says. Why does the history of Western Europe begin with the Romans, he asks, when there is an ancient written history that has been preserved? It is because the people who preserved this history were the Welsh and the Germans. Because of bitter jealousies with the English, the history of early Europe and Britain – especially Wales – was extirpated from the English school system, whilst English historians did everything in their power to label this history as 'myth'.[321] We will cover this and other related matters later in the book because, in many ways, they are part of a long history of persecution and suppression of people, which includes the denial, denegration and destruction of their histories.

We cannot insist that these kings existed, or existed by the names given to us. Whatever the truth may be it is evident that Samos is the same as Samothea, the ancient home of Druidism. Again we cannot prove that Samothes was the same person as Dis. We do know, however, that four towns in Britain were named from Magus, the supposed son of Samothes, and these are attested by Antoninus. One of these towns, Sitomagus, is actually situated in Norfolk (Samothrace) and is only 25 kilometres west of Diss. Sitomagus is the modern Thetford.[322]

IRISH AND BRITISH DRUIDS

The origin of Druids in Ireland is carried back to the earliest colonizers of the country. These were the colonies of Partholon, Neimead, the Firbolg, Tuatha De Danaan, and the Milesians. Partholon had three Druids in his company whose names were, Fios, Eolus and Fochmare, meaning 'Intelligence', 'Knowledge' and 'Inquiry'. There is no record of any performance of these Druids but, from our earlier findings, we now know their country of origin. Partholon and his Druids came from the Grecian country in the East – from Mygdonia near Thrace, or the Lincoln Wolds in the east of Britain. The colony of Neimead had not been in Ireland long before they were troubled by incursions of sea rovers, called Fomorians. Driven to despair the Nemidians assembled all their forces, from all parts of the country, on the shore opposite Tory Island. The Fomorians sent their Druids and Druidesses to confound them with Druidic spells but they were met by the Nemidian Druids and Druidesses under the leadership of Neimeads wife, Reilbeo. She was the daughter of the King of Greece and the chief of the Druidesses. A fierce contest of spells took place followed by a battle in which the Fomorians were defeated. Now, Neimead and his colony had come from Scythia having sailed through the Euxine Sea and the North Sea, which means that the country of origin of his Druids and Druidesses was also Britain.

After Neimead's death, his followers left Ireland in three bands. Beotach, the son of Iarbonel 'the prophet', the son of Neimead, went with his clan to the northern parts of Europe. They made themselves perfect in all the arts of Divination, Druidism, and Philosophy, and returned some generations later under the name of Tuatha De Danaan. As we have already located Thrace and the Euxine Sea in Bronze Age Britain, and identified the ancient boundaries between Europe and Asia, we can safely say that it was to the northern parts of Britain where this clan went.

The second clan, under Simon Breac, went to Thrace and his descendants returned to Ireland many generations later, as the Firbolg. The King of the Firbolgs, in Ireland, had a chief Druid who was called Cesarn. He is said to have had recourse to the secret agencies of his art, and to have discovered from a vision the approach of a powerful enemy. This enemy was the Tuatha De Danaan who had returned from the northern and eastern parts of Europe. Immediately prior to their removal to Ireland they were located at Dobhar and Iardobhar, that is, in the vicinity of the rivers Tay and Forth in northern Britain, or Scotland. The Tuatha De Danaan returned to Ireland perfectly accomplished in all the secrets and mysteries of the occult sciences. They had a Druidical chief called 'the great Daghda' who was their military leader, as well as three chief Druids and two chief professional Druidesses. In addition, they had a great number of private Druids and Druidesses. All of these are mentioned by name in the early accounts of their arrival in Ireland. When the Tuatha De Danaan discovered the Firbolgs in the area, they decided to move to a different part of the country. In order to oppose the Tuatha de Danaan the Firbolg hosts had assembled together in a council of war. Three of the Tuatha De Danaan Druidesses caused clouds of impenetrable darkness and mist to envelop the assembly, and showers of fire and blood to pour down upon them. For three days the business of the assembly was suspended until, finally, the spell was broken by the Firbolg Druids. During this time, however, the Tuatha De Danaan had moved to a safer place.

The tribe of the Tuatha De Danaan was in Ireland when the Milesians arrived from Spain. In the entire course of their migrations the Druids hold a conspicuous place. Among the most remarkable was Caicher, who is said to have foretold to them, on their way to Spain, that Ireland was their final destination. As well as having chief Druids in the colony, one of the Milesians' brothers, Amergin, was the Poet and Judge of the expedition, and a famous Druid. Having landed in Ireland the Milesians demanded the sovereignty from the three joint kings of the Tuatha De Danaan. These kings complained that they had been taken by surprise and if they had been given prior notice of the invasion they would have prevented it. Both sides agreed to a proposition by Amergin that the Milesians should re-enter their ships and move out to sea a distance of 'nine waves' from the land, and if the Milesians could not be prevented from landing, the sovereignty would be surrendered to them. When the ships lay at the agreed distance from the shore the Tuatha De Danaan Druids raised a tempest, which drove the fleet out to sea and dispersed them.

Now, the Milesians took their name from Milead who was the grandson of Breogan, who took possession of Spain. Breogan, as we have already determined, was of the Phrygians, Brigians or Brigantes from eastern England. Milead married Scota from whom the Scots take their name, and the Scots were Greeks who sailed via the Hellespont in eastern England to Ireland. The Milesians were a Cretan colony who founded many cities including Miletus in Asia Minor. Milead also had sons by a daughter of a King of Scythia.[323] Having located Europe and Asia in Bronze Age Britain, including the Euxine Sea, the Hellespont, and the whereabouts of various people like the Scythians and Phrygians, it becomes clear that the Milesians and their Druids had their origins in the same part of the world.

So far we have dealt with the colonies of Partholon, Neimead, the Firbolg, Tuatha De Danaan, and the Milesians, all of which inhabited Ireland at different times. The origin of these colonies however, was Britain as was the origin of their Druids and Druidessess. We now come to the Picts or Cruithne who emigrated from Thrace and went first to France, where they built the city of Poitiers, and then to Ireland. The colony was led by six brothers, one of who was Trostan the powerful diviner, the Druid of the Cruithne. After landing in Ireland the king of Leinster told them he would give them welcome on the expulsion of the Tuatha Fidhbha. Trostan, the Druid, ordered that the milk of seven score white cows should be used as a cure for the wounded. The battle was fought and all of the Tuatha Fidhbha were slain. The wounded Cruithne were bathed in the milk and the poison did not injure any of them.[324]

The Druid Abaris, mentioned by Diodorus Siculus, was a Hyperborean Priest of Apollo, but more importantly, he was a Briton. He is recorded as speaking Greek perfectly, and he visited Pythagorus at Marseilles. Chryses, mentioned by Homer in Book 1 of the *Iliad*, was also a Priest of Apollo. When the Achaean army was camped on the Trojan plain, Chryses came to recover his captured daughter. He brought with him a generous ransom and carried the chaplet of the Archer-god Apollo on a golden staff in his hand. The Achaean troops wished to see the Priest respected but Agamemnon treated him with discourtesy, insulted him and refused to free his daughter. Chryses prayed to Apollo who inflicted a deadly plague on the Achaean army. For nine days and nights innumerable fires consumed the dead.[325] There is no doubt that Chryses was a priest, probably of the Druidic order. Later, we shall find that his home was also in Bronze Age Britain, the same as the original homes of all the other Druids we have discussed.

DECLINE OF DRUIDISM

Caesar tells us that the Druidical system was thought to have had its origin in Britain, from where it was introduced into Gaul. It appears that Caesar learned all about Druidry from his friend, Diviciacus, the Aeduan Druid. Diviciacus was the acknowledged ruler of the Aedui, and a politician and diplomat of high repute. He is quoted by Cicero as having 'that knowledge of Nature which the Greeks call physiologia'. In his war in Gaul, Caesar found the Druids a main obstacle because they urged on the resistance, and were, in turn, supported by the Druids of Britain. The Roman conquest of Britain began in AD 43, directed by the Emperor Claudius. Under Nero, his successor, orders were given for the extortion of all monies possible. Roman law did not recognise matriarchal rights, which prevailed in large parts of Britain. Family fortunes were seized and female heirs to the throne were not acknowledged. Rebellion was urged on by the politically minded

Druids and the Roman governor, Seutonius Paulinus, marched to Anglesey to exterminate them.

The Pennine area, central Wales, Scotland and Ireland became refuges and racial rallying grounds. In Wales, the mountains held a number of highly intelligent, mystic-minded people who were studying the Graeco-Roman philosophies and linking with an older wisdom. In Ireland, after Padraic (St. Patrick), a disguised Druidry held some sway, customs evidently held as before. In Scotland these Druidic customs appear to have survived, unchecked. When the word 'Druid' became strictly forbidden under Christianity, the Druids became Culdees. The Druidic training colleges were taken over and called monasteries and nunneries, with schools keeping intact most of their internal arrangements. The Culdees though, however learned, could only become lesser clergy – the top positions were given only to dependable Christians. Over many centuries Druidry in the British Isles could not be explicit, although in Wales and Scotland it could be bardic. The Culdees spread a Christianised form of Druidry to Ireland and Scotland in the Celtic Church, based upon the Greek forms. The Celtic and Greek, similar at the root, again came together. Customs and ceremonies survived, but they were not to be called Druidic. Much went underground and Bards are increasingly heard of instead.

In France, there is evidence that Druidry survived the Romans and had a revival. At Poitiers is a baptizing church built on a Celtic temple foundation, but this is over a Roman temple; confirmation that the Druidic-Celtic faith was flourishing in the first and third centuries AD. It should be remembered that Poitiers, or Pictavis, was built by the Picts and their famous Druid was Trostan 'the powerful diviner'. Under Notre Dame in Paris was a Druidic circle-temple, not preserved – and one is still buried in the foundations of the new London St. Paul's. According to Davies, Gwenddoleu the Prince of the Strathclyde Britons who lived about 593 'was the head of an ancient Druidical establishment in North Britain'.[326] In the sixth century the Druids opposed Columba in Scotland. At Oxford before the foundation of the university, from about the year 800, a grove of the Pheryllt, called Cor Emrys, is found. The centre of this Oxford cult was the Mother Goddess, the mysteries of Ceridwen. Supposedly, it was suppressed by Christianity prior to 1056.

The Culdees worshipped at York as late as 936. Their chief seat in Scotland was the island of Iona, the ancient name of which was Inis Druineach, or 'Island of the Druids'. In 1171, Hywel, Prince of North Wales, was initiated into the lesser mysteries of Ceridwen, the Druidic moon-goddess. In London, a Roman temple of Diana surmounted Lud Hill. A church, then a cathedral, topped the hill, but Diana's cult continued. A ceremonial blessing of her hunt and the acceptance of a sacrifice continued at Old St. Paul's until 1557. In 1649, The General Assembly of the Church of Scotland appointed a Commission for the specific purpose of taking action against Druidism. Among other matters to which they directed their attention were the Druidical customs observed at the fires of Beltane, Midsummer, Halloween and Yuil. These customs were ordered to be abolished.[327]

Ross Nichols describes numerous Celtic-Druidic festivals and ceremonies, which survived over the centuries in France, England, Scotland, Italy, Scandinavia, Wales and Ireland. Then, with the advent of the Renaissance culture, the exclusiveness of Christianity began to break down and the wisdom of the past became more acceptable. Here was the beginning of modern Druidry.[328]

SEAHENGE

In the Spring of 1998 a circle of prehistoric timbers was found in the sands at Holme-next-the-Sea in Norfolk. The beach, part of the Holme Dunes National Nature Reserve, was eroding rapidly. A blanket of peat that had protected the timbers had almost disappeared. As the sea eroded the land the circle of timber posts became visible. Standing in the centre was an oak tree. But this was no ordinary oak. It was upside down with its roots in the air. The site, now known as 'Seahenge', was one of the most remarkable archaeological finds in Britain.

Initial fieldwork showed that the circle was early Bronze Age, made up of 55 split oak timbers with a maximum diameter of 6.78 metres. Following a great deal of debate the timbers were eventually excavated and removed to Flag Fen Laboratories in Peterborough for conservation and analysis. Using radiocarbon and dendrochronological dating methods scientists from Flag Fen and the University of Sheffield have provided dates for the central oak and the circle timbers that are astoundingly precise. The central oak and

FIG. 11. A DRAWING OF 'SEAHENGE' – SAMOTHRACE (NORFOLK)

the slender trees used for the circle were cut down in the Spring of 2049BC. They were felled with bronze axes and split with wooden wedges. Measurements of the axe-marks show that more than 50 axes were used. On the day that the great central oak was felled it was 150 years old.

The circle appears to be a religious structure with the central upturned oak acting as an alter. Its significance has been compared to that of Stonehenge. It is considered that it was deliberately placed between the North Sea and the land - between the realm of the ancestors and that of the living.[329]

If we needed further proof that Norfolk was the home of the ancient druidical religion, or the Cult of the Dead, we have it before us. 'Seahenge' is located at the extreme northwest corner of Norfolk. It is the meeting place of the Hellespont, the Helle Straits, and Morimarusa (Sea of the Dead) and, as such, no finer place could have been chosen for its location. It is also only 6 kilometres west of Brancaster, named from Bran, the early British god of Death. It may also be significant that it stands at the end of the ancient thoroughfare known as Peddar's Way, which runs right across Norfolk for a distance of 65 kilometres. The southern end, and perhaps the starting point of Peddar's Way, is located between Thetford (anciently Sitomagus) and Diss. In ancient times those who wished to be initiated into the Mysteries may well have entered from the Hellespont and travelled up the Little Ouse River from Brandon to Thetford, and perhaps even further up the river Thet to Peddar's Way.

Peddar's Way runs along the line of a Roman road and it is thought by some that it is actually Roman. But, Peddar's Way doesn't go anywhere, so why would the Romans build a road to nowhere? Andrew Mcloy, in his *Exploring Roman Britain*, asks what its original purpose was because it is a question that has long perplexed historians. Some commentators still maintain that the ancient British highways were built by the Romans whereas, in reality, they were an amazing accomplishment of the British kings Dunwallo and his son Belinus hundreds of years before the Romans

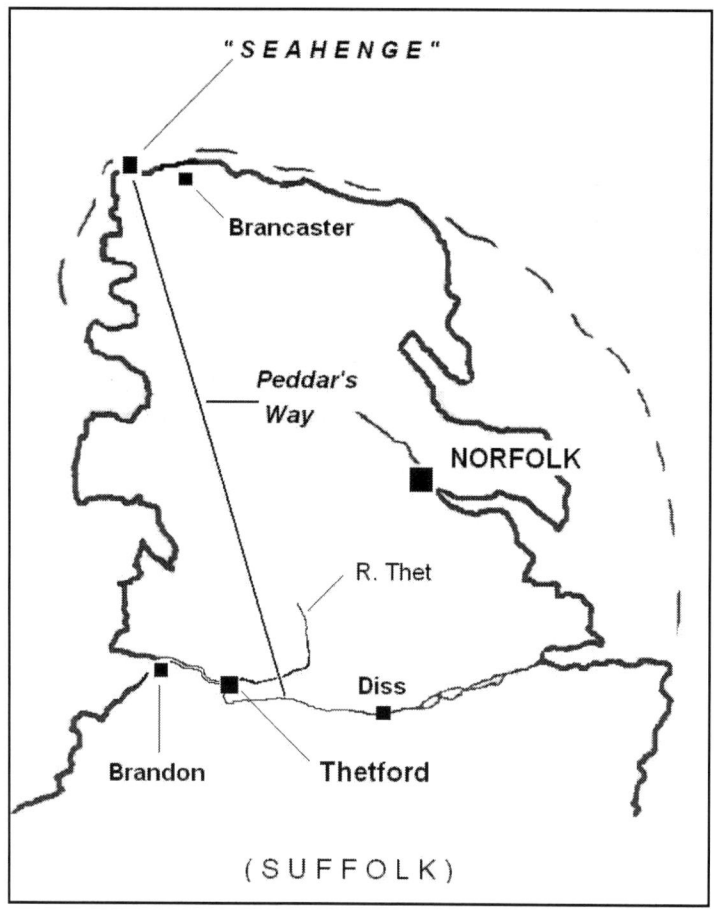

MAP 23. SEAHENGE AND PEDDAR'S WAY, NORFOLK.

arrived in Britain. Dunwallo designed and partly made the Royal British Military Roads throughout the island. They were completed by Belinus and were called the Belinian Roads of Britain. They were paved with hard stone eighteen foot wide, ten foot deep, and with huge flint stones at the bottom. These kings also made laws relating to the security of the roads and the safety and protection of the people who used them. It is found, of course, that the Roman roads and the ancient British roads constantly run in and out of each other.[330]

The name Peddar is regarded by some as coming from the Latin *Ped* or *Pedestr*, meaning foot. In this case, what does the second part of the word mean? A double *d* makes no sense in Latin but it is a normal occurrence in the British language, so could the name Peddar be British? The problem here is that the British language has many words beginning with *Ped* or *Pedd* but they are nearly all obsolete or of doubtful authority. Surprisingly though, every single one relates to the foot or travelling by foot. If we look upon the first part of the word as 'foot' or 'travelling by foot' then the British meaning agrees with the Latin. This leaves us with two options, *Pedd-ar* and *Ped-dar*. The first option, *Pedd-ar*, would mean land-walk or footway. The second option, however, gives a different meaning. *Ped* would once again mean 'foot' but the second part of the word, i.e. *dar*, means 'oak'. In this instance the meaning of Peddar is 'Oak Walk'. Is this just a coincidence or have we stumbled across the real nature of this ancient thoroughfare? If so, it would mean that the purpose of Peddar's Way was to take people directly to the great oak at Holme-next-the-Sea for religious ceremonial purposes.

ENDNOTES

[299] *The Conquest of Gaul*, vi.13-21.
[300] Spence, *The Mysteries of Britain*, p165.
[301] Frazer, *The Golden Bough*, p159.
[302] *The Mysteries of Britain*, p37.
[303] Graves, *The Greek Myths*, 1.2
[304] Apollonius of Rhodes, *The Voyage of Argo*, p65.
[305] Ibid. p66.
[306] Graves, *Greek Myths*, p19.
[307] Pliny, *Natural History*, xvi.95

[308] *The Book of Druidry*, pp. 153-154.

[309] Eugene O'Curry, 'Druids and Druidism in Ancient Ireland', pp. 15-16, in *A Celtic Reader*, Ed. John Mathews.

[310] Higgins, *The Celtic Druids*, p95.

[311] *The Mysteries of Britain*, p56.

[312] *The Celtic Druids*, pp. 95-96.

[313] *Aeneid*, 6.71-76.

[314] Ibid. 3.440-457.

[315] Ibid. 6.132-144.

[316] Ibid. 6.205-209.

[317] *The Celtic Druids*, pp. 15-24.

[318] Graves, *The White Goddess*, pp. 165-194.

[319] *Description of Britain*, p6.

[320] *The Druids*, p253.

[321] *Compendium of World History*, Vol. 1, Ch. 19. (See www. Earth-history.com)

[322] Beale Poste, *Britannic Researches*, p4.

[323] Eugene O'Curry, 'Druids and Druidism in Ancient Ireland'. See note 11.

[324] 'Irish and Pictish Additions to the Historia Britonum', in Skene, *Chronicles of the Picts; Chronicles of the Scots*.

[325] *Iliad*, 1.8-54.

[326] Edward Davies, 'The Mythology and Rites of the British Druids', p81, in *A Celtic Reader*, Ed. John Mathews.

[327] *The Mysteries of Britain*, p160.

[328] Ross Nichols, *The Book of Druidry*, pp. 76-97.

[329] See www.flagfen.com/seahenge.htm.

[330] The Tysilio Chronicle. See Roberts, *The Chronicle of the Kings of Britain*, pp. 47-49. See also Morgan, *The British Kymry*, pp. 45-46.

13

THE TROJAN BATTLE - GROUND

We have previously established that the Hellespont was the flooded plain known today as the Fenland. The Trojan War took place on the shores of the Hellespont. It had direct access to the North Sea. The Achaean ships were designed for such waters because we are told in the *Iliad* that Hector got his hands on a seagoing ship, which was 'the fast salt-water craft that had brought Protesilaus to Troy...' This was one of the ships that had sailed the ocean and, undoubtedly, both Trojans and Achaeans were familiar with conditions in the North Sea. When the Trojans finally entered the Achaean Camp, Homer tells us of these conditions when he says 'With a roar they swept across the wall, like a billow on the high seas rolling before the wind, the great wave maker, and tumbling over the bulwarks of a ship.' The Hellespont was an inland sea subject to the ocean tides. It is 'the wine-dark sea' with 'grey surf'. Aias and Odysseus walked together at the edge of 'the sounding sea', a perfect description for the continuous action of the waves against the shore. It was 'the broad Hellespont', extending some 56 kilometres across The Fens of eastern England.

THE FENS OF EASTERN ENGLAND

The Fen Country covers 3300 square kilometres of countryside and is the largest plain in England. Except for some isolated islands it is mostly flat

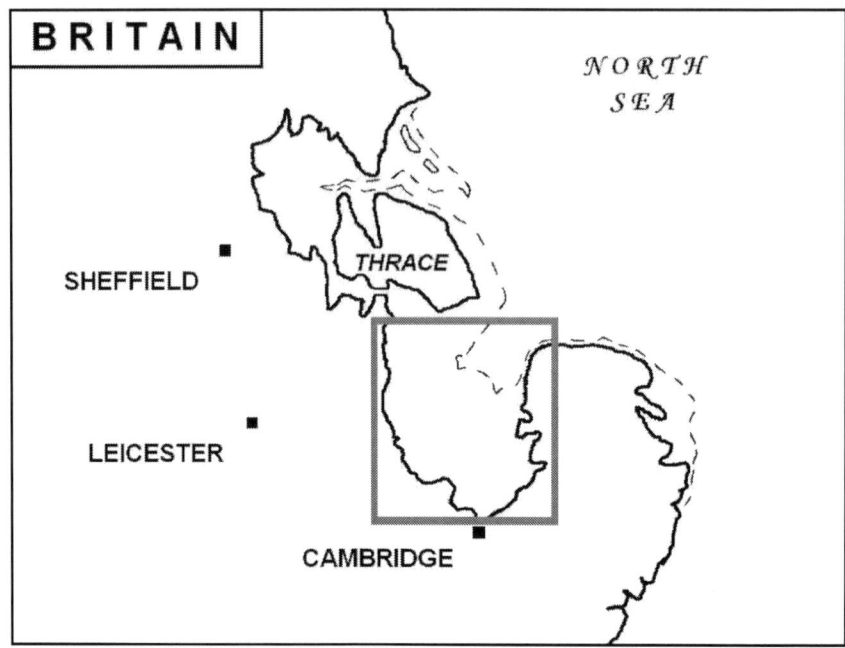

and below the level of high spring tides. It has been subjected continually to sea invasion, tidal incursion and freshwater flooding. H.C. Darby, in his book *The Changing Fenland,* tells us how the history of The Fens has often been a tale of woe. As early as 1086 AD there is a unique Domesday reference to the loss of arable land on the coast of The Wash. In the next century many men and cattle were engulfed by the sea. There were great sea floods in 1236 and again in the 1330's. In 1570 there were great inundations from the sea, drowning many villages. Corn and cattle were lost, salt-works flooded, and a ship was driven upon a house. In 1614 there was a great flood of fresh water from the uplands caused by the melting of heavy snow. The greatest risk for the Fen Country is through a combination of events, when the north or northeast winds accompany high spring tides together with freshwater floods caused by heavy rainfall or melting snow in the highlands.

In the post-Roman period the fens were a waste of sedge and water. Piecemeal reclamation of the northern silt areas appears to have commenced as far back as the early Middle Ages. It was not until the seventeenth century, however, that any widespread drainage scheme was put into place in the southern peat fens. Over the centuries some river mouths became choked with silt by the invading tides. Freshwater flooding became worse and river courses changed. Some rivers became displaced. In the seventeenth century when most of the southern fens were drained, many rivers dried up. The remains of the former waterways are known as 'roddons' and appear today as raised banks of silt meandering across the black peat fens. Reclamation of the fens is now more than complete and, undoubtedly, the most extensive flood protection scheme is the two artificial rivers, the New Bedford and the Old Bedford. These rivers run parallel to each other in a north-westerly direction across the fens from Earith to Denver, a distance of more than twenty miles (32 km). The New Bedford River saves the land through which the Ely Ouse flows from certain destruction. The tidal doors of Denver Sluice bar the Ouse to the tide and re-directs its flow. Tide-borne silt is washed back into the sea. At times of flood and high tide, the waters of the Ely Ouse and its tributaries are held back. When river levels rise, following heavy rainfall, these two artificial rivers and the 5600 acres of grassland between them act as a floowater reservoir. Such are the

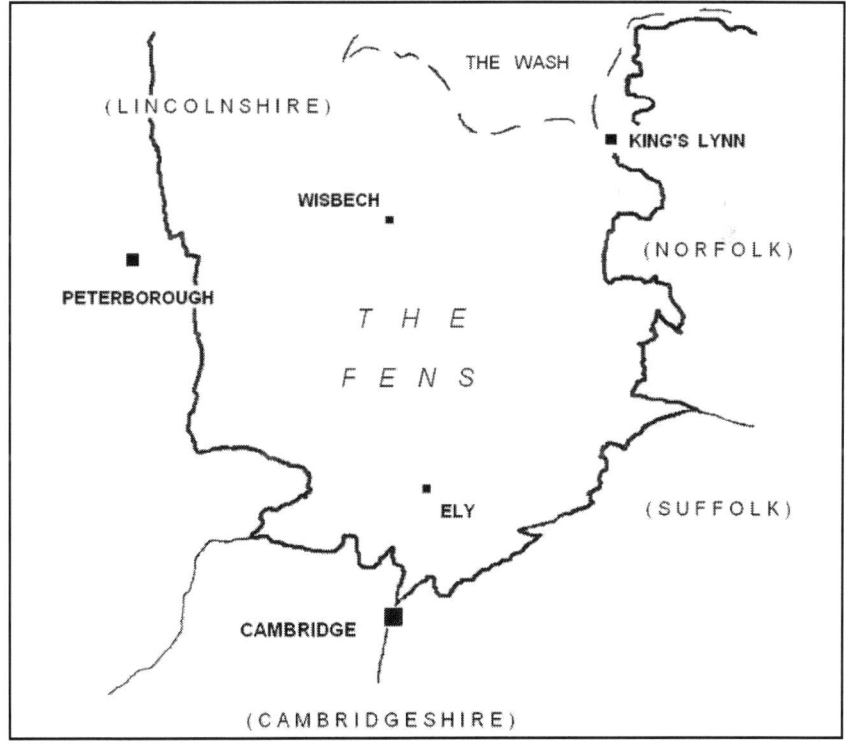

MAP 24. THE FENS OF EASTERN ENGLAND

works of man that prevent the whole of the fens from returning to the sea's domain.[331] Currently, The Wash is the last remnant of a vast inland sea, which, in the Bronze Age was called the Hellespont.

THE TROJAN PLAIN

We now need to move on and determine the actual location of the theatre of war itself. As a result of our previous work we can exclude Norfolk because we know that this was Samothrace. This leaves us with the western, southern, and south-eastern edges of the fenland as candidates for the battleground. At first, this may appear to be a daunting task but it is here that we can take advantage of a crucial piece of information provided by Homer.

At the beginning of Book IX of the *Iliad* we are told of the winds that blow from Thrace, namely 'Boreas' and 'Zephyr'. This provides us with a general location in relation to Thrace, which we have also located. As Boreas is the north wind and Zephyr is the west wind, the combined effect will be a northwest wind. If the Achaean army is subjected to a northwest wind it means that the battleground was southeast of Thrace. From this information we can establish a probability that the theatre of war was on the south-eastern shore of the Hellespont.

Most of the fighting took place on the Trojan plain, which is also called the 'Plain of Scamander', and there is such a plain on the southeast of The Fens. It extends from Cambridge in a northeast direction beyond Newmarket towards Norfolk, and it is certainly big enough to have contained the Achaean camp and the large fleet of ships on its shore. Of greater significance, however, is the chariot warfare that was employed by the Achaean and Trojan armies. By its very nature this method of fighting would mean that a vast expanse of reasonably level countryside would be required. In this respect, the plain is more than adequate for the purpose. It is about 50 kilometres in length, with at least 5 kilometres usable width. The ground rises very gently in a south-easterly direction, away from the edge of the fens. We know that the Trojan plain was not perfectly flat because Homer refers to the 'high ground', and at one stage he tells us that the Trojans were located on the plain 'above the Achaean army'. As we shall see, the Trojan War was played out on one of the largest plains in Bronze

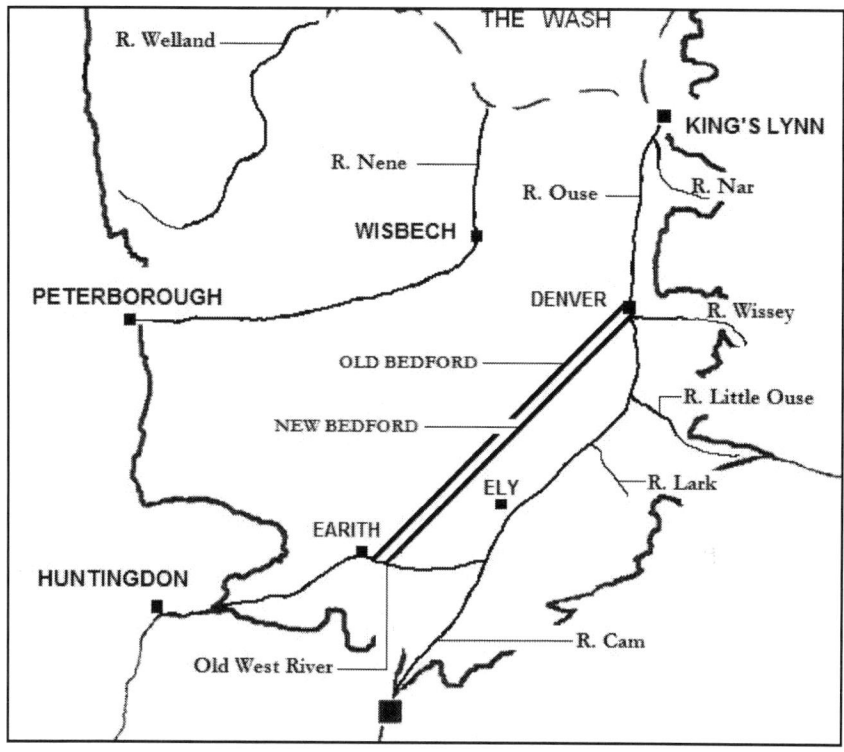

MAP 25. THE MAIN RIVERS OF THE SOUTHERN FENS.
Acknowledgement: Astbury, The Black Fens, p21.

Age Britain. The events depicted by Homer were real, and the tradition of chariot warfare survived for more than a thousand years down to the time of the Roman occupation.

SCAMANDER AND SIMOIS

In Book VI of the *Iliad* we are told that 'the battle kept swaying to and fro across the plain, with many a volley and counter-volley of bronze headed spears, midway between Simois and the streams of Xanthus'.[332] Xanthus was another name for the river Scamander. Throughout the *Iliad* it is the rivers Scamander and Simois that are given prominence over all the other rivers. They mark the extremities of the Trojan plain and there are many occasions when the location of the fighting is given with specific reference to one or other of these rivers. There are, in fact, two rivers that can be identified with Scamander and Simois in the southeast of the Fens; namely, the river Cam (Scamander) and the Little Ouse (Simois). We shall take each of these in turn and discover that not only are the geographical locations correct but that the meanings of the names are in perfect harmony with Homer's descriptions.

The river Cam is described by Homer as 'the mighty swirling river who is called Xanthus by the gods and Scamander by mankind'.[333] When Achilles enters the war and chases Hector around Troy we are told that they came to 'the two lovely springs that are the sources of Scamander's eddying stream'.[334] So the Scamander had two distinct sources and two names. And, surprisingly, so does the river Cam. In fact each source of the Cam has two names. The meaning of Scamander, (Greek: Scamandros), can be explained via the British language, as follows:

Ys:	Is, Exists i.e. life
Cam:	Crooked, Bent, Winding
An:	Vast, Great, Mighty
Dros:	Mutation of 'Tros' (Troy)

So, the Scamander was the mighty swirling (or winding) river of Troy. Homer calls his rivers 'living streams', and it can be seen that the first syllable '*Ys*' means life or existence – the first vowel has fallen away, a common occurrence in the language even today. The southeast source of the river, besides having the name of Cam, is also called Granta, a name that probably embodies a descriptive reference to the properties of its water (Gran = gloss, lustre). The waters of the Scamander apparently gave a beautiful colour to the hair or the wool of such animals as bathed in them.[335] The river was called Xanthus, and Xanthus means 'yellow'. The southwest source also bears the name of Cam but, in addition, is called Rhee, phonetically the same as the British 'Rhi', meaning 'source, sire or chief'. Rhi is a name found in Welsh mythology, as applied to the gods. The river was called Xanthus by 'the gods'.

Homer's description of the river Scamander is very much a play on words. What appear to be a few simple phrases in the *Iliad* are now shown to have

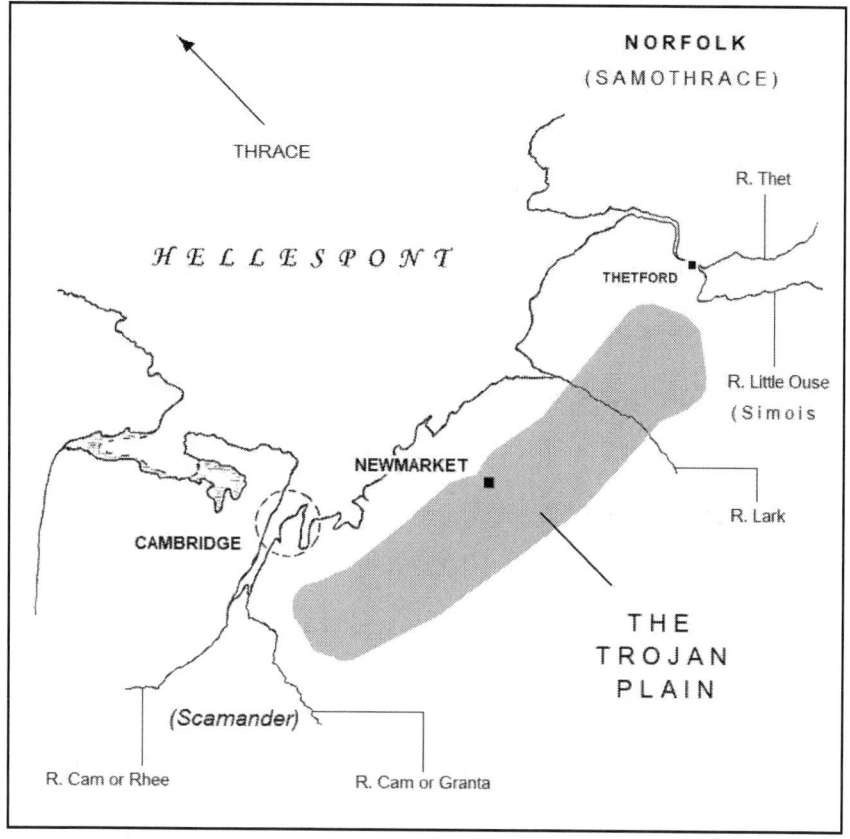

MAP 26. THE TROJAN PLAIN

a much deeper meaning and hence an intimate knowledge of the subject matter on behalf of the poet. In order that we could reveal this intimate knowledge it was necessary for us to be in the correct geographical location. Secondly, we had to identify the subject matter correctly i.e. the appropriate river, together with its tributaries. Finally, the deeper meaning of the words could only be explained via the medium of the ancient British language. All of this leads us to the conclusion that the poet was British and the *Iliad* was originally constructed using the ancient British language, which we now know was not much different to Greek.

The story of the Trojan War was transmitted orally over many centuries until finally being written down. This oral tradition demanded that the poets learn thousands of lines of poetry by heart. This tradition is typically British. Construction of such poetry required decades of learning by the poets, who appear to have distilled the whole spectrum of knowledge into their works. The poems could also be understood on different levels depending upon the learning acquired by the listener. At the superficial level a listener would be thoroughly entertained by the story and accept it at face value. Like the proverbial 'Russian Doll', however, deeper and more secret levels were concealed within, and these were understood only by those who had progressed to the higher stages of wisdom.

Further information is provided in the *Iliad* that confirms the location of the river Scamander. In Book XI the Achaeans draw up for battle outside their camp and during the morning they break the enemy battalions. By noon the Trojans are fleeing towards Troy, some even reach the Scaean gate. Zeus is watching the battle from the heights of Ida, which looks out over the Trojan city and the Achaean ships. He stabilises the battle and the Trojans turn and confront the Achaeans.

The battle moves back across the plain towards the ships. A frantic stand is made by Odysseus, who is surrounded by Trojans. Hector, however, knows nothing of this because he is still engaged where the slaughter is heaviest 'on the far left, by the banks of Scamander...' The hills having a commanding view lie immediately southeast of the plain. Seen from here the river Scamander would, indeed, be on the far left. The river that lay on the other side of the Trojan plain from the Scamander was the Simois, which we can identify as the Little Ouse. Simois is the same as Simoes in the British language, the meaning of which we can explain as follows:

Sim: What is flippant or light
Oes: Life, existence.

It can be seen that Simoes means a 'little life', or a small river. The Cornish equivalent of 'oes' is 'oys' or 'ooz', hence the English spelling of Ouse. The title Little Ouse, therefore, has the same meaning as Simois. The rivers are one and the same.

CHARIOTS AND HORSES

In chapter two we stated briefly that many scholars had been at a loss in trying to explain Homer's battle scenes. In his discussion on this topic Hans

Van Wees declares, 'There is a curious consensus that Homer does not know what he is doing when he has his heroes drive around in war chariots. For most, Homeric chariot-tactics offend against military common sense and historical precedent'.[336] Van Wees does not subscribe to this consensus view but considers the tactics to be consistent and plausible. Later, he refers to the Celts who fought along Homeric lines but, unfortunately, he did not pursue this point further. In our investigation so far we have been unable to fault Homer's reliability or accuracy, and once again on this topic he proves to be a faithful ally.

The use of chariots was a particular characteristic of British warfare. Caesar, after first landing in Britain in 55BC, records the fact that his soldiers were confounded at such an extraordinary way of fighting:

> 'In chariot fighting the Britons begin by driving all over the field, hurling javelins, and generally the terror inspired by the horses and the noise of the wheels are sufficient to throw their opponents ranks into disorder. Then, after making their way between the squadrons of their own cavalry, they jump down from the chariots and engage on foot. In the meantime their charioteers retire a short distance from the battle and place the chariots in such a position that their masters, if hard pressed by numbers, have an easy means of retreat to their own lines. Thus they combine the mobility of cavalry with the staying power of infantry; and by daily training and practice they attain such proficiency that even on a steep incline they are able to control the horses at full gallop, and to check and turn them in a moment. They can run along the chariot pole, stand on the yoke, and get back into the chariot as quick as lightning'.[337]

The British forces included cavalry as well as chariots and these had been ready to oppose the Romans when they first landed. Caesar describes in detail the very grave difficulties he faced. He tells us that the size of the ships made it impossible to run them aground. Furthermore, his soldiers were unfamiliar with the ground, and they had their hands full. He goes on to say that they had to jump down from the ships into the water and fight the enemy. We are told that the British fought on familiar ground 'boldly hurling javelins and galloping their horses, which were trained to this kind of work'. His soldiers were unaccustomed to battles of this kind and were frightened. The Romans could not keep their ranks or get a firm foothold and there was great confusion. At one stage it appears as if Caesar viewed the British tactics as extremely dishonourable because when they saw small parties of soldiers disembarking from the ships they galloped up and attacked them at a disadvantage. They surrounded them with superior numbers, he tells us, and they threw javelins at the right flank of a whole group.[338] How unsporting! How unfair!

In 54 BC Caesar organised a massive armada of 800 ships, five legions and 2000 cavalry, and invaded Britain for the second time. The British forces had assembled under the command of Cassivellaunus and the cavalry and charioteers had fierce encounters with the Romans. On one occasion we are told that when the Roman soldiers were off their guard the British forces came out of the woods, swooped upon the outpost and started a violent battle:

'Throughout this peculiar combat, which was fought in front of the camp in full view of everyone, it was seen that our troops were too heavily weighted by their armour to deal with such an enemy: they could not pursue them when they retreated and dared not get separated from their standards. The cavalry, too, found it very dangerous work fighting the charioteers; for the Britons would generally give ground on purpose and after drawing them some distance from the legions would jump down from their chariots and fight on foot with the odds in their favour. In engaging their cavalry our men were not much better off: their tactics were such that the danger was exactly the same for both pursuers and pursued. A further difficulty was that they never fought in very close order, but in very open formation, and had reserves posted here and there; in this way the various groups covered one another's retreat and fresh troops replaced those who were tired'.[339]

Even later, when Cassivellaunus gave up hope of fighting pitched battles and disbanded most of his troops, he retained 4000 charioteers for the purpose of delivering swift but effective attacks on the Romans.[340] What has been described here by Caesar was warfare according to ancient British tradition. It was no mere reminiscence of a method of fighting in a far distant land. It was, however, precisely the mode of fighting that took place in the Trojan War and is described at length in the *Iliad*.

In AD 60 Nero reigned as Emperor of Rome, and England had become a province of the Roman Empire. The land between Cambridge and Norfolk was inhabited by a tribe of ancient Britons called the Iceni. They were superb horsemen and highly skilled in the use of the chariot. Prasutagus was the last king of their royal line and when he died he bequeathed half of his property to Nero and half to his two daughters. The Romans, however, recognised only male rights to a throne and property, and attempted to seize all of the king's wealth. They maltreated his two daughters and Queen Boudicca, the widow of Prasutagus. As a result Boudicca led the Iceni into open rebellion, sacking Colchester, London, and St. Albans. The headquarters of the Iceni was at Exning, 3km from Newmarket, where Boudicca is supposed to have founded a royal stud. What little knowledge we have of their history and coinage leads us to conclude that they bred and dealt in horses. Troy was the land of horses and the Trojans' sacred animal was a mare. Iceni gold and silver coins bear on the reverse side the effigy of a horse.

According to the Venerable Bede, horse racing was also a practice among the Anglo-Saxons. He recounts how a number of people on a journey came to a plain well adapted to a racecourse. The young men were excited to prove their horses on what appears to be the plain now known as Newmarket Heath. In 1997, Suffolk County archaeologists unearthed the grave of a Saxon horse and rider buried together at RAF Lakenheath, about 19 kilometres northeast of Newmarket. The burial, which is believed to have taken place around 550 AD, was a significant archaeological discovery.[341]

In the centuries following the Norman subjugation of England Newmarket became intimately connected with royalty and reigning sovereigns. Tournaments were held at Newmarket in 1309 by a proclamation of King Edward II. The English horse, Equus Britannicus, enjoyed a great and well-merited reputation on the continent, and sovereigns lavished money on the royal stud. From 1605 James I visited Newmarket Heath on many occasions for the purpose of hunting and hawking. James and a number of subsequent kings actually moved their courts from London during their visits to the Heath. Officially, horse racing has taken place at Newmarket since the date of the first recorded match between two horses in 1622. It was here that king Charles II formally established racing in 1671 and drew up the first set of rules. The Jockey Club took up rooms in the town in

1752, and by the 1840's there were as many as 18 courses listed.[342]

Throughout the *Iliad* we are reminded of the Trojan and Achaean love for horses. They were held in high esteem by both sides, and some were even treated as gods. Homer often uses the phrase 'the horse-taming Trojans', and refers to Troy as 'the land of horses' and to Ilium as 'the land of noble horses'. We are told of their magnificent qualities, excellent breeding and, surprisingly, their genealogy. Today, this area is the centre of British horse racing and Newmarket has worldwide fame as the 'shibboleth of the turf'. Many racehorses are bred and trained here and the area is literally studded with studs. Tradition dies hard in Britain. After 3000 years this area still merits the title of 'the land of horses'.

PLAGUE, FLOOD AND FIRE

PLAGUE

Book I of the *Iliad* opens with Apollo inflicting a deadly plague on the Achaean army. The god came down in fury from Olympus with his bow and quiver to punish Agamemnon for his discourtesy to Chryses the priest:

> 'He sat down opposite the ships and shot an arrow, with a dreadful twang from his silver bow. He attacked the mules first and the nimble dogs; then he aimed his sharp arrows at the men, and struck again and again. Day and night innumerable fires consumed the dead'.[343]

Homer is describing the effects of malaria, one of the most ancient infections known. The association between swampy or marshy areas and the disease has been recognised for a long time. It was not until the 20th century, however, that the role played by the mosquito and the malarial parasite were identified. Although malaria is most common in the tropics and subtropics, it can occur in temperate regions as well. The basic method of prevention is to eliminate the breeding places of the mosquitoes by draining and filling the marshes, swamps and stagnant pools.

The location of the Achaean camp was at the edge of the sea and the Achaean forces came out from the camp directly onto the plain. Having identified the location of the Trojan plain we can now see that the Achaean

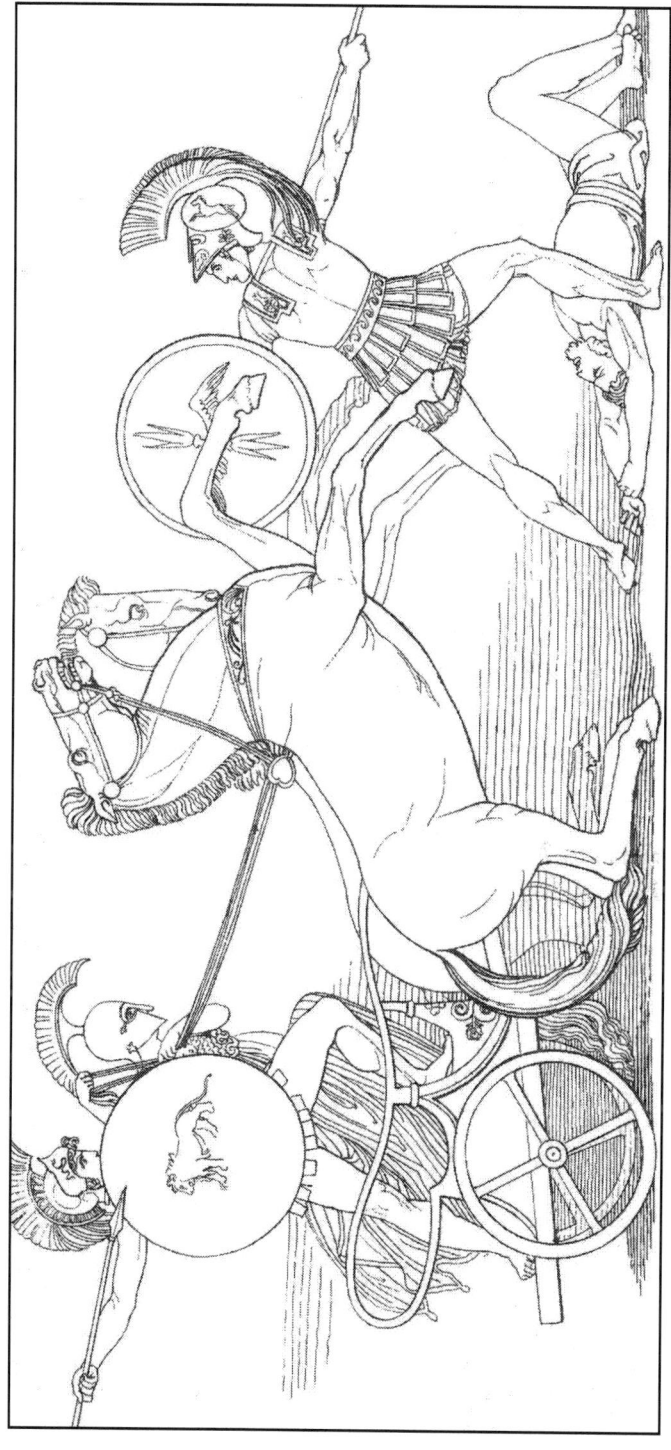

FIG. 12. CHARIOT WARFARE ACCORDING TO ANCIENT BRITISH TRADITION.
Illustration by John Flaxman, 1755-1826.

camp would be situated right at the edge of the Fens. This was a vast sedgy wasteland once afflicted by mosquitoes. Later, we will discover the precise location of the Achaean camp. We will discover also a town devastated by plague.

That town was in the middle of the land once occupied by the Achaean forces. Homer is imparting to us information about naturally occurring events in a specific geographical area. A.K. Astbury tells us that as a result of the extensive reclamation works, 'The Fens are no longer plagued by winter fogs and summer mosquitoes; and Fen Ague, a form of malaria which brought shivering, intense pain in the limbs, fever and violent thirst, is no more.'[344]

FLOOD

When Hector kills Patroclus, Achilles re-enters the battle and the Trojans are chased across the plain towards the river Scamander. When they reach the ford Achilles cuts the Trojan force in two. He drives one party across the fields and chases the rest into the deep Silver Pools. The river is cluttered with men and horses. Achilles leaps into the water, slaughtering Trojans until he is almost exhausted. Three kilometres south of Cambridge is the delightful village of Grantchester. Before the river Cam was bridged at Cambridge this was the main crossing point. Grantchester grew up on a busy east-west route that met the river where two fords were located. This is where Achilles cut the Trojan forces in two. Immediately to the south is Byron's Pool, named after Lord Byron the British poet who was an undergraduate at Cambridge. Homer refers to the river here as 'Xanthus of the Silver Pools'. How fitting it is that it should now bear the name of another poet.

Homer tells us that the ferocity of the slaughter carried out by Achilles left the dead and dying 'busily attended by eels and fish'. The river Cam is known for its eels and, historically, the whole region's economy relied on them. Bede mentions them in the eighth century. He says that the Isle of Ely was called 'the eel district' because so many eels were found there. The river Cam runs past the Isle of Ely, which is located about 22 kilometres to the north of Cambridge. The Domesday entries for Cambridgeshire villages mentions the considerable profits obtained from fishing, and these were often stated in terms of eels. In 1086 annual renders from Wisbech amounted to 33,260 eels, whilst those from Doddington were 27,150, Stuntney 24,000 and Littleport 17,000.[345] Neither was it unusual to pay rent in such a currency. Robert Fafiton's land at Grantchester included one half of the weir for which he paid a peppercorn rent of 500 eels. The weir is thought to have been where Byron's Pool is today.

Achilles continues the slaughter until the carnage becomes too much for the river:

> 'Scamander rushed on him in spate. He filled all his channels with foaming cataracts, and roaring like a bull he flung up on dry land the innumerable bodies of Achilles' victims that had choked him, protecting the survivors by hiding them in the deep and ample pools that beautified his course. The angry waters rose and seethed around Achilles; they beat down on his shield and overwhelmed him'.[346]

Achilles tries to escape from the wrath of the river Scamander but whenever he stopped a mighty wave crashes down on his shoulders. He calls to the gods for help and Poseidon and Pallas Athene appear. They tell Achilles that he is not destined to be overcome by any river, and he is not to cease fighting. Achilles takes heart and goes on across the fields, which are now completely inundated with water and afloat with armour and corpses. Again, he fights his way upstream to the fury of Scamander who calls to the river Simois for help in overpowering the man:

> 'He thinks himself a match for the gods; but I am determined not to let his strength or beauty save him now. Nor shall that splendid armour. It shall lie deep in the slime beneath my flood; and as for him, I'll roll him in the sand and pile up shingle high above him. The Achaeans will not know where to find his bones, I'll bury him so deep in silt'.[347]

Here, Homer is describing the freshwater floods that occur naturally in the Fenland.

Throughout the Fens there was an ever-present danger of flooding, both from the sea and from the uplands. William Dugdale, the 17th century historian of draining, thought that the freshwater floods presented more of a hazard than those of the sea. These floods continued longer upon the land and destroyed it by drowning. Historically, the surface of the Fenland was made up of two different areas. In the north was a silt belt, the result of the Fens being subjected continually to the action of the sea. The tides brought marine silt up the rivers, which eventually choked the river mouths. In the south was an inland expanse of freshwater peat carrying a number of lakes or meres. Essentially, it was undrained countryside. With their slow currents and gradual fall, Fenland Rivers offered little opposition to the incoming tides. As the river mouths became choked with sea-borne silt so the flooding in the southern fens became worse. Also, it was here in the southern part of the bay where there was the greatest volume of river water. In the southeast corner of the Fenland up to six lodes were cut across the peat to meet the river Cam. From the finds in these ancient waterways it appears that most of them were Roman artificially dug canals, for drainage.[348]

It is here at the edge of the southern fens where Homer describes the floods. He pictures for us the river Cam in full spate, the waters from the uplands rushing down in seething, foaming waves; the torrential waters depositing slime, piling up shingle and inundating the fields.

FIRE

Seething with foam and blood Scamander rushed upon Achilles and threatened to engulf him with a towering wave. In her terror the goddess Hera screamed to her son Hephaestus to deploy his flames against the river and the plain:

'Hephaestus responded to his mother's call with a terrific conflagration, which started on the plain and consumed the bodies of Achilles' many victims that were scattered there. The shimmering flood was stemmed and the whole plain was parched, like a freshly sprinkled threshing floor that the North Wind dries up in autumn to the farmers delight. When Hephaestus had thus dealt with the plain and consumed the dead, he attacked the River with his dazzling flames. Elm, willows, tamarisks caught fire; and the lotus, rushes and galingale that grew in profusion by the lovely stream were burnt. Down in the pools, even the eels and fish that had been tumbling about in their beautiful home were tortured by the hot breath of the Master Engineer. The river himself was scalded'.[349]

Eventually, the river admits defeat and calls to Hephaestus to stop, but the fire devoured him as he spoke. His water bubbles like melting fat. The river is consumed and his waters go up in steam. Homer describes a massive conflagration that spreads across the plain and consumes the very river itself. But the work of the gods in the *Iliad* has an earthly explanation.

In the southern peat Fens a farmer may have to face a most extraordinary hazard. As incredible as it may seem, the land he farms may catch fire. Normally, the risk is greatest in the summer but when a fire starts it is very tenacious. It can spread through the peat for hundreds of feet, perhaps only being stopped by a drain or watercourse. Peat fires can also burn downwards, and they can destroy trees from underneath by destroying their foundations. These fires cannot be smothered because the burning fibres have to be separated and mixed with water almost particle by particle. In 1871 the peat in Conington Fen caught fire and burned for a number of weeks. More recently, one fire burned for months, and another for almost two years. In a sycamore spinney in Prickwillow the peat burned twelve feet under the roots of the trees, and in the night they were blown down by a high wind. But what of the possibility that such a fire could consume a river? With reference to this particular point I believe that sufficient confirmation of Homer's words are provided by A.K.Astbury in his description of peat fires when he says, 'I have heard it suggested that an unbroken peat fire is hot enough to burn water…'[350]

THE ISLANDS OF THE HELLESPONT

Homer mentions Tenedos, Lemnos, Imbros, Chryse and Cilla in association with the war on Troy. But where exactly were they? The higher sea levels in the Bronze Age meant that The Fens of Eastern England were completely flooded, forming the Hellespont. The sea level at that time was five to seven metres higher than it is today. This transformation in the landscape means that a certain number of highland areas would have been islands at the time of the Trojan War. The surface of The Fen basin is clay and the more resistant rocks are on either side; chalk to the east and Jurassic Limestones to the west. After the Ice Age the sea broke into The Fens and the higher parts of the basin became the 'islands'. These are capped with boulder clay.[351] It seems that there were about fourteen of these islands, which are referred to as 'Original high ground of the Fens'. Some of these were very small indeed whilst others rose to only a few metres in height, so they would have been below the surface of the Hellespont. Nevertheless, there are still a number of highland areas that would have been islands of some significant size in the Bronze Age.

Some of these are located north of Cambridge. They include the Isle of Ely. Others are found to the north west of Ely, where now the modern towns of Chatteris and March are situated. It must be admitted that for a number of reasons we cannot be sure of the exact heights of these islands as they were at the time of the Trojan War. This is because from about 7500 BC the Fen basin has been filling up with various agents of deposition. Marine silt has continually encroached upon the inland fresh-water peat, and as if this wasn't enough, the encroachment of inland peat onto the silt has been taking place in a reverse fashion. Vertical sections frequently show an alternation of silt and peat beds.

This whole process has been further complicated by changes in the relative level of the land and the sea.[352] Also, in more recent times since more effective means of draining the Fens have been employed, the peat tends to evaporate and the land sinks further. Erosion of the islands' boulder clay capping since the Bronze Age is also difficult to ascertain. So, we cannot guarantee that where some islands are very close together they were or were not physically joined above the surface of the Bronze Age Hellespont.

Homer does not tell us where these islands were but he provides clues throughout the *Iliad*. One piece of information that is imparted to us is contained in Chryses' prayer to Apollo. Chryses was a priest of Apollo who came to the Achaeans imploring them to set free his captured daughter. Agamemnon refused and insulted the priest. Later, the priest implored Apollo to bring a plague upon the Danaans:

'Hear me, god of the Silver Bow,
Protector of Chryse and holy Cilla,
and Lord Supreme of Tenedos'.[353]

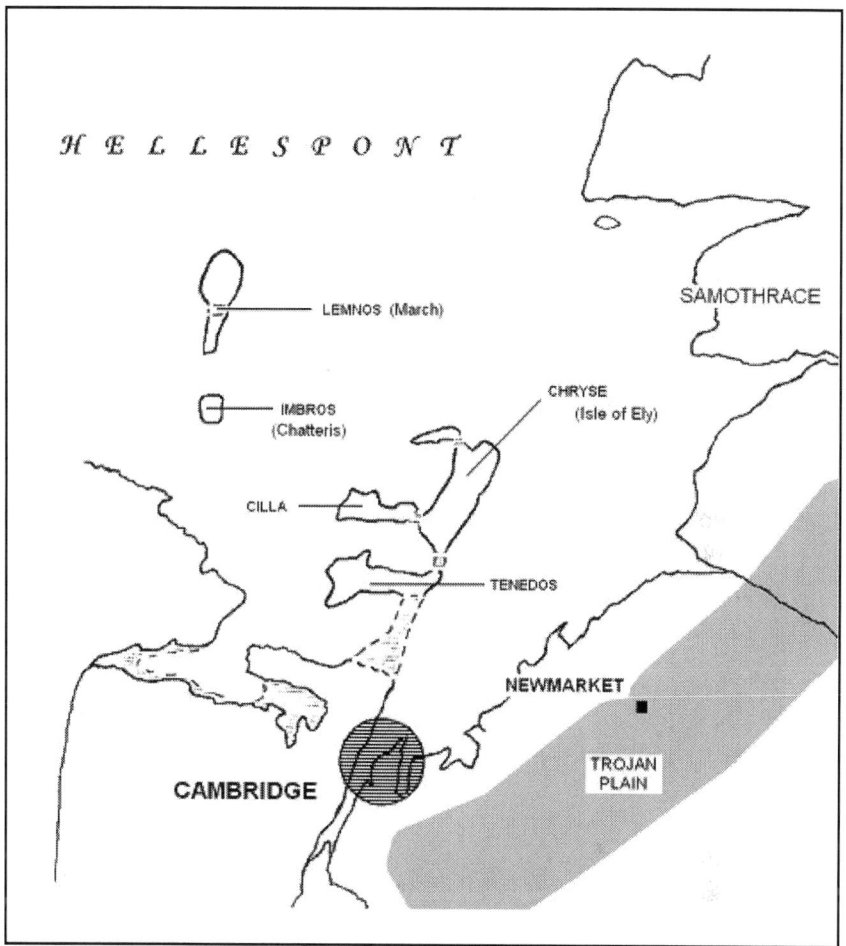

MAP 27. THE ISLANDS OF THE HELLESPONT

Although no further information is imparted to us about Cilla it appears from Chryses' prayer to Apollo that Tenedos, Chryse and Cilla were three islands in close proximity. The Trojans worshipped Apollo so it would not be surprising if these islands had the same god, particularly if they were very close to Troy.

Clearly, Chryses was priest for the three places. There is only one group of highland areas in the Fens that could have been three islands close together and close to the Trojan Plain. These are the ones to the north of Cambridge.

TENEDOS

Virgil tells us that on the night that Troy fell, the invading forces came ashore from Tenedos. It appears to have been a port of Troy and was where Paris disembarked when he came back with Helen, the wife of Menelaus. When the Achaean fleet arrived in the Hellespont they sacked Tenedos and afterwards sent an embassy from the island to King Priam of Troy to demand Helen's return. The day before Troy was taken the Achaeans burnt their camp and put out to sea. Unknown to the Trojans, however, the fleet had secretly anchored off Tenedos and in the night the squadrons came ashore and took the city.[354] Virgil also tells us that Tenedos 'lies in sight' of Troy so it must be the current highland area south west of the Isle of Ely, where the modern towns of Haddenham and Wilburton are situated. This would have been the island closest to the shore of the Hellespont, and it has direct access by land. It was along this neck of land that the Romans built a road more than a thousand years later.

CHRYSE

The home of Chryses, the priest of Apollo, must have been the current Isle of Ely. Chryses had gone from here to the Achaean camp to ransom back his daughter who was a prize of Agamemnon's, taken in Achaean raids. When Agamemnon refused the ransom and insulted the priest Apollo brought a plague upon the Achaean army. Seeing his men dying all around him Agamemnon eventually relented and agreed to return Chryseis of the fair cheeks to her father. Calchas the seer had advised that Apollo would not remove the plague until the girl was returned without price or ransom, and accompanied by sacrifice. Agamemnon drew a fast ship down to the water, put Odysseus in charge of twenty rowers, and the girl was returned to her father. On the island of Chryse the Achaeans sacrificed to Apollo and Chryses the priest prayed to the God to remove the plague. All day long they propitiated the god with song.

The following morning they returned to the Achaean camp.[355] If they spent all day on the island of Chryse then it certainly did not take long to get there from the Achaean camp so the isle of Chryse could not have been all that far from the mainland. As we can see, the Isle of Ely is not far from any point on the southeast shore of the Hellespont. Chryse was clearly an important place because at least three faggot causeways were built across the fens to this island in the Bronze Age.[356] Today, Ely is a thriving cathedral city. In the eighth century though Bede says that it was an island surrounded by marsh and water. Ely still retains the descriptive title of 'Isle', and is it mere coincidence that Ely is the English spelling of Ili, from whom Ilium took its name?

CILLA

The highland area to the west of the Isle of Ely is probably Cilla, but we have no further information to go on. It may have been joined to the Isle of Ely by a small neck of land, but the name of 'Witchford' between the two areas suggests that it was separated by water although possibly not very deep.

IMBROS AND LEMNOS

To the northwest of the Isle of Ely are March and Chatteris. These areas can only be Lemnos and Imbros. As can be seen they are close together, and Homer indicates that they were almost one place. He tells us that Hera, in one of her schemings, came down to Lemnos and encountered Sleep, the brother of Death. The goddess asks him to put to sleep the shining eyes of Zeus, and promises him one of the younger Graces for him to marry if he does her bidding. At length Sleep agrees and 'the two went away from Lemnos, and the city of Imbros'.[357] In addition, we are told that Achilles had sold Lycaon in Lemnos and he had been bought by Eetion of Imbros. This suggests that the two places were adjacent. They were certainly not regarded as being close to Troy because Hecabe, the wife of King Priam, laments the fact that Achilles had sold her sons as slaves 'far across the unresting salt water into Samothrace, Imbros, and Lemnos in the gloom of the mists'.[358] March and Chatteris are indeed further away from the southwest shore of the Hellespont than all the other islands.

There is no description given of Lemnos but Homer does tell us something about Imbros. He uses a word that means steep or rugged. In the flat Fen Country anything higher than an anthill is regarded as a mountain, and there is a difference between the heights and appearance of March and Chatteris. March covers about nine square kilometres, hardly rising to more than six metres, but then extends south a further four kilometres to Doddington where it rises another two metres. In comparison, Chatteris covers only about four square kilometres but rises to eleven metres. Seen from a distance they would look distinctly different. The highland area of March would have been about three times as long as Chatteris and much flatter. Chatteris, therefore, must be Imbros and March must be Lemnos.

Lemnos is said to have been the island where the Achaean army had left Philoctetes at the start of the war. Immediately after the Achaean victory at Tenedos, Philoctetes had been bitten by a malignant water snake and Odysseus was ordered to put him ashore on the isle of Lemnos to recover. There are a number of accounts of the accident and Philoctetes' wound has been associated with many different localities. Lemnos was also the island visited by the Argonauts prior to their initiation into the mysteries at Samothrace. About a year before their arrival the Lemnian men had quarrelled with their wives. The Lemnian women had denied Aphrodite her due honours so they were visited by an offensive smell. The men complained that their wives stank, so they made concubines of Thracian girls that they had captured on raids. Thus dishonoured, the Lemnian women killed the entire male population.[359] Robert Graves suggests that perhaps the Lemnian women stank because they worked in woad – which has such a nauseous and lingering smell that Norfolk/Lincolnshire woadmaking families have always been obliged to intermarry.[360] This is a remarkable suggestion considering the fact that the Lincolnshire/Norfolk boundary ran through the Fens to the north of Wisbech, in the middle of what was the Hellespont. Wisbech is only about ten kilometres north of March.

We are told that the woad was used by the Thracians for tattooing, and we have already identified the Lincoln Wolds as the Thrace of the Bronze Age. It lay immediately to the north, near the entrance to the Hellespont. Thrace was the home of the Picts before they went to Ireland, and the Picts were known for their tattoos. It is believed that Lemnos retained a gynocratic form of society (rule by women) but the visiting Hellenes could understand this anomaly only in terms of a female revolution. Presumably, it was for this reason that it became known as the isle of women. The Domesday name for March was 'Mercha' or 'Merche', which is almost the same as the Welsh word *Merch*, meaning daughter, girl, or woman. *Merched* is the plural for women.

ENDNOTES

[331] See Darby, *The Changing Fenland;* and Astbury, *The Black Fens.*
[332] *Iliad,* 6.1-4
[333] Ibid. 20.73-74
[334] Ibid. 20.147
[335] Lemprier's Classical Dictionary.
[336] Van Wees, 'The Homeric Way of War: The Iliad and the Hoplite Phalanx (1)'.
[337] Caesar, *The Conquest of Gaul,* iv. 33
[338] Ibid. iv. 24 and 26
[339] Ibid. v. 16
[340] Ibid. v. 19
[341] East Anglian Daily Times, 8th October 1997.
[342] See Onslow, *The Heath and the Turf,* and Siltzer, *Newmarket: Its Sport and Personalities.*
[343] *Iliad,* 1.47-51
[344] *The Black Fens,* p7.
[345] *The Changing Fenland,* pp. 8 and 22.
[346] *Iliad,* 21. 234-241
[347] Ibid. 21. 314-321
[348] *The Changing Fenland,* pp. 1,2, and 22.
[349] *Iliad,* 21. 342-356
[350] *The Black Fens*
[351] *The Changing Fenland,* p1.
[352] Ibid.
[353] *Iliad,* 1.36-38
[354] *Aeneid,* 2. 254-267
[355] *Iliad,* 1. 430-486
[356] *The Black Fens,* p80.
[357] *Iliad,* 14. 224-282
[358] Ibid. 24. 753
[359] See Apollonius of Rhodes, *The Voyage of Argo,* p52, and Apollodorus, *The Library,* I.ix.17.
[360] See *Greek Myths,* 149.1, and *The White Goddess,* p241.

THE ACHAEAN CONFEDERACY.

Under the leadership of Agamemnon, the imperial overlord of Greece, the invading forces were a confederacy, an alliance of Lords and Kings who brought and led their own battalions. Nowhere in the *Iliad*, however, does Homer call the invading forces 'Greek'. He uses the names 'Achaeans', 'Danaans', and 'Argives'. He also uses the term 'Hellenes' on a number of occasions. Thucydides says that before the Trojan War the people inhabiting Greece had no comprehensive name, that they were called by the name of their tribe such as Danai and Achaeans. So, who were these people and from what lands did they come to Troy?

We had seen in Chapter 5 that the Achaeans, Danaans, and Argives were the ancestors of the Irish and Scots. These tribes came originally from Britain. After the coming of Danaus to Argos some of the Achaeans took the name of Danaans. The inhabitants of the city of Argos were called Argives. The Achaeans lived in the vicinity of Argos but also broke into Thessaly as did the Aeolians. We have already equated the Danaans with the Tuatha de Danaan, a confederacy of tribes that invaded Ireland from Britain in the middle Bronze Age. According to the Irish histories they lived in Boetia (Boeotia) in the north of Europe but left that country in fear of a Syrian invasion. Having identified the boundary between Europe and Asia in Bronze Age Britain we can say with a reasonable amount of accuracy that the north of Europe must be the north of Britain, the original home of the Danaans. The Argives came from Argos, the ancient capital city of Argolis. In the north of Britain, on the west coast of Scotland, is the county of Argyll, which appears to indicate their territory. Indeed, it is quite remarkable that Scotland appears to be an upside-down image of the mainland of Greece and the Peloponnese in the Mediterranean. Menelaus, the husband of Helen, was king of Sparta, which was also known as Lacedaemon. He led the Lacedaemonians to Troy. The unicorn was the emblem of the Lacedaemonians and, in heraldry, it figured in the arms of Scotland. Together with the lion it became one of the national supporters of the British coat of arms. So it appears that we have further indications that the invasion forces came from the north of Britain.

Homer mentions 'Thoas, Andraemon's son, who was king of all Pleuron and mountainous Calydon and was worshipped by the Aetolians he ruled.[361] Calydon means Caledon, or Caledonia, in Scotland. Further proof is given by Homer when he describes Meleager, on whom kingship over the Aetolians had devolved, as being 'red-haired'. Red hair has always been particularly ascribed to the Caledonians. Menelaus was redheaded, and so was Pyrrhus the son of Achilles.

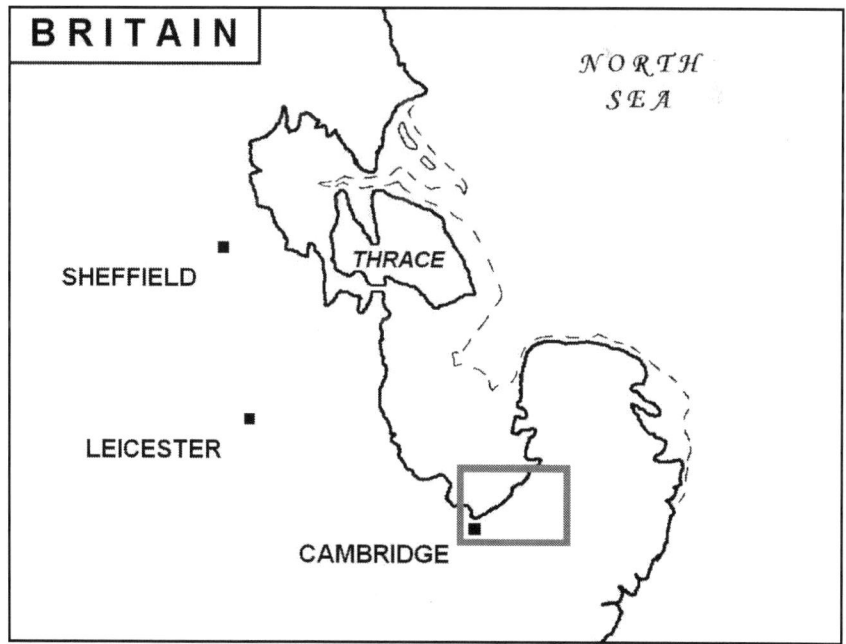

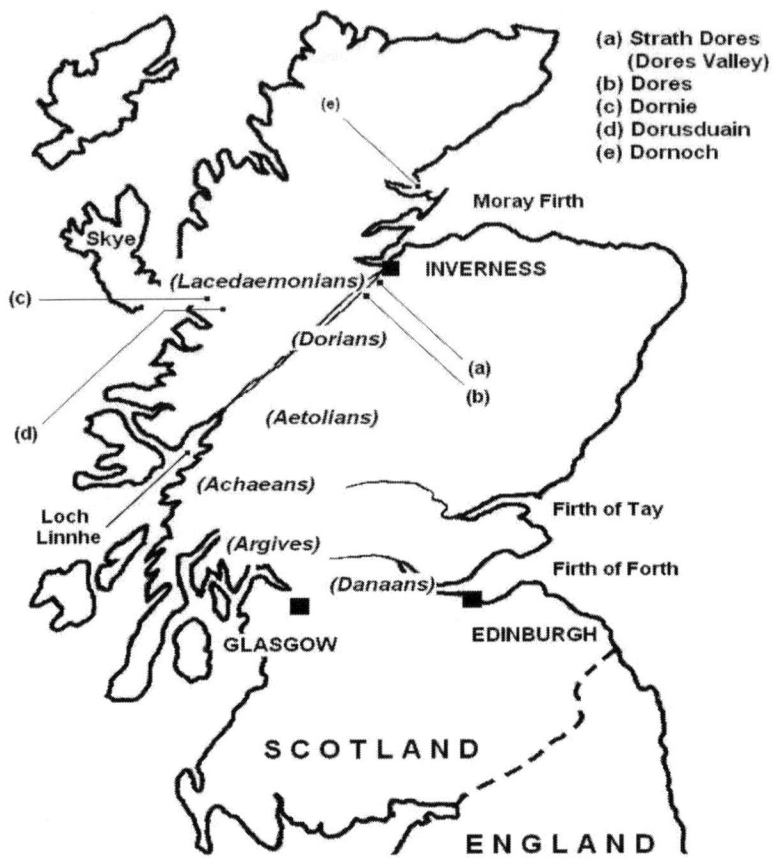

(a) Strath Dores
    (Dores Valley)
(b) Dores
(c) Dornie
(d) Dorusduain
(e) Dornoch

MAP 28. ACHAEAN CONFEDERACY (1)
Irish Tuatha de Danaan (Daans) returned from Scandinavia
to the Rivers Tay and Forth, then migrated to Ireland. The Scots are
descended from Argus Nealus, the 4th king of the Argives.

The day before Troy was taken the Trojans discovered that the invading forces had left so they went to see the empty Achaean camp. In the *Aeneid* Virgil calls the camp 'Dorica',[362] which could either refer to part of Achaia or to the Dores (Dorians), but is normally seen as an epithet applied to all the Greeks in general. The Dorians took their name from Dorus, the son of Hellen. According to Apollodorus[363] Dorus first received the country over against the Peloponnese and called the settlers Dorians after himself.

In the north of Scotland Glen Albyn, or Glen Mor, cuts the country in two, from Loch Linnhe to the Moray Firth. From our recent findings the Highland Region of Scotland to the northwest of this line must be the Peloponnese of the Bronze Age. Lying opposite, on the shore of Loch Ness about 12 kilometres from Inverness, is the hamlet of Dores and the valley of Dores. At the point where the Isle of Skye meets the Scottish mainland at Loch Alsh and Loch Duich are the hamlets of Dornie and Dorusduain. North of Inverness is the town of Dornoch on the shore of the Dornoch Firth. In addition to the place-name evidence for the existence of the Dorians in Scotland, the term 'Doric' is used as an appellation of the dialect of the Scots.

The Tuatha de Danaan lived in Boeotia in the north of Britain. Boeotians formed part of the invasion forces at Troy.[364] The lesser Aias led the Locrians, but Homer tells us that they were neither Hellenes nor Achaeans.[365] The Locrians were Lloegrians, a small, dark, hardy people who formerly inhabited Lancashire. They were called Lloegrwys by the Welsh and gave their name to Lloeger, which is the Welsh name for England.

Although the Achaean Confederacy was under the supreme command of Agamemnon, Achilles may have had special responsibility for the naval expedition to Troy. It appears that whilst the land forces were commanded by Agamemnon the Hellenic fleet was commanded by Achilles.[366] This naval aspect is worthy of some attention. Achilles' prowess on the battlefield is legendary but did he really have naval experience and skills for this crucial role? When he was a young boy Achilles was instructed by Cheiron the Centaur in all the arts, including riding, hunting and healing. I can find no information, however, which indicates that he learned anything about sea-faring. In the Trojan War Achilles led Myrmidons, Hellenes, and Achaeans from Pelasgian Argos in Thessaly,[367] but neither these Hellenes or Achaeans appear to have been knowledgeable about maritime affairs. This leaves us with Achilles' Myrmidons who were for some obscure reason also called 'ants'. In order to learn something about the Myrmidons we must go back two generations to Achilles' grandfather, Aeacus.

The *Myth of Aeacus*[368] tells us that Aegina was carried off by Zeus to the island of Oenone and ravished. Aegina bore a son called Aeacus who became king of the island and re-named it Aegina. When Hera discovered

Zeus' affair she brought famine and pestilence to the island in order to destroy the inhabitants. Aeacus prayed to Zeus and begged him to replenish the land with as many people as there were ants climbing a nearby oak tree. That night he dreamt of ants falling from the sacred oak and springing up as men. The following day a host of men appeared and the deserted island was thus repopulated. Aeacus called them Myrmidons meaning 'ants'. It is interesting that the Old Welsh word *Myr* (substantive plural) means 'ants' whilst *Mudw* means 'moving or wandering', hence the *Myr-mid*-ons would be 'wandering ants'. *Myr*, however, also means 'seas' so it appears that in reality the Myrmidons were wandering sailors or 'sea-rovers'. These Myrmidons followed Aeacus' son, Peleus, into exile from Aegina to Thessaly where they became warriors. Achilles, as son of king Peleus, led these sea-warriors to Troy. So, as son of the king he may have commanded the fleet but the knowledge and experience of the seas was clearly that of the Myrmidons.

Having dealt with some of the main tribes in the Achaean Confederacy we can see that at the time of the Trojan War they were to be found in a geographical area covering western Scotland and two counties in northwest England, namely Cumbria and Lancashire. We shall now try to establish the territory of the Myrmidons, Hellenes, and Achaeans, from Thessaly. Surprisingly, a Greek ceramic black-figured water jar (520-510 BC) in the Museum of Fine Arts in Boston provides us with an important clue to their location. Shown on the water jar is a scene from the Trojan War in which Achilles is dragging Hector's body behind a chariot. The story behind the Trojan War scene is Achilles' refusal to lead the Myrmidons into battle against the Trojans because Agamemnon, the commander-in-chief, has taken his war prize and concubine, Briseis, from him. Patroclus is Achilles' best friend and companion and he prevails upon Achilles to let him lead the Myrmidon army in disguise, wearing Achilles' armour.

Patroclus leads the army out onto the plain of Troy but he disregards Achilles orders and is killed by Hector. In a rage Achilles returns to the battlefield to avenge Patroclus. He kills Hector and desecrates his body by dragging it behind his chariot around the walls of Troy. The drawing here shows the scene painted on the Greek water jar. To the left is king Priam of Troy and Hecuba, Hector's parents, in mourning for their son. On the

MAP 29. ACHAEAN CONFEDERACY (2)

Acaeans, Hellenes, and Myrmidons, are led by Achilles from
Thessaly. The Myrmedions came originally from the Isle of Man (Aegina).
The Triskelion, the ancient symbol of the Isle of Man, is displayed
on the shields of Achillies and his Myrmidons. The Locrians, called Lloegrwys
by the Welsh, gave their name to Lloeger, the Welsh name for England.

FIG. 13. ACHILLES DRAGGING HECTOR BEHIND A CHARIOT.

right is the tomb of Patroclus, shown in white behind the horses, with a snake at its base. Above the tomb is the soul of Patroclus now released from death. The female winged figure is Iris, the messenger of the Olympian gods. She has been sent down to earth to implore both sides to agree a ransom for Hector's corpse. In the centre is a mounted charioteer shown holding the reins for the chariot's four horses. Hector's dead body is in the foreground of the picture, on the left. Achilles is the warrior in the process of mounting the chariot. He has one foot on the ground and is staring scornfully at Hector's parents. The important clue spoken of earlier is depicted on Achilles' shield. It is a triskelion symbol; three running legs bent at the knee, conjoined at the crotch.

This, however, is not the only clue available to us. There is another black-figured hydria (510-500 BC) in the British Museum that shows Achilles carrying the dead body of the Amazon Penthesileia away from the battlefield. This time the triskelion is on the shield of one of Achilles' warriors. Logically, this makes perfect sense because although it is not incorrect on Achilles' shield it is more correctly the symbol of the Myrmidons. Both

Aeacus and his son, Peleus, are associated with the island of Aegina. Peleus, of course, left the island and went to Thessaly on the mainland and the Myrmidons went with him. In Britain there is only one place where the triskelion symbol belongs and that is the Isle of Man, located in the Irish Sea off the coast of Cumbria. The triskelion is the ancient symbol of the Isle of Man and is still carried on the island's flag. Bronze Age Aegina, therefore, can only be the Isle of Man, so ancient Thessaly must be on the mainland opposite, in the Cumbrian –Lancashire area.

THE ACHAEAN CAMP.

For nine years the Achaean forces were encamped beside their ships on the shore near the Trojan plain. Throughout this period they were unable to sack Troy. Whilst the Trojans were penned up in their city the Achaeans plundered the surrounding countryside and looted the towns. Eventually, the Achaean forces were put on the defensive and, as a result, they had to build extensive fortifications around their camp to protect themselves and their ships. The Achaean camp was situated on the Trojan plain somewhere between the rivers Scamander and Simois. The whole Achaean fleet had been pulled up onto dry land at the edge of the sea and the camp lay nearby. But where exactly was it located? Throughout the *Iliad* we are given clues, but because the information is widely scattered it is not always readily apparent. When the Trojans were fighting by the ships Athene and Hera came down from Olympus to help the Achaeans. The two goddesses stopped their flaming chariot at the waters meet of Scamander and Simois and then set out on foot 'strutting like pigeons' in their eagerness to get to the battle.[369] Why should the two goddesses have to strut like pigeons? The answer is because they had to walk across the sedgy waste to reach dry land. The action of walking in the waterlogged fens is likened, therefore, to strutting pigeons. Also, it is in this southern part of the basin that fen penetration into highland is known to have been deepest.[370] Probably, Athene and Hera arrived at low tide when the sea had receded a little way to the north, across the fens.

Locating the Bronze Age waters meet of Scamander and Simois is not a simple process. Since 7500 BC, the Fenland has been subjected to complicated changes in the relative level of land and sea.[371] In recent times drainage and cultivation has transformed the area, and the peat in the Fens has shrunk as much as 5 metres or more. In ages past most of the rivers appear to have found their way to the sea near Wisbech, where a large estuary opened towards the Wash. During the thirteenth century however, there was a drastic alteration in the network of the ancient watercourses. The Wisbech estuary became choked by silt and sand brought in by the tides, and many rivers began to flow to the sea by the estuary at Kings Lynn.[372] Fortunately, the pattern of the ancient river systems is preserved by raised banks of silt, known as 'Roddons', and from these remains many of the former waterways have been traced. Of all the rivers draining into the fens it appears that the courses of the rivers Cam (Scamander) and Little Ouse (Simois) are the ones that have remained most constant.[373] That of the Cam appears to be of considerable antiquity.[374] The formation of these 'Roddons' is a process explained by Fowler. We begin with an original river course running through the peat fens (some silt forms the river bed). Over time, the deposition of silt by the tides continues and eventually fills the river bed. As the peat shrinks in the fens the silt river bed becomes a convex roddon and appears to rest on top of the peat. By this time the river has been forced to change its course.

From these Roddons and maps of the extinct waterways we can establish the old courses of the Cam and the Little Ouse so that we now know where the two rivers met. It is clear from Homer's description that the two goddesses Athene and Hera were able to walk from this point, over the fens to the Achaean army that was locked in battle with the Trojans somewhere near the ships. Afterwards, when the two goddesses had left the battlefield, the Trojans and Achaeans were left to carry on the struggle alone, 'midway between Simois and the streams of Xanthus'[375] – another important clue to the location of the Achaean camp.

The distance between the river Cam immediately south of Cambridge and the river Little Ouse near Thetford is approximately 52 kilometres. The halfway point lies about 2km northeast of Newmarket, which itself is within 6 kilometres of the edge of the fens, or the Bronze Age shore of the Hellespont. It is in this area near the edge of the fens where we will find the location of the Achaean camp.

There is only one place which answers the descriptions given by Homer. The Bronze Age location of the Achaean camp was immediately northwest

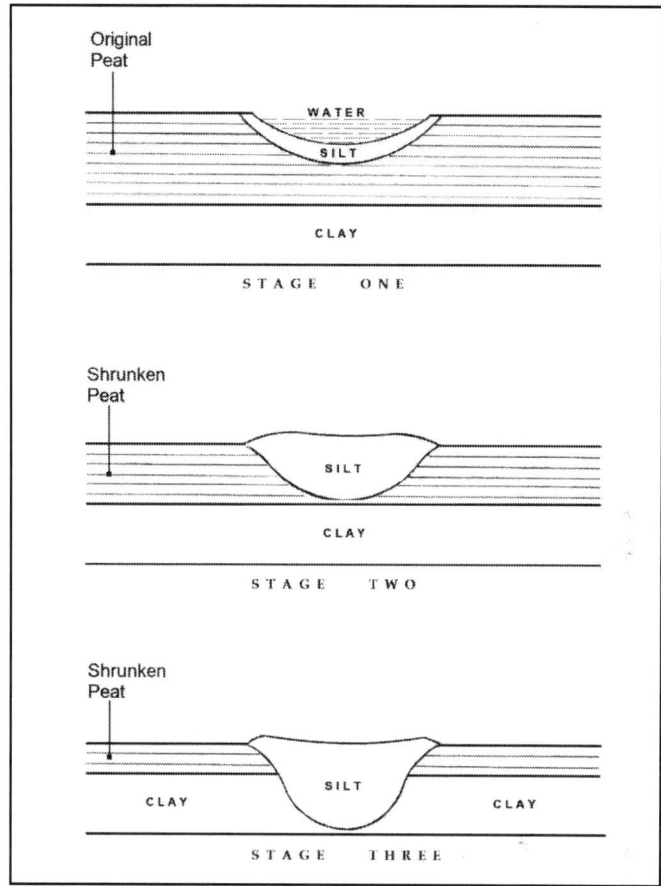

FIG. 14. RODDONS: RAISED BANKS OF LAMINATED SILT
DEPOSITED BY TIDAL ACTION. THERE IS DIFFERENTIAL SHRINKAGE
BETWEEN THE PEAT AND THE SILTY BEDS AND BANKS. THE
SHRINKAGE OF THE PEAT TURNS A CONCAVE RIVER BED INTO A
CONVEX RODDON.
Acknowledgement: Fowler, Fenland Waterways Past and Present.

of Newmarket and northeast of Devils Dyke. A geological survey map
showing mineral soil of highland and island enhances the more general
picture provided by an ordnance survey map. In Book XVI of the *Iliad* the
Trojans had broken through the wall that the Achaeans had built to protect
the fleet and some of the ships had been set on fire. Patroclus had entered
the fight at the head of Achilles' troops and the Trojans had fallen back in
confusion. The Trojan withdrawal from the ships had turned into a noisy

rout:

> "Patroculus had by now cut up the nearest companies and was heading them off in their own tracks towards the ships. He defeated all their efforts to take refuge in the city, and there, between the ships, the river and the high wall, he kept charging in and killing men, in compensation for the Achaean dead".[376]

Devils Dyke is a massive linear defensive earthwork comprising a large bank with a deep ditch on its southwest side. We shall discover later that it matches Homer's descriptions perfectly. The river in question is the River Snail. It flows down from the highland area south east of Newmarket and runs close to Devil's Dyke for about 2 kilometres. It then alters course to the northwest, flows through Newmarket and on to Fordham. The Achaean ships had been pulled up onto dry land around Soham Meer (now extinct), referred to as mineral soil of highland and island. The area of land taken up by the ships extended most of the way towards Devil's Dyke.

In the previous chapter we dealt with the plague that was inflicted upon the Achaean army and saw how this was caused by mosquitoes in the Fens. Apollo shot his arrows at the men near the ships so we now know the exact location where the plague occurred. History often repeats itself and once again, in 1227, a devastating plague occurred in exactly the same place. This was at the village of Exning in the middle of the land once occupied by the Achaean army. Subsequently, all the inhabitants moved away and settled what was then called the 'New Market'. Exning lay 'between the ships, the river and the high wall'.

THE ACHAEAN FLEET

The Achaean fleet comprised almost 1200 ships. Some of these held fifty men, others as many as one hundred and twenty. From these figures it appears that more than sixty thousand warriors may have arrived originally with the fleet. Homer provides us with information in the *Iliad*, however, which indicates that the total numbers were far in excess of this. As the Trojan War lasted for ten years it is quite conceivable that reinforcements may have arrived on a number of occasions. At one stage during the war Agamemnon, the Commander-in-Chief, had considered sailing home with

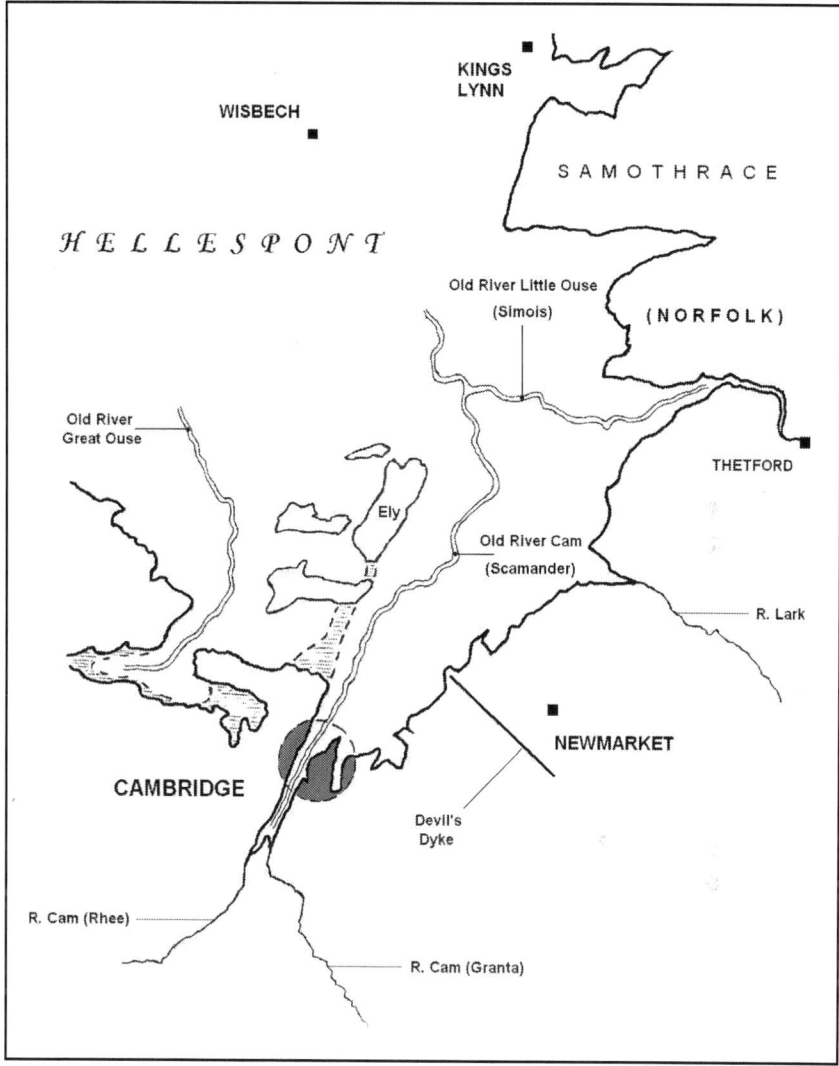

MAP 30. WATERSMEET OF SCAMANDER AND SIMOIS

half his army lost. The Achaeans, it seemed, were locked in an unsuccessful struggle with a weaker enemy – they outnumbered native Trojans by more than ten to one.[377] Later, we are told how many Trojans there were camped on the plain at night:

> "There were a thousand fires burning on the plain, and round each one sat fifty men in the light of its blaze ..."[378]

This means that there were fifty thousand native Trojans and more than five hundred thousand Achaeans. If half of Agamemnon's army had been lost by the tenth year of the war then the total number of Achaean warriors may have exceeded a million. According to Dares Phrygius, the Trojan War lasted ten years, seven months and twelve days, with lives lost totalling 300,000 Trojans and 600,000 Achaeans.[379]

Although Dares' history of the war gives the Trojan viewpoint, the loss of life on the Achaean side is remarkably close to the information provided by Homer.

When the fleet first arrived there was not enough room in the bay for all the ships. Homer tells us how the problem was resolved in Book XIV of the *Iliad*, after the Trojans had broken through the great Achaean wall and were advancing towards the huts and ships. Nestor heard the sounds of battle growing louder by the ships and became alarmed at the sight of the Achaeans in full rout. Seeking out Agamemnon, his Commander-in-Chief, he found him in the company of Diomedes and Odysseus:

> "They were coming up from their ships, which were stationed on the shore of the grey sea a long way from the present fighting, being the first row that was drawn up on land, whereas the wall was built along those farthest from the sea. For the beach itself, wide as it was, had proved unable to hold all the ships, and the Achaeans, cramped for room, had drawn them up in tiers, covering the whole seaboard of the long bay from headland to headland".[380]

Having established the exact location of the Achaean camp we can see that Homer's account really does make sense. The ships that were drawn up near the wall were indeed on the plain, and may have been as much as three or four kilometres from the sea. The main area of the Achaean camp was at least 6 kilometres in width and more than 4 kilometres in depth. There must have been large open tracts of land between the rows of ships for the movement of such a large army as well as horses and chariots. It appears that there were many huts built near the ships, particularly for the many Achaean leaders. Achilles' hut, for instance, was a substantial size that could sleep three or four people. It had a portico and was enclosed by a fence with an entrance gate. The Achaeans held their assemblies and legal

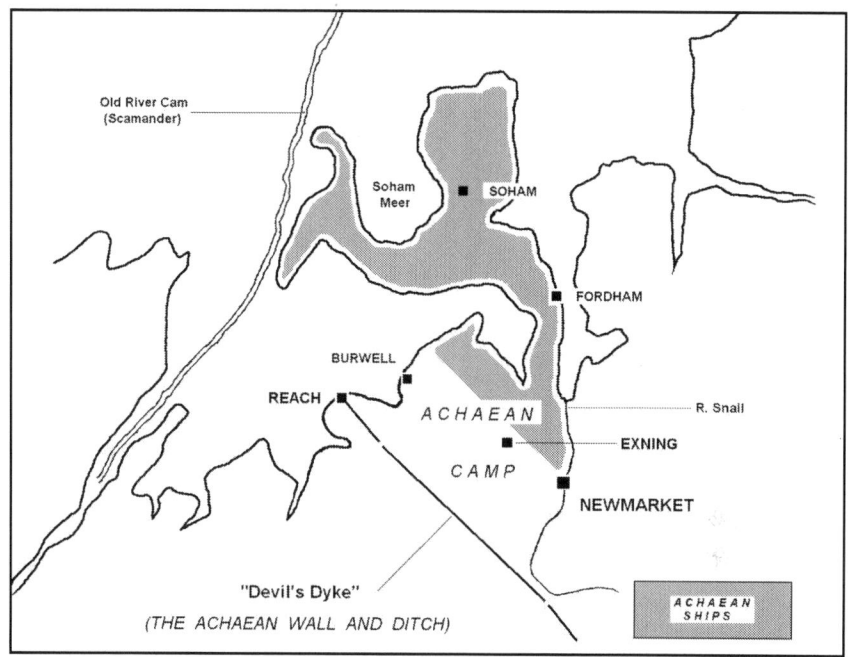

MAP 31. THE ACHAEAN CAMP

sessions near the ships of Odysseus. It was here too that they put up their altars for worship.

The location of the Achaean camp is exactly as Homer tells us. It is situated midway between the river Cam (Scamander) and the Little Ouse (Simois). It is bounded by the wall and ditch, the sea, and the river. We must now determine whether Devils Dyke, or Devils Ditch as it is sometimes called, is the same wall and ditch which is described in the pages of the *Iliad*.

THE ACHAEAN WALL

Devils Dyke is a massive linear defensive earthwork comprising a large bank with a deep ditch on its southwest side. It extends from the edge of the Fens at the village of Reach, at 3m o.d. (ordnance datum), to the upland area near Wood Ditton, at 112m o.d. In general terms it is laid out in three major alignments. The central and longest section is approximately straight, whereas the two shorter end sections are both deflected slightly from the main alignment. Both deflections appear to have been imposed by the topography, indicating that they were necessary in order to retain tactical control. The Dyke formed a continuous line of defence from the forest in the southeast to the river Cam in the northwest. Undoubtedly, it was constructed to prevent access from the southwest. At its northwest end it was deliberately positioned to extend on to a bulb-shaped promontory at Reach.

This basic description is taken from the *Inventory of Historical Monuments in the County of Cambridge*.[381] It is the most comprehensive information available on Devils Dyke. Using this reference we will compare the key features of the Dyke with the information provided in the *Iliad*. Let us start by finding out exactly what was built by the Achaeans, and if it fits the general description.

In Book VII of the Iliad the Trojans and Achaeans agree a truce in order to burn the bodies of the dead. There were heavy losses on the Achaean side and Nestor advises that the bodies be brought in and burnt not far from the ships:

> "Over the pyre, let us make them a single barrow with such material as the plain provides. Then, with this mound for a base, let us quickly build high walls to protect the ships and ourselves, with strong gates let into them, leaving carriageway for the chariots. And a little way outside, let us dig a deep trench parallel with the walls, to serve as an obstruction to chariots and infantry, in case the Trojans get out of hand someday and press us hard".[382]

The trench and the walls were built according to Nestor's scheme, and what was built matches the basic description of Devils Dyke. It started from the burial mound, which was heaped over the pyre near the ships. The burial mound was positioned on a 15 metre high dome-shaped promontory at the village of Reach. The trench was dug on the outside of the wall, away from the camp, on the southwest side.

THE WALL

The *Inventory* describes the Wall as a massive bank, usually 3.5 metres to

5.4 metres high above the adjacent ground level, and up to 21 metres wide. It maintains its dimensions throughout its length, other than at its extreme northwest end.

Homer tells us that the wall had high, well-built ramparts. It was a 'thick wall', a 'stone wall', and it was equipped with towers and battlements along its length. Eventually Hector and the Trojans managed to storm the wall:

> "...they now made determined efforts to breach the great Achaean wall, tearing at the parapets of the towers, pulling down the battlements, and levering up the projecting buttresses that the Achaeans had let into the ground outside to support the towers, in the hope that by undermining these they might bring down the wall itself".[383]

The *Inventory* tells us that nothing now remains of the first 300 metres of the Dyke at the village of Reach. Until 1968 a small fragment of the bank, 9 metres wide, then 1.4 metres high existed here but this has since been destroyed.

Generally speaking this linear defensive earthwork is considered to be in good condition, other than at its extreme northwest end. Why is it then that there are such meagre remains at this point along the dyke? Surprisingly, the answer lies in the pages of the *Iliad*. In Book XII, Homer tells us that in order to enter the Achaean camp the Trojans and their allies had to abandon chariot warfare and storm the wall on foot. Asius, one of the princes, objected to this and drove his chariot at the left flank of the ships, 'where the Achaeans had a causeway that they used themselves when returning from the plain'. When he reached the gateway he found that the doors had not been closed. The Trojans massed around prince Asius and a fierce battle ensued in front of the gate:

> "Then Sarpedon got his mighty hands on the battlement. He gave a pull, and a whole length of the breastwork came away, exposing the top of the wall. He had made a breach big enough for a company".[384]

Massing together, the Trojans charged at the rampart and began to scale the parapet. Here, Homer tells us that Hector broke down the doors and

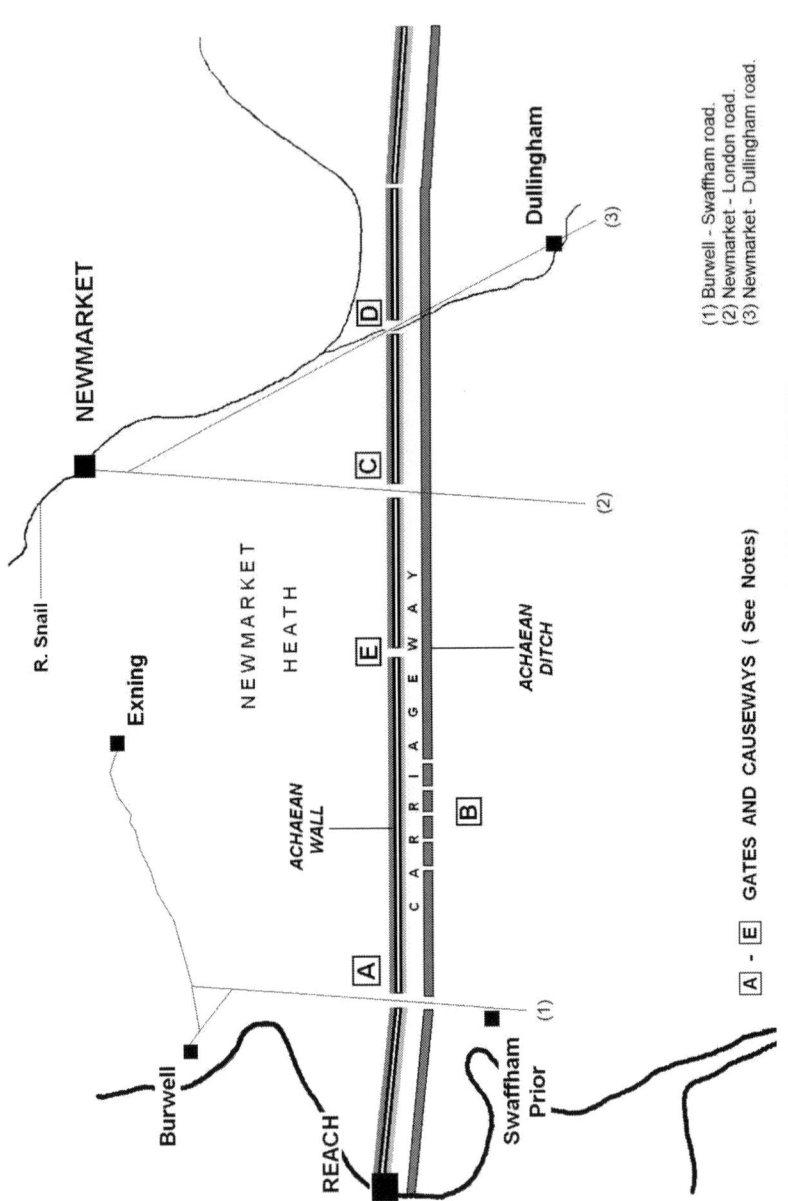

A - **E** GATES AND CAUSEWAYS (See Notes)

(1) Burwell - Swaffham road.
(2) Newmarket - London road.
(3) Newmarket - Dullingham road.

FIG 15. THE ACHAEAN WALL AND DITCH.

TABLE 2
THE ACHAEAN WALL: GATES AND CAUSEWAYS

A. (CAUSEWAY & GATE):

A Causeway and Gate to the far left of the Wall and near the sea was used normally by the Achaeans when returning from the plain. Here, the Swaffham – Burwell road cuts the Dyke at right angles and the alignment of the Dyke changes at this point.

B. (CAUSEWAYS):

Here, 5 Causeways up to 27 metres wide cross the Ditch at right angles on a broad, flat – topped spur of chalk. Homer tells us that the Trojan Army could not cross the Ditch in their chariots. They separated into 5 Companies and stormed the Achaean Wall on foot.

C. (GATE):

This is the line of the Newmarket – Old London road and presumed line of the ancient Icknield Way. An original opening is suggested by a slight change in the alignment of the Dyke.

D. (GATE):

This is the line of the Newmarket – Dullingham road. The gap is possibly original. At this point the Dyke crosses a broad valley with a chalk stream having a considerable flow in winter and wet weather. There is a small change in alignment of the Dyke and the ends of the bank are not directly opposed.

E. (GATE):

Possible gate, but the evidence is not conclusive. 4 gaps in the Dyke are identified south west of Newmarket Heath. We are informed that they were cut to take tracks across Newmarket Heath, perhaps in the Medieval Period. But, no evidence is provided for this. One of the openings, called the King's Gap, is more than 18 metres wide but is not considered original. It is stated, however, that no road, track, or course is known to have passed through it, but its date and purpose remain unknown. It is suggested that this gap was one of the gates in the Achaean Wall. Without it, chariots would have to travel 3 kilometres to reach the first gate if they turned right over one of the causeways. A gate in this position automatically centralises the 5 causeways between gates A and E, with travel distances being 1.25 kilometres in either direction.

leapt inside. His men swarmed over the wall and through the gate, and the battle continued inside the camp:

> "So Hector was still on the offensive in that part of the front where he had broken the shield-bearing Danaan companies and stormed the gate and wall, and where the ships of Aias and Protesilaus were drawn up on the shore of the grey sea. There, the protecting wall had been lower than anywhere else and the Danaan infantry and chariots were putting up the fiercest defence".[385]

The causeway near the left flank of the ships was very close to the village of Reach. It was here that Hector broke down the gate and the battle continued near the ships on the shore of the sea. It was here that a whole length of the breastwork was pulled down from the wall, which was already lower than anywhere else. Homer also tells us that after the war there was a great flood that lasted for nine days and the waters of all the rivers united to destroy the wall. All the wooden and stone foundations were washed out to sea, and the shore of the Hellespont was levelled.[386] These then are the reasons why this part of the wall suffered so badly.

THE GATES

The *Inventory* enumerates 16 gaps of various forms and dates through the Dyke. They include two cut for railways in the 19th century, four for roads, a number for footpaths and one apparently for a watercourse. Whilst most of these are not original openings, there are three or four which cannot be excluded from such a possibility. The first of these is where the Burwell-Swaffham Prior road cuts the Dyke almost at right angles, and there is a change in alignment of the Dyke. The second is where the Newmarket-London road (A1304) crosses the Dyke, following the presumed line of the ancient 'Icknield Way'. The change in alignment of the Dyke might suggest an original opening. The third is where the Newmarket-Dullingham road crosses the Dyke. Here, there is a slight change in alignment again, and the ends of the bank are not directly opposed. We shall see later that, in addition to these, there was probably a fourth opening.

We know that the wall had been fitted with 'strong gates'. Homer indicates that the number of openings was at least three by telling us that when Asius and the Trojans were fighting at one gateway, 'other Trojan companies had carried the fighting to other gates'.[387] When Hector broke through one of the sets of doors with an enormous rock, he broke the hinges off on either side. Homer tells us how the doors were constructed:

> "... he lifted up the rock and brought it to bear on the panels that filled in the morticed framework of the high double doors, which were held on the inner side by two sliding bars locked by a single bolt".[388]

THE DITCH

The *Inventory* explains that Devils Dyke also comprises a ditch, running parallel with the wall, which measures up to 5.1 metres deep and 19.6 metres wide. It varies between a v-shape with its bottom only 60 to 90 centimetres wide, and a broad flat-bottomed ditch up to 5.5 metres across. Most variations are due to natural slumping of the ditch sides, and to ploughing.

Homer tells us that the trench was parallel with the wall and it was 'a little way outside'. When the Achaeans built the wall they also dug 'a deep trench, and along this broad and ample ditch they planted a row of stakes'.[389] When Hector and the Trojans came up to the ditch they found that the horses could not break in with a chariot trundling after them:

> "Thus Hector darted to and fro among his men, goading the charioteers to cross the trench. But when it came to the point, his own fast horses jibbed. They were frightened by its width and halted at the brink, neighing shrilly. Indeed the dyke was by no means easy to take at a bound or to cross at all. Both banks were overhanging all along, and on top there was a row of pointed stakes, close-set and strong, which the Achaean troops had planted there to keep out their enemies".[390]

Homer provides us with a lot of detail about the construction of the wall and ditch, but it is magically woven into the narrative:

> "It would be folly", said Polydamas, "to cross the trench in our chariots. The palisade on top makes it well-nigh impossible; and close behind comes the Achaean wall, leaving the charioteers no room whatever to

dismount and fight – in fact, so narrow a strip that I am certain they would come to grief..." [391]

Homer does not say that there was not enough room for charioteers to drive between the palisade and the wall, only that there was not enough room for them to dismount and fight. This narrow strip of land had been purposely designed to allow the passage of a chariot but prevent the opposing forces from using chariot warfare tactics. When Nestor first proposes the wall and trench he says it should be built 'leaving carriage-way for the chariots.'

Other than the reference to Asius driving over the causeway and coming to the gateway near the left flank of the ships we are not told directly how the Achaeans and their chariots managed to cross the trench and enter the camp. We know that there were at least three gateways in the wall so it is logical to suppose that all of them were capable of being used. Did this narrow strip of land allow access to all the gates in the wall? Was this the 'carriage-way for the chariots'? If so, then a number of causeways over the trench would be necessary in order to cope with such vast numbers of combatants and the horses and chariots.

In theory it would be perfectly logical for causeways to be located midway between the gates. But this does not take account of local conditions such as the nature of the terrain, river courses, and so on. Causeways would be needed across the ditch in the areas of the plain subject to most use by chariots, horses and men.

On advice from Polydamas the Trojans and their allies abandoned chariot warfare at the edge of the trench and massed in full war gear behind their own captains:

> "Of these, the best and biggest was that which Hector and the peerless Polydamas commanded. None showed greater eagerness to breach the wall and fight by the hollow ships. Cebriones, in whose stead Hector had left a less valuable man with his chariot, was third in command. The second company was led by Paris, Alcathous, and Agenor; and the third by two of Priam's sons, Helenus and the godlike Deiphobus, and as third in command, the noble Asius son of Hyrtacus, whom his big and glossy horses had brought from Arisbe and the River Selleis. Aeneas, the

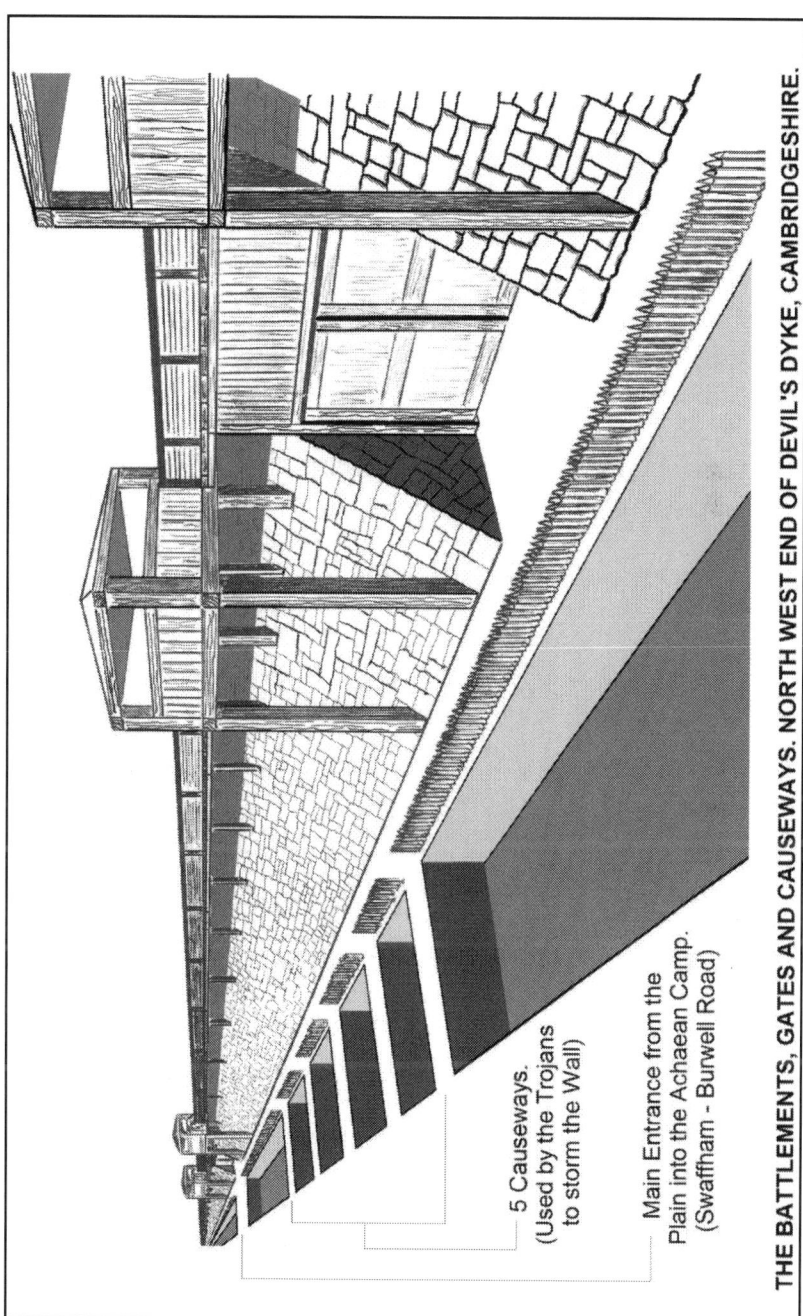

THE BATTLEMENTS, GATES AND CAUSEWAYS. NORTH WEST END OF DEVIL'S DYKE, CAMBRIDGESHIRE.

FIG 16. HOMER'S ACHAEAN WALL.

5 Causeways.
(Used by the Trojans
to storm the Wall)

Main Entrance from the
Plain into the Achaean Camp.
(Swaffham - Burwell Road)

handsome son of Anchises, led the fourth company, supported by two sons of Antenor, Archelochus and Acamas, men with experience in every kind of fighting. Sarpedon commanded the glorious allies, and had appointed under him Glaucus and the warlike Asteropaeus, whom he considered beyond question the best men among the allies next to himself, he being the finest soldier of them all. Thus they drew up, shield touching oxhide shield, and resolutely advanced on the Danaans, in the confidence that nothing could stop them now from swooping down on the black ships".[392]

It is here that Homer tells us indirectly that the actual number of causeways over the Achaean trench was five. The whole Trojan army had assembled into five separate fighting units with one objective – to cross the trench and attack the wall. There was no other way across the trench other than by using a causeway. Homer is telling us that five companies attacked the wall, each using a separate causeway.

Amazingly, there are a number of features connected with the ditch that are highly significant and support this assertion. These are located about one-third of the way along Devils Dyke from the village of Reach.

The *Inventory* informs us that at this point the dyke is on a broad, flat-topped spur of chalk. The ditch has been under cultivation for many centuries with the result that it is ploughed down and largely filled in. In at least five places there are what appear to be low causeways up to 27 metres wide crossing it at right angles. They are thought to be former headlands between furlongs in the common fields.

The number of causeways and their width would meet the requirement for use by a large number of chariots. There are no openings in the Dyke opposite these causeways, which means that the chariots would have to travel between the ditch and the wall until they reached the nearest gateway. However, the fact that such a carriageway would be needed would be consistent with Homer's description and the defensive design. There appears to be no doubt that these low causeways are the ones that allowed access from the Trojan plain over the ditch to the carriageway immediately in front of the Achaean Wall. They are the five causeways used by the five Trojan companies. Homer also tells us that Asius did not obey the general command. He objected to leaving his chariot behind with his charioteer in charge. Instead, he drove in his chariot at the left flank of the ships where the Achaeans had a causeway that they used when returning from the plain. He drove his horses over straight at the gateway and found that the doors had not been closed. He was killed near the ships by Idomeneus' spear.[393]

In relating the story about Asius' refusal to obey the general command Homer is telling us that there was an exception to the massed infantry storming the wall using the five causeways. The exception was Asius and he used another causeway. This was the one that was normally used by the Achaeans when they returned from the plain. It allowed direct access straight through the gateway into the Achaean camp. It was on the far left of the ships, or the northwest end of Devil's Dyke. This must be the gap where the Burwell-Swaffham Prior road cuts the Dyke at right angles and where there is a change in alignment of the Dyke.

THE LENGTH OF THE WALL AND DITCH

Homer provides us with information which helps us understand how long the wall and ditch were when the defences were completed. But, he does not tell us directly using a known unit of measurement. The knowledge is available as part of the narrative but it is necessary for the listener (or reader) to recognise the significance of the information being presented.

At the beginning of Book IX of the *Iliad*, darkness has fallen and the day's fighting has come to an end. The Trojans are camped on the plain and the Achaeans inside the camp are in the grip of panic. At a meeting of their Assembly there is disagreement among the Achaeans whether they should sail home or carry on the war. Eventually, on Nestor's advice, the meeting is terminated so that supper can be prepared. Agamemnon then invites the senior commanders to his hut for a banquet and to listen to their advice. Meanwhile, sentries are posted outside the wall:

> "Armed sentries went out at the double under the command of Prince Thrasymedes, Nestor's son; Ascalaphus and Ialmenus, children of the War-god; Meriones, Aphareus, and Deipyrus; and the noble Lycomedes, Creon's son. There were seven captains of the guard, and a hundred young men marched behind each, with long spears in their hands. They

took their posts midway between the ditch and the wall, and there each party lit a fire and everyone prepared his supper".[394]

The total number of sentries needed for guard duty was 700, which indicates the wall and trench to have been an extraordinary length. In addition, Homer informs us that the sentries had to be 'posted at intervals along the trench outside the wall.'[395] The actual length of Devils Dyke is 12 kilometres, which means that the sentries would have been posted at 17 metre intervals, a distance which is both realistic and practicable.

MAKING SENSE OF THE PAST

Why and when Devil's Dyke was built are questions that have never been answered satisfactorily. The scale of the earthworks is truly breathtaking and it can be understood why it has confounded many minds. It is clearly part of British history but the events that brought it about are not known. It is not too long ago that massive structures of unexplained origin such as this were called works of the devil, and this is probably the reason why it is known as Devil's Dyke. The Historical Monuments report accepted that the date and function of the Dyke remained problematical. It concluded that its great size and careful planning designed to achieve strategic and tactical advantages would indicate that it was constructed essentially for military defence. The report declared that there had been many attempts to date the construction of the Devil's Dyke and to explain its purpose, though none had been conclusive.

ENDNOTES

[361] *Iliad*, 2.638-643
[362] *Aeneid*, 2.27
[363] *The Library*, I.vii.3
[364] *Iliad*, 2.498-510
[365] Ibid. 2.527-535
[366] Graves, *Greek Myths*, 160 n
[367] *Iliad*, 2.681-685
[368] See Graves, *Greek Myths*, 66
[369] *Iliad*, 5.773-780

370 Astbury, *The Black Fens*, p5

371 Darby, *The Changing Fenland*, p1

372 Ibid. p31

373 Seale, *Ancient Courses of the Great and Little Ouse in Fenland*, pp. 2 and 8

374 Fowler, *Fenland Waterways, Past and Present*. Part 1.

375 *Iliad*, 6.4

376 Ibid. 16.394-398

377 Ibid. 2.119-130

378 Ibid. 8.560-563

379 Dares Phrygius, Translated from the Welsh copy in *The Book of Basingwerke*. Dares Phrygius may be found as part of The Chronicle of the Kings of Britain. These were translated into English by Peter Roberts in 1811.

380 *Iliad*, 14.27-36

381 See Vol. 2, *North East Cambridgeshire*, Appendix, The Devil's Dyke, pp. 139-144.

382 *Iliad*, 7.336-343

383 Ibid. 12.256-262

384 Ibid. 12.397-399

385 Ibid. 13.679-684

386 Ibid. 12.19-33

387 Ibid. 12.175

388 Ibid. 12.453-462

389 Ibid. 7.440-441

390 Ibid. 12.49-57

391 Ibid. 12.61-66

392 Ibid. 12.88-107

393 Ibid. 12.108-126

394 Ibid. 9.80-88

395 Ibid. 9.66-67

15

THE LAND OF TROY

The war in Troy was fought in Britain on the plain at the edge of the Fens, between Newmarket and the river Cam. It was fought between Bronze Age tribes living in Britain. Having located the battleground we were able to identify the Achaean camp, the Achaean wall and ditch, and explain the significance of Homer's descriptions of the plague, the floods and the fire on the plain. We now need to locate the land of Troy.

When Achilles re-entered the battle the Trojans were chased across the plain until they came to the river Cam. One party was driven into the pools whilst the other party was driven across the fields in the direction of Troy. But how far to the west of the river Cam was Troy located? According to Homer it was not far because he tells us that there were stone troughs near the river where Trojan wives and daughters washed their clothes.

PRIAM'S JOURNEY TO THE ACHAEAN CAMP

Priam travels all the way from Troy to the Achaean camp when he goes to ransom Hector's body so we can use this information to our advantage. In Book 24 of the Iliad Homer describes the preparations, together with Priam's journey to the Achaean camp, and his return.396 But Homer does much more than this – he gives us reference points so that we can verify distances travelled and he also provides indications of time during the journey. As we now have the necessary Bronze Age geographical details we can re-trace Priam's journey. This will serve two purposes: it will be a final check on the accuracy of our previous findings, and will also help in locating the land of Troy.

Sometime during the day King Priam left Troy with a ransom that would melt Achilles' heart; twelve beautiful robes, twelve single cloaks and as many sheets, white mantles and tunics to go with them. He also took ten talents of gold, two shining tripods, four cauldrons, and a treasured Thracian cup. The ransom was put into a smooth-running mule-cart with a wicker body lashed on top, and it was pulled by two sturdy mules that had been trained to work in harness. Priam left the city in his chariot preceded by the mule-cart, which was driven by his herald. They drove through the town, down through the streets to open country and struck out across the plain. They continued past the great barrow of Ilus and then stopped the mules and horses for a drink at the river. Homer tells us that it was now dark. Hermes had been sent by Zeus to conduct Priam in secret to the ships and during the whole journey not a single Danaan saw him. The sentries were having supper when Priam reached the Achaean ditch and wall, and shortly afterwards he arrived at the hut of Achilles.

The King prayed and beseeched Achilles to release the body of his son, Hector, and to accept the ransom he had brought. Eventually, Achilles agreed. Hector's body was washed, wrapped in a mantle and put onto the mule-cart. Meanwhile, the mules and horses had been unyoked and food prepared for Priam and the herald. After the meal beds and blankets were provided in the portico and Priam fell asleep. In a short while he was awakened by Hermes who was worried about getting them past the sentries unchallenged. Hermes yoked the mules and horses and drove them out of the camp. At dawn they had reached the ford in the river, and from here they made their way back to Troy.

We do not know the time of the year when the journey was made but the most likely time for the occurrence of peat fires, mentioned by Homer, would be during the summer months of July and August. This means that sunset would occur around 7.50 pm and sunrise about 4.20 am. As darkness is about one hour after sunset and dawn one hour before sunrise, this gives us 8.50 pm as the time when Priam left the river Cam on the

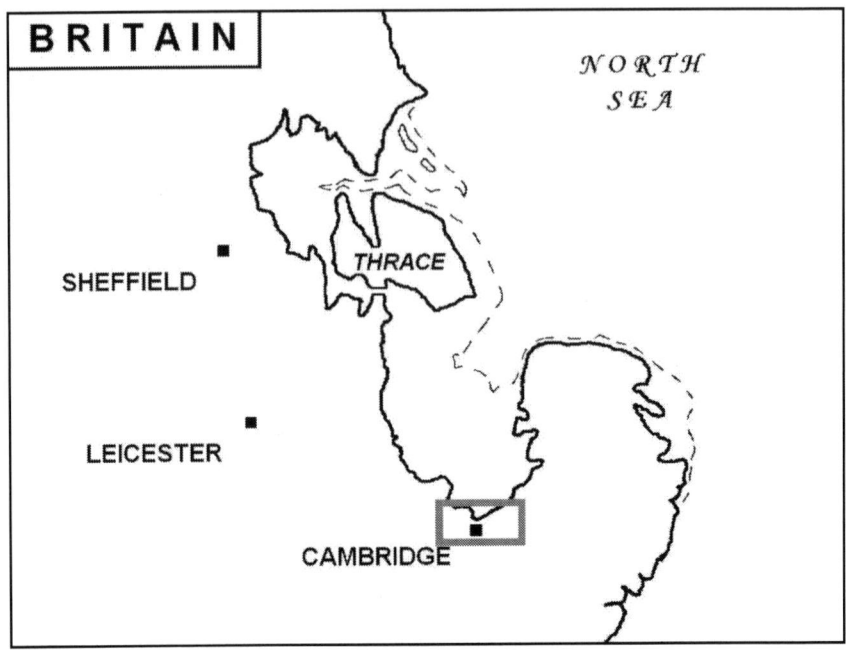

outward leg, and 3.20 am when he arrived back at the same place, a duration of 6.5 hours. If we allow 2 hours at the Achaean camp then 4.5 hours are left for travelling. The distance from the river Cam to the Achaean camp and back again is 48 kilometres, which would require an average speed of 10.6 kilometres per hour for the mule-cart. Surprisingly, this is not excessive because mules have such tremendous strength, stamina and resilience. For example, in 1881, in New Mexico, a pack train travelled 136 kilometres under the desert sun in twelve hours.

The mule has hybrid vigour. Weight for weight they are stronger than horses, are much longer lived and have much longer working lives. They rarely become ill or lame. They can withstand extremes of temperature, and can live on frugal rations. Mules are highly intelligent and are very quick to learn. Also, during rest periods mules return more rapidly to their normal conditions. If the load is on a wheeled vehicle mules can pull twice their own body weight and it would not be unusual for a two-mule team to be expected to pull a load up to 900 kilograms[397], probably eight times Hector's body weight. John Green is a long time experienced horse and mule owner in Wales and a number of years ago I discussed Priam's journey with him. He saw no problems in the mules doing this journey. Two hours would be a good rest period for the mules, and if food had not been taken along on the cart they would have taken advantage of whatever vegetation was available. 'But', he said, 'the horses may have been in a worse condition than the mules at the end of the journey'. He explained, 'Some mules can travel 130 kilometres in a day, sun-up to sun-down. It is not appreciated though that mules have a very fast walk. They have a peculiar gait and what can only be described as an additional gear in between a walk and a trot. Horses would have to trot to keep up with them'. 'So that explains why king Priam laid the lash on the horses[398] when the chariot followed the mule-cart out of the city', I said. 'Exactly', he declared, 'because he had to force the horses into a trot in order to keep pace with the mule-cart'.

THE LAND OF TROY

Now that we know that Priam's journey was a realistic one in terms of complying with Homer's descriptions and the geography of the area, we can follow Priam on his way back from the river Cam to Troy. In order to do this we need to reverse the information we were given when Priam first departed. This means that shortly after leaving the river he would pass the barrow of Ilus; shortly after this he would leave the plain; then he would drive up through the streets; and finally through the town.

The ford in the river Cam was at Grantchester. If we travel west from here along the line of the Bourn brook we come to a tumulus alongside the B1046 road, near the Joddrell Bank radio telescopes. This must be the Barrow of Ilus from whom Ilium took its name. A short distance beyond the tumulus we start to leave the plain, although the land is still low-lying at about 20 metres above sea level. A little further west are the villages of Kingston and Toft. From here the gradient becomes steeper in all directions. If we travel northwest along the line of the Bourn brook we gradually rise about 20 metres over a distance of 7 kilometres until we reach the village of Caxton. Travelling north or southwest, however, means a much steeper climb and almost immediately we would rise about 30 metres in less than 1.5 kilometres before levelling out onto the flatter parts of the uplands.

Regardless of the direction in which we travel from the villages of Kingston and Toft, we end up on the uplands of west Cambridgeshire. This is a large triangular block of land that extends to about 26 kilometres east to west, and 20 kilometres north to south. Most of the area is between 30 metres and 75 metres above sea level. The peripheral edges of the uplands are all sloping to a lesser or greater extent and on the southeast edge is a steep scarp 30 metres high. It is bounded by the river Great Ouse to the west and the river Cam (or Rhee) to the south and east. We have shown that in the Bronze Age the Hellespont extended as far as the southern edges of the Fens, hence the northern edge of the uplands would have been bounded by the sea. This gently undulating countryside complies with Homer's descriptions in every respect. It was the 'deep-soiled land of Troy' and it was so extensive that it provided enough room for Troy's own population and all of Troy's allies. Homer also tells us that the gods had built the walls of Troy, indicating that the land had been fashioned by nature. The land bears witness to this with its peripheral slopes and escarpments, and its two rivers and tributaries having cut down through chalk, gault, glacial deposits and clays.

Previously, we identified Homer's Simois with the river Little Ouse. Homer also mentions the Satniois which can only be the other river of that name, the Great Ouse. Satniois or *Sath-ny-oes*, means a river that is 'trampling' and 'spreading' – a powerful river, correctly termed 'Great'. In Book 20 of the *Iliad* Aeneas recalls the time when Achilles sacked the towns of Lyrnessus and Pedasus and raided Aeneas' cattle. Pedasus was the home of Altes, the king of the Leleges, and it was situated on the banks of the Satniois. Therefore, it appears that Aeneas lived near the Satnioise, or the river Great Ouse, on the west side of Troy.

TROY TOWN MAZES

In the area of west Cambridgeshire and the Isle of Ely are a number of mazes or labyrinths. Normally, these maze patterns are found on the ground, cut into the turf, or laid out with stones but they have also been found cut into rocks. The labyrinth pattern has found its way into churches although the stereotype existed long before the Christian era. The practice of placing labyrinths in churches does not appear to have been common in Britain and moreover, there is no written ecclesiastical evidence of their use or significance in the service of the church. Conversely, turf mazes appear to be peculiar to Britain, and were formerly of general occurrence throughout

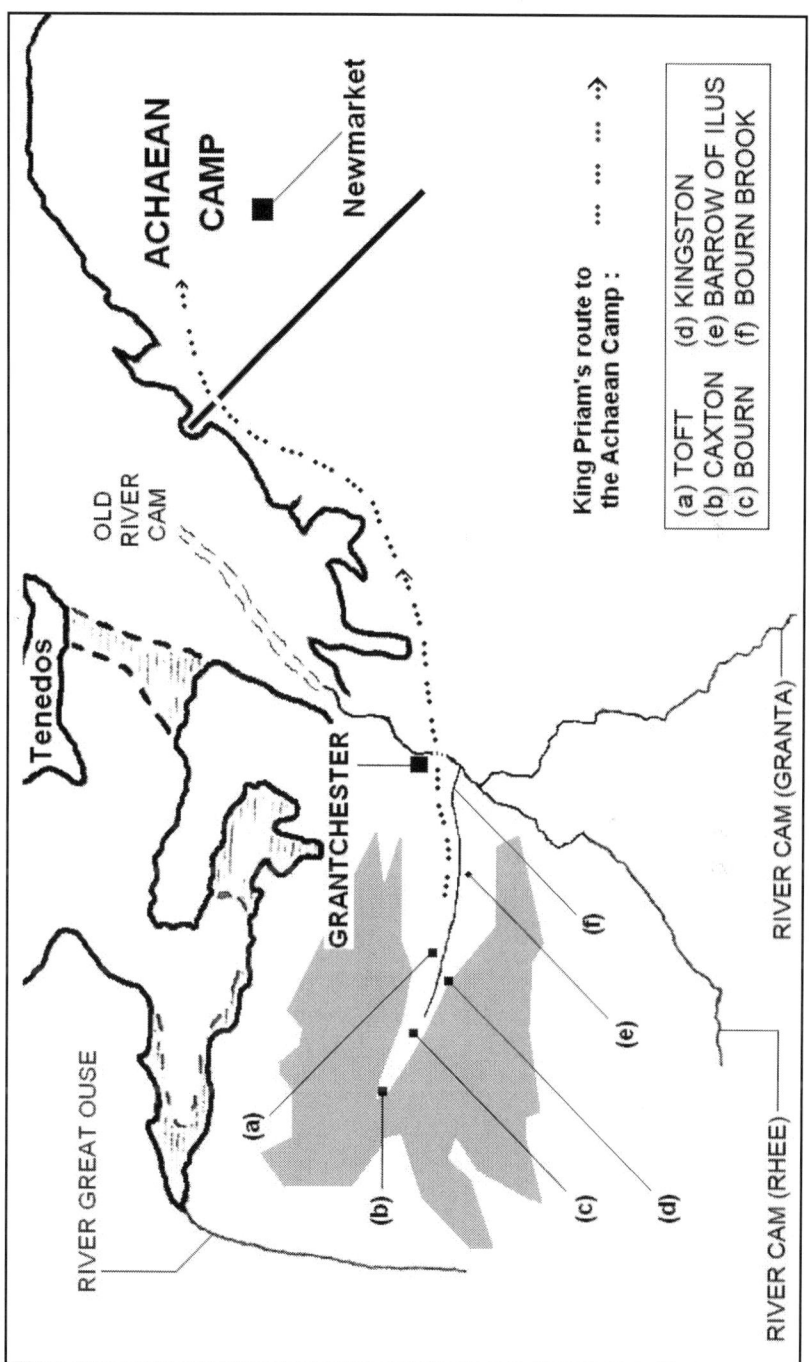

MAP 32. PRIAM'S JOURNEY TO THE ACHAEAN CAMP

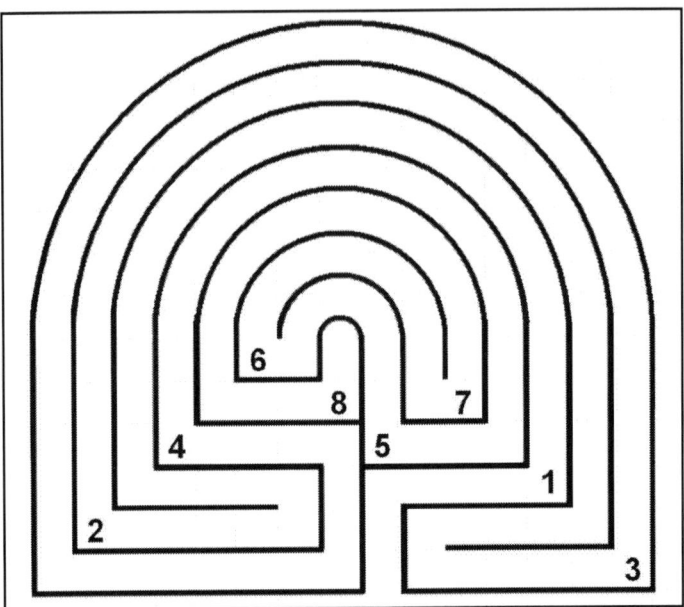

FIG. 17. A TYPICAL MAZE PATTERN

the country. Many of them are in close proximity to ancient ecclesiastical sites. In Wales, these maze patterns were called *Caerdroia* or 'City of Troy', and in England 'Troy Town'.

There is a modern specimen of a maze on the floor of the cathedral at Ely, the isle we identified as Chryse. In the church at Bourn, in the middle of the upland area that we have now identified as the land of Troy, is another maze of a comparatively modern design. In the village of Comberton, directly north of the barrow of Ilus, there existed a turf-cut maze in the northeast corner of the crossroads. This survived until recently on the green which was evidently subjected to progressive encroachment. Also, in the northwest of the area in a low-lying district approaching the river Great Ouse, there is another turf-cut maze in the village of Hilton. Located in a corner of the green, the maze is extremely well preserved but has a curious design.[399]

The maze or labyrinth design was described by P.O. Roberts in his *Cambrian Popular Antiquities*, published in 1815. It referred to the custom among Welsh shepherds of cutting the maze pattern in the turf. A number of 19th century writers also described labyrinth designs in Finland, Lapland, and

Sweden, which had been formed from stones or large pebbles. The Swedish antiquarian Rudbeck wrote about similar objects in his *Atlantica* in 1695, and the 17th-century Danish antiquary, Olaf Worm, shows the design engraved on an ancient cross in Denmark.[400]

The labyrinth is depicted on coins of Knossos of the fifth century BC and also on an Etruscan wine jar of the seventh century BC. The wine jar, from Tragliatella, shows two horsemen emerging from a womb-like labyrinth, which is marked with the letters 'Truia' or 'Troy'. The scene depicts the ritual death of a sacred king.

The labyrinth takes its name from the Labrys, or double axe. It is both the underworld of the dead and the womb from which the dead are reborn. It is also a ritual calendar. As tomb, womb and underworld, it is spatial, but as a solar-lunar calendar it represents the cyclical nature of sun, moon, seasons, birth, maturity, mating, death and rebirth. It also presents a quest relating to the mysteries of initiation. This is a test of the conscious ego in the face of the 'underworld' forces of the unconscious.[401]

Only exceptional heroes like Daedalus and Theseus entered the labyrinth and came out alive. The existence of such a calendar has been amply demonstrated by Charles F. Herberger in his two books, *The Thread of Ariadne* and *The Riddle of the Sphinx*. A solar-lunar calendar that reconciled solar and lunar time had been achieved by 1500 BC, which later developed into an eight-year calendar. Afterwards, a nineteen-year solar-lunar cycle was discovered which permitted an even closer reconciliation of solar and lunar years.

King Priam of Troy had fifty sons, and nineteen of these were legitimate. Graves states that this suggests that the length of the King's reign was governed by the nineteen-year Metonic cycle.[402] The king would then undergo a sacrificial death. In the last book of the *Iliad* Helen says that she has been at Troy for nineteen years, hence Homer confirms the knowledge of such a calendar at Troy. Helen was the same divine character as Helle, or Persephone, a Goddess of Death and Resurrection.[403] On the reverse of the Tragliatella wine-jar is a ceremonial procession that precedes the sacrificial death of the sacred king. A priestess of the moon-goddess offers the king an apple, his passport to immortality, whilst he holds out an egg, the egg of rebirth or resurrection. The Easter egg is the egg of resurrection, and Easter was the season when Troy Town dances were performed in the turf-cut mazes of Britain.[404]

As far as the mysteries of initiation are concerned it requires eight circuits to enter the labyrinth. The inner cell is counted as the eighth circuit because an initiate has to turn around in order to get out again. This means 'turning around' the centre in an alternate clockwise and counter clockwise direction. The Welsh verb *Tro* means 'to turn' or 'to revolve', but it also means 'to convert'. The land of Troy was also called

FIG. 18. DANISH RUNIC STONE CROSS WITH LABYRINTH DESIGN.
(O.Worm, 1651.)

the 'Troad', meaning 'a turning' or 'a conversion', hence the name *Caerdroia* or 'Troy Town' for the labyrinths or mazes. It is equally applicable to initiation into the mysteries or to the study of the heavens. To turn or revolve is the esoteric meaning behind the labyrinth as well as the names of Tros, the Troad, and Troy.

MEMORIALS TO ILUS

The memory of people and events are celebrated in a number of ways. These include poetry, song, plaques, paintings, sculptures, monuments, and so on. The most effective though may be that of place-names. Think of Thermopylae, Waterloo, and Hiroshima. The associated historical events come immediately to mind. In its day the Trojan War was an event of gigantic proportions, never equalled in the ancient world. But Troy itself was equally renowned even before the war.

Homer informs us that 'the opulence, the gold and the bronze, of Priam's city was the talk of all the world'.[405] Above all others it appears that the names of Tros and Ilus were the most celebrated in connection with the land of Troy and the city. Troy takes its name from Tros, the father of Ilus and grandfather of Laomedan. Ilus, the son of Tros, built the citadel of Troy, and from him it was called Ilium. Homer refers to both Troy and Ilium throughout the *Iliad*. In this area of west Cambridgeshire, which we have identified as the land of Troy, there are a number of places that still testify to the name and renown of Ilus, as follows:

Hatley (Hatley St. George, East Hatley)
Eltisley
Thriplow   (Hundred)
Tadlow
Madingley
Childerley
Graveley
Wetherley   (Hundred).

At first glance there is nothing which would suggest a connection between these places and the name of Ilium. Yet place names endure much longer than most people imagine. Some will change out of all recognition, but the greater proportion will allow the serious investigator considerable success in tracing their original meanings. The *Domesday Book*, William the Conqueror's record of his survey of England, gives the spellings of these places as they were known in 1086 AD:

Current Name	Domesday Name
Hatley	Hatelai, Atelai
Eltisley	Hecteslei
Thriplow	Trepeslav, Trepeslai
Tadlow	Tadelai
Madingley	Madingelei
Childerley	Cilderlai, Cildrelai
Graveley	Gravelei
Wetherley	Wederlai, Wedrelai

All of the above names contain the ending *Elei* or *Elai*. Where a word is difficult to say, it often happens that letters become interchanged, as in 'Cildrelai/Cilderlai'. Sometimes letters are dropped, as in 'Trepes(e)lei'. All of these names have meanings but, for the time being, it is enough to show that these names still exist in the area we have identified as the land of Troy, and that they all have one word in common. That word is *Elei* or *Elai*, (the pronunciation is the same) and equates to the English 'Ely' or the Latin 'Ili'. It is the Welsh name for Ilus. These place names stand as testimony to the renown of Elai (Ilus) and Ilium in the Uplands of west Cambridgeshire.

PRIAM'S RETURN

We can continue now with Priam's journey from the river Cam (Scamandros) back to the city of Troy. Following the route of the Bourne Brook he would first pass the barrow of Ilus. Having identified the Uplands of west Cambridgeshire as the land of Troy we can see the significance of the location of the barrow. It stands at the entrance to the Uplands, the

FIG. 19. THE TRAGLIATELLA WINE JAR
Horsemen emerging from a 'Troy' Labyrinth.
(Deecke, acknowledgement Mathews.)

entrance to the land of Troy - a magnificent grave-mound, memorial, and landmark. And just as it helped to guide Priam back to the city so it will help guide us too.

A little way past the barrow are the modern-day villages of Great and Little Eversden which, in the *Domesday Book*, are described as a single unit. It is interesting to note that the Parish church at Little Eversden is dedicated to St. Helen. About 5 kilometres further is the village of Bourn, its location, extent and relatively large and handsome church suggesting that its past status may have been that of a 'mother parish'.[406] Again, perhaps it is not mere coincidence that the church is dedicated first to St. Helen, and only secondly to St. Mary. On the floor of the church tower is a maze but, as we observed before, these mazes served no purpose in churches. Knowing that the stereotype is pre-Christian we can only conjecture that the church at Bourn may have been erected on an ancient ecclesiastical site and that a representation of a pre-existing maze was installed in the church.

In the south chapel are two carved panels, one of the Virgin and Child, the other an emblematic female figure, both supposedly Flemish and of the 16th century. It is plain to see that they are important artefacts with great religious meaning. The carving of the Virgin and Child needs no discussion other than to state the obvious, that Mary is the Virgin and the church is dedicated to her. The second panel is unusual and demands closer attention. It shows a fully clothed but beautifully attired young adult female figure. What is unusual about the way that this female figure is being portrayed is that both her arms are being pulled outwards, away from her body, by sturdy restraints attached to her wrists. In one hand she holds a dagger, pointing into her body and upwards to her breast. There is no doubt here that the restraints are preventing her from killing herself. But who is this beautiful figure intent on her own death?

These carvings are a matching pair with the central figures set inside a circular wreath on a square panel. The Virgin and Child is highly significant and, by implication, so too is this terrifying female figure in the second panel. If the Virgin in the one panel is Mary, then the female in the other panel must be Helen. Both are named in the joint dedication, but Helen is given precedence by being named first. If we accept the fact that she warranted this position then it must be because she was regarded as being superior and in existence prior to the worship of Mary the Virgin. We are dealing, therefore, with a pre-Christian divinity of considerable importance. Bourn could be considered to be the geographical centre of the Uplands, which also means that it was the centre of the land of Troy. As a 'mother parish' it would have been regarded as the spiritual centre too. Is it beyond the bounds of possibility that the Helen to whom the church is dedicated is the same Helen over whom the Trojan War was fought? And is this the same Helen depicted in the carved panel? Let us explore this matter a little further.

HELEN: WISDOM, DEATH AND RESURRECTION

The cause of the Trojan War is generally ascribed to the abduction of Helen of Sparta by Paris, the second son of King Priam of Troy. Paris' responsibility remains uncertain, but no source argues that Helen is kidnapped against her will.[407] Throughout Homer's portrayal of Helen there is not one consistent view and he leaves matters in doubt as to her complicity.[408] Stesichorus had, apparently, told the story of Helen's journey to Troy in a poem and he had, afterwards, lost his eyesight. It was not restored until he recanted with the words 'You never sailed on a benched ship. You never entered the city of Troy'.[409] Euripides, however, has Helen sojourn at the court of King Proteus in Egypt, and we are told that Hera had fashioned a breathing image of her

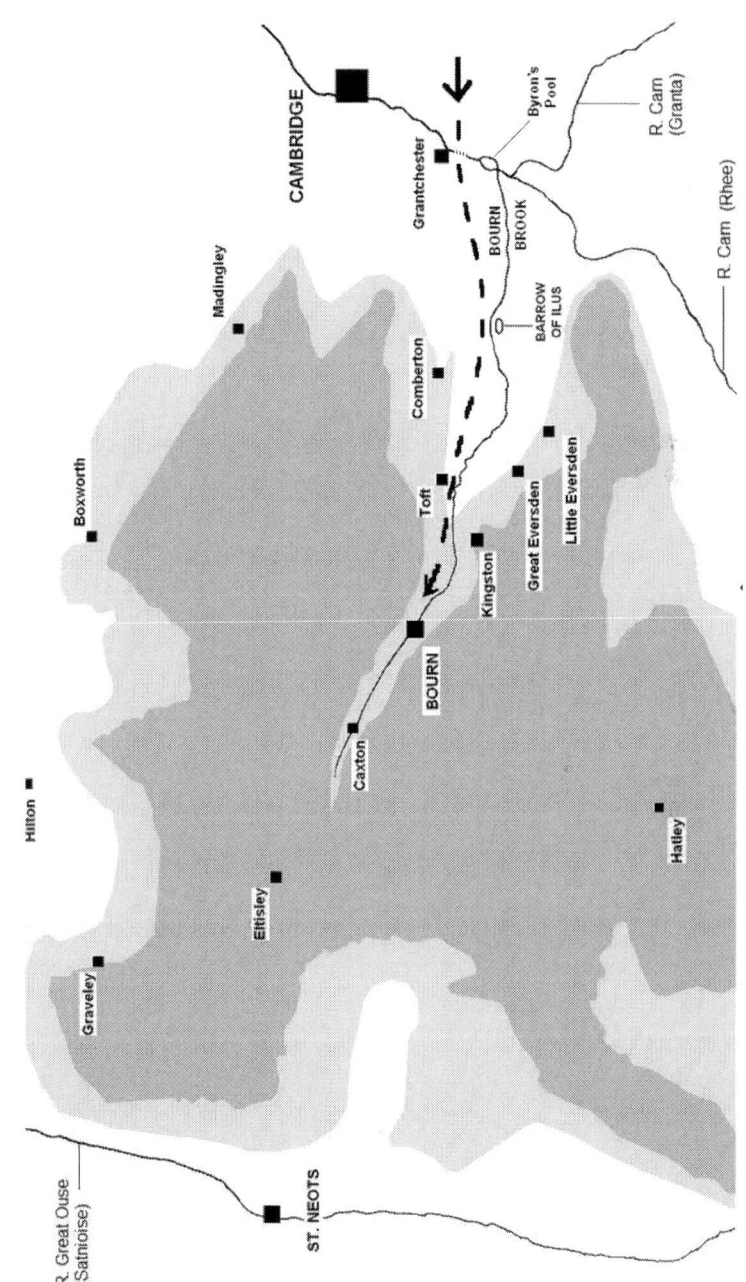

MAP 33. KING PRIAM'S RETURN FROM THE ACHAEN CAMP: HIS ROUTE BACK TO TROY.

out of the air. Paris had taken the image to Troy, and the Greeks and Trojans had fought over a phantom.[410] So who was Helen? Was she imaginary or real? A supernatural power or an earthly being? Although Helen was cursed for the War, Aphrodite has a key role in it, and we shall see that Helen and Aphrodite are intimately and mysteriously connected.

It was Aphrodite who promised Paris the hand of Helen if he awarded her the prize of beauty over the goddesses Hera and Athene.[411] And it was Aphrodite who suggested that Paris build ships in order to go to Sparta. In Euripides' *The Trojan Women*[412] Helen explains that she was powerless to prevent Paris from taking her away because Aphrodite was helping him. While Paris is alive he is protected by Aphrodite and at one stage in the war, she removes him from the battlefield in a thick mist.[413] The only mortal that Aphrodite sleeps with is Anchises and it is his son, Aeneas, who is destined even before his birth to rule the Trojans after the War.[414] The gifts of Aphrodite overwhelmed mortal men and all gods and goddesses, and even Zeus succumbed to a potion that she gave to Hera.[415] But she was a jealous goddess and punished Helen's father when he forgot to sacrifice to her, by making his daughters twice and three times married and deserters of their husbands.[416] This darker, vengeful side of her nature is hinted at by Homer when Helen refuses to do the goddess's bidding, and Aphrodite tells Helen not to provoke her lest she deserts her in anger and hates her as much as now she loves her terribly.[417]

These sentiments appear rather strange and obscure, but this great love which Aphrodite has for Helen needs explanation. Aphrodite, or Venus Cytheraea, was probably a lunar goddess, whilst Helen was a lunar goddess particularly associated with Cythera.[418] Helen appears to be another face or aspect of Aphrodite the moon-goddess, but her character is an enigma. In the *Iliad* Aphrodite is called 'the shining,' whereas Helen is described as 'shining among women.' Helen veils herself in 'shining' or 'luminous' robes and the Trojan elders compare her likeness to 'immortal goddesses.'[419] Graves says that Helen was priestess of the Spartan Moon-goddess, and Helle (the goddess who gave her name to the Hellespont) and Helen are the same divine character.[420] We are told that Helen's name had spread throughout the world and the 'all-wise' came to seek her hand in marriage.[421] All who came were heroes in their own right so there appears to be a connection between heroism and wisdom. In this respect it is interesting to look at the Welsh equivalent, *El-en,* in order to gain an insight into what may be a unique meaning behind the name:

El - intelligence, spirit, angel.

En - source of life; deity, soul.

It is possible, therefore, that the name *Elen* means 'a deity of intelligence'. Two of the greatest heroes were Theseus and Heracles who were said to have 'harrowed hell'. Theseus had penetrated to the centre of the Cretan Maze, where death was waiting, and came safely out again.[422] Theseus won Ariadne when he was in Crete, but his guide and companion for the voyage was, of course, Aphrodite.[423] Besides being closely associated with Ariadne, Theseus had abducted Helen when she was young. Richer[424] tells us that Ariadne and Helen are two names of a single earth-moon goddess, perhaps of Cretan origin. Aphrodite was the goddess of Death-in-life,[425] and her other face, the face of Helen, seems to have brought either death or destruction for the hero or else death and rebirth.

It was Helen that brought death and destruction to Troy, but Helen was not a mortal woman. She was Helle, or Persephone, a Goddess of Death and Resurrection.[426] In discussing heathen festivals of divine death and resurrection, Frazer[427] informs us that Attis, the god of vegetation, received a self-inflicted death under a pine tree. The priest who played the part of Attis at the spring festival of Cybele was regularly hanged or otherwise slain upon the sacred tree. The human victims dedicated to Odin were strung up to a tree and hanged or stabbed with a spear. The great goddess Artemis appears to have been annually hanged in effigy in her sacred grove.

Helen was worshipped in Rhodes as 'Helen of the Tree', because she caused her handmaidens to string her up to a bough. Coins of Ilium also show sacrifices of an ox or a cow hanging on a tree and stabbed with a knife. And this is exactly what the carved panel in the church at Bourn represents. It depicts the self-inflicted death, by stabbing, of Helen, the Goddess of Death and Resurrection. We can now see that she was a pre-Christian divinity of great importance, and we can also understand why she has precedence in the joint dedication. Frazer says that the coincidences of the Christian with the heathen festivals are too close and too numerous to be accidental. This was the compromise that the church was compelled to make with its vanquished yet still dangerous rivals.

In this chapter we have been able to retrace king Priam's journey from the river Cam (Scamander) to the Achaean Camp and back again as far as the village of Bourn. Priam's journey is exactly as Homer describes it. We have discovered also that the Uplands of West Cambridgeshire is rich in supporting evidence that we are now in the Bronze Age Land of Troy. This evidence comes in the form of the continued existence of Troy Town Mazes in the area and the place-names containing the name of Ilus who built the citadel of Troy. In addition, we have churches dedicated to St. Helen. It is particularly significant that the church at Bourn, located in the centre of the Uplands and apparently its 'mother church', gives precedence to St. Helen in its joint dedication. From our study of the carved panels in the church we now know who Helen was. She was the original goddess of Death and Resurrection.

ENDNOTES

[396] *Iliad*, 24.228-697

[397] Travis, *The Mule*. See also British Mule Society Journals.

[398] *Iliad*, 24.325

[399] See *An Inventory of Historical Monuments in the County of Cambridgeshire*, Vol.1, West Cambridgeshire, under Bourn, Comberton, and Hilton.

[400] See Mathews, *Mazes and Labyrinths*.

[401] Herberger, *Riddle of the Sphinx*, pp.37,39, and 174

[402] Graves, *Greek Myths*, 158.7

[403] Graves, *The White Goddess*, p257

[404] Graves, *Greek Myths*, 104.4

[405] *Iliad*, 18. 288-290

[406] See Note 4, under Bourn.

[407] Gantz, *Early Greek Myth*, p568

[408] Groten, 'Homer's Helen', p38

[409] Atchity, *The Classical Greek Reader*, p64

[410] Euripides, Helen, 16-48 and 605-615

[411] Hesiod, The Cypria, 1

[412] Euripides, The Trojan Women, 923-933

[413] *Iliad*, 3.380-382

[414] Hesiod, Hymn to Aphrodite, 191-201

[415] *Iliad*, 14. 198-314
[416] Hesiod, Catalogues of Women and Eoiae, 67
[417] *Iliad*, 3. 413-415
[418] Richer, *Sacred Geography of the Ancient Greeks*, pp. 15 and 113
[419] *Iliad*, 3. 141, 158, 171, 228, 413, and 419
[420] Graves, *Greek Myths*, 58.3
[421] Hesiod, Catalogues of Women and Eoiae, 67
[422] Graves, *Greek Myths*, 103. 1-6
[423] Ibid. 98
[424] Richer, *Sacred Geography of the Ancient Greeks*, p122
[425] Graves, *Greek Myths*, 18.4
[426] Graves, *The White Goddess*, p257
[427] Frazer, *The Golden Bough*, pp. 352-362

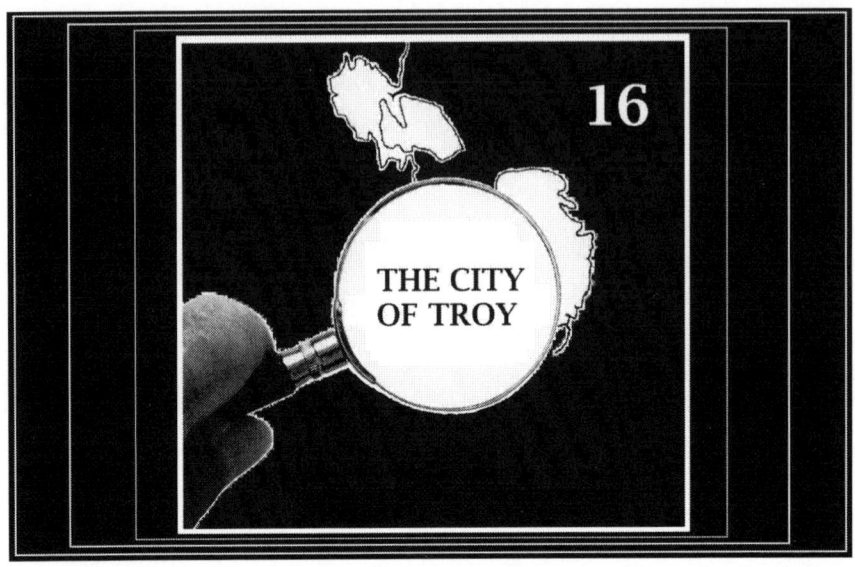

16

THE CITY
OF TROY

'More interesting than the disappearance of the city is the total disappearance of the Trojans themselves'. So states Finley in his discussion on the Archaeological Troy in Turkey. 'Trojan allies are historically identifiable whereas the Trojans themselves have vanished completely', he continues. He goes on to declare, 'It is hard to discover a parallel for the mysterious failure of the people themselves to leave any traces'.[428] As we have found, Homer's Troy was not in Turkey and neither were the Trojans. Troy was located in Britain, and the traces that Finley so desperately sought are to be found in Britain too. But in order to answer the questions that arise quite naturally as a result of Finley's statements we need to know who the Trojans were. Only then can we begin to appreciate the part they played in the ancient tapestry that was Bronze Age Britain. Finally, we will be able to identify the city of Troy itself and discover that it had not disappeared at all; not disappeared, that is, from its original location. We will find that the city had been there all the time, if only someone had taken the time to look.

WHO WERE THE TROJANS?

The foundation of Troy is generally ascribed to Dardanus but opinions differ as to whether he came from Greece or the country afterwards known as Tyrrhenia.[429] It is generally agreed, however, that after coming first to Samothrace he then went to Phrygia, was received hospitably by a King called Teucer, and married the princess Bateia. The Phrygians, the Brigantes of Britain, were the posterity of the Kymry, and in his book *The British Kymry*[430] Morgan states that the King of Phrygia reigning at the time of Dardanus' arrival was Athus. Dardanus exchanged his rights in Umbria for a part of Phrygia and Tyrrhi, the son of Athus, sailed and took possession of that portion of Umbria and called it Tyrrhenia.[431] We have previously located the Tyrrhenian Sea in the English Channel, so Tyrrhenia may be on the south coast of Britain too. Dardanus married Bateia, the daughter of Teucer, the King of Llydaw (Lydia). Llydaw it seems was adjacent to or a part of Phrygia and was a Kymric or ancient British name. For example, the Gallic Lydia was called *Llydaw Ar y Mor Ucha*, (Lydia, the Land on the Upper Sea). The name *Ar y Mor Ucha* in Gaul was eventually Latinized and became Armorica. But, we can see now that the ancient Phrygia was located in the lands occupied by the Brigantes of Southern Britain.

Dardanus was succeeded by his son, Ericthonius, who inherited the kingdoms of his father and his father-in-law, Teucer. Ericthonius was followed by his son Tros who removed the capital to Troy. Tros, it seems, had an illustrious reign of sixty years and to commemorate the splendour of his career the Kymry of Italy who had followed Dardanus took the name of Trojans. Tros had three sons: Ilus, Assaracus, and Ganymede. Tros was succeeded by Ilus who built the citadel of Troy, and Ilus by his son, Laomedon. In the reign of Laomedon, the citadel and walls of Troy were rebuilt by Belin and Nev, architects of Crete, after the model of the Cretan Labyrinth, which was also an exact representation of the Stellar Universe.[432] Priam was the son of Laomedon and it was during king Priam's reign that the Trojan War took place. From Assaracus the second son of Tros came Anchises the father of Aeneas of Troy. Aeneas was the head of the royal tribe of Dardanidae (the Kymry) and patriarch of the Trojan lines of Britain and Rome. Aeneas' great grandson, Brutus the Trojan, would become the first king of the Britons after the Trojan War. He would build his 'New Troy' on the bank of the river Thames and, later, it would be called London.

Graves says that Troy seems to have been peopled by a federation of three tribes and this was a usual arrangement in the Bronze Age. He calls these elements Trojan, Ilian and Dardanian.[433] We have dealt with the Dardanian element and have seen that it relates to the ancient Kymry of Britain and

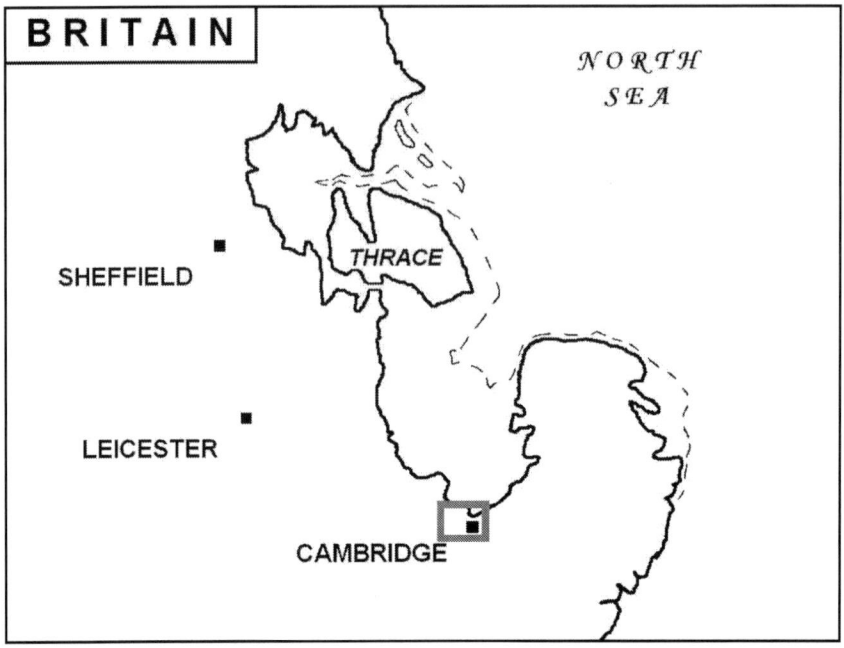

their descendants, the Phrygians, or Brigantes. The Ilian element seems to have been provided by Locris, a pre-Hellenic Lelegian district. There was at least one Locrian colony in Thrace and a tribe of Leleges at Pedasus in the Troad. Dionysius tells us that the Locrians were previously called Leleges and this is confirmed by Hesiod who says, 'For Locrus truly was the leader of the Lelegian people'.[434] Of the invading forces at Troy the lesser Ajax was lord of the Locrians, and Homer describes them as lightly armed archers. Patroclus was yet another Locrian. After the fall of Troy the Locrians returned home with difficulty and afterwards suffered a plague. An oracle instructed them to propitiate Athena at Ilium by sending two maidens as suppliants for a thousand years.[435] The Locrians of ancient Greece were a sister tribe of the Kymry, their name and dialect being the same as those of the Ligurians, Locrians or Lloegrians.[436] We saw in chapter 14 that they formerly inhabited Lancashire. The Welsh call this people Lloegrwys, and a portion of Britain was named Lloeger after them. This part of Britain is now called England.

The Trojan or Phrygian is the third element comprising the make-up of Troy. Throughout the *Iliad* it is Hector, the son of King Priam, who leads the Trojans. These must be Trojans who lived in the city and the wider geographical area of the Troad. We saw earlier that these forces may have numbered fifty thousand men. There were other Trojans brought to Troy who were led by Pandaros. He walked to Troy from Zeleia where his men of wealth drank the waters of Aesepos.[437] It appears that Pandaros ruled over a tribe of Trojans on the Aesepos and came to Troy as a friend of Hectors rather than as a subject of King Priam's. We identified the Aesepos as the river Ashop, which flows through Derby and Nottingham to Newark-on-Trent. Phrygians were brought from Ascania by the Lords Phorkys and Askanios. Ascania is generally considered to be the Ashkenaz of scripture and was inhabited by the descendants of Gomer. It is usually held that its river drained into the Propontis.[438] As we have also identified the Propontis we can confirm that this is once again in Phrygian (Brigantean) lands and that the descendants of Gomer, the descendants of the ancient Kymry, are the Phrygians.

Edwin Guest tells us that in the poems of the Homeric cycle the distinction between the Trojans and Phrygians is clearly marked. Priam, he says, led his Trojans to the aid of the Phrygians, Mugdon and Otreus, so he evidently looked on his allies as a distinct people.[439] Further, when Aphrodite slept with Anchises she reveals that she is not immortal but the daughter of Otreus who governs Phrygia.[440] At this point in time it may be impossible to draw minute distinctions between Trojans and Phrygians. What we can say, however, is that the people who followed Dardanus to Phrygia were the ancient Kymry and they changed their names to Trojans. The Phrygians were also descended from the Old Kymry. Jordanes informs us that Telefus was the husband of a sister of Priam and after his death his son, Eurypylus, succeeded to the throne. For the love of Cassandra and to help her parents Eurypylus took part in the Trojan War but was killed soon after his arrival. Jordanes, however, does not refer to Priam as King of the Trojans. He calls him 'King of the Phrygians'.[441]

Now that we are more aquainted with the Trojans we can see that they were the indigenous people of Britain. They were the Kymry, or the 'ancient' Britons. We should no longer be surprised, therefore, to find that the native histories that assert their descent from the ancient Kymry and from Aeneas of Troy are correct. The only two national names acknowledged by the ancient Britons are Kymry and *Y Lin Troia*, the race of Troy.[442] We now know that the aftermath of the Trojan War included, in particular, mass migrations from Britain to Gaul. Yet, in less than a generation Trojan princes would begin to rule in southern Gaul and the Low Countries, and more migrations would follow afterwards. Communications and intermarriages between the British-Trojan royal families and those of the continent would continue into the current era, and these events are attested to in both the British and continental records.

So, there really was no mysterious failure of the Trojans to leave any traces of themselves in the Aegean because it was not necessary. The Trojans did not disappear from Turkey because they were never there. And neither was their city. It was where it had always been. In the country where the Trojan War took place and where the Trojans lived. That country was Britain. It was in the Uplands of West Cambridgeshire, which we have identified as the Land of Troy. But, in order that we can finally locate the City of Troy we now need to return to king Priam who is travelling back from the Achaean Camp.

PRIAM'S RETURN TO THE CITY

In the previous chapter we left king Priam in the village of Bourn on his journey back to Troy with Hector's body. Utilising an Ordnance Survey map we can check the details of Priam's journey against Homer's descriptions. Immediately upon leaving Bourn, Priam has a steep climb uphill for about 330 metres, rising from 36 metres to 50 metres o.d. (ordnance datum). Over the next 550 metres he climbs a further 10 metres in height. The Ordnance Survey map calls this incline Moulton Hills. After travelling another 1300 metres he is almost at the highest point, at 70 metres o.d., where he makes his way across the 'Great Common'. If we recall Priam's outward journey he left the city, driving 'through the town and down through the streets.' The journey from the Great Common down to Bourn is exactly as Homer describes it. He tells us of the 'steep streets' of Ilium and also of Troy with its 'broad ways.' The road from Moulton Hills to the Great Common is actually called 'Broadway.'

Hesiod[443] and Dares[444] both tell us that it was after first arriving at Tenedos that the confederate forces sent envoys to King Priam demanding the return of Helen. Having previously located Tenedos (Chapter 13) we can see that it is quite straightforward for envoys to travel from here to the

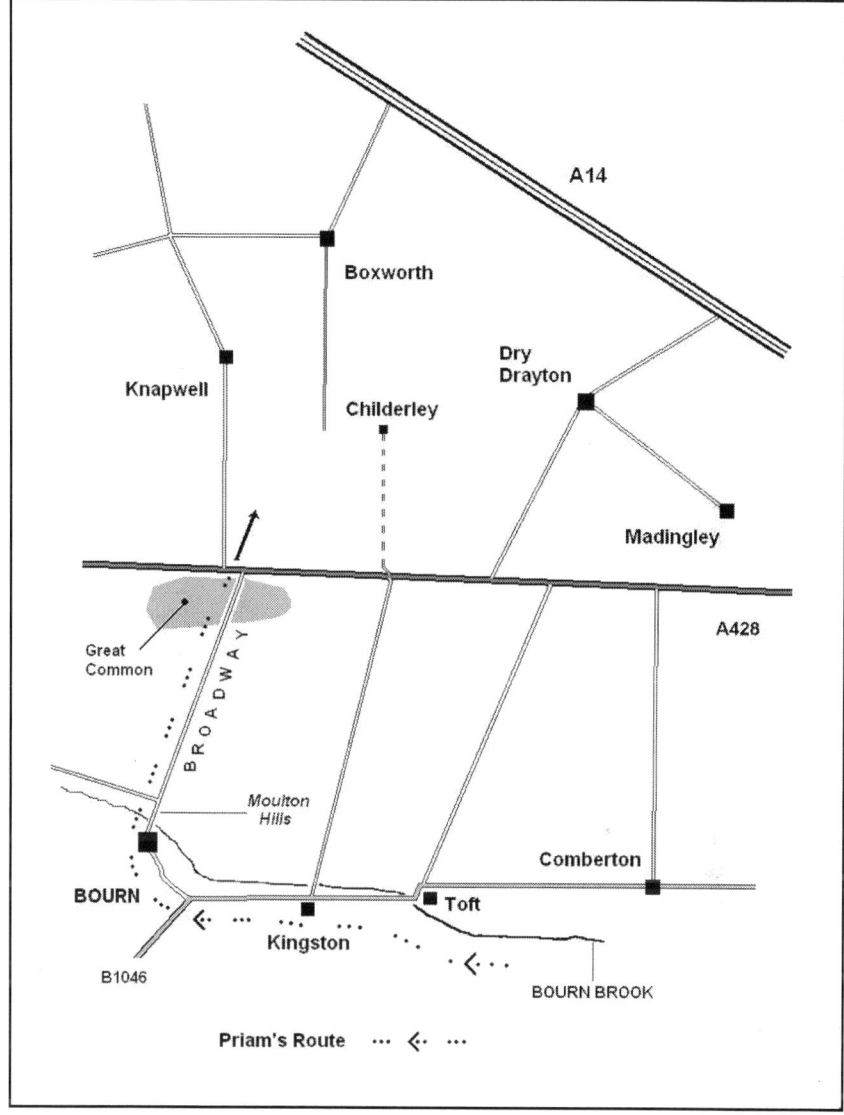

MAP 34. THE LOCATION OF THE CITY OF TROY.

mainland. Virgil tells us that[445] so it must be close to the Hellespont and to the west of Cambridge.

Homer refers to the city as 'windy Ilium' and 'steep Ilium',[446] and we have discovered that the location of Priam's city is somewhere on the

Uplands of West Cambridgeshire, north of the village of Bourn and the Great Common. For the city of Troy to comply with all of these requirements it must be located near the brow of the northern uplands escarpment between the villages of Boxworth to the west, and Madingley to the east, a distance between the two villages of only 6 kilometres. The northern Uplands escarpment terminates immediately south of the modern A14 dual carriageway. Within this confined area we will find the Bronze Age city of Troy.

CHILDERLEY

The Childerley Estate is located in the northern uplands on land that is more than 65 metres above o.d. and extends down over the brow at the northern escarpment. Its highest point is near Childerley Gate where it is 72 metres above o.d. It lies about 2.5 kilometres from Boxworth and 4 kilometres from Madingley. It was long ago described as one of the most absolute and complete estates, if not the best, in the whole shire. It is thought, however, that it was subsequently reduced in size. Childerley Hall is centrally positioned with Grove Park to the west, Great Park to the south and east, and Black Park to the northeast.

From the main barn at Childerley it is possible to see the spire of Ely Cathedral, some 26 kilometres to the northeast (In other words, beyond Tenedos). Two villages, Great and Little Childerley, existed in mediaeval times, but the parishes were not differentiated at Domesday. In the 17th century the villages became deserted. There is a possibility that Great Childerley was depopulated in order to enlarge a deer park, and a private chapel replaced the parish churches. Charles I was confined by Cromwell at Childerley Hall for a few days in June 1647, and Cromwell may have dined with him when he was there. Almost nothing is known about Childerley before the *Domesday* survey. Shortly afterwards, however, the Countess Judith, a niece of King William, was a landholder here.[447] The Childerley Estate is on the north side of the A428 Cambridge to St. Neots road, a very short distance from the Great Common.

Homer describes Priam's city as 'Troy of the broad ways' and 'windy Ilium'. The temple of Athena stood in the upper part of the city, and there was a temple of Apollo high in the citadel in the holy Pergamos.

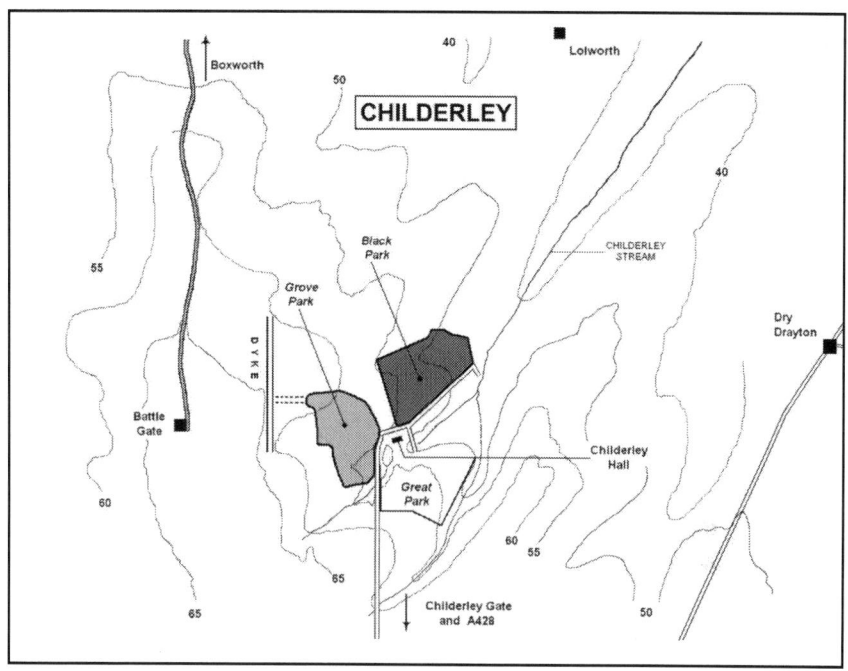

MAP 35. CHILDERLEY: THE CITY OF TROY..

It can be seen that the higher portions of the Childerley estate are to the west of Childerley Hall. This includes Grove Park. A 'Grove' can be a cluster of trees shading an avenue but very often it can mean a wood or forest sacred to a divinity. I believe that in this instance 'Grove Park' was a sacred grove. It is only the northwest corner of Grove Park that rises to above 60 metres. Undoubtedly, this would be the favoured location for Apollo's temple. Earthworks have been identified in this corner of Grove Park but it seems that they were destroyed by ploughing. At one time there was a straight east-west track here about 275 metres long and 6 metres to 9 metres wide with a continuous line of rectangular platforms on either side.

Immediately opposite the northwest corner of Grove Park, at a distance of about 200 metres to the west, can be found the remains of a linear earthwork. This earthwork consists of a bank and ditch facing west, and running north - south for a distance of 550 metres. In 1968, the Royal Commission on Ancient Monuments reported that 'where best preserved, the bank is 11 metres wide and 1.8 metres high with a flat top 3 metres wide; the ditch is

9 metres wide, 1 metre deep and 1.8 metres across the bottom; the outer bank is 3 metres wide and 0.5 metres high.' This linear earthwork was built for defensive purposes against attack from the west side. It can be seen that it was strategically positioned almost on the 65-metre contour line, thereby negating any advantage to those attacking from slightly higher ground. A further 500 metres to the west is the place-name 'Battle Gate', which would appear to indicate an event of historical significance.

THE GATES OF TROY

Troy had a number of different gates but it is not known through which of these the Achaean forces entered the city. The Trojans had been told that the invading forces had sailed for home, so they went to see the deserted Achaean camp for themselves. Unknown to the Trojans, however, the Achaean fleet had anchored off Tenedos,[448] unseen, and on that fateful night the squadrons came ashore and took the city. The Isle of Tenedos lies to the north east of Childerley and it is certainly possible that the Achaeans could have marched from there. But even the most direct route from Tenedos would have entailed a journey in excess of 30 kilometres. There is, however, a portion of the Bronze Age Hellespont that is much closer than this, and it may solve the question of where the Achaean forces came ashore and where they entered the city. This is where the Satniois (the river Great Ouse) entered the Hellespont a little to the east of Huntingdon.

In ancient and more modern times the river Great Ouse was navigable by sea-going vessels. They travelled up the river without difficulty as far as St. Ives, and the town became prosperous as a result of its ancient international markets and fairs. Swavesey was also a river port, with a navigation channel that ran north-west from the town to meet the river. The Romans carried out drainage works in the area so that the land could be cultivated. About 1200 AD all the rents and rights of the port were granted to Swavesey Prior, and in 1232 AD half the tolls from traffic between Swavesey and the Ouse were also given to the head of the priory.[449] In more modern times Swavesey thrived as a commercial centre with a necklace of wharves linked to the river Great Ouse. Barges laden with coal and building materials for the 'upland' villages reached their journey's end in Swavesey.[450]

It is possible that the inland port of Swavesey was the original port of Troy.

It is only 7 kilometres from Childerley. The Achaean fleet could easily have moved there from Tenedos under cover of darkness before finally disgorging its malign forces on the very threshold of the city. Achaean forces coming ashore at Swavesey would then have the least distance to travel overland. Their passage would take them first to Boxworth, about 4.5 kilometres, and then direct to Battle Gate at Childerley. A standard road now runs from Boxworth to Battle Gate, but south of Battle Gate it becomes narrower and ends up as a track. It should be noted that the roadway from Boxworth to Battle Gate is called 'Battle Gate Road'.

So, do the names 'Battle Gate' and 'Battle Gate Road' really refer to this cataclysmic event or are they just a coincidence? Would evidence such as this really survive for more than three thousand years even though the knowledge of the event may have been lost? And do we know that this really was the route taken by the Achaean forces on the night that Troy fell? To reduce the chances of coincidence there must be at least a probability that the battle took place at this gate and this was the actual route taken by the invading forces from the port at Swavesey. This relies on the fact that the fleet is then required to move to this point from Tenedos. But do we know that this is what really happened? Fortuitously, there are two pieces of information that help shed a little light on the matter.

In *The Sack of Ilium*[451] we are told that 'the Greeks sailed in from Tenedos' which, although we are not told where they landed, it does at least confirm the movement of the fleet towards Troy. In the *Aeneid* Virgil allows Aeneas himself to relate the events of that particular night:

> "We the wretched people to whom that day was our last, hang the shrines of the gods with festal boughs throughout the city. Meanwhile the heavens wheel on, and night rises from the sea, wrapping in her vast shadow earth and sky and the wiles of the Myrmidons; about the town the Teucrians are stretched in silence; slumber laps their tired limbs. And now the Argive squadron was sailing in order from Tenedos, and in the favouring stillness of the quiet moon sought the shores it knew; ..."[452]

Virgil confirms that the fleet sailed from Tenedos in the night. Again, he does not tell us where the invading forces disembarked, but clearly it must have been near to Troy. As we can see, the nearest place to the Uplands of west Cambridgeshire is Swavesey, and there would be no point in the fleet moving from Tenedos unless it could bring the Achaean army closer to Troy than it was already.

In his history of the war Dares tells us that the names of the gates of Troy were, the Antenoridas, Dardanides, Iliacides, Thymbrians, and Troianas.[453] So it appears that there were five gates in total. We may recall that Dares was a Phrygian (i.e. British) priest and he was involved in the war on the Trojan side from the start to the finish. He would have known the city of Troy intimately so there is no reason why he should provide us with false names for the gates. For our purposes though it is the number of gates that is important and of these it seems that Battle Gate was one. A second gateway into the city of Troy was the one used by King Priam when he returned with Hector's body after his journey to the Achaean camp. From the 'Great Common' he travelled the route currently marked on the Ordnance Survey map as a 'Byway' and entered the city from the southwest. It connected with the 'Bridleway' from Battle Gate and led to the centre of Childerley. A third route is indicated by the 'Bridleway' that goes from Childerley to Lolworth. Significantly, it goes direct from Black Park, which we will discuss later, and is once again called 'The Broadway' (Troy of the broad ways). The fourth route is the entrance road into the estate from Childerley Gate. On the east side of Childerley is another 'Bridleway', extending from Black Park to the Dry Drayton road. This Bridleway passes through 'Thoroughfare Pasture', indicating that this may have been the principal or most frequently used route. It appears to have had an alternative title of 'Gate Pasture'. From Dry Drayton the road leads to Oakington and Cottenham in the direction of Tenedos, so it is possible that this is the route traversed by the Achaean envoys when they first came to Troy.

THE MAIN GATE AT TROY

Whenever the Trojans go out from Troy onto the plain they go out through one particular gate. Homer refers to it as the 'Scaean' Gate. This is possibly an additional gate to the five we have identified, but it is not a specific name. In fact, I believe it is a general descriptive term using the British word *cae*, meaning field or enclosure – something that is fenced or walled around. The term would be applicable to the main fortress gate or city gate. Priam and Antenor drive their chariot through this gate to the plain to

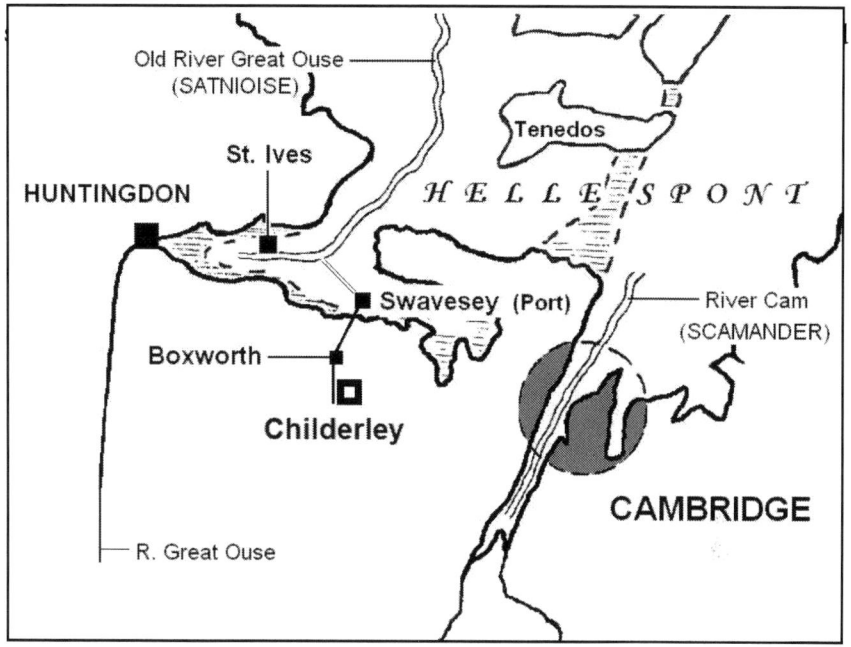

MAP 36. THE PORT OF TROY.
(The Armada sailed in from Tenedos)

Menelaus prior to their duel.[454] Hector came back from the plain through this gate and returned afterwards the same way.[455] At one stage the two armies were fighting by the Scaean Gate and the walls before the Trojans reversed the onslaught and chased the Achaeans back towards their ships.[456]

But it is not until the end of the *Iliad*, when Hector comes face to face with Achilles, that Homer provides us with the information that is necessary to identify this particular gate.

Achilles had finished slaughtering Trojans in the Pools of Scamander, (at Grantchester). Now the Trojan army was being driven back to the very walls of Troy. King Priam climbed one of its bastions and saw the gigantic Achilles and the panic-stricken Trojans being driven before him. He shouted in alarm for the watchmen to open the gates. The troops made straight for the city and the high wall and sweeping in as a mass sought the safety of the massive battlements. Outside, the Achaeans advanced on the wall. But fate had dealt a deadly blow. Hector was still outside the gate. King Priam begged his son to come inside the walls and not to stand up to the savage Achilles. But Hector, debating inwardly if he should take the course of the hero or the coward, let the monstrous Achilles approach him.[457] Trembling with fear he left the gate and ran, but Achilles was in hot pursuit:

> "...Hector fled before him under the walls of Troy, fast as his feet would go. Passing the lookout and the windswept fig-tree and keeping some way from the wall, they sped along the cart-track, and so came to the two lovely springs that are the sources of Scamander's eddying stream. In one of these the water comes up hot; steam rises from it and hangs about like smoke above a blazing fire. But the other, even in summer, gushes up as cold as hail or freezing snow or water that has turned to ice. Close beside them, wide and beautiful, stand the troughs of stone where the wives and lovely daughters of the Trojans used to wash their glossy clothes in the peaceful days before the Achaeans came".[458]

One of the significant pieces of information that Homer reveals is that at this time Achilles and Hector were actually 'under' the walls of Troy. To be under or below the city would mean that we would be to the north of Childerley, on much lower ground. And this is where a detailed knowledge of the topography is needed. It can be seen that there are three spurs, three fingers of land, stretching beyond Childerley to the northeast. These spurs are between 40 metres and 50 metres above o.d. At the ends of the spurs the land drops quickly away from 40 metres down to 20 metres where it meets the A14 dual carriageway. This is built along the line of a Roman road, which previously was an ancient British highway. Here is the cart track along which Hector fled, pursued by Achilles. They passed the lookout point, at the end of the spur, and came to the springs near where the Trojan women washed their clothes. Undoubtedly, this place was at Madingley, and it has a plentiful supply of natural spring water. It is possible that the place where the Trojan women washed their clothes is now the lake immediately north of the Church of St. Mary Magdalene. I am unable to find a warm spring near here but the Historical Monuments Commission's report on Madingley has some interesting things to say in connection with the other spring mentioned by Homer. We are told, 'A powerful spring' near Moor Barns Farm 'doubtless supplied the famous Bath'. It was 'thought to be one

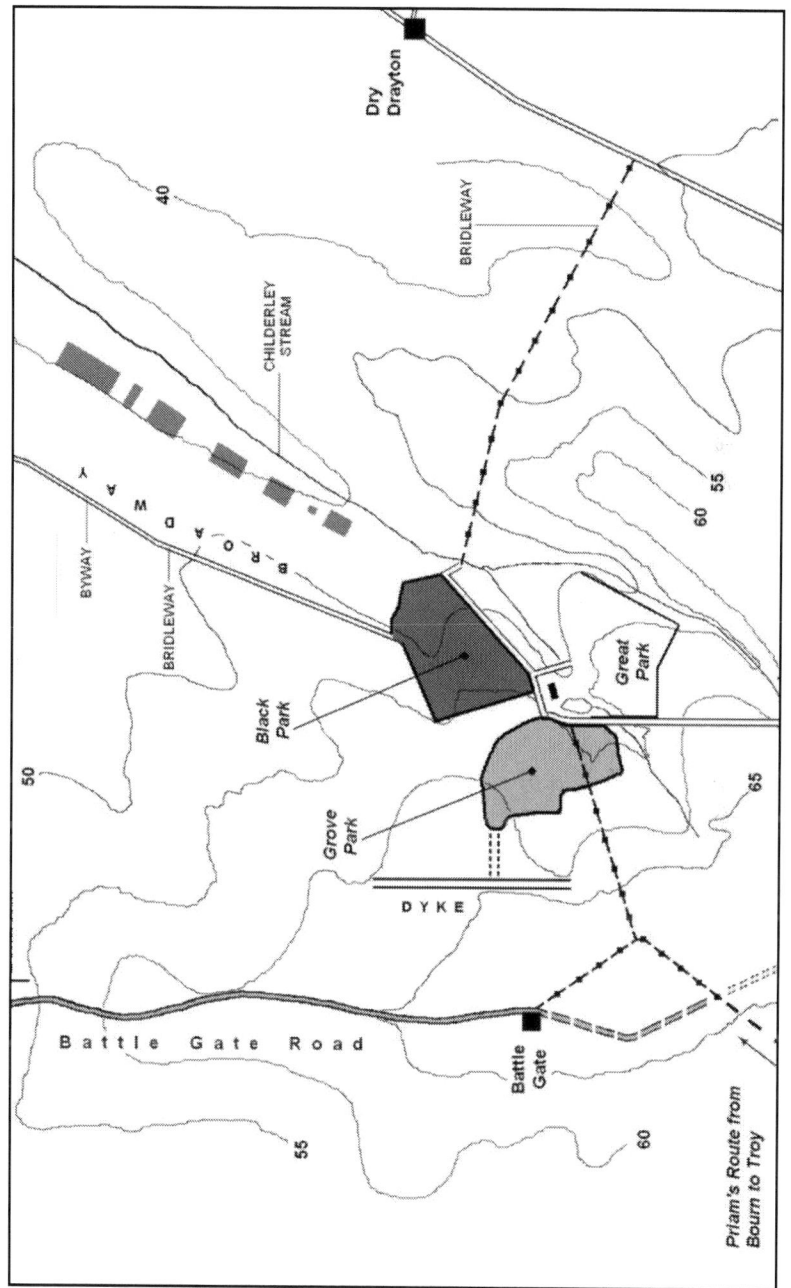

MAP 37. CHILDERLEY; ROUTES AND GATES.

of the coldest in England'.[459]

Homer mentions one gate by name but he only refers to it once, when Achilles is chasing Hector around Troy:

> "More than once Hector made a dash for the Dardanian Gates, hoping as he slipped along under the high walls to be saved from his pursuer by the archery of those above; but Achilles, keeping always to the inner course, intercepted him every time and headed him off towards the open country".[460]

The 'Dardanian' Gate can only be at the end of the bridleway or 'Broad Way' that leads from Childerley to Lolworth along the westernmost of the three spurs. We have already identified this as one of the gates. So it seems that the walls of Troy were built following the contours of the ground around these three spurs. How far around Troy they extended we do not know. But Homer refers to the city as 'strong-walled Ilion' so we can only believe that the walls completely enclosed the city. The walls were 'steep' with 'massive' battlements and the main gate was 'strong' and 'lofty'. When the Trojan warriors flooded back from the plain to the city they came from the River Cam at Grantchester following the cart track, or the ancient highway, skirting to the north of the Uplands of West Cambridgeshire. They passed the village of Madingley heading towards Dry Drayton. King Priam, from his vantage point along the north-eastern spur, had an uninterrupted view and saw them approaching from the southeast. The gates were opened and the panic-stricken warriors flooded into the city. And there really is only one position where the Main Gate could have been. That is its most strategic position, where the village of Dry Drayton is located and where the ground slopes gently upwards from the lower-lying land. Immediately south of Dry Drayton there is a footpath across the fields, which joins the bridleway to Childerley. Immediately south of the footpath there is also a track across the fields. Either of these may have been the route from the Main Gate to the city. A third possibility, however, is that the actual route from the Main Gate has been replaced by the road coming south from Dry Drayton.

It can be seen that in the Bronze Age Childerley was truly of a vast size, probably around 26 square kilometres. It extended from the A428 in the south to the A14 in the north, and from Boxworth in the north west to Dry Drayton in the south east. There is also a possibility that the walls of the city in the north extended from Dry Drayton towards or beyond Madingley. It appears now beyond question that Childerley is the actual Bronze Age city of Troy. Even the land at Childerley matches Homer's account. He says that Troy was 'deep-soiled', and this description is confirmed by the owners of the Childerley Estate.

PRIAM'S PALACE.

When Homer tells us that the temple of Athena and the temple of Apollo were situated in the upper part of the city he is separating out Priam's domain and providing us with a visual picture of the layout. In this way he tells us that Priam's palace and the other buildings were not in the upper part of the city. They were located, therefore, on lower ground. Black Park is situated on the lower ground at Childerley, parts of which are as much as 15 metres below Grove Park. Black Park extends about 500 metres in a north-easterly direction, away from Childerley Hall. The land at Childerley drains north towards the fen, and Black Park loses about 9 metres in height over its length. The north eastern portion extends over the brow of the escarpment. A palace in this position would be strategically positioned to take advantage of the topography and the commanding views from the northwest to the northeast. Specifically, the Trojans would have been able to view the mouth of the Satniois (11 kilometres) and the port of Troy, Tenedos (17 kilometres) and its port, the mouth of the Scamander (15 kilometres), and the southern Hellespont.

Homer informs us that King Priam's palace was a magnificent house fronted with marble colonnades. It contained the King's private apartments, with a courtyard, stables for horses and mules, and accommodation for chariots and carts. Here, I believe, is the site of King Priam's palace where, after being burnt to the ground, it was forever afterwards known as 'Black Park'. But the city was still more extensive than this. Homer tells us there were buildings behind the palace. There were fifty apartments of polished stone, adjoining each other, where the King's sons slept with their wives. Paris had a house near the palace, which had sleeping quarters, a hall and a courtyard.

Hector also had a house nearby with many rooms and spacious halls. In addition, there were twelve adjoining bedrooms for his daughters and sons-in-law, as well as the house of Deiphobus.[461] Of course, present day Childerley shows no obvious signs of its magnificent Bronze Age past, so where are all these buildings likely to have been? Probably the most important clue to their location is the knowledge that many of them were 'behind the palace,' and we may have indications from aerial photography that something extensive is present in the fields to the northwest of Black Park. These markings run along the 40-metre contour line, between the Childerley-Lolworth bridleway and the Childerley stream. Even if the houses of Hector and Paris were contained within the boundaries of Black Park, there is a possibility that these markings may be the site of the fifty apartments belonging to King Priam's sons.

THE NAME OF TROY

The Trojan War took place in Britain 1,100 years before the Romans visited the island. 1,500 years would pass by before the coming of the Angles and the Saxons, and 2,300 years before the arrival of the Normans. Original British names would be passed on to these new people but they would be pronounced slightly differently. Even if these people were literate it is highly unlikely that they would write or pronounce the British names correctly. But place-names continue to exist over very long periods of time despite being altered slightly. Many of them, although they are now anglicised, are still recognisable.

When pronounced in English the difficult sounds are dropped so that the words become easier to say. Of course, the words then have no meaning in English as they did before, but this is what happens. Fortunately, we are not choosing names at random. In fact, it is quite the reverse. We are coming to the end of a very long journey where the focus of our investigation has continually contracted until it is now at its end point. That end point is the Bronze Age city of Troy, and the meaning of the name of Childerley itself.

The final clues to confirming the location of the city of Troy comes from the modern name of 'Childerley' and the Domesday names 'Cildrelai' and 'Cilderlai'. All of these are correct to a certain extent but it requires a small amount of work to discover the original name and its related meaning.

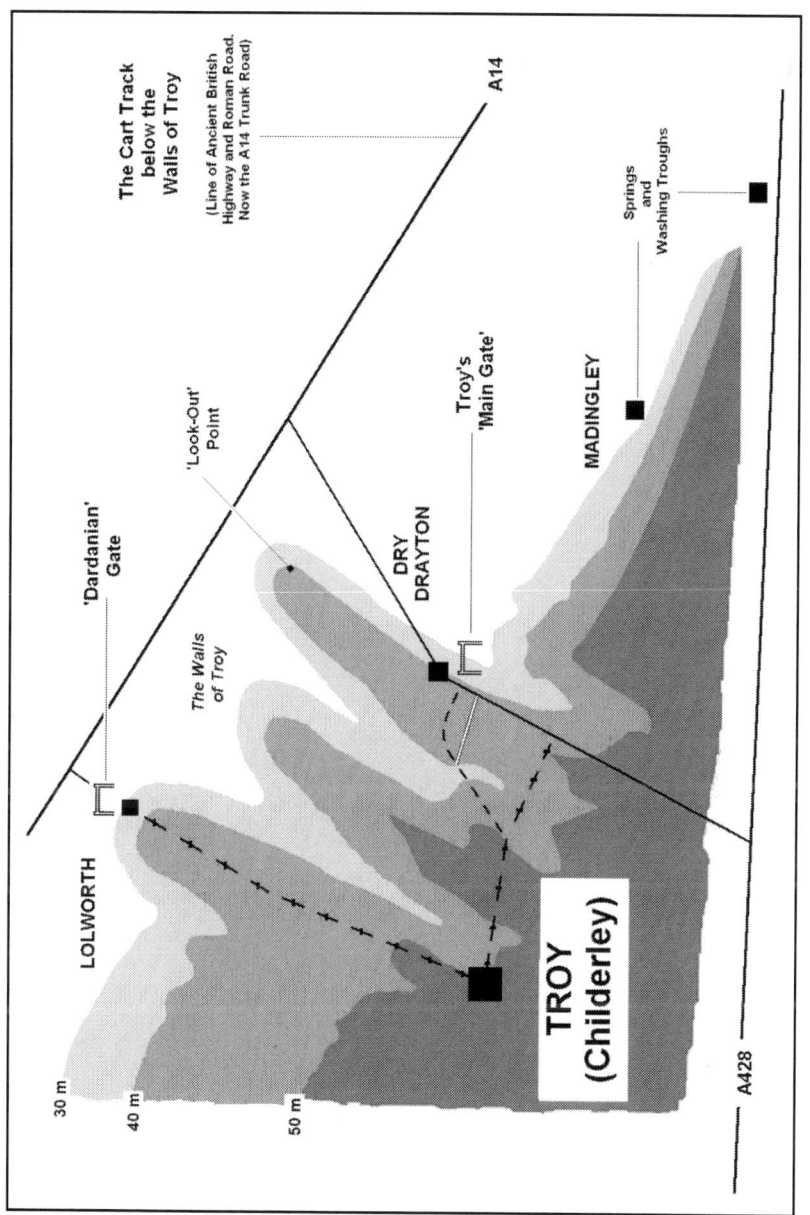

The Cart Track
below the
Walls of Troy

(Line of Ancient British
Highway and Roman Road.
Now the A14 Trunk Road)

A14

'Dardanian'
Gate

'Look-Out'
Point

The Walls
of Troy

Troy's
'Main Gate'

Springs
and
Washing Troughs

MADINGLEY

DRY
DRAYTON

LOLWORTH

30 m

40 m

50 m

TROY
(Childerley)

A428

MAP 38. TOPOGRAPHY.

Let us reconstruct the original name, and then show how the changes have taken place over time:

Original Name = 'CHWILDRELAI'

1st change: → CHIL-DRELAI   ('w' sound dropped)

2nd change: → (a) CHIL-DERLAI   ('r' + 'e' swapped)

or

(b) CIL-DRELAI ('h' sound dropped)

3rd change: → (a) CHIL-DERLAI becomes CHILDERLEY

or

(b) CIL-DRELAI becomes CILDERLAI

As we can see the changes are quite logical with the most difficult sounds tending to be the first to be dropped, and so on. The second change of name (b) to Cildrelai is that found in the *Domesday Book* of 1086 and is the earliest written reference to the name of Childerley.

Let us now look at the original (reconstructed) name and its meaning:

CHWILDRELAI is a shortened version of

CHWIL DRE–ELAI (The two 'e' sounds merge into one)

Which gives:

Name	Meaning
CHWIL	Whirling, turning, revolving.
DRE	Town

ELAI   Ilium

The meaning equates approximately to 'Turning Town Ilium'. This description will be understood better if we look at some other words associated with **Chwil**. For example, *Chwil* (substantive) means 'a search' or a 'scrutiny', and *Chwiliog* means 'a sorcerer' or a 'seer'. A related word *Chwyl* can mean 'an orbit' whereas the verb *Chwylo* means 'to turn' or 'to revolve'. All of this would seem to indicate the fact that Troy was renowned for its study of the heavens. It is also in agreement with Morgan's statement that the city of Troy was associated with a representation of the stellar Universe. The verb *Chwylo* has exactly the same meaning as the verb *Tro*, which we dealt with earlier. It was the esoteric meaning behind the labyrinth and the names of Tros and Troy.

The name of CHILDERLEY then can be interpreted as 'Turning Town Ilium'. More correctly, however, it is **Troy Town Ilium**, and this is the reason why Homer uses the two names for the city in the *Iliad*. Why Homer consistently used the two names of Troy and Ilium throughout his work has never before been satisfactorily explained. It was, of course, impossible to explain because the original name of the city was an ancient British name. And, of course, it is definitive proof not only of the location of Troy but also of its identity. Childerley (Chwyldrelai) is Troy Town Ilium, Homer's Bronze Age city of Troy.

ENDNOTES

[428] Finley, *The World of Odysseus*, pp. 43-44
[429] See Graves, *Greek Myths*, 158; Diodorus 4, Dionysius 1.
[430] Morgan, *The British Kymry*, p25
[431] Ibid. pp. 23-25
[432] Ibid. p23
[433] Graves, *Greek Myths*, 158.1
[434] Dionysius 1.17; Hesiod, Catalogues of Women and Eoiae, 82
[435] Apollodorus, Epitome, vi. 20-22
[436] Morgan, *The British Kymry*, p19
[437] *Iliad*, 2.824

438 Guest, *Origines Celticae*, p23

439 Ibid. p229

440 Hesiod, Hymn to Aphrodite, 109

441 Jordanes, The Origin and Deeds of the Goths, IX

442 Morgan, *The British Kymry*, p24

443 Hesiod, The Cypria.

444 Dares Phrygius, pxxxix.

445 *Aeneid*, 2.21

446 *Iliad*, See for example 3.305, 9.419, and 15.71

447 See Royal Commission on Historical Monuments, West Cambridgeshire, under Childerley.

448 Hesiod, The Little Iliad.

449 See *A History of the County of Cambridge and the Isle of Ely*, Vol. 9, Chesterton, Northstowe, and Papworth Hundreds, pp. 386-392, Eds. Wright and Lewis.

450 See the series of articles on Station Road, Swavesey, Published by Stephen Bull in Swavesey's Meridian Magazine.
       Also available on www.swavesey.org.uk/meridian/s_bull_station_rd

451 Hesiod, The Sack of Ilium.

452 *Aeneid*, 2.246-246

453 Dares Phrygius, pxxvii

454 *Iliad*, 3. 259-263

455 Ibid. 6.237 and 393

456 Ibid. 11.170

457 Ibid. 21.520 - 22.138

458 Ibid. 22. 143-156

459 See Royal Commission on Historical Monuments, West Cambridgeshire, under Madingley.

460 *Iliad*, 22. 194-199

461 Ibid. 6. 242-250 and 312-317

17

**TROY:
THE LOST
HISTORY**

At the beginning of this book my original intention of learning something about the early history of the Cymry in Asia and about Aeneas of Troy was subjected to a very early setback. In fact any expectation that existed at all was blown out of the water by the results of the initial investigation. At this early stage it was almost impossible to believe that Troy could not have been in the Aegean and the voyage of Aeneas could not have taken place in the Mediterranean. It would be many years later that the true origins of the Cymry and of Aeneas of Troy would be discovered. By this time history, as generally perceived, would be turned on its head. In reality, of course, it was not the history that had been turned on its head but the geography. The Bronze Age world in which the Trojans lived was not in the Aegean or the Mediterranean. In Chapters 1 to 8 it became evident that it was in a completely different place altogether, whereas chapters 9 to 16 revealed how this corrected Bronze Age environment helped restore the true nature of the geography of Homer's world.

The world in which the Trojans lived was in Britain. It could be said that such a simple statement does not do justice to the years of investigative work that this book has entailed. Nevertheless, it is the plain unadorned conclusion. Recalling the painstaking work that was necessary, however, to get to this point it is somehow difficult to comprehend the achievements. Yet, in practical terms, every step along the way provided more detail about

Homer's Bronze Age geography.

THE GEOGRAPHY OF HOMER'S WORLD

Homer's Thrace was in eastern England where the Bronze Age sea levels were different. The topography of eastern England had changed drastically resulting in the formation of two inland seas. These were the Bronze Age Euxine (Black Sea) and the Hellespont. Having located the river Aesepus and the Nepeian Plain, the Phasis river and the ancient city of Aea at York, this led in turn to the identification of the river Don in England as the ancient division between Europe and Asia. In the Bronze Age these were merely regions of Britain. There were two routes from the Black Sea, with a Thracian Bosporus and a Cimmerian Bosporus. They were distinctive physical boundary markers in Bronze Age Britain but the boundaries made no sense at all when the names were later transferred to the modern Aegean area. The Cimmerian Bosporus had taken its name from the Cimmerians, the ancient British Cymry of Wales. They were not from the modern continent of Asia but from the Bronze Age Asia in Britain. The Cymry can be considered an indigenous race, and their own history is correct in stating that they were 'Men of Asia'. The Brigians or Phrygians were the Brigantes of Britain who called themselves Bryttas, later Britones. The Cimmerian Bosporus allowed passage from the Black Sea into the Cronian Sea whereas the Thracian Bosporus connected the Black Sea with the Hellespont and the Sea of Marmara, or Morimarusa, the Cymric name for the North Sea. The Helle Straits separated Thrace from Samothrace, the modern county of Norfolk. Samothrace, famous for its mysteries, was the ancient home of the Cult of the Dead, or Druidism.

As it transpired this detailed geography was crucial to everything that followed. It enabled the Trojan Plain and Troy's main rivers to be identified. Homer's use of chariots reflected exactly the peculiar characteristics of British warfare. The Trojan War took place in Bronze Age Britain, on the largest plain in England. Historically, the region where the Trojan War took place was always, and continues to be, 'the land of horses'. The correct geography also allowed Homer's descriptions of the plague, the flood, and the fire on the Trojan plain to be explained. The work of the gods in the *Iliad* was due to natural phenomena occurring only in this specific location in England. The invading forces at Troy were an alliance of lords and kings leading their own battalions, and the majority of these came from Britain. Normally referred to as the Achaean confederacy the location of the camp and refuge for the fleet was duly identified. Amazingly, it was also discovered that the Achaean Wall and Ditch perfectly matches the massive defensive earthwork system surviving to the present day in the exact location across the plain.

These discoveries led in turn to the identification of the Land of Troy. Here it was found that king Priam's journey from Troy to the Achaean Camp, in order to ransom Hector's body, could now be re-traced in accordance with Homer's descriptions and the detailed geography of the area. Troy Town Mazes and memorials to Ilus add to the evidence available, and dedications to Helen exist in the very heart of the Land of Troy. Priam's Troy was eventually located and the question of the total disappearance of the Trojans finally resolved. The city of Troy was exactly as Homer described it, and its size was truly vast. The city's topography, the gateways, and the probable port and route taken by the Achaeans on the night that Troy fell have all been determined. Final definitive proof of the location and identity of Homer's Troy is contained in the ancient British name for the city itself.

Homer's geography was the principal means by which the history and the story of Troy have been recovered. But how was it that the history was lost in the first place? There are many reasons for the state of total confusion that existed with regard to the history of Troy.

THE EARLY HISTORY OF WESTERN EUROPE

It may sound incredible but the early history of Western Europe is recorded and documented. These histories stretch back thousands of years, in some cases to within a few generations of the Great Flood. Many of these have been brought together by Herman L. Hoeh in his *Compendium of World History*.[462] They make fascinating reading. These histories contain information about kings and princes of nations and notable events that are either unknown to the classic historians or else receive passing mention only as a myth or legend. Taken together one distinct advantage is the simple fact that they can be cross-checked. Many of the histories mention persons or events connected with the story of Troy, its early history, or the aftermath of the war. Others provide additional evidence for Homer's

Bronze Age geography in northwest Europe.

EARLY IRISH, SCOTS, AND BRITISH HISTORIES

These histories were instrumental in establishing the Bronze Age geography of Homer's day. Yet, to many modern historians they are unbelievable. The Irish maintain Greek origins whilst the Scots derive theirs from Greece and Egypt. On the other hand the ancient British claim descent from Troy and from Gomer, the eldest son of Japeth. To echo a familiar phrase, it all seems too preposterous for words. Writing in 1934 Henry Hubert said that these Celtic peoples 'forged' Mediterranean pedigrees for themselves at the expense of their Celtic inheritance. He then continues:

> "They took bits from the Bible and the Latin historians and geographers. They placed themselves among the great peoples of the world. The only connection they did not boast was the Celtic. They claimed kinship with the Iberians because they called themselves Hiberni, and with the Scythians because they called themselves Scotti. They credited their forbears with the wildest of wanderings, but they did not make them come from the lands which really were the Celtic cradle. So the Celts assumed an illustrious classical pedigree, which they could share with the great civilized peoples, but disowned themselves and their forefathers".[463]

This is only one of the disparaging comments made about these histories. Often they are the result of pure dogma; a dogma which if applied consistently would remove the histories from all the nations of the world. Hubert clearly sees these people as grossly inferior to other people of the world, and regards a classical pedigree as the pinnacle of achievement and the mark of a civilized society. His reasoning allows for no other possibility other than that of forging the histories. The Irish, Scots, and ancient Britons, all have illustrious pedigrees and authenticated histories. They were among the great peoples of the world even before the so-called 'classical civilization' was born.

Comments such as these are also often repeated without the application of reason and, seemingly, with little or no actual knowledge of the histories themselves. Michael Wood tells us that the old world had 'invented' the tale of Troy. He informs us that in the declining days of the late Roman Empire evidence is first found of the Troy tale being appropriated by barbarians as a way of becoming more closely identified with the ancient and superior Roman culture. The Franks also appropriated the tale, he says, and invented their mythical eponymous founder, Francus the Trojan. The Troy tale then found its way to Britain where it was related by Nennius and popularised by Geoffrey of Monmouth. Wood dismisses it all as 'a good story'.[464]

The findings of this book demonstrate quite clearly that the story of Troy is authentic. As far as the ancient accounts of the peoples of the British Isles are concerned they have been thoroughly vindicated. It has also been shown in this book that these histories proved to be surprisingly accurate and trustworthy regarding their geographical and historical accounts. Yet, these histories are part of what Bill Cooper declares is a very large body of historical evidence that is mostly passed over in silence by today's scholars.[465] He refers to Flinders Petrie who, in front of the British Academy in 1917, presented a paper entitled *Neglected British History*. It was Petrie's view that a considerable body of historical documentary source-material was being overlooked if not wilfully ignored by modern historians.[466] Bill Cooper and Flinders Petrie, however, are not alone when it comes to these discoveries. Sadly, the causes of why the history of Troy was lost go much deeper than this.

Herman L. Hoeh explains that the history of early Western Europe, as preserved by the Welsh and the Germans is today almost wholly unknown, having been literally erased from the consciousness of men. He tells us that the history of early Europe and Britain, especially Wales, was extirpated from the English school system.[467] Bill Cooper further informs us that the records that the early Britons have left us are omitted in their entirety from modern history books, the media and the classroom. He goes on to say:

> "I cannot think of any other literate nation on earth that has managed to obliterate from its own history books two thousand years or more of recorded and documented history".[468]

Adrian Gilbert also comments on these tragic affairs. He says that it is clear to the unbiased researcher that Welsh historical records have, through the ages, been deliberately suppressed by the English establishment. It had its early roots in the reign of George I who was the first Hanoverian king of

MAP 39. CELTIC KINGS IN BRITAIN AND GAUL
Celtic kings ruled in Britain from 2094 BC down to the Fall of Troy.
Afterwards, vast numbers migrated to the Low Countries. By the sixth
century BC they had spread across Gaul.

Great Britain and Ireland, and Court historians were worried about nationalistic feelings towards this king. Later, when Queen Victoria married Prince Albert of Saxe-Coburg-Gotha the cleansing of history was taken to a new level. Bishop William Stubbs totally reformed the teaching of British history and established his new curriculum for the teaching of this history in schools.[469] Bill Cooper relates that the final result was that whilst Roman, Saxon, and Norman accounts of history were taught in schools throughout the land the recorded history of the Britons was consigned to oblivion.[470]

EARLY HISTORIES OF GAUL AND THE LOW COUNTRIES

These histories were discussed in chapter 7 and, again, they are not generally known. They commence immediately after the fall of Troy in Britain and cover the various migrations to Gaul and the Low Countries (See Appendix 4). Basically, this is the early history of what would become the modern Western Europe, and covers Isauria, Sicambria, Pannonia, Agrippina, Brabant, Frisia, Belgium, and Gaul itself. The records include those of the Celts, the Franks, the Hapsburgs, the Dukes of Gaul, and the later Kings of France. As previously discussed these records correlate to a remarkable degree whilst they also independently verify the authenticity of the British histories and the history of Troy itself.

As a result of the discoveries made in this book it is now possible to add some additional remarks. Previously, the first notice that existed of the Celts related to the end of the sixth century BC when they were to the north of Marseilles in southern France. We now know that they arrived in the Low Countries as fugitives from Britain immediately after the fall of Troy (See Appendix 8). It is clear then that in the intervening six centuries the Celts had spread right across Gaul. The Celts, however, had been in Britain prior to the Trojan War, and it has always been maintained in the British histories that the Celtic kings were the first kings of Britain. *The Antiquities of Ancient Britain* by Aylett Sammes, 1676, lists all of the kings of Britain from 2094 BC down to the Romans.[471] The first king was Samothes, the founder of the Celtic kingdom. The Celtic kings ruled in Britain for 900 years until the fall of Troy (For further information see Appendix 9).

Surprisingly, there is confirmation that the Celts were in Britain prior to the Trojan War, and it comes from an unexpected quarter. In chapter 10 it was seen that the Argo's voyage to the Black Sea had, in reality, taken place in Bronze Age Britain. Apollonius of Rhodes actually tells us that when the Argonauts commenced the voyage home they passed through the unchartered country of the Celts.[472]

We know that the majority of the fugitives from Troy went to Gaul and the Low Countries. One of the interesting things to emerge from these histories, however, is that a number of different groups went to the Black Sea area first. As the Bronze Age Black Sea was in Britain this means that they went to another part of this country. In the records of the Trojan kings of Isauria (See Appendix 5) we are told that immediately after the Trojan War Francio, the son of Hector, flees from Troy with his brother Turcus to Maeotis, where they rule for 21 years.[473] Maeotis lay to the north of Thrace, east of the modern Yorkshire Wolds. In the records of the Spanish Hapsburgs we are informed that the descendants of Helenus, son of Priam, recaptured Troy and reigned until another war ended the city in 677 BC (See Appendix 10).

Members of the Trojan royal family fled to the northern shores of the Black Sea where they stayed until 439 BC, before migrating to the mouth of the Rhine.[474] The northern shores of the Black Sea in Britain are close to the modern city of York and the Yorkshire Wolds. There is also another reference to 12,000 Trojans going to the northern shores of the Black Sea immediately after the fall of Troy. We are told that some of these settled on the mouth of the Danube. This cannot be the Danube of modern times but the Bronze Age Danube, which the Greeks called Ister. It was situated in Thrace in Britain, immediately south of the Yorkshire Wolds. All of this indicates that these Trojans all went to the same area, in the vicinity of the Cimmerian Bosporus, and near to the Yorkshire Wolds. It indicates that they may have returned to their motherland where the Cymry and the Phrygians were. This particular facet of history, however, does not end here. In the records of the kings of Sicambria and Pannonia we are told that Palamides reigned for 52 years (663-611 BC), and that one of his sons called Parriis went to some islands in the Pontus.[475] The Pontus is the Black Sea again, and the tribe of Pariisi were actually located in Britain between the modern city of York and the North Sea.

The river Danube, the Greek Ister of Thrace in Britain, is a common feature of the histories of the Trojan migrations, except that of Franco who departed from Troy with Aeneas and Antenor. After the Trojan War Priamus II, of the line of Francio son of Hector, commenced his reign on the Danube in 1063 BC and built the city of Sicambria. Clearly, it is from here that the Sicambrians take their name. Over the next nine centuries this line of kings sent settlers to many parts of Europe, including Poland, Russia, France and Ireland for example, so it appears that Sicambrians were in Sicambria for a very long time. There was a large Sicambrian migration in 439 BC for the line of Helenus but, for the Trojan line of Francio, the Sicambrian history continues beyond this down to 118 BC when the account ceases.

Bavo, the Trojan priest-king of the Belgians, commenced his reign on the Rhine in 1179 BC. He had conducted his Trojan fugitives here from the same Danube, a relatively straightforward journey from the shores of eastern England (See Appendix 7). Francus, the king of the Celts in Britain, continued to govern the remnants of the Celts in the Danube basin. Their migration from the same location to Gaul took place about 1045 BC. Francus is attested in the histories of the Celts in Gaul and also in the records of the Celtic kings of Britain.

Trojan fugitives of the line of Helenus went to the Black Sea after the last Trojan War in 677 BC. Marcomirus I then settled these people on the Danube in 441 BC. Evidently, this was in Sicambria because Marcomirus was king of the Sicambri (See Appendix 11). Before he led a migration of Sicambri to the mouth of the Rhine in 439 BC, however, he received a prophecy in council from a pagan priest. Marcomirus was told to go west where Brutus of Troy had previously gone, and he was promised victory over the Gauls and the Romans. Brutus the Trojan had indeed gone west, to the Loire river in France and to Totnes in the south-west peninsular of Britain.

The point to be made here is that Brutus the Trojan is a purely British King. He is not mentioned in Greek or Latin histories. In fact, he is completely unknown to the classic historians. In 439 BC this pagan priest clearly knew the details of Brutus' travels that took place some six and a half centuries earlier, and only a priest or druid who was British could have known this information as a matter of national historic significance. By independently verifying the existence of Brutus the Sicambrian histories indirectly confirm the river Danube to have been in Britain.

THE EARLY HISTORY OF DENMARK. [476]

Danish written history reveals that the first king to rule over the Danish or Cymbric peninsular was Danus. Denmark had originally received its name from the tribe of the Danaan and it passed to the king who took the name of his subjects. The present kings of north-western Europe are all related to him. Danus commenced his reign in 1040 BC, which was the break-up

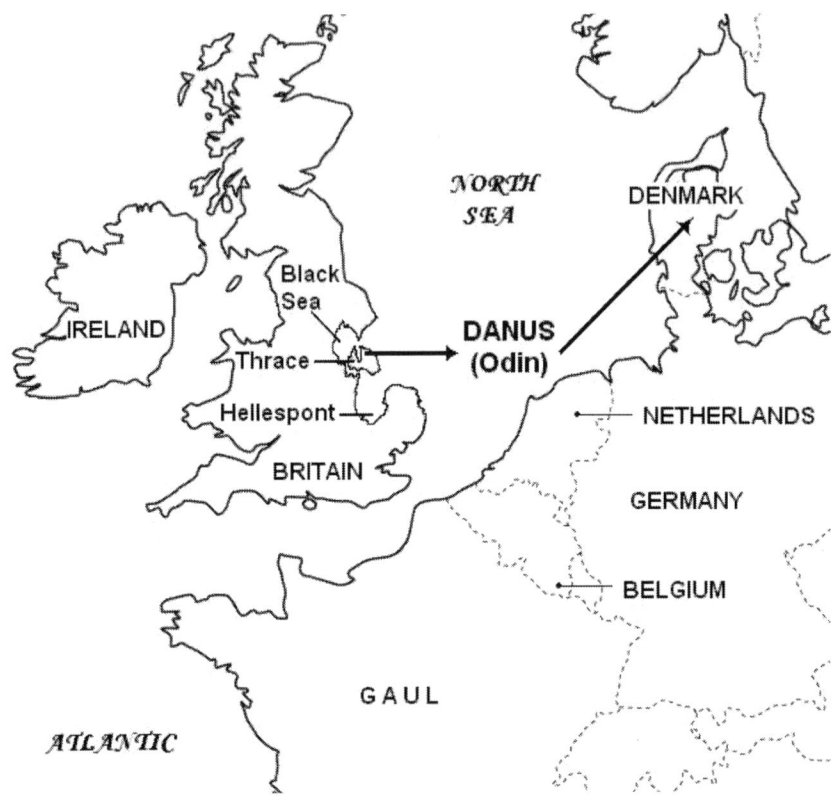

MAP 40. DANUS AND THE DANISH KINGS
Denmark was named after the Irish Danaan (Homer's Danaans).
In 1046 BC Danus (Odin) left Thrace to reign over the Danish people. Danus
was of the House of Troy and eighth in descent from king Priam.

of the German realm when the seafarers of northwest Europe were left without leadership. The inhabitants of Denmark asked the heir to the Trojan House to reign over them. That person was Danus and he lived in Thrace. Danus, also known as Odin, was eighth in descent from king Priam. His genealogical and historical line continues down to 1035 AD to Canute II who united all of Scandinavia and became king of England (See Appendix 16). Herman L. Hoeh informs us that for centuries the Danes revered the history of their nation but it was discarded when the atheistic educational philosophy of German schools permeated their country.

How did the Danaans give their name to Denmark if Homer's Danaans were in Greece in the Bronze Age? Equally, why would the inhabitants of Denmark ask for a king from the Trojan House in the Aegean? The answers are that in reality Homer's Danaans and the Irish Danaan were the same people, and we know from the Irish histories that they went to Denmark. In Homer's corrected Bronze Age environment it is also evident that Danus actually came from Thrace in Britain, and it is only a short distance across the North Sea to Denmark.

THE EARLY HISTORY OF THE GERMANS.[477]

It was mentioned briefly in chapter 12 that the history of Western Europe had been preserved by the Welsh and the Germans. Effectively, the Welsh histories had originated the whole investigative process towards finding Troy. Additionally, they played an important part in reconstructing Homer's Bronze Age geography and thereby authenticating the Trojan history. The early history of the Germans is no less remarkable. It begins with Saturn, the Nimrod of Scripture, and continues down to the time of the Emperor Augustus when anarchy reigned among the German tribes and the ruling families killed each other off (See Appendix 17). After this time, a period of more than 2,000 years, Germany was governed by the royal house of the Sicambrian Franks.

The original beginner of the German (Assyrian) nation was Tuitsch, otherwise Shem. He came with twenty-two descendants plus eight from Japeth and two from Ham. These were the earliest settlers of Europe. Tuitsch made his headquarters at Deutz (Koeln-Deutz) and the country was called Deutschland after him. In the twenty-fifth year of his reign (2190-2189 BC) he held a state assembly, divided lands among his descendants, and ordained laws.

In many ways the German histories are difficult to get to grips with. Their kings include those of Dacia, Mysia, Phrygia, Bithynia, Istria, Arcadia, Emathia, Thrace, the Netherlands, Denmark, the Balkans, and Greece. The German family of nations is also very large, including those of the Getae, Goths, Sabines, Rheinlanders, Hermanduri, Schwabians, Wends, Vandals, Teutones, Bavarians, Huns, Helvetti, Mediomatrices, Franks, Schordisci, and Angles. Much of the geography too is very confusing. Tuitsch, for example, lived in Deutschland (Germany) but brought more colonies

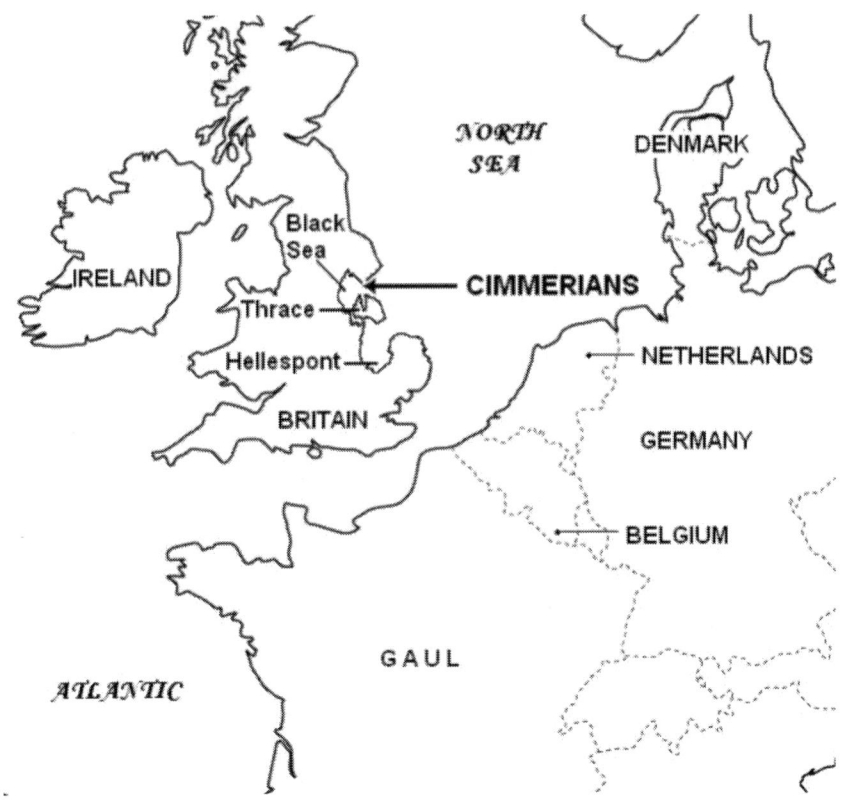

MAP 41. THE ANCIENT CIMMERIANS (KYMRY) OF BRITAIN
German histories give the earliest recorded date for the Cimmerians,
the ancient British Cymry, in the reign of Baier (1489-1429 BC).

from Mesopotamia. Dicla, one of the Dukes of Tuitsch, is thought to have lived on the Rhine, but his descendants migrated to Persia. Baier reigned 1489-1429 BC. He sent an army of Germans and Wends from Germany, Denmark and Gothland to the Balkans. It is evident that in some circumstances modern names have replaced the ancient ones. For example, Brenner II reigned 589-479 BC but he is called an 'Englander' whereas England would not be known for at least a thousand years. In 1978 BC Mannus sends out colonies to France when the country did not yet exist. If Dicla's descendants migrated to Persia, where did they go? The empire of Persia would not be founded for another 1500 years. There is also some confusion with the names of the rivers Don, the Ister, and the Danube. These histories state that Sarmata's son, Tanaus, gave his name to the river Tanais, but it was afterwards called the Don. The Danube was originally called the river Thonau.

In Homer's Bronze Age world the Ister flowed into the Euxine that we now know was in Britain. The Danube that flows into the modern day Black Sea was not originally called the Danube but the Ister. According to Lemprier's *Classical Dictionary* it was the Romans who gave it the name Danube for half its course. The German histories, however, only use the later name of Danube. The previous names, either of Thonau or Ister, must have been changed. These are some of the difficulties that have to be faced by anyone reading these histories. In many ways they are similar to the Irish histories inasmuch that on first reading them the wild wanderings and absurd geography makes no sense at all. Many other places mentioned in the German histories would have added to the confusion were it not for the fact that it is now known that they were in Bronze Age Britain. The German histories deserve detailed study in their own right. Herman Hoeh's work and the various chronicles referred to should be given particular attention.

It should be said at this point that the German histories actually provide material that greatly increases our knowledge of the story of Troy. Evidently, modern historians know nothing about it. This material contains a number of surprises.

One of the first pieces of information that is worthy of attention is that the German king, Herman, is said to have established the kingdoms of Phrygia, Mysia and Bithynia, around 1945-1944 BC. It makes no sense that a king in Germany establishes kingdoms in the Aegean whereas it is only a short crossing from Germany to Britain in the corrected Bronze Age environment. Phrygia had always been in Britain. The German histories also relate that in the reign of Eingeb (1906-1870 BC) 'Myrein, queen of the African Amazons advanced up the Danube but was defeated and slain by Eingeb's generals Seiphyl and Mopser'. This is exactly what we find in the *Greek Myths*, where we are told that the Amazonian queen crossed over from Samothrace to Thrace. Here she encountered king Mopsus and his ally, the Scythian Sipylus, who worsted her in fair fight, and she was killed.[478] It can be seen that it would be straightforward for the German king and his generals to be fighting in Bronze Age Britain but not the other side of the world in the Aegean area. This battle took place in Thrace, the modern Lincoln Wolds, where was the Ister (German Danube).

In the reign of Baier (1489-1429 BC), we are told that a migration occurred that included the German Amazons. They proceeded down the Danube to the Black Sea, on through the Crimea and the Palus Maeotis to Armenia and Cappadocia and the Taurus mountains. 'Here they were known as Cimmerians'. Clearly, this reference to the Danube is the same as before. It means the Greek Ister. Again, it is not the familiar modern-day geography that we have become accustomed to but Homer's Bronze Age geography in Britain. And it places the Cimmerians exactly where, in Chapter 10, they were discovered to have been. This is extraordinary confirmation of our previous findings.

It should be noted too that the histories lay claim only to the Amazons being German, although at a later date they were all called Cimmerians. So who were these Cimmerians before they migrated? They can only have been descendants of the family of Japeth and Gomer who had originally accompanied Tuitsch (Shem) on his initial wanderings. The children of Gomer are the Cimmerians, the Cymry of ancient Britain.

The following information, however, is so astounding that it is given exactly as found in Hoeh's work. It begins with Larein, the fifteenth king of the Germans (1328-1277 BC), and continues down to Wolfheim Siclinger, the twentieth king (1114-1056 BC). See Table 3.

These histories claim that Laertes, Odysseus, and Hector, were all German kings, which comes as something of a revelation. Brenner is otherwise unknown. Yet, these entries are no more than simple statements that the Germans knew the Trojans, they knew and had dealings with king Priam, they knew about the Trojan War, and they took part in it themselves. Evidently, they also married into the Trojan Royal House. What is important is the fact that, once again, these histories independently verify the authenticity of the history of Troy.

TABLE 3
GERMAN KINGS FROM LAREIN TO WOLFHEIM SICLINGER

15. Larein (1328-1277 BC)
Son of Adalger. This is the Laertes of Trojan fame, mentioned by the Roman historian Tacitus. During his rule an army set out from Germany and went via Poland and Ruthenia to the Danube valley. Here it was joined by Germans who had come to the area some 150 years earlier, and the combined forces fell into Asia Minor under their leader Mader and their queen Aloph. They passed through Phrygia and settled in Armenia.

16. Ylsing or Ulsing (1277-1224 BC)
Son of Larein. This is the Trojan Ulysses of Tacitus. He is also the Greek Odysseus who sailed out to the Atlantic and up to the Rhine. Built Emmerick on the Main. During his reign the Germans under Galter again invaded Asia Minor and settled on the banks of the river Sangarius. Priam of Troy tried in vain to expel them, finally made a treaty, and they later helped him against the Greeks.

17. Brenner or Breno (1224-1186 BC)
Son of Ylsing, in whose reign Prichs ruled the Germans on the Black Sea and the women under queen Themyschyr conquered Bithynia, Paphlagonia and Cappadocia.

18. Heccar (Hykar or Highter) (1186-1155 BC)
Son of Brenner. He is the famous Hector of the First Trojan War. He was of great help to Priam. Teutschram, king of the Germans of Transylvania and son-in-law of Priam also sent help.

19. Frank (Francus or Franco) (1155-1114 BC)
Son of Heccar. From him descended the German Franks or Franconians. In his days Amar, queen of the German Amazons burned the temple in Ephesus.

20. Wolfheim Siclinger (1114-1056 BC)

Son of Frank. He sent another great migration of settlers from Germany to the Black Sea.

THE HISTORY OF LATER TIMES

The Trojan War took place in Britain. It is, primarily, a part of the history of Britain and the British Isles. In the three thousand years that followed, however, numerous events would contribute to the loss of knowledge of these Trojan times. Indeed, it could be said that the whole history had been lost. These times were often the times of war, of subjugation by foreign nations, of injustices inflicted on people in the name of religion, and of persecution by monarchies and governments. These events would have far-reaching consequences. It is both ironic and lamentable that, unknown to the perpetrators, they were destroying not only the knowledge relating to the history of Troy but that which related to their own early history as well.

THE ROMANS.

The Trojan War devastated the country and there was vast migration to the continent. The first major event to affect Britain after this was the Roman Invasion, and it had repercussions on a national scale. As Peter Beresford Ellis remarks, 'It is a traditional imperialist maxim that to conquer a nation you must first subvert or remove the class which is most dangerous to your objectives, that is – the intellectuals.'[479] In Britain this was the Druidic class so the Romans did their utmost to exterminate them. The account of the massacre of the Druids in Anglesey, Wales, has been recorded for posterity by Tacitus (Annales XIV) to the everlasting shame of the Romans.

The Druids were Britain's historians and the source of all wisdom in the country. They were the teachers of the people and the country's philosophers. They had particular duties to ensure that the nation's history, genealogical record, customs and laws were recorded and preserved. We will never know the extent of the damage or the loss to the country as a result of this Roman policy.

THE SAXONS.

No sooner had the Romans left than Britain was subjected to the Saxon Invasion. Vortigern, the British king, has gone down in history as the infamous ruler who committed treason by inviting them into the country. In contrast to the Romans they never went home. Nennius tells us that the more the Saxons were vanquished, the more they sought for new supplies of Saxons from Germany. Kings, commanders, and military bands were invited over from almost every province, and this practice continued until the time of Ida.[480] When the Roman Occupation of Britain came to an end the country was left depleted of all its fighting men and, as a result, the Britons were eventually pushed to the western extremities of the country, and the British crown was lost. Ethelwerd's Chronicle relates that so greatly did the invasion of those nations spread and increase, that they by degrees obliterated all memory of the inhabitants.[481]

The Saxons, of course, were not averse to treachery. The *Tysilio Chronicle* records how they came to a peace conference with the Britons where it would be decided how many Saxons would be permitted to remain in the country. The Saxons took knives concealed in their clothing and, on a prearranged signal, slew four hundred and sixty kings and chieftains of the Britons.[482] The same chronicle also records how the Saxons extended their ravages from sea to sea, destroying the churches and slaying the men of learning. Gildas laments the fact that if there were any writings and records of Britain they have been consumed in the fires of the enemy, or have accompanied his exiled countrymen into distant lands.[483]

THE CHURCH OF ROME

It may surprise many people to learn that Christianity was first introduced into Britain in 137 AD, by the British king Lucius. He sent to Eleutherius, the bishop of Rome, and requested teachers of the Christian faith. Two learned men arrived, called Dyvan and Fagan. Temples were consecrated and ordinances made for the maintenance of religious worship. Throughout the country Lucius installed thirty-eight bishops, with an Archbishoprick at London, York, and Caerleon.[484] After the Diocletian persecution died out Christianity flourished to such an extent that at the Council of Arles in 314 AD the British Church was actually represented by bishops from the three Archbishopricks in Britain.[485]

The conquests and settlement of the Saxons, however, had overthrown all of British Christianity in the eastern and central parts of the country.[486] What followed was the introduction of a new Christianity with the arrival in the sixth century of Augustine, bishop and emissary of the Pope. Roman domination had reappeared in a new guise.

The Britons were entreated to jointly preach the gospel to the Saxons, and submit to Roman Catholic obedience and papal authority. They refused. Augustine threatened them that if they refused peace they would suffer death at the hands of the Saxons. Instigated by this so-called 'man of god' the Saxons slew 1,200 distinguished scholars and monks of the celebrated monastery at Bangor.[487] This educational institution never recovered. The original British Church refused to capitulate. It was first condemned as non-Catholic and was afterwards openly declared heretical by Rome. The clergy of the British Church were gradually removed and its property transferred to the Roman hierarchy. Eventually, it was completely dispossessed.[488]

C.F. Cusack relates that in Ireland St. Patrick is said to have destroyed all the remnants of pagan writing. She cites material stating that one hundred and eighty tracts of the doctrine of the Druids were condemned to the flames.[489] In England, from 1100 AD onwards, large numbers of Welsh historical records were transferred to the Tower of London, usually as the personal libraries of Welsh princes held captive there. Around 1300, most of these were burned by a monk of the Roman Church.[490]

THE NORMANS

In the reign of Henry II of England the Anglo-Normans became owners and lords of all Ireland. Their tenure was the tenure of the sword. Families were dispossessed of their lands and the natives deprived of everything. Castles were built as a means of controlling the population and the Irish were taxed to pay for the garrisons that supplied them. Castle battlements were generally adorned with the heads of the Irish who had been slain. For more than 600 years the Irish suffered poverty and inhuman deprivation of the most immoral and disgraceful kind. Regardless of who was on the

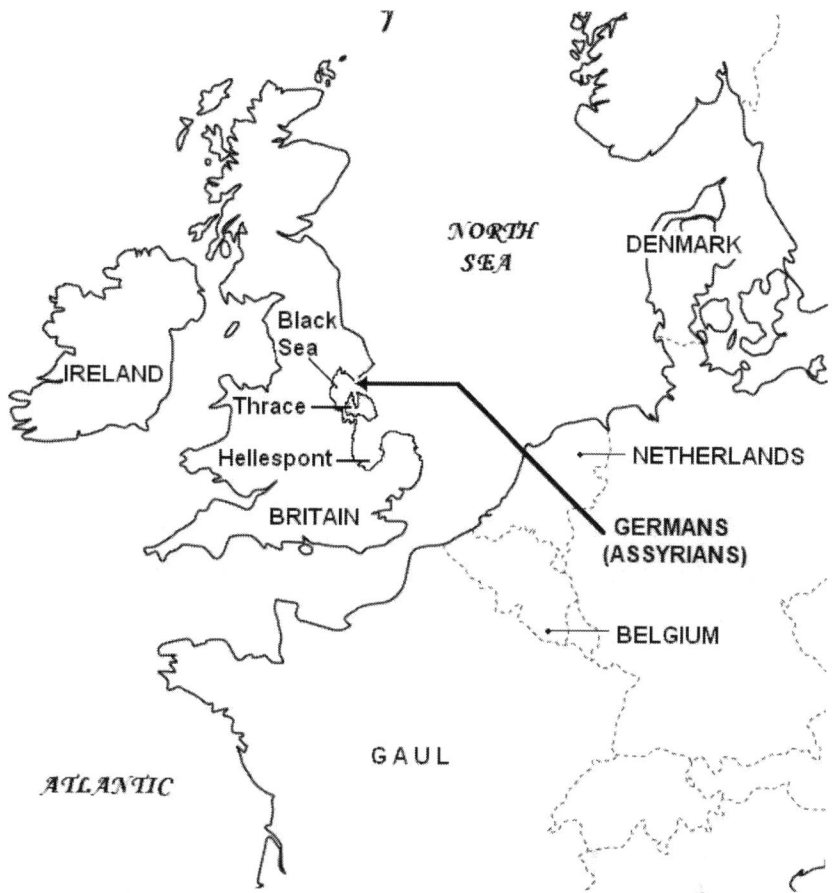

MAP 42. THE ANCIENT GERMAN (ASSYRIAN) KINGS.
German kings sent many migrations of settlers to the Black Sea. Their histories record their knowledge of the Trojan War, their assistance to the Trojans, and intermarriage with the Trojan Royal House.

throne of England Irish poverty and misery were treated with contempt and indifference.

The Irish people were shut out from the law, civil society, and religion. In the reign of Henry VIII a scheme was put into effect to kill or carry away their cattle and to destroy their corn. Cathedrals were destroyed, abbeys plundered, and monks and friars put to the sword or hanged. Every effort of Queen Mary and her emissaries was directed to dispossess the Irish Catholics of their property and exterminate them. Cromwell landed in Ireland in 1649, and the majority of the Catholic nobility and gentry were soon banished. The rest of the nation was sent to Connaught, the most wasted province of Ireland. All the property of the Irish people was declared to belong to the English army. Of the thousands of young children left destitute 6,000 boys and girls were sent as slaves to the West Indies. The Irish who refused to surrender their houses and lands were punished as 'rebels' in the courts known as 'Cromwell's Slaughter-houses', and hanged.

The majority of the Irish nation had by now been disposed of, either by banishment, transportation, or hanging. Yet, this was not the end of their purgatory. Further penal laws continued to be enacted against the Catholics, which were of the grossest atrocity. These laws prohibited the Irish from practising their religion and educating their children. Trade laws prevented them from earning a living, whereas embargo laws prohibited the merchants from trading with foreign nations. For the Irish that were left there was no option but to emigrate, steal, or starve to death. In 1739 about half a million people starved when severe frost destroyed the potato crops.[491] Over all these years the Irish were locked in a living hell. It is a miracle that we have an Irish nation today let alone any surviving Irish historical records. Peter Beresford Ellis tells us that most of the Irish pedigrees and family histories were scrupulously kept until the devastating English conquests of the seventeenth century when the native intelligentsia and the ruling families were destroyed or driven into exile. Most of the written records were also destroyed.[492]

The ancient Britons had been shut up in the western extremity of Britain that came to be called 'Wales' by the English (from the Saxon Wealas), a disparaging term meaning 'foreigners'. Through ignorance the English do not even know the meaning of this derogatory term and how hypocritical it is for them to call the Cymry foreigners in their own land. It could be said with some justification that the Cymry of 'Wales' could never have hoped to withstand the might of the Normans and their technology. They were, however, fighting for the last remnants of their country. It was an inequitable struggle for the Cymry but the Norman conquest of Wales took more than 200 years to complete. Llywellyn, the last native prince, met his death in 1282 AD. His head was cut off and taken to King Edward who had it borne through London on the point of a lance and then set up over the gateway of the Tower. Like the Red Men of North America the Cymry were dispossessed of their lands. In 1485 Richard III, the last Norman king, was killed at the Battle of Bosworth. Henry Tudor became king. Ironically, Henry Tudor was of Welsh descent.

MORE MODERN TIMES

It was the ancient Britons (Welsh) who consistently asserted their Trojan descent. The final observations as to why knowledge of the history of Troy was lost is restricted to them and relates to events from the Normans into more recent times. These events would have consequences that are still immeasurable.

In his *History of Wales* B.B. Woodward tells us that in the twelfth century AD the most illustrious scholars of the Cymry studied in England, or at Paris. It was thus, in 1169, that Henry II issued an edict requiring that 'If any Welshman, cleric or laic, shall come into England, unless he have passports from our lord the king, let him be apprehended and put in prison; and let all Welshmen who are in the schools in England be turned out'.[493] Two hundred years later an outright attempt at suppressing the Welsh language was put into effect by Richard II who attempted to prohibit writing in Wales. His immediate successor, Henry IV, was no different. He had an act of Parliament passed that prohibited writing materials and equipment from being imported into Wales. Richard III was crowned in 1483. He prohibited the use of printing presses outside London, and particularly in Wales. It would take more than two hundred years for the Welsh nation to be allowed such equipment.[494] This barbarism continued under Henry VIII when the so-called 'Acts of Union' were passed by the English Parliament in 1536 and 1542. In truth, they were not Acts of 'Union' but 'Annexation', which were their original title.[495] As a result, all Welsh laws and customs different to England were abolished, and all legal procedures conducted in Wales in the Welsh language were prohibited. The Acts specifically forbade the enjoyment of every kind of office throughout the king's dominions to persons using the Welsh tongue.[496]

Even in the nineteenth century these outrages continued. In 1846 the English Parliament set up a 'Commission' to investigate teaching in Welsh schools. Three monoglot Anglican barristers from England, knowing little about Wales and even less about the Welsh language, reported that the Welsh language was hindering the improvement of education. After the commissioners reported an act of Parliament was duly passed. The teaching of the Welsh language in Welsh schools was prohibited. All Welsh teachers were removed and replaced with English ones. All children were to be taught only in English and any child who uttered a Welsh word was punished. Adrian Gilbert explains how the system worked in the schools:

> "To enforce the ban, the 'Welsh not' was introduced into the classroom. This was a heavy piece of wood strung onto a length of rope, which struck fear into the hearts of the children. Any child who inadvertently uttered the forbidden language had the dreaded 'Welsh not' placed around his or her neck. The next child to make the same mistake had the feared token passed over to them, and so it went on for the rest of the day. At the end of classes the one unfortunate enough to be wearing the infamous collar was caned as an example to the rest".[497]

In this respect, it is interesting to look at a Log Book of the times, from one of the schools in Wales. It is written by the Headmaster who had the job of exterminating the Welsh language in his school.[498] In this Log Book there are continuous references to pupils being punished for speaking their own language, and in the playground as well as in the classroom. On one occasion he writes, the 'Welsh Stick was rather effective this afternoon'. On another he says, 'By continual application and diligence I have prevailed at last as regarding Welsh speaking during school time'. The excerpts from

TABLE 4
EXCERPTS FROM TOWYN SCHOOL LOG BOOK 1863-1876

9th March 1865:

"I was much troubled today with the Welsh speaking, which is a continued impediment in our Welsh schools – I have tried all imaginable plans but have totally failed in the case of many children – nothing will cause them to yield – I must consult H.M.Inspector".

2nd November 1865:

"Much trouble is given me by the continual practice of some of the children in speaking Welsh in the playground and even in the schoolroom. It is very difficult to discover a just punishment for the crime".
12th July 1866:

"Welsh is spoken too freely in and without the school. Have had occasion to refer to this ---- drawback, and cannot --- a suitable process of punishment to get rid of the evil".

the Towyn School Log Book show quite clearly the Headmaster's endeavours to eliminate the Welsh language for what he sees as the greater good. Unfortunately, they also show the extent of his indoctrination.

The system was clearly effective, resulting in the majority of the population being unable to speak their own language or read their own histories. Gilbert says that this was a gross violation of human rights. It was much more than this. It was oppression and persecution of a nation and it disgraces and dishonours the English establishment. In recent years a number of world leaders have publicly apologised on behalf of their nation for the wrongs inflicted on others. In 1993 Russia apologised for the 1968 invasion of Czechoslovakia. In 1995 Jacques Chirac apologised for the involvement of French people in persecuting Jews during the German occupation of France. The American President, Bill Clinton, publicly apologised for slavery in the United States. More recently, the Australian government apologised to the indigenous Australian people for the injustices committed by successive parliaments. Whether or not there is ever a public acknowledgement of the wrongs inflicted on the Irish and Welsh remains to be seen. In the meantime it would be prudent to heed the warning given by Peter Beresford Ellis:

"Language is the highest form of cultural expression. The decline of the Celtic languages has been the result of a carefully established policy of brutal persecution and suppression. If these Celtic languages die then it will be no natural phenomenon. It will be as the result of centuries of a careful policy of ethnocide. Once these languages disappear then Celtic civilization will cease to exist and the cultural continuum of three thousand years will come to an end. The world will be the poorer for one more lost culture".[499]

HOMER: THE BEGINNING AND THE END

To say that this book is indebted to Homer is something of an understatement. Nevertheless it is true. He has been the fountain of knowledge by which the story of Troy has been seen through to its conclusion. Surprisingly, almost nothing is known about him. It is not known, for example, who Homer was, where or when he lived, or even if his name really was Homer. It is generally considered that his work, the *Iliad*, was orally composed between 850 and 950 BC and first written down about four hundred years later. Most of the surviving manuscripts are from the fourteenth and fifteenth centuries AD. It was at this time that Italians brought back a large number of them from the Byzantine Empire. The first printed version appeared in Florence in 1488 AD, followed by many others that permeated Europe after the sixteenth century.

In Michael Wood's examination of the legend of Troy he declares that Homer's *Iliad* and *Odyssey* 'stand at the beginning of European literature – and these beginnings are unexcelled masterpieces'.[500] It comes as no surprise now to be able to confirm that the *Iliad* is a masterpiece, but in so many different ways. Clearly, it is the greatest reference work on the Bronze Age world. Homer describes with great accuracy an infinite number of matters relating to the natural world and the environment of the Greeks and the Trojans. He gives flawless accounts of the oceans and the climate, the landscapes, people and cultures. He identifies and locates the land of Troy by astronomical means, before ever maps were available or known. His descriptions of metals, priests and prophets, chariot fighting, and the combatants in the war were all instrumental to locating Troy and determining Homer's Bronze Age geography. Homer also perfectly describes the place where the Trojan War took place, the land of Troy, and Priam's city.

As a reference work the subject matter covered in the *Iliad* is truly monumental. It includes anthropology, zoology, sociology, biology, cosmology, and theology, but to refer to its contents as encyclopaedic does not do it justice. Homer provides information that embraces technology, arts and crafts, history, geography and climate, ornithology, philosophy, mythology, and much more besides. His work is kaleidoscopic. Above all, he distils and purifies the knowledge into the narrative of his work in such a way that the *Iliad* will forever remain an enigma.

Now that it is clear that the *Iliad* is the authoritative record of the Trojan War that took place in Britain it follows that Homer must have been British. There is no other way that he could have recorded a myriad details in the *Iliad* that only apply to Britain in specific locations and in very specific ways. And it is this fact that helps identify who he was. At the beginning of this book the search for the origins of the Cymry commenced its long and tortuous journey. It is only fitting, therefore, that the book ends with them because the Cymry and Homer are inextricably linked:

> "Homer is one of the mutatative forms of the word Gomer – the 'g' being under certain laws dropped. The *Iliad*, assigned to Homer, is a collection of the Heroic Ballads of the Bards of the Gomeridae or Kymry on the great catastrophe of their race in the east. It was originally composed in the Kymric or Bardic characters. These were afterwards changed by the Greeks into the Phoenician, and in so doing they were compelled to drop the Kymric radical 'Gw'. Hence the metrical mutilation in the present Greek form of the *Iliad*".[501]

In very simple terms Gomer, in English, becomes Omer in Greek, and is given the ending –os. So, Omeros (Homer) is Gomer. Homer, therefore, may not necessarily be a name as such but the actual title of the poet of the race of Gomer. Equally, it also means Gomer, the Cymry of Britain.

The Greeks revered Homer. As Lattimore informs us in the introduction to his *Iliad* they believed that one of the episodes of their own early history was the Trojan War. For most of them it was genuine history and not a myth.[502] Their belief in this history has finally been vindicated.

This book changes nothing about the story of Troy. Only the geography has changed. The great difference is that Troy has been found and its history has been duly authenticated. Furthermore, the early histories of many European nations provide the ultimate verification. So, was the Trojan War the greatest catastrophe of the ancient world? Is it the greatest story ever told? There is no dilemma here because the answer to both questions is yes. And what of the accounts that the Trojan War devastated Europe and Asia and plunged the known world into a Dark Age that lasted five hundred years? Nothing could be further from the truth. The Trojan War is the cardinal point in both British and European history and British and continental records prove there was never any 'Dark Age'. The evidence shows that the historical account is continuous down to modern times. Consequently, the Story of Troy can now be removed from the realm of myth and be placed firmly into the historical arena.

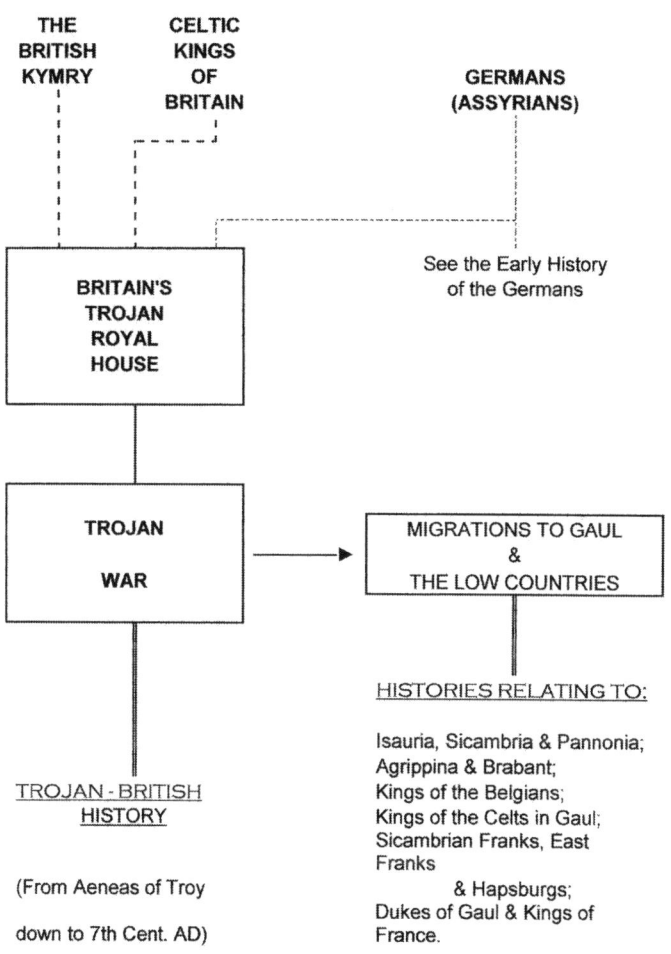

TROY: THE LOST HISTORIES

THE BRITISH KYMRY

CELTIC KINGS OF BRITAIN

GERMANS (ASSYRIANS)

See the Early History of the Germans

BRITAIN'S TROJAN ROYAL HOUSE

TROJAN WAR

MIGRATIONS TO GAUL & THE LOW COUNTRIES

TROJAN - BRITISH HISTORY

(From Aeneas of Troy

down to 7th Cent. AD)

HISTORIES RELATING TO:

Isauria, Sicambria & Pannonia;
Agrippina & Brabant;
Kings of the Belgians;
Kings of the Celts in Gaul;
Sicambrian Franks, East Franks
    & Hapsburgs;
Dukes of Gaul & Kings of France.

FIG. 20. TROY: THE LOST HISTORIES.
British and continental histories prove there was no
'Dark Age' following the Trojan War.

ENDNOTES

462 Pub. 1963, Ambassador College, Pasadena, California, and on www.earth-history.com

463 Hubert, *The History of the Celtic People*, pp. 26-27

464 Wood, *In Search of the Trojan War*, pp. 39 and 42

465 Cooper, *After the Flood*, p36

466 Ibid, p54

467 Hoeh, *Compendium of World History*, Vol. 1, Ch. 19, p2

468 Cooper, *After the Flood*, pp. 42-43

469 Gilbert, Wilson, and Blackett, *The Holy Kingdom*, pp. 6 and 30

470 Cooper, *After the Flood*, p43

471 Sammes, *The Antiquities of Ancient Britain*, pp. 145-146

472 *The Voyage of Argo*, trans. Rieu, p164

473 Hoeh, *Compendium of World History*, Vol. 2, Ch. 12, p3

474 Ibid. Vol. 2, Ch. 12A, pp. 2-5

475 Ibid. Vol. 2, Ch. 12, p4

476 Hoeh, *Compendium of World History*, Vol. 2, Ch. 5

477 Hoeh, *Compendium of World History*, Vol. 2, Ch. 11

478 Graves, *Greek Myths*, 131n and o

479 Ellis, *The Druids*, p16

480 Nennius 50

481 Ethelwerd, in *Six Old English Chronicles*, p5, Ed. Giles

482 *The Chronicle of the Kings of Britain*, pp. 116-117, trans. Roberts

483 Gildas 4, in *Six Old English Chronicles*, p301, Ed. Giles

484 *The Chronicle of the Kings of Britain*, pp. 90-91

485 Elder, *Celt, Druid and Culdee*, p109

486 Woodward, *The History of Wales*, p80

487 *The Chronicle of the Kings of Britain*, pp. 176-179; Bede, Bk. 2, Ch. 2; *The Anglo-Saxon Chronicle* p23

488 Elder, *Celt, Druid and Culdee*, pp. 129-132

489 Cusack, *The Illustrated History of Ireland*, p148

490 Gilbert, Wilson, and Blackett, *The Holy Kingdom*, p30

491 See Cusack's *Illustrated History of Ireland*

492 Ellis, The Druids, p201

493 Woodward, *The History of Wales*, pp. 302-303

494 See *The Holy Kingdom*, p32

[495] Ellis, *The Druids*, p198

[496] Woodward, *The History of Wales*, p576

[497] Gilbert, Wilson, and Blackett, *The Holy Kingdom*, pp. 34-35

[498] Log Book of the Towyn British School, Merionethshire, 1863-1867. (From Merionydd Archives, Gwynedd Archive Services, Wales)

[499] Ellis, *The Druids*, p280

[500] Wood, *In Search of the Trojan War*, pp. 136-141

[501] Morgan, *The British Kymry*, p34

[502] *Iliad*, trans. Lattimore, Intro. P12

PLATE 1: TENBY, SOUTH WALES. TIDE IN.
BRITISH TIDES: MENTIONED BY VIRGIL (*Aeneid*) AND HOMER (*Iliad*)

PLATE 2: TENBY, SOUTH WALES. TIDE OUT.
BRITISH TIDES: MENTIONED BY VIRGIL (*Aeneid*) AND HOMER (*Iliad*)

PLATE 3. APOLLO
Acknowledgement: Wikimedia Commons.
APOLLO WAS A PURELY BRITISH GOD, CALLED MABON
IN WELSH, MEANING 'BOY'. HE WAS THE YOUTHFUL SUN GOD.
IN ROMAN DEDICATIONS IN BRITAIN HE IS IDENTIFIED
AS APOLLO-MAPONUS.

PLATE 4. DRUID STATUE: CROOME PARK, WORCS, UK.
Acknowledgement: Wikimedia Commons
THE DRUIDS CLAIMED DESCENT FROM DIS, KNOWN ALSO AS HADES
OR SAMOTHES. HE WAS THE FIRST KING OF CELTICA, IN BRITAIN,
AND HE LAID THE FIRST FOUNDATIONS OF DRUIDISM IN BRONZE AGE
SAMOTHRACE, NOW NORFOLK IN ENGLAND.

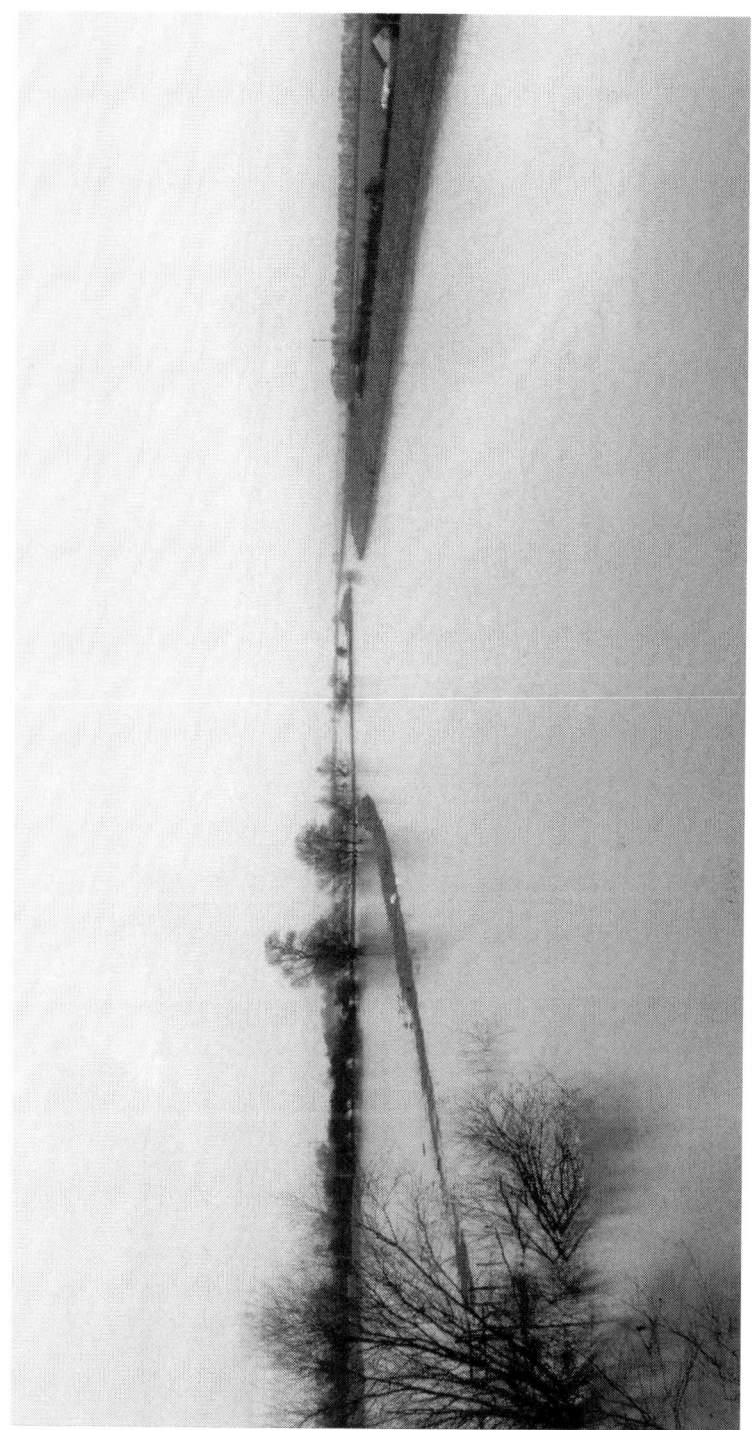

PLATE 5. FLOODING IN CAMBRIDGESHIRE, UK. 2014.
THE BEDFORD RIVERS AND THEIR DYKES SAVE THE LAND FROM DEVASTATION.
HOMER MENTIONS BOTH FLOODING AND DYKES IN THE ILIAD.

PLATE 6. GREEK WATER JAR, BRITISH MUSEUM.
Acknowledgement: JESS BYGD.
ACHILLES CARRIES THE DEAD PENTHESILEIA FROM THE
BATTLEFIELD. TO HIS RIGHT IS A MYRMIDON WARRIOR. HIS SHIELD
DISPLAYS THE TRISKELION SYMBOL OF THE ISLE OF MAN.

PLATE 7. RIDERS ON BROADWAY, CHILDERLEY.
(ONE OF TWO 'BROADWAYS' IN THE LAND OF TROY) HOMER DESCRIBES TROY AS 'TROY OF THE BROAD WAYS'.

PLATE 8. TROY TOWN MAZE: HILTON, CAMBS. (ONE OF A NUMBER OF MAZES IN THE AREA)

PLATE 9. PLOUGHED LAND AT CHILDERLEY.
HOMER USES THE EPITHET 'DEEP-SOILED' LAND OF TROY.

PLATE 10.
A CARVED PANEL OF HELEN IN THE CENTRE OF THE LAND OF TROY.
HELEN WAS A GODDESS OF DEATH AND RESURRECTION.

PLATE 11. DEVIL'S DYKE, CAMBRIDGESHIRE.
(HOMER'S ACHAEAN WALL AND DITCH) VIEW LOOKING SOUTH EAST.

PLATE 12. DEVIL'S DYKE, CAMBRIDGESHIRE.
(HOMER'S ACHAEAN WALL AND DITCH) VIEW LOOKING NORTH WEST.
(MY WIFE STANDS AT THE TOP OF THE MASSIVE EARTHWORK)

Bibliography

Primary Sources

Apollodorus, *The Library*, (1995) trans. Frazer, J.G., London: Harvard University Press.

Apollonius of Rhodes, *Jason and the Golden Fleece*, (1998) trans. Hunter, R., Oxford: Oxford University Press.

Apollonius of Rhodes, *The Voyage of Argo*, (1978) trans. Rieu, E.V., Penguin Books.

Apollonius Rhodius, *Argonautica*, (1967) trans. Seaton, R.C., London: William Heinemann.

Bede, *A History of the English Church and People*, (1988) trans. Sherley-Price, L., London: Penguin Books.

Caesar, *The Conquest of Gaul*, (1982) trans. Handford, S.A., London: Penguin Books.

Cicero, *De Natura Deorum*, (1933) Loeb. Text in the public domain (see penelope.uchicago.edu/Thayer/E/Roman/Texts/Cicero/de_Natura_Deorum/2A*.html)

Dares Phrygius, (1811) translated from the Welsh copy in the Book of Basingwerke, Roberts, P., London.

Diodorus Siculus, (1960) trans. Oldfather, C.H., Loeb Classical Library, Cambridge, MA: Harvard University Press.

Dionysius of Halicarnassus, *Roman Antiquities*, (1960) trans. Cary, E., London: William Heinemann.

Euripides, (1959) Grene, D. and Lattimore, R. (eds) *The Complete Greek Tragedies*, Vol. III., Chicago, Illinois: University of Chicago Press.

Geoffrey of Monmouth, *The History of the Kings of Britain*, (1966) trans. Thorpe, L., London: Penguin Books.

Gerald of Wales, *The Journey through Wales/The Description of Wales*, (1978) trans. Thorpe, L., London: Penguin Books.

Herodotus, *The Histories*, (1972) trans. De Selincourt, A., London: Penguin Books.

Hesiod, *The Homeric Hymns and Homerica*, (1914) trans. Evelyn White, H.G., London: William Heinemann.

Homer, *Iliad*, (1961) trans. Lattimore, R., London: University of Chicago Press.

Homer, *Iliad*, (1973) trans. Rieu, E.V., Norwich: Book Club Associates.

Homer, *Iliad*, (1999) trans. Murray, A.T., London: Harvard University Press.

Homer, *Odyssey*, (1999) trans. Lattimore, R., New York: Harper Collins.

Josephus, *Jewish Antiquities*, (1930) trans. Thakeray, H.St.J., Loeb Classical Library, Cambridge, MA: Harvard University Press.

Lebor Gabala Erenn, (1938-1956) 5 parts, trans. Stewart Macalister, Dublin: Irish Texts Society.

Livy, *The Early History of Rome*, (1971) trans. De Selincourt, A., London: Penguin Books.

Nennius, *History of the Britons*, (1938) Wade-Evans, A.W., London: Church Historical Society.

Pliny, Natural History, (1957) trans. Haberly, L., New York: Frederick Ungar Pub.Co.

Sidonius Apollinaris' Letters, (1915) trans. Dalton, O.M., *www.tertullian. net/fathers/sidonius_letters*

Six Old English Chronicles, (1891) Giles, J.A. (ed), London: George Bell & Sons.

Tacitus, *On Britain and Germany*, (1967) trans. Mattingley, H., London: Penguin Books.

The Ancient Laws of Cambria, (1823) trans. Probert, W., London.

The Anglo-Saxon Chronicle, (1986) trans. Garmonsway, G.N., London:

Dent.

The Chronicle of the Kings of Britain, translated from the Welsh copy attributed to Tysilio, (1811) Roberts, P., Facsimile Reprint, Lampeter, Wales: Llanerch Publishers.

The Gothic History of Jordanes, (2006) Merchantville, NJ: Evolution Publishing. Also available online as Northvegr edition.

Virgil, *Aeneid*, (1927) trans. Mackail, J.W., London: Macmillan and Co.

Virgil, *Aeneid*, (1998) trans. Lewis, C.D., Oxford: Oxford University Press.

Virgil, *Eclogues, Georgics, Aeneid*, (1986) trans. Fairclough, H.R., London: William Heinemann.

Secondary Sources

Astbury, A.K. (1987) *The Black Fens*, Providence Press

Atchity, K.J. (1998) *The Classical Greek Reader*, Oxford: Oxford University Press

Baigent, M., Leigh, R. and Lincoln, H. (1993) *The Holy Blood and the Holy Grail*, London: Corgi Books

Beaumont, C. (1945) *The Riddle of Prehistoric Britain*, London: Rider & Co

Beaumont, C. (1948) *The Key to World History*, London: Rider & Co

Blegen, C.W. (1963) *Troy and the Trojans*, London: Thames and Hudson

Boedeker, D. (ed) (1997) *The World of Troy: Homer, Schliemann, and the Treasures of Priam, Proceedings from a Seminar sponsored by the Society for the Preservation of Greek Heritage*, Washington, D.C: Society for the Preservation of Greek Heritage

Bromwich, R. (1961) *Trioedd Ynys Prydein*, Cardiff: University of Wales Press

Bull, S. (   ) *Station Road, Swavesey*: A series of articles published in Swavesey's Meridian Magazine.

See *www.swavesey.org.uk/meridian/s_bull_station_rd*

Burn, A.R. (1990) *The Penguin History of Greece*, London: Penguin Books

Cooper, B. (1995) *After the Flood*, England: New Wine Press

Darby, H.C. (1983) *The Changing Fenland*, London: Cambridge University Press. *Development of the East Riding Coastline*. See *www.eastriding. gov.uk/aspirelinks/coastal/1development*

Dillon, M. and Chadwick, N. (2000) *The Celtic Realms*, London: Phoenix Press

Dinan, W. (1911) *Monumenta Historica Celtica*, London: David Nutt

Drews, R. (1988) *The Coming of the Greeks*, Princeton, New Jersey: Princeton University Press

Easton, D. (1977) *The Quest for Troy*, London: Orion

Elder, I.H. (1994) *Celt, Druid and Culdee*, London: Covenant Publishing Co. Ltd

Ellis, P.B. (2002) *The Druids*, London: Robinson

Elton, C. (1882) *Origins of English History*, London: Bernard Quaritch

Evans, J. Gwenogvryn, Ed. and Pub. (1916) *The Book of Taliesin*, Llanbedrog.

Fearn, J. *Thatch and Thatching*, Bucks. U.K: Shire Publications Ltd

Finley, M.I. (1964) 'The Trojan War', *Journal of Hellenic Studies* Vol. LXXXIV. 1-9

Finley, M.I. (1979) *The World of Odysseus*, 2nd Edn. London: Penguin Books

Fowler, G. (1933, 1934) 'Fenland Waterways, Past and Present', Part I, *Cambs. Ant. Soc. Comm.*, XXXII, 1933; Part II, *Cambs. Ant. Soc. Comm.*, XXXIV, 1934

Frazer, J.G. (1990) *The Golden Bough*, London: Macmillan

Gantz, T. (1993) *Early Greek Myth*, London: John Hopkins University Press

Gilbert, A., Wilson, A. and Blackett, B. (1998) *The Holy Kingdom*, London: Bantam Press.

Giles, J.A. (ed) (1891) *Six Old English Chronicles*, London: George Bell & Sons

Graves, R. (1961) *The White Goddess*, London: Faber and Faber

Graves, R. (1992) *The Greek Myths*, Complete Edition, London: Penguin Books

Groten Jr, F.J. (1968) 'Homer's Helen', *Greece and Rome*, 2nd series Vol. XV. 33-39

Guest, E. (1883) *Origines Celticae*, London: Macmillan and Co

Herberger, C.F. (1970) *Riddle of the Sphinx*, New York: Vantage Press

Higgins, G. (1829) *The Celtic Druids*, Facsimile Reprint 1977, Los Angeles, California: The Philosophical Research Society Inc

Hinde, T. (ed) (1997) *The Domesday Book*, Godalming, Surrey: Bramley Books

Hoeh, H.L., (1963) *Compendium of World History*, Pasadena, California: Ambassador College. See also *www.originofnations.org*

Holinshed (1976) *Chronicles of England, Scotland and Ireland*, New York: AMS Press inc.

Howorth, Sir Henry H. (1896) 'The Destruction and Shattering of the Chalk of Eastern England', *Geological Magazine*, 58-66. See also *www. sentex.net*

Hubert, H. (1993) *The History of the Celtic People*, London: Bracken Books

Keating, G. (1902) *The History of Ireland*, London: Irish Texts Society

Markale, J. (1999) *The Druids*, Rochester, Vermont: Inner Traditions International

Mathews, J. (ed) (1991) *A Celtic Reader: Selections from Celtic Legend, Scholarship and Story*, England: The Aquarian Press

Mathews, W.H. (1970) *Mazes and Labyrinths*, New York: Dover Publications

May, V.J. & Hanson, J.D. (2003) *Coastal Geomorphology of Great Britain*, Geological Conservation Review Series, No.28, Peterborough: Joint

Nature Conservation Committee.

Morgan, R.W. (1857) *The British Kymry*, Caernarvon, Wales: H. Humphreys

Morris, J. (1981) *Domesday Book: Cambridgeshire*, Pub. Phillimore

Nash, D.W. (1858) *Taliesin: The Bards and Druids of Britain*, London: John Russell Smith

Nichols, R. (1990) *The Book of Druidry*, England: The Aquarian Press

Onslow, R. (1971) *The Heath and the Turf: A History of Newmarket*, London: Arthur Baker.

Poste, B. (1853) *Britannic Researches*, London

Rankin, D. (1996) *Celts and the Classical World*, London, Routledge

Richer, J. (1994) *Sacred Geography of the Ancient Greeks*, New York: State University of New York Press

Roberts, N. (2002) *The Holocene; an Environmental History*, Oxford, UK; Blackwell

Royal Commission on Historical Monuments (1968) *An Inventory of Historical Monuments in the County of Cambridge*, Vol.1, West Cambridgeshire, Pub. H.M. Stationary Office

Royal Commission on Historical Monuments (1972) *An Inventory of Historical Monuments in the County of Cambridge*, Vol.2, North East Cambridgeshire, Pub. H.M. Stationary Office

Sammes, A., (1676) *Britannia Antiqua Illustrata or The Antiquities of Ancient Britain*, London: Thomas Roycroft.

Seale, R.S. (1979) 'Ancient Courses of the Great and Little Ouse in Fenland', *Proceedings of the Cambridge Antiquarian Society*, 69, 1-19

Siltzer, F. (1923) *Newmarket: Its Sport and Personalities*, London: Cassel.

Skene, W.F. (1867) *Chronicles of the Picts; Chronicles of the Scots*, Edinburgh: H.M. General Register House

Skene, W.F. (1880) *Celtic Scotland*, Edinburgh: David Douglas

Spence, L. (1994) *The Mysteries of Britain*, London: Senate

Steers, J.A. (ed) (1965) *The Cambridge Region*, Pub. The British Association for the Advancement of Science.

Travis, L. (1990) *The Mule*, London: J.A. Allen.

Van Wees, H. (1994) 'The Homeric Way of War: The Iliad and the Hoplite Phalanx' (1), *Greece and Rome*, 2nd series, Vol. XLI, No.1, April 1994, pp 1-18

Waddell, L.A. (1925) *The Phoenician Origin of Britons, Scots and Anglo-Saxons*, London: Williams and Norgate

Wareham, A.F. and Wright, A.P.M., (2002) *A History of the County of Cambridge and the Isle of Ely*: Vol. 10, Cheveley, Flendish, Staine and Staploe Hundreds, (north-eastern Cambridgeshire) pp. 1-27

Wilkens, I. (1990) *Where Troy Once Stood*, London; Rider.

Wood, E.S. (1995) *Historical Britain*, London: Harvill Press.

Wood, M. (2005) *In Search of the Trojan War*, London: BBC Books.

Woodward, B.B. (1853) *The History of Wales*, London: Virtue & Co.

Wright, A.P.M. and Lewis, C.P., (1989) *A History of the County of Cambridge and the Isle of Ely*: Vol. 9, Chesterton, Northstowe, and Papworth Hundreds, pp. 386-392

APPENDIX 1:
THE NATURAL WORLD IN HOMER'S *ILIAD*

AGRICULTURE

Barley 1.449, 5.196, 11.67, 11.631, 20.496.

Bread 24.625.

Carts 24.190.

Cheese 11.638.

Corn 2.148, 5.613.

Farms 4.433, 5.556, 16.641, 18.575.

Fishing 16.406.

Grain 19.223.

Herbs 11.740.

Herdsmen 4.275, 12.302, 15.325.

Honey 10.495, 11.631.

Markets 18.274, 18.497.

Meat (see Animals).

Milk 4.434, 13.5, 16.641.

Orchards 20.185, 21.36.

Ploughing 2.751, 6.142, 10.352, 13.704, 18.541, 20.185, 23.835.

Reaping 11.67, 18.550.

Rye 5.196.

Sheaf-binders 18.553.

Shepherds 3.11, 5.237, 12.451, 18.160, 23.834.

Straw 19.222.

Threshing 5.499, 13.5, 20.496.

Vineyards 3.184.

Water 6.457.

Wheat 5.613, 11.67, 12.312, 15.372, 21.601.

Wine 6.258, 7.467, 9.71, 10.579.

ANIMALS

Boar 4.253, 5.782, 7.256, 11.293, 12.42, 17.20.

Bulls 1.41, 16.487.

Cattle 5.161, 9.466, 11.244.

Deer 1.125, 3.23, 10.361, 11.474, 22.1.

Dogs 12.147, 15.351.

Ferret 10.335.

Goats 1.41, 1.66, 10.485, 11.244.

Hare 10.361, 22.310.

Horses 2.838, 4.500, 7.361, 8.185, 9.407, 10.491, 16.576.

Lions 3.23, 5.136, 5.782, 7.256, 10.297, 10.485, 11.113, 11.293, 12.42, 16.487, 17.20, 22.262.

Mules 1.49, 2.852, 7.333, 10.351, 17.742.

Oxen 2.448, 6.235, 7.333, 8.505, 10.351.

Sheep 1.66, 2.551, 3.102, 8.505, 9.466, 10.485, 11.244, 22.262, 22.310.

Swine 9.466.

Wolves 4.471, 10.334, 11.72, 13.103, 16.156, 22.262.

See also:

'Nestor's Booty'- (cattle, sheep, swine, goats and mares) 11.677-681

'Iphidamus' Bride-Price'- (cattle, goats and sheep) 11.244

BIRDS

Cranes 2.459, 3.3, 15.691.
Doves/Pigeons 2.502, 5.778, 22.140, 23.853.
Eagle (black/dusky) 21.252, 24.315.
Eagle (fiery, yellow/tawny) 15.690.
Eagle 12.201, 13.822, 22.308.
Falcon 13.819, 15.237, 16.682, 17.755, 22.139.
Geese 2.459, 15.691.
Hawk 13.62.
Jackdaws 17.755, 16.582.
Nightjar 14.290.
Starlings 17.755, 16.582.
Swans 2.459, 15.691.

CLOTHING

Bracelets 18.401.
Bright clothes 22.155.
Brooches 14.180.
Cloaks 10.131, 16.224, 24.228.
Coverlets 24.228.
Dresses 6.294.
Earings 14.182.
Ferret skin 10.335.
Leopard skin 10.25.
Lion skin 10.25, 10.177.
Long robes 18.595.
Mantles 24.228.
Necklaces 18.401.
Ox hide 10.155.
Robes 6.289, 22.105, 24.228.
Sandals 2.44, 14.186.
Trailing gowns 6.442, 7.297.
Tunics 13.685, 16.223, 24.228.
Wolf skin 10.334.

DEATH

Bier 24.589.
Burial mound 7.79, 16.456, 23.45, 24.797.
Cremation 6.418, 7.79, 7.376, 7.408, 7.427, 22.343.
Funeral feast 23.29.
Funeral fire 23.45, 24.786.
Funeral games 23.262-897.
Funeral urn 23.91, 24.795.
Mourning 18.315, 24.664, 24.718.

FISH

Dolphin 21.22.
Eels 21.203.
Fish 21.122, 21.203.
Oysters 16.747.

GENEALOGY

Achilles 20.203.
Aeneas 20.213.
Argives 7.128.
Asteropaeus 21.153.
Combatants 10.68.
Diomedes 14.112.
Glaucus 6.144.

LANDSCAPE

Arcadia beneath the steep mountain 2.603.
Argos: cornlands and orchards 14.122, wheat-bearing 15.372.
Bold headlands of the coast 12.282.
Calydonia vineland and ploughland

9.577.

Cities rich in flocks and cattle 9.149.

Cornlands of Buprasion 11.755.

Deep-soiled: Larissa 2.840, Tarne 5.44, Thrace 11.222, Ascania 13.793, Larissa 17.172, Paeonia 17.350.

Delightful woods 20.8.

Dykes & Embankments 5.87.

Eteonus; the high hills 2.497.

Fertile countryside of Hyle 5.708.

Flowery Pyrasus 2.695.

Grassy: Asopus 4.383, Haliartus 2.503.

High hills and forestlands 13.18.

High hilltops 12.282.

Iphiclus: rich in flocks 2.705.

Lycia: vineyards and cornfields 6.194, wheat-bearing ploughland 12.312.

Meadows: deep 9.151, flowery 2.467,

grassy 20.9, low-lying 15.631.

Mother of flocks: Iton 2.696, Phthia 9.479, Thrace 11.222.

Orchomenus: rich in flocks 2.605.

Paesus: rich in wheat fields 5.613.

Paturelands of horses: Argos 2.287, 9.246, 15.30; Dardania 20.219; Trica 4.202.

Pedasus: hill town by the lovely waters of Satniois 6.34.

Peneius and Pelion covered with waving forests 2.757.

Phrygia: rich in vines 3.184.

Phthires dense with leafage.

Pteleus deep in grass 2.697.

Rocky Calydon 2.640.

Rolling lands of Lacedaemon 2.581.

Rugged Olizon 2.717.

Shores and inlets of the sea 12.284.

Spreading lawns of Mycalessus 2.498.

Steep slopes of Tereia 2.829.

The Bountiful Earth: 8.277, 11.619, 14.272.

Valleys 18.588.

Wheat-bearing plain of Troy 21.601

Wooded hill of Placus 6.396.

METALS

Bronze 1.240, 6.48, 6.235, 9.137, 9.365, 10.315, 10.379, 11.133, 13.305, 13.612, 18.474, 23.561.

Copper 4.187.

Gold 2.872, 6.48, 6.235, 9.122, 9.137, 9.365, 10.315, 10.379, 11.124, 11.133, 18.474, 23.196.

Iron 4.123, 4.485, 6.48, 9.365, 10.379, 11.133, 23.261, 23.826.

Lead 24.80.

Silver 1.219, 2.857, 3.331, 7.303, 11.17, 11.31, 18.474, 19.369.

Tin 11.25, 11.32, 18.474, 23.562.

PLANTS

Crocus 14.347.

Galingale 21.351.

Hyacinth 14.347.

Lotus (clover) 2.776, 14.347, 21.351.

Parsley 2.776.

Poppy 8.306.

Rushes 21.351.

THE SEA

Battering waves descend on a fast ship 15.624.
Blue seawater 11.298.
Boiling waves 13.798.
Crashing waves and salt wash 4.422.
Dark waves 9.6.
Fish-delighting sea 9.4.
Great billows 11.307.
Great billows overtop the ships 15.381.
Grey salt water 13.351.
Mighty waves roar 17.264.
Salt sea beach 24.14.
Salt sea waves 6.136.
Ship smothered in foam 15.626.
Surging waves 13.798.
The black deep 7.64.
The dark sea 24.79.
The deep of the grey sea 21.59.
The grey sea: 13.682, 14.31, 15.619, 19.268, 23.374.
The loud-resounding sea: 6.347, 9.182, 13.798, 23.59.
The roaring sea: 2.210, 6.346, 14.394.
The salt sea 12.26.
The salt sea bellows 17.265.
The thunder of the invading sea 17.264.
The wine-dark sea: 7.88, 23.143.
Thundering waves 4.422.
Towering waves 15.626.

TREES

Ash 16.767.

Beech 16.767.
Cedar 24.192.
Cornel 16.767.
Elm 6.419, 21.350.
Fir 5.560.
Oak 5.693, 11.494, 13.389, 16.482, 23.118.
Olive-wood 13.612.
Pine 11.494, 13.389, 16.482.
Plane trees 2.307.
Poplar 4.482, 13.389, 16.482.
Tamarisk 6.39, 10.466, 21.18, 21.350.
Wild Fig 6.433, 11.167, 21.37.
Willow 11.105, 21.350.

TROY

Apollo's temple 5.446.
Athene's temple 6.88.
Broad realm of Troy 13.433.
Broad-wayed Troy 9.28, 14.88.
Citadel of Troy 5.445, 6.297.
Deep Soiled Troy 3.257, 16.461, 18.67, 23.215.
High City of Troy 15.71, 22.383.
House of Paris 6.312.
Ilium famed for horses 16.576.
Land of Horses 5.551.
Priam's famed city 18.288.
Priam's palace 6.242.
Sacred Ilium 4.46, 21.128.
Steep Ilium 9.419, 13,773, 15,71, 17.328.
Troy of the high gates 16.698.
Wealthy Ilium 9.402.
Well-peopled city of Ilium 13.380.
Windy Ilium 8.499, 12.115, 13.724,

18.174, 23.64.

WARFARE

Aprons 4.187.
Armour 1.371, 2.47, 4.285, 6.235, 7.206, 10.439, 11.25, 12.353, 19.357, 19.368.
Arrows 4.123, 8.297, 13.650, 15.313.
Axes 23.851.
Bows 3.18, 4.105.
Chariots 3.143, 4.226, 4.486, 5.838, 6.39, 10.322, 10.431, 10.438, 11.47, 14.431, 15.355, 17.481, 23.263-533.
Corselet 15.529, 23.560.
Greaves 3.331, 11.17, 19.369.
Helmets 7.12, 10.32, 11.41, 12.183, 16.137, 17.293, 22.315.
Mace 7.141.
Quiver 4.116.
Shields 5.452, 6.319, 7.219, 11.32, 11.545, 12.105, 12.295, 13.405, 13.804, 15.479, 15.646, 20.281.
Spears 2.543, 4.165, 4.469, 6.319, 22.225, 22.328, 23.799.
Swords 2.45, 3.361, 7.303, 11.30, 13.577.

WEATHER

Blazing meteor 4.76
Clouds: dark 12.157, black as pitch 4.277
Fog 17.368, 17.644, 17.655
Frozen water 22.150
Hail 10.6, 15.170, 22.150
Lightning 8.75, 17.595
Mist: 3.10, 5.186, 15.308, 21.7, dense 3.381, 16.790, 20.444
Rain: 13.138, heavy 5.91, torrential 16.385, unspeakable 10.6, unceasing 3.4
Rainbow 17.548
Sky: stormy 16.384, copper 17.425
Snow: 3.222, 10.6, 12.156, 12.278, 15.170, 19.357, freezing 22.150
Thunder 8.75, 17.595
Wind: blustering 13.334, gales 11.305

MISCELLANEOUS

Currency 23.703.
Homes 12.301, 17.738, 18.589, 23.832.
Insects: bees 12.167, flies 19.25, Wasps 12.167, 16.259.
Snake 3.33, 12.202.
Towns 17.738, 23.835.
Wages 12.435.

APPENDIX 2:
EARLY IRISH KINGS

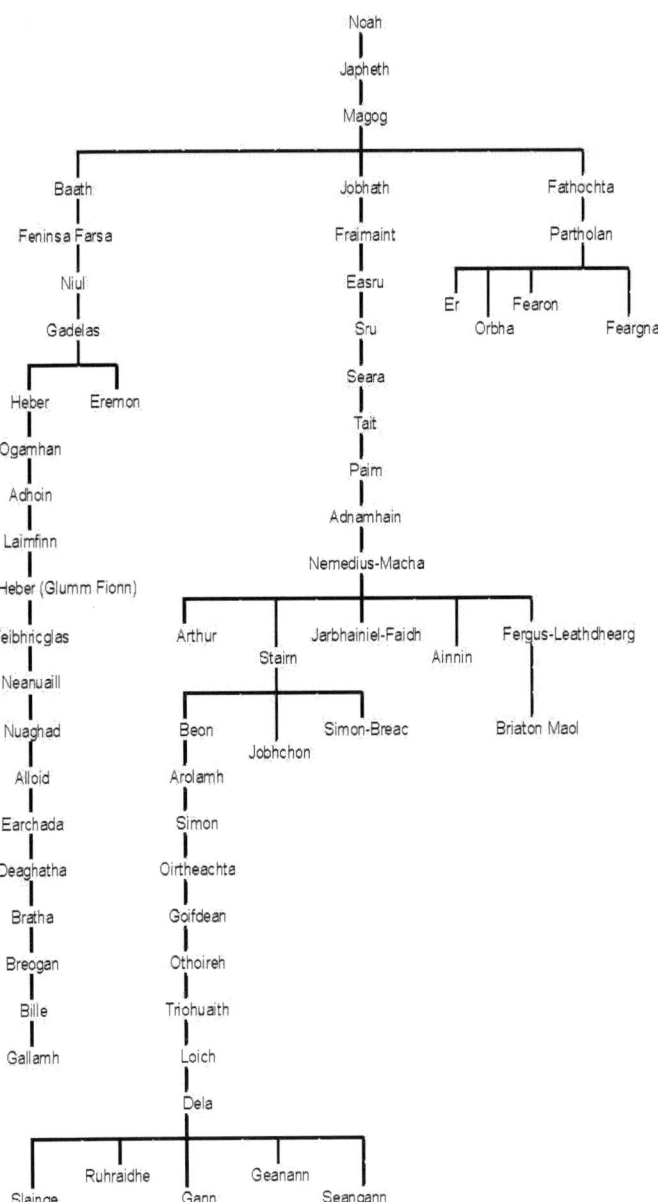

APPENDIX 3:
EARLY BRITISH KINGS

The genealogy of the Early British Kings is reproduced as per Bill Cooper's excellent example in *After the Flood*. It shows their descent traced down from Japeth, the son of Noah. The information is taken from Nennius's *History of the Britons; The Chronicle of the Kings of Britain*, attributed to Tysilio, *and Geoffrey of Monmouth's The History of the Kings of Britain*.

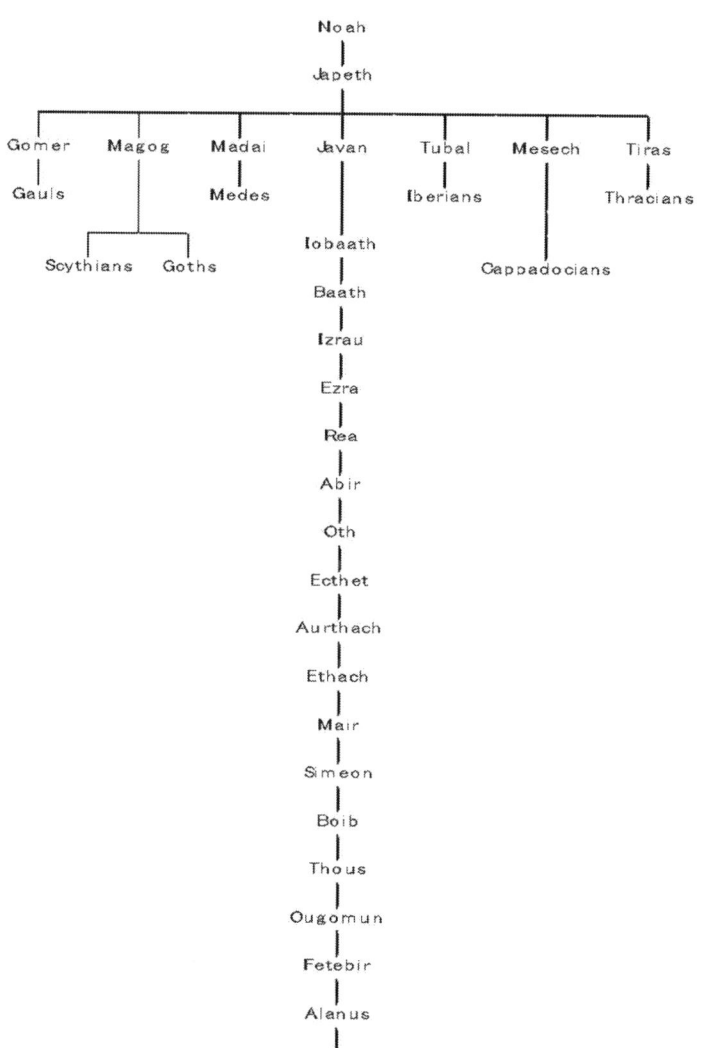

EARLY BRITISH KINGS (2)

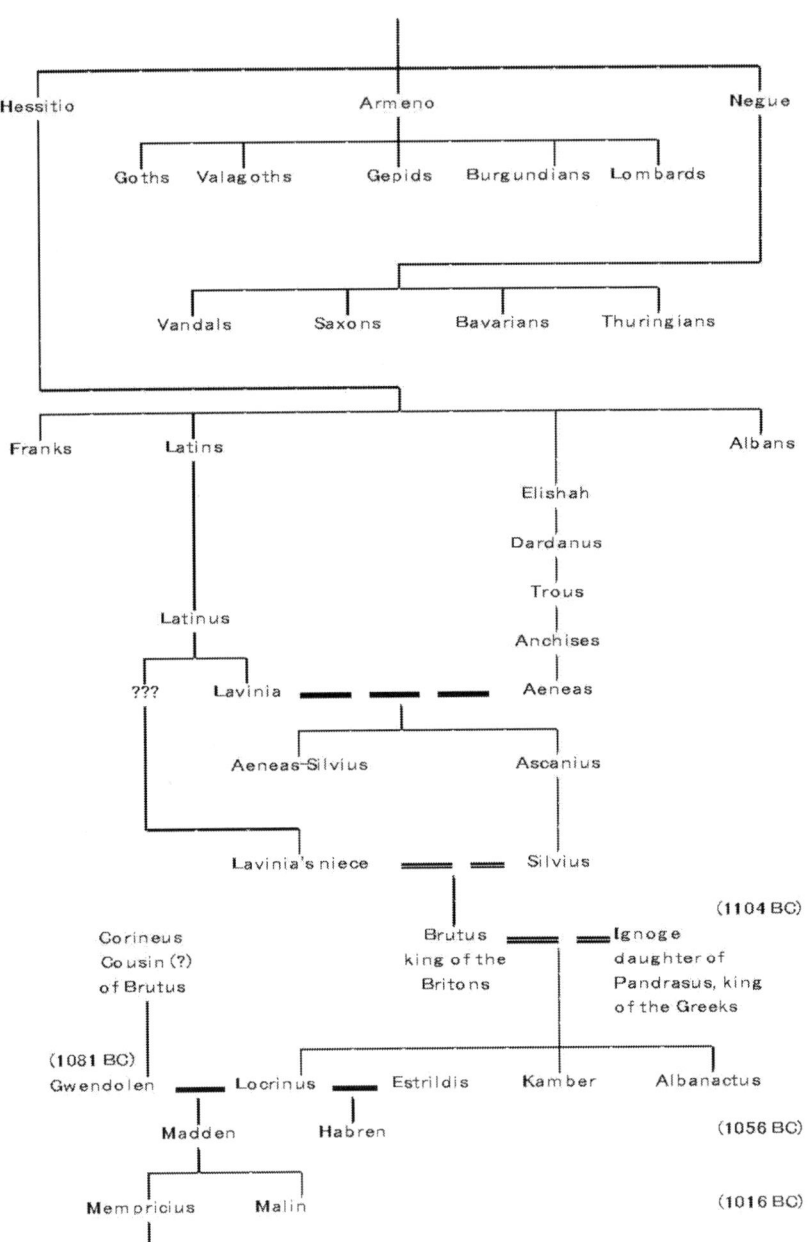

EARLY BRITISH KINGS (3)

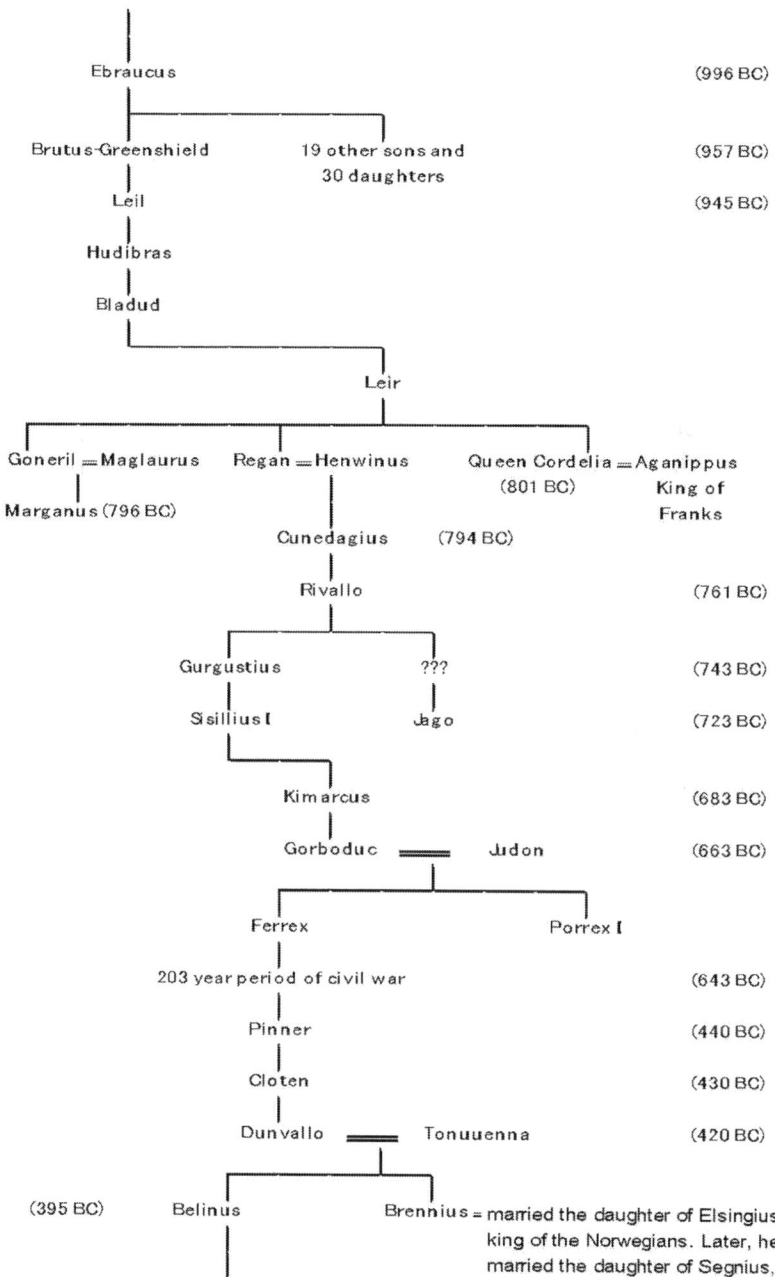

Ebraucus	(996 BC)
Brutus-Greenshield 19 other sons and 30 daughters	(957 BC)
Leil	(945 BC)
Hudibras	
Bladud	
Leir	
Goneril ═ Maglaurus Regan ═ Henwinus Queen Cordelia ═ Aganippus	
Marganus (796 BC)	(801 BC) King of Franks
Cunedagius (794 BC)	
Rivallo	(761 BC)
Gurgustius ???	(743 BC)
Sisillius I Jago	(723 BC)
Kimarcus	(683 BC)
Gorboduc ═══ Judon	(663 BC)
Ferrex Porrex I	
203 year period of civil war	(643 BC)
Pinner	(440 BC)
Cloten	(430 BC)
Dunvallo ═══ Tonuuenna	(420 BC)
(395 BC) Belinus Brennius = married the daughter of Elsingius, king of the Norwegians. Later, he married the daughter of Segnius,	

EARLY BRITISH KINGS (4)

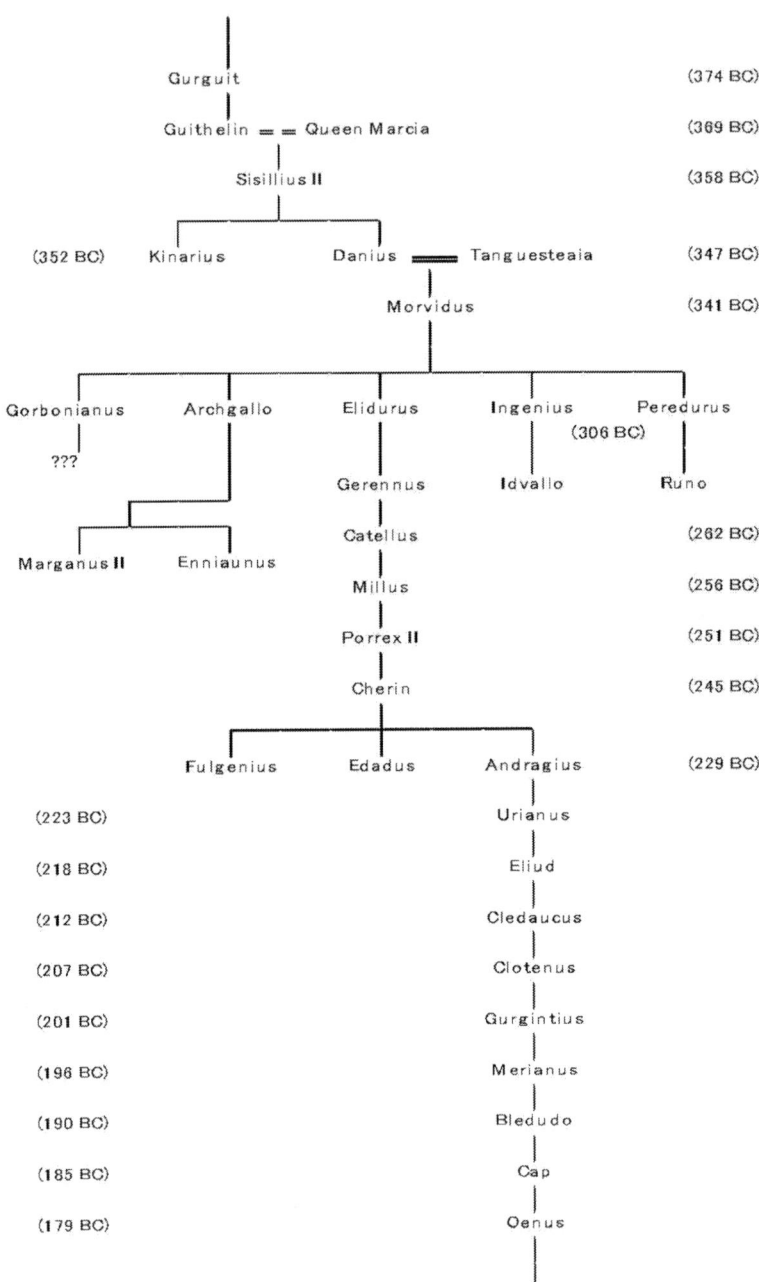

Gurguit (374 BC)

Guithelin == Queen Marcia (369 BC)

Sisillius II (358 BC)

(352 BC) Kinarius | Danius === Tanguesteaia (347 BC)

Morvidus (341 BC)

Gorbonianus | Archgallo | Elidurus | Ingenius | Peredurus

??? (306 BC)

Gerennus | Idvallo | Runo

Marganus II | Enniaunus

Catellus (262 BC)

Millus (256 BC)

Porrex II (251 BC)

Cherin (245 BC)

Fulgenius | Edadus | Andragius (229 BC)

(223 BC) Urianus

(218 BC) Eliud

(212 BC) Cledaucus

(207 BC) Clotenus

(201 BC) Gurgintius

(196 BC) Merianus

(190 BC) Bledudo

(185 BC) Cap

(179 BC) Oenus

330

EARLY BRITISH KINGS (5)

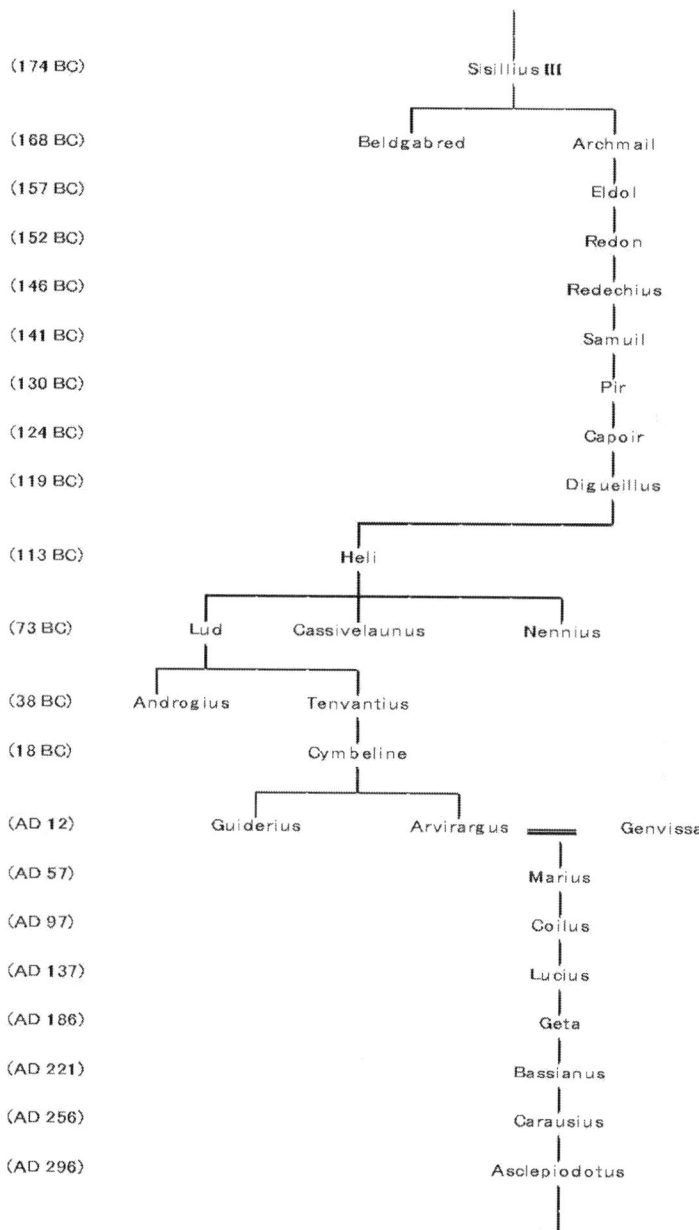

(174 BC)	Sisillius III
(168 BC)	Beldgabred — Archmail
(157 BC)	Eldol
(152 BC)	Redon
(146 BC)	Redechius
(141 BC)	Samuil
(130 BC)	Pir
(124 BC)	Capoir
(119 BC)	Digueillus
(113 BC)	Heli
(73 BC)	Lud — Cassivelaunus — Nennius
(38 BC)	Androgius — Tenvantius
(18 BC)	Cymbeline
(AD 12)	Guiderius — Arvirargus ═══ Genvissa
(AD 57)	Marius
(AD 97)	Coilus
(AD 137)	Lucius
(AD 186)	Geta
(AD 221)	Bassianus
(AD 256)	Carausius
(AD 296)	Asclepiodotus

EARLY BRITISH KINGS (6)

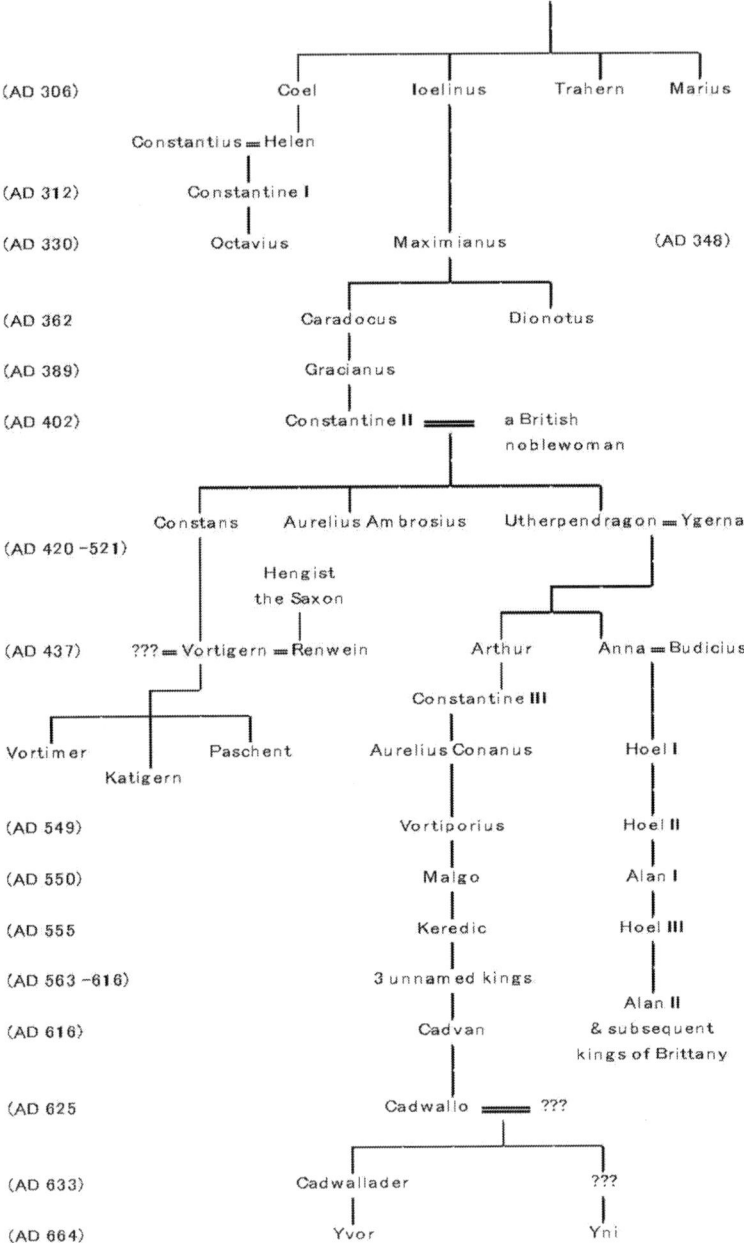

(AD 306)   Coel   Ioelinus   Trahern   Marius

Constantius ═ Helen

(AD 312)   Constantine I

(AD 330)   Octavius   Maximianus   (AD 348)

(AD 362   Caradocus   Dionotus

(AD 389)   Gracianus

(AD 402)   Constantine II ═══ a British noblewoman

Constans   Aurelius Ambrosius   Utherpendragon ═ Ygerna

(AD 420 –521)

Hengist the Saxon

(AD 437)   ??? ═ Vortigern ═ Renwein   Arthur   Anna ═ Budicius

Vortimer   Paschent   Constantine III   Hoel I

Katigern   Aurelius Conanus

(AD 549)   Vortiporius   Hoel II

(AD 550)   Malgo   Alan I

(AD 555   Keredic   Hoel III

(AD 563 –616)   3 unnamed kings

(AD 616)   Cadvan   Alan II & subsequent kings of Brittany

(AD 625)   Cadwallo ═══ ???

(AD 633)   Cadwallader   ???

(AD 664)   Yvor   Yni

APPENDIX 4:
TROJAN MIGRATIONS

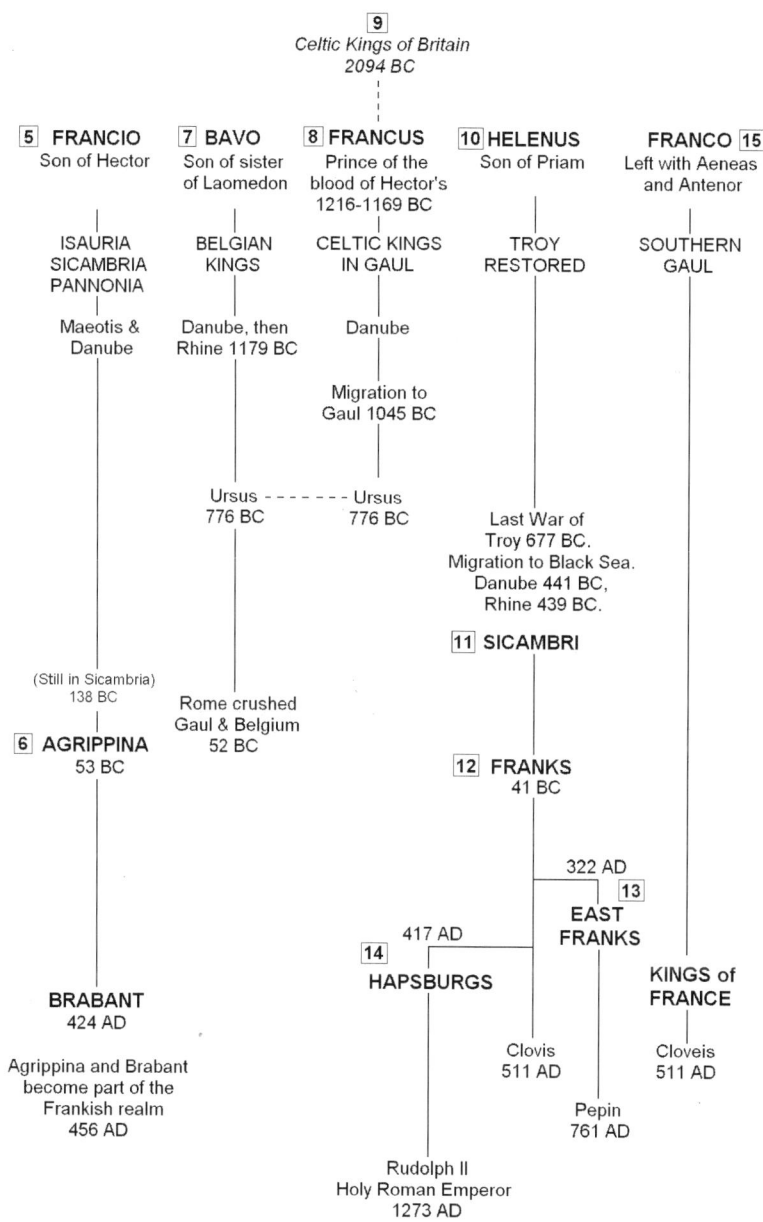

9
Celtic Kings of Britain
2094 BC

5 FRANCIO
Son of Hector

ISAURIA
SICAMBRIA
PANNONIA

Maeotis &
Danube

(Still in Sicambria)
138 BC

6 AGRIPPINA
53 BC

BRABANT
424 AD

Agrippina and Brabant
become part of the
Frankish realm
456 AD

7 BAVO
Son of sister
of Laomedon

BELGIAN
KINGS

Danube, then
Rhine 1179 BC

Ursus - - - - - - Ursus
776 BC   776 BC

Rome crushed
Gaul & Belgium
52 BC

8 FRANCUS
Prince of the
blood of Hector's
1216-1169 BC

CELTIC KINGS
IN GAUL

Danube

Migration to
Gaul 1045 BC

10 HELENUS
Son of Priam

TROY
RESTORED

Last War of
Troy 677 BC.
Migration to Black Sea.
Danube 441 BC,
Rhine 439 BC.

11 SICAMBRI

12 FRANKS
41 BC

322 AD

13
EAST
FRANKS

417 AD

14
HAPSBURGS

Clovis
511 AD

Rudolph II
Holy Roman Emperor
1273 AD

FRANCO **15**
Left with Aeneas
and Antenor

SOUTHERN
GAUL

KINGS of
FRANCE

Cloveis
511 AD

Pepin
761 AD

APPENDIX 5:
TROJAN KINGS OF ISAURIA, SICAMBRIA AND PANNONIA

After the fall of Troy Francio, the son of Hector, flees to Maeotis (near the Cimmerian Bosporus and Black Sea).

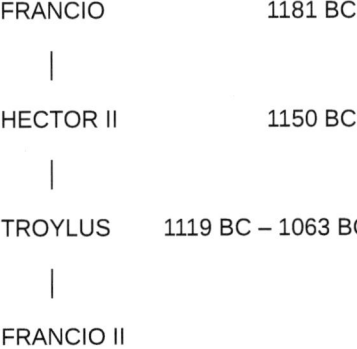

FRANCIO	1181 BC
HECTOR II	1150 BC
TROYLUS	1119 BC – 1063 BC
FRANCIO II	

(Francio's brother, Priam, led a migration to Isauria). His son, Priamus II, commences his reign on the Black Sea and builds the city of Sycambria.

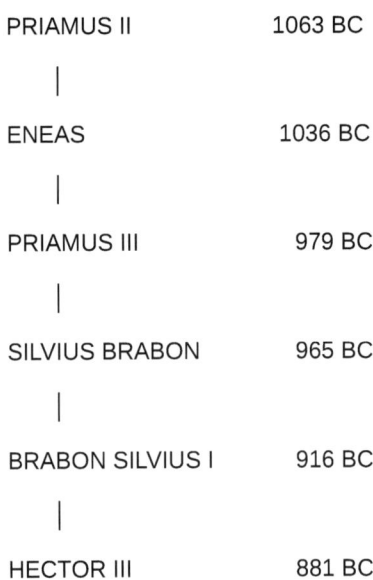

PRIAMUS II	1063 BC
ENEAS	1036 BC
PRIAMUS III	979 BC
SILVIUS BRABON	965 BC
BRABON SILVIUS I	916 BC
HECTOR III	881 BC

|

FRANCIO BRABON   847 BC

|

TROYLUS   771 BC

|

BRABON II   739 BC

|

SILVIUS BRABON II   732 BC

|

HECTOR BRABON   700 BC

|

PALAMIDES   663 BC

|

BRABON III   611 BC

|

PRIAMUS IV   554 BC – 522 BC

|

PHILYMEUS   552 BC – 522 BC

|

PRIAMUS V   522 BC

|

BRABON IV   502 BC

|

LAOMEDON   452 BC

|

PELIUS   428 BC

|

TROYLUS II   370 BC

|

PRIAMUS VI   332 BC

|

FRANCIO III   325 BC

|

BRABON V   316 BC

|

SILVIUS BRABON III   312 BC

|

BRABON TROYLUS VI   291 BC

|

BRABON VII   258 BC

|

BRABON VIII   236 BC

|

PRIAMUS VII   220 BC

|

HECTOR IV   192 BC

|

BRABON IX   161 BC

|

PRIAMUS VIII   157 BC

|

FRANCIO IV   138 BC

The account of the kings of Sycambria and Pannonia ceases with Francio IV.His youngest son, Brabon junior, had a son called Brabon Silvius who accompanied Caesar in the Roman conquest of Gaul. Caesar conquered the kingdom of Agrippina (Cologne), killed the king, and gave the kingdom to Brabon Silvius. (See Appendix 6.)

APPENDIX 6:
KINGS OF ALGRIPPINA, PRINCES AND DUKES OF BRABANT

The kingdom of Agrippina was given to Brabon Silvius by Julius Caesar. Brabon Silvius was the grandson of Frankio IV.

KINGS OF AGRIPPINA (COLOGNE)

BRABON SILVIUS

|

KAROLUS I   53 BC – 39 AD

|

KAROLUS II   39 AD

|

KAROLUS III   80 AD

|

KAROLUS IV   145 AD

|

KAROLUS V   155 AD

|

KAROLUS VI   260 AD

| |

KAROLUS VII   263 AD

|

BRABON   325 AD

|

KAROLUS VIII   366 AD

|

ANGISUS

Angisus was captured by the Romans. He had two sons, Brabon and Karolus. Maximus, a rival emperor to Theodosius, devastated parts of northern Gaul and gave these to Brabon. It was called Brabant. Karolus succeeded his father in the kingdom of Agrippina. In the days of Brabon the Franks destroyed Agrippina and annexed Brabant. Brabon and his descendants become servants of the Franks (456-459). See Appendix 12.

PRINCES OF BRABANT

BRABON I	424 – 456 AD
BRABON II	459 AD
BRABON III	519 AD
KAROLOMANNUS	570 – 615 AD

After the death of Karolomannus Brabant becomes a dukedom.

DUKES OF BRABANT

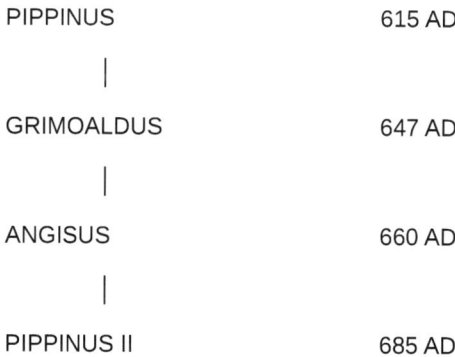

PIPPINUS	615 AD
GRIMOALDUS	647 AD
ANGISUS	660 AD
PIPPINUS II	685 AD

|

KAROLUS MERTELLUS   715 AD

|

PIPPINUS III 'the Short'   747 AD

Pippinus inherits Brabant, Austrasia, Thuringia, Burgundy, Neustria, and Provence.

|

KAROLOMANNUS   768 AD

|

KAROLUS MAGNUS 771 – 814 AD

Karolus Magnus became Roman Emperor in 800 AD.

APPENDIX 7:
TROJAN KINGS OF THE BELGIANS

Under the Trojan priest-king, Bavo, Trojans migrated to the Danube (Black Sea) and then on to the mouth of the Rhine, where they arrived in 1179 BC.

BAVO	1179 BC
|	
BAVO the Belgian	1166 BC
|	
BAVO the Lion	1122 BC
|	
BAVO the Wolf	1102 BC
|	
BAVO BRUNUS	1052 BC
|	
BRUNEHULDIS	1017 BC
|	
BRUNO	950 BC
|	
AGANIPPUS I	914 BC
|	
AGANIPPUS II	885 BC
(Married British Queen Cordelia)	
|	
AUDENGARIUS	835 BC
|	
HERISBRANDUS	796 BC

End of rule of priest kings. Ursus, a warrior-king came to the throne.)

URSUS	776 BC
URSA (Daughter of Ursus)	742 BC
GURGUNCIUS	741 BC
(British king Gurgust)	
SISILLIUS	713 BC
FRISCEMBALDUS I	703 BC
FRISCEMBALDUS II	672 BC
WARINGERUS	640 BC
LEONIUS	625 BC
LEOPARDUS I	615 BC
LEOPARDUS II	610 BC
LEOPARDINUS	580 BC
CAMBER	546 BC

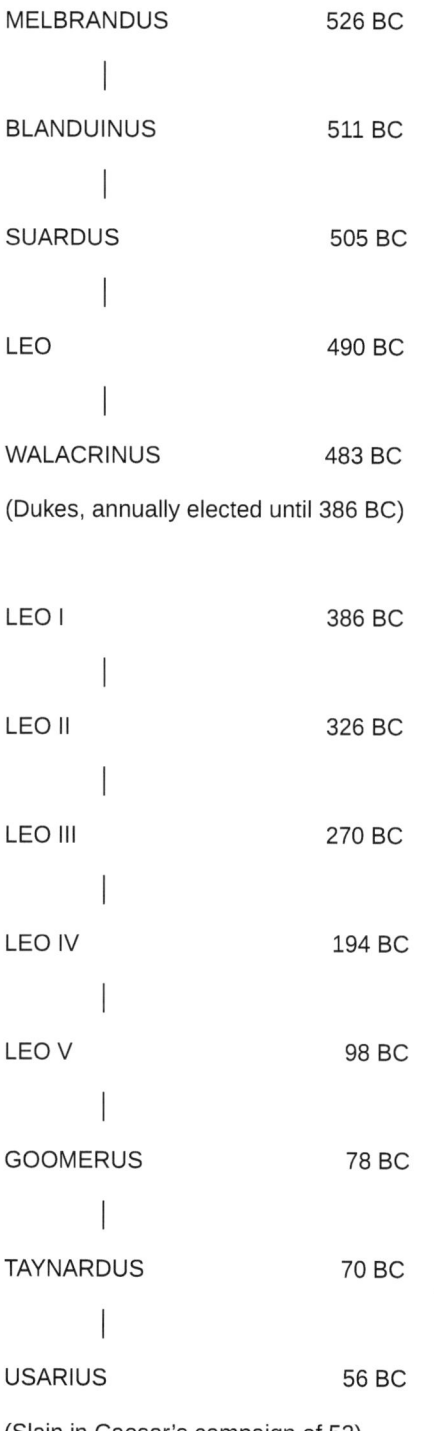

MELBRANDUS   526 BC

BLANDUINUS   511 BC

SUARDUS   505 BC

LEO   490 BC

WALACRINUS   483 BC

(Dukes, annually elected until 386 BC)

LEO I   386 BC

LEO II   326 BC

LEO III   270 BC

LEO IV   194 BC

LEO V   98 BC

GOOMERUS   78 BC

TAYNARDUS   70 BC

USARIUS   56 BC

(Slain in Caesar's campaign of 52)

|

ANDROMADUS   52 BC

Rome crushed Gaul and Belgium 52 BC.

APPENDIX 8:
KINGS OF THE CELTS IN GAUL

After the Trojan War Francus continued to govern the Celts on the Danube basin in Britain. In 1181 BC he led a migration to the Low Countries where kings of this Trojan line ruled until 776 BC, when the warrior-king, Ursus, came to power. Francus was a Celtic king in Britain at the time of the Trojan War. See Appendix 9.

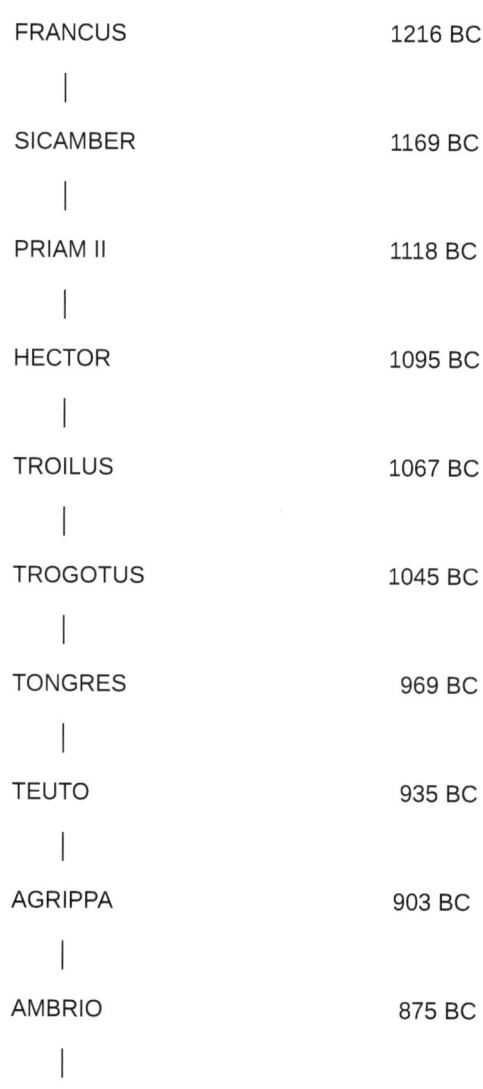

FRANCUS	1216 BC
SICAMBER	1169 BC
PRIAM II	1118 BC
HECTOR	1095 BC
TROILUS	1067 BC
TROGOTUS	1045 BC
TONGRES	969 BC
TEUTO	935 BC
AGRIPPA	903 BC
AMBRIO	875 BC

THURINGUS   842 BC

|

CAMBER   808 BC

Ursus comes to power 776 BC. See Appendix 4.

APPENDIX 9:
THE CELTIC KINGS OF BRITAIN

SAMOTHES   2094 BC

|

MAGUS   2048 BC

|

SARRON   1997 BC

|

DRUIS   1936 BC

|

BARDUS   1922 BC

|

LONGHO   1847 BC

|

BARDUS II   1819 BC

|

LUCUS Protector   1782 BC

|

CELTES   1771 BC

|

HERCULES   1758 BC

|

GALATHES   1739 BC

|

NARBON   1690 BC

|

LUGDUS	1672 BC

|

| BELIGIUS | 1621 BC |

|

| IASIUS | 1601 BC |

|

| ALLOBROX | 1551 BC |

|

| ROMUS | 1483 BC |

|

| PARIS | 1454 BC |

|

| LEMANES | 1415 BC |

|

| OLBIUS | 1353 BC |

|

| GALATHES II | 1348 BC |

| NAMNES | 1300 BC |

|

| REMUS | 1256 BC |

|

| PHRANICUS | 1216 – 1149 BC |

In the British histories Phranicus is stated to be a prince of the blood of Hector's. He held the sceptre in right of his wife, the daughter of Remus. He left Samothes to be governed by the druids and betook himself to the continent. The reason for his departure has been lost to British history but is found in that of the Kings of the Celts in Gaul. Phranicus led one of the migrations out of Britain after the Trojan War.

APPENDIX 10:
TROJANS AT TROY AND THE BLACK SEA

Spanish histories record the names of the descendants of Helenus who recaptured Troy in 1149 BC. After a third Trojan War in 677 BC members of the Trojan royal family and most of the population fled to the northern shores of the Black Sea.

HELENUS

ZENTER

FRANCUS

ESDRON

ZELIUS

BASAVELIAN

PLASERIUS

PLESRON

ELIACOR

ZABERIAN

PLASERIUS II

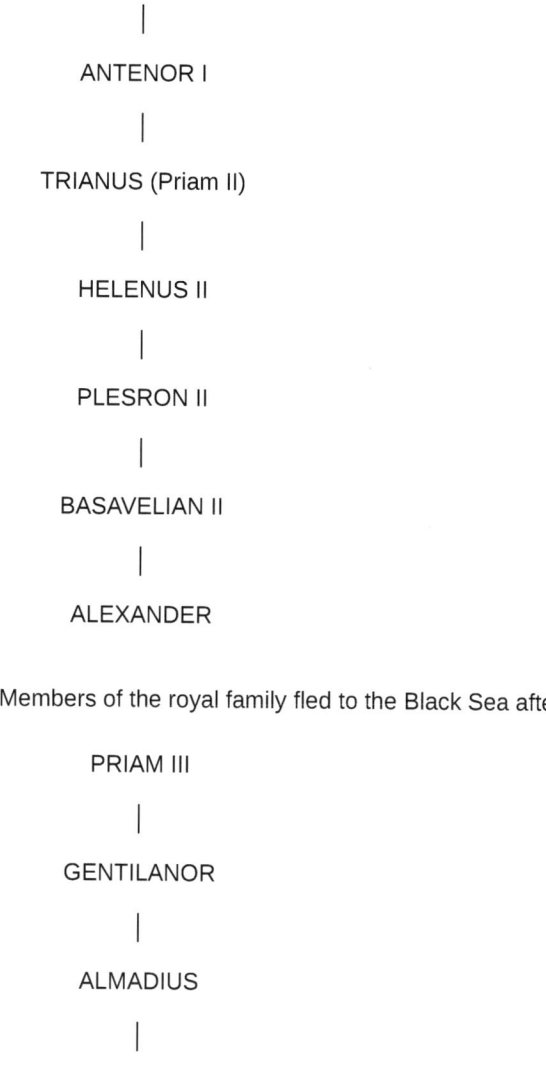

|

ANTENOR I

|

TRIANUS (Priam II)

|

HELENUS II

|

PLESRON II

|

BASAVELIAN II

|

ALEXANDER

The last war against Troy. Members of the royal family fled to the Black Sea after 677 BC.

PRIAM III

|

GENTILANOR

|

ALMADIUS

|

DILULIUS

|

HELENUS III

|

PLASSERIUS III

|

DILULIUS II

|

MARCOMIR

|

PRIAM IV

|

HELENUS IV

|

ANTENOR II (Died 445 BC)

Marcomirus, the son of Antenor II, led a migration of almost half a million people to the mouth of the Rhine. They settled West Friesland, Gelders and Holland. See Appendix 11.

APPENDIX 11:
TROJAN KINGS OF THE SICAMBRIANS

Marcomirus was told by a pagan priest to go west where Brutus of Troy had Previously gone. A pagan prophecy promises him victory over the Gauls and the Romans. In 439 BC he leads half a million people to the mouth of the Rhine and they settle West Friesland, Gelders and Holland. He crossed the Rhine and conquered part of Gaul. Later, the conquest of all Gaul was completed.

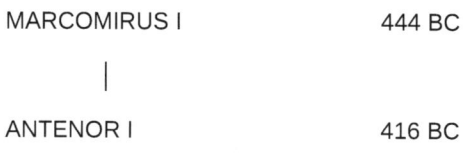

MARCOMIRUS I	444 BC
ANTENOR I	416 BC

Antenor married Cambra, the daughter of Belinus, king of Britain.

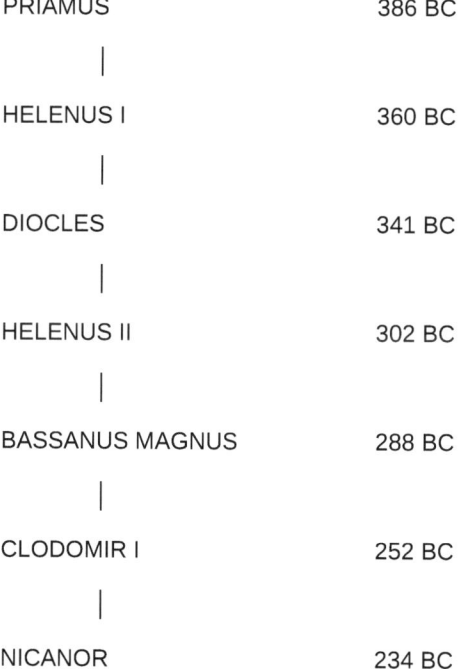

PRIAMUS	386 BC
HELENUS I	360 BC
DIOCLES	341 BC
HELENUS II	302 BC
BASSANUS MAGNUS	288 BC
CLODOMIR I	252 BC
NICANOR	234 BC

Nicanor married Constantina, thedaughter of the king of Britain.

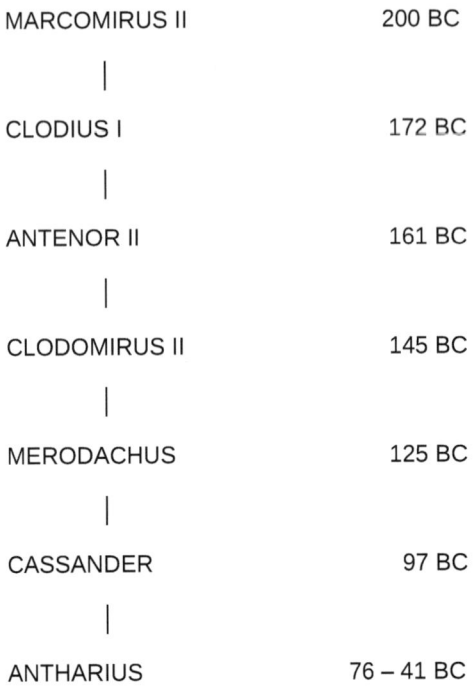

MARCOMIRUS II   200 BC

|

CLODIUS I   172 BC

|

ANTENOR II   161 BC

|

CLODOMIRUS II   145 BC

|

MERODACHUS   125 BC

|

CASSANDER   97 BC

|

ANTHARIUS   76 – 41 BC

In Antharius' twentieth year some of Caesar's soldiers revolted to the Sicambri who refused Caesar's demand to deliver them up. In revenge, Caesar entered their country and marched all the way to Britain. In 41 BC Antharius and 2000 of his men were slain by the Gauls. Afterwards, the Sicambri were called Franks after the name of his son and successor, Frankus. See Appendix 12.

APPENDIX 12:
THE KINGS OF THE FRANKS

Antharius, the last king of the Sicambri, was slain in Caesar's revenge 55-54 BC. (See Appendix 11.) His son Francus afterwards took the throne. The name of Sicambri was changed to Franci.

FRANCUS	41 BC
|	
CLODIUS	13 BC – 18 AD
|	
HERIMERUS	18 AD
|	
MARCOMIRUS	30 AD
|	
CLODOMIRUS	48 AD
|	
ANTENOR III	60 AD
|	
RATHERIUS	66 AD
|	
RICHIMERUS I	87 AD
|	
ODOMAR	111 AD
|	
MARCOMIRUS IV	125 AD
|	
CLODOMIRUS IV	146 AD

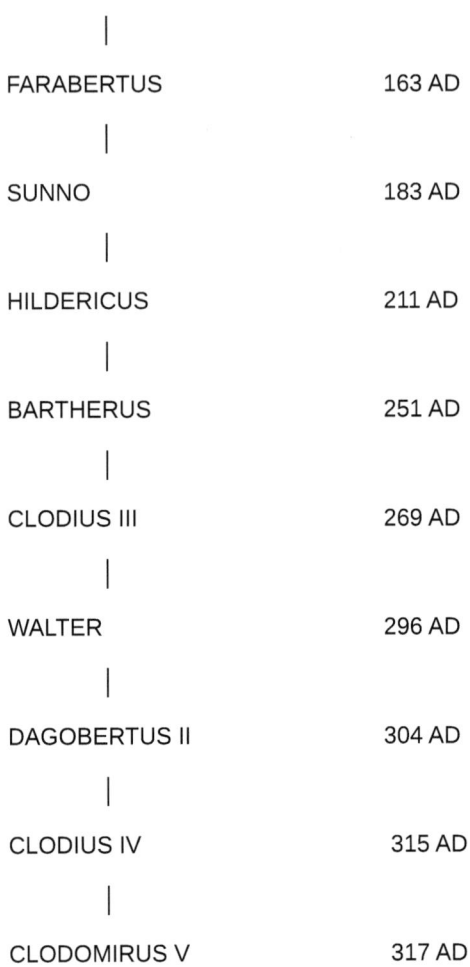

FARABERTUS	163 AD
SUNNO	183 AD
HILDERICUS	211 AD
BARTHERUS	251 AD
CLODIUS III	269 AD
WALTER	296 AD
DAGOBERTUS II	304 AD
CLODIUS IV	315 AD
CLODOMIRUS V	317 AD

In 322 AD Clodomirus V sends 30,000 Colonists to the river Main and establishes the Dukedom of Frankonia. See Appendix 13

RICHIMER II	335 AD
THEODOMIRUS	348 AD
CLODIUS V	358 AD

Pepin and Charlemagne are descended from his third son.

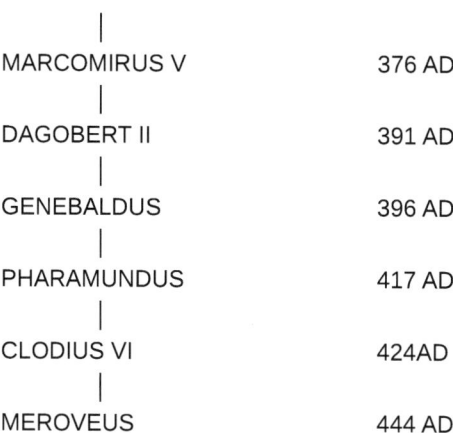

MARCOMIRUS V	376 AD
DAGOBERT II	391 AD
GENEBALDUS	396 AD
PHARAMUNDUS	417 AD
CLODIUS VI	424AD
MEROVEUS	444 AD

After whom the Franks were called Merovingians.

HILDERICUS	455 AD
CLOVIS	481 – 511 AD

APPENDIX 13:
DUKES OF THE EAST FRANKS

Clodomirus V established the Dukedom of Frankonia in 322 AD. The Franks were permitted to resettle where Holland, Utrecht, Gelders, part of Friesia, Westphalia and Brabant now lie. The Franks now split and Genebald, the brother of Clodomirus V becomes their first duke.

GENEBALD   322 AD

|

MARCOMER   352 AD

|

CLAUDIUS   373 AD

|

MARCOMER II   383 AD

|

PHARAMUND   399 AD

|

MARCOMER III   414 AD

|

PRIAMUS   432 AD

|

GENEBALDT II   444 AD

|

SUNNO   464 AD

|

CLODIUS II   487 AD

|

CLODOMIR   503 AD

|

HUGBALD   524 AD

|

HELENUS   550 AD

|

GOTTFRIED   580 AD

|

GENEBALDT III   604 AD

|

CLODOMIR II   624 AD

|

HERIBERT   647 AD

|

CLODOUEUS III   677 AD

GROSSWERT   689 AD

|

GOSSPERT   715 AD

|

HETAN   729 AD

Interregnum under Pepin 749 – 761 AD
From this point see modern history of the Franks.

APPENDIX 14:
THE HAPSBURGS

A ruling line from Pharamund, king of the Franks, intermarried with Austrian royalty.

CLODION

|

MEROVEUS

|

CHILDERIC

|

CLODOVIUS

|

CLOTARIUS

|

SIGIBERT

|

CHILDUBERT

|

THEODOBERT

|

LIGIBERT

|

OTHOBERT

|

AMPRINETUS

|

HECTOBERT

|

RAMPERT

|

GUNTRAMUS I

|

LUIFFRIDUS I

|

LUIFFRIDUS II

|

HUNDIFRIDUS

|

GUNTRAMUS II

|

BERTUS

|

RAPATUS

|

WERNER

|

OTHO

|

WERNER II

|

WERNER III

|

ALBERT I

|

RUDOLPH I

|

ALBERT II

|

RUDOLPH II

Holy Roman Emperor 1273 AD

APPENDIX 15:
THE DUKES OF GAUL

This group of fugitives was led by Franco the son of Hector. He left Troy with Aeneas and Antenor. Franco and his followers settled in southern Gaul.

FRANCO I	1181 BC
|	
MELUS	1171 BC
|	
BOSSES	1120 BC
|	
ECTOR	1096 BC
|	
ALEMAINE	1080 BC
|	
CASTOR	1058 BC
|	
YLION I	1028 BC
|	
ALIENOIR	988 BC
|	
GOSSAIN	960 BC
|	
ECTOR II	948 BC
|	
ATHANAISE	929 BC
|	

FRANCO II   908 BC

|

YBORUS I   898 BC

|

ANTHENOIRE   883 BC

|

YOLENS   866 BC

|

PRIAN I   823 BC

|

YBORUS II   797 BC

|

ECTOR III   775 BC

|

YLION II   725 BC

|

NAY   685 BC

|

ALYMODES   651 BC

|

ORLINS   577 BC

|

AVRENGNAS   523 BC

|

YBORUS III   509 BC

|

FRISONES   469 BC

|

FLAMBO   441 BC

|

FLANDROC   393 BC

|

TURRUS   360 BC

|

BRUGEN   301 BC

|

DUANUS   276 BC

|

CAMBERACION   260 BC

|

BRETANGES   205 BC

|

CLETUS   195 BC

|

FRANCO III   173 BC

|

PRIANS II   120 BC

|

YBORUS IV   64 BC

|

FRANCIO IV   28 BC

|

TROIELUS   5 AD

|

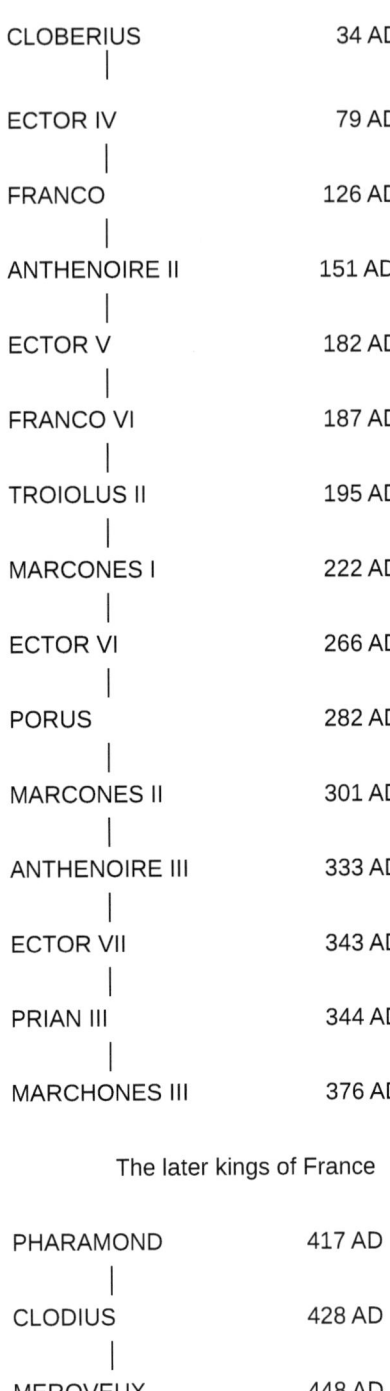

CLOBERIUS	34 AD
ECTOR IV	79 AD
FRANCO	126 AD
ANTHENOIRE II	151 AD
ECTOR V	182 AD
FRANCO VI	187 AD
TROIOLUS II	195 AD
MARCONES I	222 AD
ECTOR VI	266 AD
PORUS	282 AD
MARCONES II	301 AD
ANTHENOIRE III	333 AD
ECTOR VII	343 AD
PRIAN III	344 AD
MARCHONES III	376 AD

The later kings of France

PHARAMOND	417 AD
CLODIUS	428 AD
MEROVEUX	448 AD

CELDRUS   458 AD
|
CLOVEIS   481 AD

APPENDIX 16:
ODIN, TROY AND DANISH HISTORY

PRIAM

King of Troy

|

MINON (MEMNON)

Married Priam's daughter

|

TROR (THOR)

|

EINRIDI

|

VINGETHORR

|

VINGENER

|

MODA

|

MAGI

|

SESKEF (ODIN) or DANUS I

1040 BC

|

CANUTE II

1014 – 1035 AD

United Scandinavia and became King of England 1016.

Denmark received its name from the Irish Danaan. The name passed to the king who took the name of his subjects. Danus I (Odin) commenced his reign in 1040 BC. This followed the break-up of the German realm when the seafarers of northwest Europe were left without leadership. Danus ame from the Trojan royal house in Thrace, in Britain. He was eighth in descent from king Priam.

APPENDIX 17:
ANCIENT KINGS OF THE GERMANS (ASSYRIANS)

The German histories detail their knowledge of the Trojan War, their assistance to king Priam, and marriage into the Trojan royal house.

TUITSCH (Shem)   2214 BC

|

MANNUS   1978 BC

|

EINGEB   1906 BC

|

AUSSTAEB   1870 BC

|

HERMAN   1820 BC

|

MERSE   1757 BC

|

GAMPAR   1711 BC

|

SCHWAB   1667 BC

|

WANDLER   1621 BC

|

DEUTO   1580 BC

|

ALMAN   1553 BC

|

BAIER   1489 BC

|

INGRAM   1429 BC

|

ADALGER   1377 BC

|

LAREIN   1328 BC

|

YLSING   1227 BC

|

BRENNER   1224 BC

|

HECCAR   1186 BC

|

FRANK   1155 BC

|

WOLFHEIM SICLINGER   1114 BC

|

KELS, GAL & HILLYR   1056 BC

|

ALBER   1006 BC

|

WALTER, PANNO & SHARD   946 BC

|

MAIN, ZNGEL & TRIEBLE   884 BC

|

MYELA, LABER & PENNO   814 BC

|

VENNO & HELTO   714 BC

|

MADER   644 BC

|

BRENNER II & COENMAN   589 BC

|

LANDEIN & SONS   479 BC

|

BRENNER III   399 BC

|

SCHIRM   361 BC

|

THESSEL   279 BC

|

DIETH I   194 BC

|

BAERMUND & SYNPOL   172 BC

|

BOIGER, KELS & TEUTENBUECHER 127 BC

|

SCHEIRER   100 BC

|

ERNST & VOCHO   70 BC

|

PERNPEIST   50 BC

About the author

Bernard Jones was, until recently, a multi-disciplinary professional; a Chartered Practitioner and Chartered Fellow with a lifetime of scientific, technical, investigative and research work behind him. In addition to his professional vocation he is a historian of some 35 plus years.

He completed his post graduate research in ancient philosophy/mythology and ancient history. For the last three decades he has applied his professional skills to his work as a historian, the result of which is two extraordinary books. *The Discovery of Troy and its Lost History* is the first of these.

His second book, *The Voyage of Aeneas of Troy*, is scheduled for publication in 2019.

Preview:
The Voyage of Aeneas of Troy

This sequel commences where *The Discovery of Troy and its Lost History* finishes. As discussed in Chapter 9, Aeneas's voyage was instrumental in determining the Bronze Age geography of eastern England and, as a result, the eventual discovery of Troy.

Scheduled for publication in 2019

Index

Printed in Great Britain
by Amazon